A⁰ 1801.

J.P.Gabler sc.

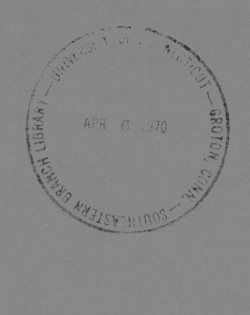

THE EARLY SPANISH MAIN

THE
EARLY SPANISH MAIN

by Carl Ortwin Sauer

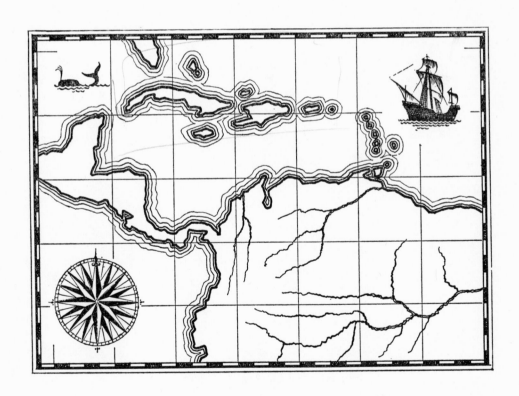

UNIVERSITY OF CALIFORNIA PRESS, BERKELEY AND LOS ANGELES

1966

University of California Press
Berkeley and Los Angeles, California

Cambridge University Press
London, England

Foreword

A Midwestern geographer who came to California as I did in 1923 might well have been tempted to turn south across the international boundary that runs straight across the grain of the continent from the Rio Grande to the Pacific coast. The same mountains and deserts, pine forests, oak woodlands, scrub, and grasslands extend north and south; the difference is in the people and their ways. On this side, change has been accelerating and innovation has become the dominant order of living. On the other side, ways of past experience and acceptance have been retained in gradual modifications.

Northwest Mexico was richly rewarding to study Spanish institutions of agriculture, stock ranching, and mining. Its colonial development rested mainly on missions and to understand these it became necessary to learn about the native peoples. There was time and opportunity to continue field work in repeated observations and by improving identifications and to become conversant with the documents of the past. Northwest Mexico provided the primary school to study the making of Spanish America, based on native peoples of different customs. The continuing and expanding theme thus was to learn what the Spaniards found of nature and culture at their coming and what they did in accepting, adapting, and replacing prior conditions.

The farther south the earlier was the meeting of Spaniard and native. In Sinaloa it was by the brutal conquest of the country that Nuño de Guzmán called Nueva Galicia. Here a high culture was quickly and thoroughly destroyed and was forgotten until we found its remains. Still farther on, we came to the Pacific coast that captains of Hernán Cortés took, and so to the western fringe of the Tarascan Indian state, where copper and silver had been mined and smelted by native skills. Here there were other Indian towns, in former times of merchants trading afar, speaking Nahua, and kinsmen of those who had built the state we call the Aztec empire. In Colima and Jalisco there was thus additional rediscovery of what native civilization had been like at the coming of the white man and what had happened to it. From the borders of Arizona to Michoacán we had the opportunity to trace, by field work and written document, the native cultural geography and its overriding by Spanish colonization.

Having gotten as far back as Cortés and the conquest of Mexico, it seemed proper to turn to the first Spanish entry into the New World by similar inquiry: what was seen and thought of the new lands and their inhabitants, how control was taken, and how possession was extended. Important lineaments of Spanish America were well drawn before Cortés began his march into Mexico. That span of a scant thirty years of discovery and domination gave not only geographical but large economic and political directions to Spanish empire. I have tried here to outline and interpret the historical geography of this brief period and narrow region of the New World.

That such a job needed doing came to me, I regret to say, as an afterthought. Mexico took the most and the best years, when field work was unrestricted by endurance or time. Mexico also provided some experience of tropical life, especially of plants under the care or attention of man. When later there was occasion to visit the West Indies, Colombia, and Venezuela I was most interested in such plants and their uses. I made acquaintance with physical features of tropical coasts and of the limestone country of the islands. I have looked somewhat at savannas, from palm to pine. At the time I gave little and casual attention to the places where the Spaniards had first lived because I was uninformed about the manner of their coming. It has since been possible to read the early records with the aid of modern maps made by air photography, as for the Dominican Republic and Panama. By such pieces of information a preliminary reconstruction of status at and after discovery is here attempted, an introduction to land and life in the first decades of Spanish America.

The record of those early years has been preserved in many and diverse documents. Spanish bureaucracy was attentive to keeping files of instructions, of inquiries into the conduct of affairs, of reports on discoveries and revenues. These have been mainly collected into the vast Archive of the Indies at Sevilla. The most important ones have been published in series; others have been winnowed and given in excerpt by scholars who continue to search colonial history.

The strange newly-found world and its people were of immediate interest to all western Europe, quickly informed by numerous versions of the first letter of Columbus and the accounts of Vespucci. Others who participated overseas got into print early, Fernández de Enciso with his *Suma de Geografía*, and Oveido with his *Sumario de la Natural Historia*, both descriptions of land, biota, and the natives. Las Casas wrote his very lengthy *Historia* in later years, based on early, long, and intimate knowledge of country, natives, and Spanish personalities, and dealt with the same area and period as this study. Peter Martyr never saw the New World, but was one of its best reporters, interviewing those who returned for the famous letters of his *Decades*. The official cosmographer Alonso de Santa Cruz and the biographer of Cortés, López de Gómara, came later, relied on the observations of others, and preserved other knowledge of the early years. Less well known witnesses and reporters are available in number for information.

The materials on the nature of the new Indies and the life of their people are abundant, fairly adequate, and rarely in serious contradiction. Columbus himself is the most difficult informant, less in what he saw than in the extravagance of what he thought he heard. Testimony on the conduct of Spaniards in positions of responsibility, on the other hand, is widely divergent and often self-serving and partisan, but it may not be disregarded so far as such conduct determined the direction and result of colonization.

There is a large secondary literature on the beginnings of Spanish America. Much of it is narrative history centered on leading personalities. A good deal has been written about political institutions, less about economic organization and returns. There are local histories in some number and of varying merit. What the Spanish Indies were like at their beginning and what was done to them has had least attention. There is a wealth of first-hand observations that have remained unnoticed and which provide supporting materials from which a human geography of those years of fateful alterations can be written.

It is necessary to consider as well the role of the principals, for it was they rather than manifest destiny of place and time that determined the results. The natives were the main resource; the manner of their exploitation outlines the successive changes of the map of the Spanish Indies. To most of those who held power in the early years the Indians were manpower and nothing else. It is significant that the first census in the New World was a statistic of native numbers as to age suited to labor. What happened to the natives determined the character of the Spanish colonies. The responsibility for the course of events is divided between those in charge in the new possessions and those who gave directions in Spain. That things went so very badly is due in part to inexperience in administering a suddenly acquired and unexpected colonial empire, to its remoteness and poor communications, to internal troubles in Spain, and to involvement in European quarrels. We may not forget that Spaniards were the severest and most insistent critics of the sad state of their own colonies and that gradually they brought about admirable reforms.

The gross shortcomings and misconduct of those who took and governed the new possessions are clearly on record and must be taken into account in the decline and failure of the enterprises. These men stand against a background of personalities and manipulations in Spain of which I know little beyond the occasional disclosure of the hand of King Ferdinand, of the all-powerful Bishop Fonseca, and of the great and good regent, Cardinal Cisneros. These political maneuvers are important to the colonial theme, but they are largely beyond my competence and purpose.[1]

I have made use of the original accounts in the form of abstracts and excerpts. Most of these are in Spanish; a few in Italian and Latin. They are given here in my own translation. All are taken from printed editions, for the most part available to me in the Bancroft Library of the University of California. Enciso, Oviedo, and Herrera have been at hand in the printed forms of their time; the rest in standard modern editions.

A good many Indian terms passed into Spanish usage—names of plants, animals, physical features, artifacts, whatever lacked a name in Spanish. Such borrowing was mainly from Arawak islanders, some was from Caribs, and a little from the form of Chibchan speech that was met with in Panama. The words were written as they sounded to the hearer and in the wide latitude of orthography of the

---

[1] Manuel Giménez Fernández, *Bartolomé de las Casas* (Sevilla, vol. I, 1953; vol. II, 1960), is engaged in an impressive inquiry into the conduct of Spanish affairs of state by scrutiny of official documents of legal character. He has shown how orders were arrived at or circumvented, how decisions were passed into particular hands, the contentions between factions, the placing of partisan supporters in key positions overseas. Only one thus versed in the procedures and persons of that time can undertake to interpret the actions behind the scene. Fernández traces the commitments of partisanship in their ramifications of family ties and of *criados* attached to high personages. The longlived Fonseca–Conchillos–Cobos "machine" is sharply outlined, with King Ferdinand as their earlier supporter, followed later by William of Croy as the power behind the throne of the young King-Emperor, Charles V.

time. Georg Friederici has collected the range of spellings in his dictionary of Americanisms.[2] For the most part I have followed the spelling preferred by Friederici wherever we lack an Anglicized form. All non-English words are italicized only when first used. The English use of one word needs comment. In English, "cassava" applies both to plant and to product. In Spanish America the plant (*Manihot utilissima*) and its fleshy rootstock were and are known by the Arawak name *yuca;* only the unleavened bread made from the root is cassava (at first *cazabí*). I have retained the Indian and Spanish meaning.

The greatest variation is in the spelling of proper names, both of places and persons. They were likely to be polysyllabic and difficult to catch. The cursive writing of the time blurred individual letters. The names were meaningless to the copyists who made the transcriptions. I have used the more common forms, placing special confidence in Las Casas, who had a didactic interest in native names and some competence in Indian speech.

Accents on native names have been omitted unless they are still used. Except for Las Casas, writers and copyists usually omitted stress. In all three of the major Indian languages the accent seems to have been most commonly on the last syllable. In Spanish usage the tendency has been to move it to the penultimate, as cazabí to cassava.[3]

Special acknowledgment is due to Mrs. A. D. Morgan for the able designing and drafting of the maps and to the Department of Geography and its Chairman, James J. Parsons, for clerical facilities.

---

[2] Georg Friederici, *Amerikanistisches Wörterbuch und Hilfswörterbuch für den Amerikanisten* (Hamburg, reprinted 1960), hereafter cited as Friederici. Errors and omissions are easy to find. The compendium remains the invaluable guide to the vocabulary Europeans picked up from contact with Indians, recording place and date of earliest use, and the spread of such terms.

[3] In reading proof I find accents still somewhat elusive. Names unaccented in the documents were to remain so, as were those that shifted stress in passing from Indian to Spanish language. These directives have exceeded our observance.

Contents

List of Illustrations

Abbreviations

Alba: *Mapas españoles de América*, portfolio in facsimile (Madrid, 1951) under auspices of the Duke of Alba and Berwick.

Altolaguirre: Angel Altolaguirre y Duvale, *Vasco Núñez de Balboa* (Madrid, 1914), collected the documents about that person and the Isthmus of his time.

CDI: *Colección de documentos inéditos relativos al descubrimiento, conquista, y organización de las antiguas posesiones españolas de América y Oceanía* (Madrid, 1864–1884), 42 vols.

CDU: The succeeding series of the same title but ending . . . *posesiones españolas de ultramar* (Madrid, 1885–1932), 25 vols. The two-volume index to both series by Ernst Schäfer, *Indice de documentos inéditos de Indias* (Madrid, 1946–1947) has been invaluable.

Enciso: Martín Fernández de Enciso, *Suma de geographia*, originally published in Sevilla in 1519.

Harrisse: Henry Harrisse, *The Discovery of North America* (Paris, 1892), with maps.

Herrera: Antonio de Herrera y Tordesillas, *Historia general de los hechos de los castellanos, en las islas, y tierra-firme de el Mar Oceano* (1601–1615), 4 vols.

Kretschmer: Konrad Kretschmer, *Die Entdeckung Amerikas in ihrer Bedeutung für die Geschichte des Weltbildes* (Berlin, 1892), with atlas.

Las Casas: Bartolomé de las Casas, *Historia de las Indias*, 1520–1561, the main work utilized in manuscript by Herrera and others, not printed until 1875–1876 in Madrid.

Las Casas, *Apologética*: His *Apologética historia de las Indias* remained in manuscript until 1909, when it was published in Madrid by Marcelino Menéndez y Pelayo in *Historiadores de Indias*.

Navarrete: Martín Fernández de Navarrete, *Colección de los viages y descubrimientos que hicieron por mar los Españoles* (Madrid, 1825–1829), 3 vols.

Oviedo, *Historia:*   Gonzalo Fernández de Oviedo y Valdés, *Historia general y natural de las Indias;* had partial publication in 1535 and 1547, but was not printed in complete form until 1851–1855 in Madrid.

Oviedo, *Sumario:*   His *Sumario de la natural historia de las Indias* (1526). Republished in 1950 in Mexico with introduction by José Miranda.

Peter Martyr: Pietro Martire d'Anghiera, *De Orbe Novo, the Eight Decades of Peter Martyr d'Anghira,* transl. by Francis MacNutt; originally written in Latin between 1493 and 1525. I have found the Spanish translation by Joaquin Torres Asensio (Buenos Aires, 1944) most satisfactory, checking occasionally with the Latin.

Raccolta: The inclusive collection of documents concerning Columbus made by the R. Commissione Colombiana, *Raccolta di documenti e studi* (Rome, 1892–1896), in six parts.

Santa Cruz: Alonso de Santa Cruz, Cosmógrafo Mayor, *Die Karten von Amerika in dem Islario general, ca.* 1541, published with maps by Franz, R. v. Wieser (Innsbruck, 1908).

Velasco: Juan López de Velasco, *Geografía descripción universal de las Indias, recopilada . . . desde el año de 1571 al de 1574,* first published 1894 by the Sociedad Geográfica de Madrid.

I

INTRODUCTION

•

NAMING THE DISCOVERIES

The geographical preconceptions of Columbus attached the name Indies to the newly discovered lands. His original authorization of April 30, 1492, spoke only of "Islands and Tierra Firme in the Ocean Sea." The official documents drawn up after his return repeat the phrase, and some add "toward the side of the Indies." When Ovando was appointed governor in 1501 it was to "the islands and mainland of the Indies of the Ocean Sea." The House of Trade, set up in 1503, was called simply "Casa de Contratación de las Indias." Whatever lay west across the ocean was officially and popularly the Indies because the anticipatory name of Columbus was the one first learned. Other nations and languages might speak of the New World, but in Spanish this name was late, uncommon, and unofficial.

"Islas y Tierra Firme" were written into the authorization for Columbus to go exploring, a blanket provision to find whatever he might, so long as there was no trespass on Portuguese premises. He found, or thought that he had found, both islands and mainland. The phrase stuck in the official division of the new lands in two parts. The islands we still know as the West Indies. Florida at first was thought to be one of them. By 1500 it began to be apparent that a land of continental proportions lay south of the islands. This was named for a time by particular parts, but soon was called Tierra Firme, the Mainland. When its political organization was put into effect, Tierra Firme was the proper and official name of lands along the south coast of the Caribbean Sea, from the peninsula of Paria, opposite the island of Trinidad, westward into Central America. "Islas" meant the Antilles; "Tierra Firme," the southern littoral of the Caribbean.

For two decades after the discovery the sea was still held to be one, the Ocean Sea. Then Balboa announced "the other sea," a great sea shown as such by its very great tides. Having found it by crossing the narrow land of Darién from north to south, he named it Mar del Sur. The newly found sea having been thus named, the other one thereafter became Mar del Norte. The east-west orientation of the Isthmus of Panama provided the names for the two oceans. The official geography of López de Velasco of 1574 thus defined the South Sea, Mar del Sur, as lying along the western side of the Indies from the Strait of

Magellan to California and beyond into the undiscovered north; also, that which is called "del Norte" as all the sea to the east of the "Indies" discovered by Spain, from the provinces of Labrador, Newfoundland, and Bacalaos by way of Florida and New Spain and Tierra Firme to the Equator and the provinces of Brazil and thence down to the Strait of Magellan. This was the established Spanish usage: the whole Pacific Ocean was the South Sea, the Atlantic from north to farthest south was the Mar del Norte. It is not uncommon to find "north" and "south" in colonial documents referring not to compass direction but to the respective ocean, omitting the word *mar*.

Delineation of the new discoveries by maps improved rapidly. The navigators employed compass and quadrant, kept logs and charts. The coastal outlines and landmarks were recorded and named in useful detail. It was in the common interest to know the position and form of islands, reefs and shoals, harbors, bays, and capes and to identify these by name. The configuration of the western side of the Atlantic Ocean was first shown with some realism on the map of Juan de la Cosa in 1500, in fair representation of the West Indies islands, the north coast of the southern continent, and a discreetly masked great gulf to the west of the islands, a first adumbration of an unnamed enclosed tropical sea. Possibly this had nothing to do with a prior discovery of Central America. Seamen knew that tides were features of the open ocean and they had seen that there was hardly any tide inside the island chain.

The men who sailed the sea and entered the new lands had need of a proper topography of coast and land but not of names for parts of the sea greater than reëntrants that marked a terminus of route. The Gulf of Mexico was well known and well shown on maps long before it had a name. It is first recorded in 1544 on the Sebastian Cabot map as Golfo de la Nueva España, then as Golfo Mexicano on the Zaltieri map (1566?) and the famous Mercator map of 1569. In Velasco's *Geografía* it was Golfo de la Nueva España y Florida. All such early inclusive names were given by cartographers and compilers in Europe, were not derived from local usage, and were not used by those who sailed on such waters.

Although the best-known sea of the New World, the Caribbean remained nameless longest. It was the original Mar del Norte, a term promptly extended to all parts of the western Atlantic. Velasco tried to find a proper name for it, saying: "de los Canibales llaman el golfo grande del mar Océano desde la Deseada y Dominica por toda la costa de Tierra Firme, Yucatán, Golfo de Tierra Firme y de las islas del mar del Norte." This compiler in Spain, regarding the maps before him, made the distinction we do between Caribbean Sea and Gulf of Mexico. (Gulf of Tierra Firme was that of Darién.) Velasco remained in manuscript until the ninteenth century, and I do not know that his Gulf of the Cannibals was ever thus known. In the introduction to his *West Indies Atlas* (1773) Thomas Jefferys wrote, two centuries later: "It has been sometimes called the Caribbean-Sea, which name it would be better to adopt, than to leave this space quite anonymous"; he did so on his map. North European nations at the time were in possession of the Carib islands (the Lesser Antilles) and it is perhaps thus that Jefferys introduced the designation that was to become standard on maps but was not adopted in Spanish lands.

Tierra Firme continued to be the common name for the south side of the Carib-

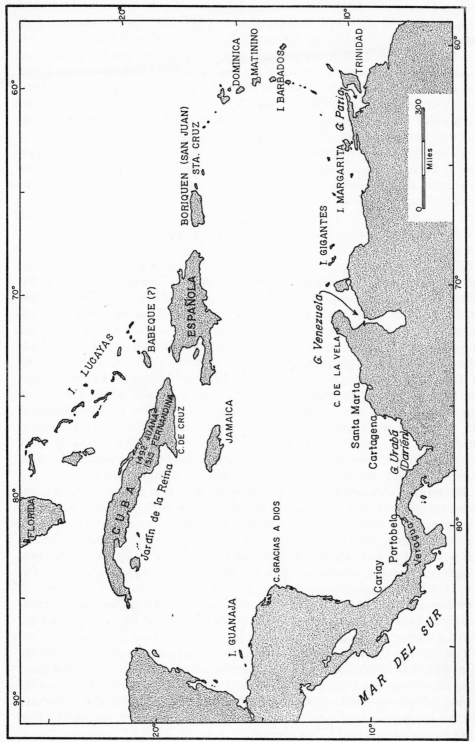

Fig. 1. The West Indies: Islas y Tierra Firme.

bean. It was translated into English as the Spanish Main, the ports of which were raided by English ships. It was easier to take Spanish ships at sea than to attack their towns. Pirates and privateers lurked in various Caribbean waters where a Spanish ship might be expected to pass, and while waiting camped and provisioned themselves ashore. They knew the approaches and exits of Tierra Firme and where they might best lie in wait. The whole of the Caribbean area came to be known in English as the Spanish Main, including the sea. Thus sailing *to* the Spanish Main became called sailing *on* the Spanish Main. By this extension and transfer of meaning the English language acquired the first inclusive name for Tierra Firme, the West Indies islands, and the intermediate sea. It is used here as the most compact and convenient term, the equivalent of Islas y Tierra Firme de las Indias, and is preferred to the neologism of the Circumcaribbean Region (fig. 1).

THE SPANISH MAIN AS A REGION

The area qualifies as a natural region, fuzzy about the edges but having common characteristics: it is the rim of land about a mediterranean sea; it is the double corridor between North and South America; and it is the region of tropical climate to the north of the Equator that is stirred by the trade winds.

As the northern flank of the American tropics, it is marked by small seasonal range of temperature, by seasonal contrast of rainfall, and by a brisk flow of air. The trade wind blows west out of the Atlantic across the islands, along the coast of Tierra Firme and piles the waters of the Caribbean against the Central American shores. It was in this reach of the trade wind that Spaniards had their first experience of life in the tropics. They liked it. They suffered neither from cold nor from heat, the sensible temperatures being further reduced by the freely moving air. The rains fall at the time when the sun stands high. However, having come from a land of winter rains, the Spaniards called the time of rains winter (*invierno*), though it is summer and fall by the calendar.

The contrast of season is expressed as wet and dry. It is summer when it rains. There are parts where it rains very little and others where it rains very heavily. The eastern end of the traditional Tierra Firme is the peninsula of Paria, a lush rain forest. Going west about a hundred miles it becomes the arid peninsula of Araya, a land of poor thorn scrub and salt pans (fig. 1). Continuing on west, rainfall is scanty for a thousand miles, the islands and land that jut out into the sea being the most arid. Beyond Cartagena the rainfall increases in amount and period to and beyond the Gulf of Darién. Here, in the Atrato basin to its south, and in the Isthmus beyond is one of the rainiest regions of the tropics, supporting tropical rain forests and swamps, still however with a short dry season.

The islands from Trinidad to the Bahamas lie athwart the trade wind during part or all the year. Their geographical pattern of rain and drought is complex, affected by relief and exposure. For the most part the rainy season on the islands is adequate and not excessive. The largest arid tracts are in the island of Haiti, the first occupying the long structural depression from Port-au-Prince to the Bay of Ocoa; the second, the lower part of the basin of the Río Yaque del Norte; and the third, the northwestern peninsula. One is found on the south coast, an-

4

other on the north coast, and the third on the Windward Channel across from a similar area in Cuba. Their pattern of precipitation is better known from the aspect of the vegetation than from rain gauges.

On the islands the bird life attracted the attention of the newcomers. It was very abundant and diverse, especially during winter. (I shall not follow the reversal of seasons of Spanish usage, but stay with the calendar.) That many birds came south to the islands to overwinter was understood in the first landfall of Columbus, which witnessed the beginning of fall migration, incidentally of interest as to the implied presence of land to the north. The islands are part of the great eastern flyway by which ducks and geese came in very large numbers, to be hunted by both Indians and Spaniards. Of the many tropical birds the parrots (*papagayos*) were of greatest interest, as food, for their plumage, and by the ease with which they were tamed and taught to speak. In contrast, the poverty of mammalian and reptilian land fauna was noted, many in number but of few kinds, rabbit-like rodents such as the *hutias* and the great lizards called iguanas. Most of the plants were wholly strange. Pines, grapevines, and other northern elements were, however, seen in Cuba and Haiti as pleasing reminders of a familiar vegetation. As Spanish occupation extended to Tierra Firme the identifications that had been learned in the islands sufficed for much of the biota encountered. The natural history of the islands is mainly a reduced extension of adjacent South America. The island arc is a corridor freely open to organic dispersal at the south and almost blocked at the north at the Florida Straits.

On Tierra Firme a far greater diversity of land animals was found—deer, peccaries, tapirs, and felines they called tigers and lions, which were jaguars, pumas, and ocelots. This fauna of large land mammals was recognized as proper to a mainland and not to islands. The acquaintance with Central America was by way of its tropical lowlands that still confirmed the southern nature of the biota. The Isthmus, beyond which exploration hardly passed except in the last voyage of Columbus, again had the same familiar flora and fauna known farther east.

The native people who lived about the Caribbean were South American in stock and culture. Arawaks had spread from the mainland to almost every habitable island of the Antilles and had increased to large populations. They were followed by Caribs, who had taken over most of the Lesser Antilles, seemingly only a few generations before the discovery. In Panama, Chibchan languages were spoken and the culture was cognate to that of the highlands of Colombia. Ruder peoples, also of Chibchan speech, occupied the farther Caribbean coast of Central America almost to the Bay Islands of Honduras.

To the north of the West Indies the Straits of Florida formed a very sharp ethnic boundary between South and North America. In Central America a sort of boundary between Caribbean and Mesoamerican native peoples and ways runs from Cape Camarón on the Gulf of Honduras south-southeast to the Pacific coast of westernmost Panama. To the west of the Gulf of Panama an invasion of people from the north was taking place at the time; the ethnical frontier of South America was in process of retreat and mixing.

The ethnic affiliations of coastal Colombia and Venezuela are most obscure. The natives were not well described. If they were hostile they were called Caribs, which some of them were and others were not. The situation is most

5

confused for the coast of Colombia. In the Spanish view, a Carib was one who practiced cannibalism, a habit that is not supported for the Colombian coast. Also, the use of poisoned weapons was held to be a Carib trait, but it is of doubtful validity. The so-called Caribs of Colombia are dubious, nor was the language they spoke identified. Northeastern Venezuela was open to contacts from other parts—here a mixing of stock, skills, customs, and political institutions makes simple classification as Carib or Arawak questionable.

The bona fide Caribs differed from the Arawak and Chibchan groups in political organization. Both of the latter had a society of classes in which, for the most part, status was hereditary; these groups constituted states under hereditary rulers for whom the Spaniards adopted the term *caciques* from the Arawak islands. The Caribs lacked such aristocracy. Columbus and those who followed him were quick to see that control or elimination of the caciques left the native people exposed to the will of their new masters.

The native economy was much the same throughout the Caribbean. Starch and sugar were produced by planting; protein and fat were secured by fishing and hunting. I have called these people tropical planters and fishermen by a generalization that is only slightly exaggerated. The main tillage was of starchy root crops which were vegetatively reproduced. These were ancient domesticates of Tierra Firme and nearby parts. Seed crops, principally maize, were of least importance in the islands. On the mainland these were of increasing significance toward Central America, out of which they are indicated as having come. Fishing in sea and stream provided abundant food. Fishing skills and aquatic hunting were excellent and general. In all parts the Indians were adept makers and handlers of canoes, accustomed to voyaging in them and thus able to occupy the farther regions of the Caribbean from their earlier homelands in Tierra Firme.

The Spanish Main was the original nucleus of the Spanish empire. It was here that the obsession with gold began. Here the first tragic confrontation of Europeans and American natives took place and here also the first concern about human rights found insistent expression. From here entry was made to Florida and the Gulf coast of the United States, to Mexico, to Peru, and beyond. What happened on the Spanish Main in the first quarter of a century had great and lasting effects on the colonization and institutions of Spanish America. The present study is limited to this opening stage which ended by 1520, after which the area became subordinate to other parts of the New World, important as guarding the approaches to New Spain, Peru, and New Granada, but of minor interest in other ways.

KNOWLEDGE OF THE WESTERN OCEAN

The all-encompassing Ocean Sea of Greek cosmography was accepted into the thought of the late Middle Ages. The spherical form of the Earth and its approximate size had been demonstrated by Greek scholars, who also construed climatic zones by latitude belts encircling the Earth, and thought to define its habitable limits. In the revival of learning, familiarity with classical cosmography took an important place. The world ocean, it was held, could be sailed to any shores that were not blocked by ice. The Earth was round and one might get to its other side by sailing east or west. Terrestrial globes were made, such as that of Martin Behaim in 1492. The theory of an uninhabitable torrid zone was long obsolete. The authority of learning favored rather than opposed venturing into unknown seas.

The compass had been in use for centuries by mariners in Europe, with some knowledge of its magnetic deviation. Astrolabe and quadrant gave the means of determining latitude without large error. Longitude was reckoned by crude measures. Portolan and Catalan charts were providing progressively better representations of direction and distance and thereby of the configuration of land and sea.[1] Both northern and Mediterranean Europe had developed hulls and riggings of ships that were stoutly seaworthy and of good steerage and speed. Navigation had become well able to go across the wide seas and was engaged in doing so.[2]

The West had learned of the lands of a distant East by the precious goods brought from there: spices, essences, jewels, and fine fabrics that came by way of Italian merchants. Arabia Felix, and India on the near side of the Ganges and another India beyond including Cathay and Tartary, the Golden Chersonese (Malaya) and Java, the seat of the Great Khan and the home of Prester John, were attractive facts or fictions of this farther world. It had been visited on occasion and its places and scenes described, as in the vivid and informed account of Marco Polo, who had returned by sea from China to the Persian Gulf. The approaches from the Mediterranean across the lands of the Levant had fallen into Muslim hands, to the growing injury of the Italian cities. If the great Orient trade was to be restored it would be by finding an all-sea route. The Ptolemaic version of a closed Indian Ocean notwithstanding, the belief in the universal ocean prevailed. Maritime effort of the fifteenth century was directed to getting to the east by sailing south around Africa, which was done by Portuguese initiative, aided by Italian tutors.

The ocean to the west of Europe, stormy and cloud-covered as it often was, did not hold back the inhabitants of its shores from bold and early venturing. It was, on the contrary, the greater proving ground of European seamanship, which has had less attention because it was marginal to the intellectual centers of the Middle Ages and left few literary documents. When Norsemen reached the Faeroe Islands and Iceland in the ninth century they found that Irish monks had preceded them. The discovery of Greenland followed promptly, its settlement late in the tenth century. The North American mainland was reached by about A.D. 1000 in Labrador and Newfoundland. A Norse village is at present being excavated in Newfoundland. Norse landings and settlements farther south are still in dispute. The last settlements in Greenland were probably abandoned late in the fifteenth century. Hanseatic ships were at their busiest in the fourteenth and fifteenth centuries carrying bulky cargoes about the North Sea and the Norwegian Sea, and got as far as Iceland, as did English trade in salt fish. For more than five hundred years before Columbus, ships had made the formidable crossings of the Norwegian Sea to Iceland at will, nor were all these Norse.

Voyages to Greenland ceased after the failure of that colony. The last expedi-

---

[1] George T. H. Kimble, *Geography in the Middle Ages* (London, 1938).
[2] E. G. R. Taylor, *The Haven-Finding Art* (London, 1957).

tions to the American continent remain undetermined; they may have continued into the fifteenth century. About 1473 King Christian I of Denmark sent an expedition to Greenland under the captains Pining and Pothorst, with a pilot named Scolvus.[3] Larsen has inferred that it got beyond, into the Gulf of St. Lawrence. A part of the argument depends on the obscure and important question of the meaning and origin of the term "Terra do bacalhaos" (*bacalaos*, stockfish, cod) as the land adjacent to the Grand Banks of Newfoundland. Larsen showed repeated relations between the Danish and Portuguese kings during that century and gave some evidence that the father of the Cort Real brothers was sent to take part in the Danish voyage. The voyages of the sons to the northeast coast of North America began in 1500 and are construed as entering on their patrimony; the Portuguese interest being to find another route to the Far East, later known as the Northwest Passage. The data at the least show that in the fifteenth century Portugal was in communication with Scandinavia about the western sea.

There is new light on English seafaring through a document discovered by Vigneras, which he has presented competently and discussed with modesty.[4] The letter, written toward the end of 1497 by John Day, is mainly an account of the John Cabot voyage of that year from Bristol to the coast of Newfoundland and Nova Scotia. It was made in one ship of fifty tons with twenty men; the crossing of the Atlantic took thirty-five days, and a month was spent in exploration of the coast. They got to the lower part of the Seven Cities (a land or island of familiar medieval legend), in another passage called "Brasil" (Brazil) (another legendary island, for which Vigneras cites a representation on maps as early as 1325). The First Admiral of Spain to whom Day was writing had inquired also about a previous voyage, to which Day answered that a ship had gone, but turned back on account of bad weather, poor provisions, and the discontent of the men. (This was the first attempt by John Cabot of 1496, otherwise documented.) The John Day letter is our best information about the earlier voyages of Cabot, who may have come to England in 1495 or shortly before. The letter also refers to earlier discovery out of Bristol: "It is considered certain that the *cabo* of the said land had been found and discovered by those of Bristol in other times (*en otros tiempos*), who had discovered *el Brasil* as Your Lordship knows. It is called the island of Brasil and thought and believed to be mainland, which those of Bristol discovered." *Cabo* may mean cape, extremity, or farther end. The point apparently was that John Cabot had gotten to one end of a country which had been found by men of Bristol years before and was thought to be the Brazil of medieval lore. This earlier discovery had been known previously to

---

[3] Sophus Larsen, *The Discovery of North America Twenty Years Before Columbus* (Copenhagen, 1925).

[4] L. A. Vigneras, "New Light on the 1497 Cabot Voyage to America," *Hispanic American Historical Review*, XXXVI (1956), 503–509. This is a letter from the Englishman, John Day, resident in Spain, addressed to the First Admiral of Spain, thus identified correctly by Vigneras as Fadrique Enríquez, grandee of Castile, Marqués de Tarifa. The document and the comments by Vigneras are used in the subsequent studies of David P. Quinn, "The Argument for the English Discovery of America between 1480 and 1494," in *Geographical Journal*, CCXVII (1961), 277–285, and J. A. Williamson, "The Cabot Voyages and Bristol Discovery under Henry VII," *Hakluyt Society* Second Series, CXX (1962). Quinn prefers to consider the letter as addressed to Columbus, and says that Vigneras is of the same mind. He is in error. Williamson says it was "addressed to a Spanish notable who was most likely Columbus himself," which is contradicted by the address, form, and content of the letter.

the Admiral of Spain, the Marqués de Tarifa. The new knowledge showed that Brazil was not an island but mainland.

Other items relevant to western ventures from Bristol have been collated by Williamson and Quinn. The first is from 1480, when a ship left Bristol for the "island" of Brasil to the west of Ireland. It was forced to turn back by bad weather. A second attempt was made in 1481 by two ships with results unknown. A Spanish emissary in London, Pedro de Ayala, reported to Ferdinand and Isabela in 1498 that "for the past seven years those of Bristol annually had equipped two, three, or four caravels to seek the island of Brasil and the Seven Cities, according to the fantasy of this Genoese [Cabot]." The last phrase is obscure and has been the subject of discussion. It may mean that Cabot attached Brazil and the Seven Cities to the same quest. The voyages indicated began before Cabot came to Bristol and they had been in search of Brazil as early as 1480. Whatever their success, seamen of Bristol, undeterred by wind and weather, had been sailing west into the Atlantic for years before Cabot or Columbus.

Southern Europe turned its attention to the Atlantic early in the fourteenth century. Genoese and Venetian merchants were settled in numbers from Sevilla to London, their ships carrying the sea trade of southwestern Europe. The Genoese in Portugal opened ways into the ocean to the west and south.[5] The Genoese merchant family of Pessagno had such a leading part for a century. By compact of 1317 with the King of Portugal it secured trading rights with northwestern Europe, the assignment to train captains and pilots for Portuguese service, and a commission to explore the ocean. Under Genoese command the Canary, Madeira, and Azores islands were reached during that century. A Genoese captain founded a settlement in midcentury on one of the Canary Islands, which still bears his name, Lanzarote.[6] The early discovery of the Azores, a good third of the way across the Atlantic, without intermediate land, and mainly upwind and upcurrent from Portugal, speaks for the sailing skill and the confidence of the men who headed into the unknown ocean. These brave beginnings might well have given Portugal control of the Atlantic in its middle and lower latitudes and have led from island bases to the discovery of the New World. They were lost toward the end of the fourteenth century through the war with Castile, which invaded Portugal repeatedly, and also through the Black Death. Here, as in the north, which was also ravaged by the great epidemic, discovery ceased and what had been discovered was partly forgotten or became woven into legends of lost lands.

In 1402 the Norman Bethencourt, in belated Viking manner, established himself in the Canaries. In 1418 Madeira was "rediscovered" by Portuguese of the entourage of Prince Henry the Navigator, soon to become the first base of the grand design to which Henry devoted his life.

THE PORTUGUESE EXAMPLE

The year 1420 may serve for the beginning of the Portuguese century of commitment to far ocean enterprise. It was then that Prince Henry built his institute

---

[5] Charles Verlinden in *Historia Mundi*, III (Bern, 1959), 278–300.
[6] *Ibid.*, p. 281.

of ocean studies and seafaring at Sagres, facing south and west on the Atlantic. It was about 1420 that the settlement of Madeira began, soon to be denuded of the forest that had covered it and to be planted to fields of sugar cane and to vineyards. Twenty years later the Azores were in process of settlement, with grainfields, orchards, cattle and pig raising, and fishing. Both previously uninhabited island groups were divided into feudal donatories; from their beginnings they were extensions of the mother country in their government, economy, and inhabitants. Madeira developed the plantations that supplied Europe with sugar as a new household commodity of rapidly growing demand, requiring many cargo ships. It also provided a proper location for the support of ventures farther south.

Prince Henry is thought to have had the original purpose of turning the western flank of Islam and rolling it back. The period from 1420 to 1460, during which he directed the expansion of Portugal at sea, was also a sober and persistent succession of limited objectives of exploration and commerce, mainly sugar and Negro slaves. The ships under his orders reached the Guinea coast, in first contact with a source of African gold. He lived to know the eastward turn of that coast that gave promise of a sea route around the south of Africa to the Indies. A generation later the return of Batholomeu Dias in 1488 brought assurance of success by passing the Cape of Good Hope.

Before 1492 the Portuguese knew the whole Atlantic coast of Africa, had a highly profitable trade in sugar and slaves, and also in gold, ivory, and pepper grains, and had developed or adapted a variety of ships, especially the light and speedy caravels of lateen sails and three masts,[7] able to go to windward as they returned against the northeast trades. They had wide experience of the wind systems of the Atlantic and knew how to lay their course across, against, or with them. Whatever Columbus learned of the ocean he picked up mostly from the Portuguese while living in Madeira and Lisbon, and on his trip to the Guinea coast.

SPANISH OUTPOST IN THE CANARY ISLANDS

The Norman claims to the Canaries were ceded around 1418 to the Crown of Castile. The island history is obscure for the next sixty years, with an occasional Spanish appearance and a few Portuguese attempts at a foothold. The conquest of the Canaries for Castile began in 1479 and was completed in 1496. Unlike the other islands, these had a numerous native population, known as Guanches, who put up stout resistance at times. The islands were taken by conquest, the people subjugated, and in part transported as slaves. The Spanish occupation of the Canaries has been considered a continuation of the drive that was then nearing its end in the reconquest of Moorish Spain. The participants were given grants of land and natives in service. As had been the case in Andalusia, people of all classes came in numbers to colonize. Over a thin base of surviving Guanches another province was added to Castile, with the institutions and ways of the homeland.

The ports of Andalusia that lie on the Atlantic coast benefited most from the

---

[7] Björn Landström, *The Ship* (Garden City, N. Y., 1961), pp. 103, 106–108.

embarkations for the Canaries and the new opportunities of trade. They acquired the ships, crews, and master mariners who could sail a thousand miles across the open ocean to the Canaries and find their way back to their home ports. Going out, ships were likely, and in summer almost sure, to have benefit of the *alisios*, the northeast trades. Returning, they had to work their way against the wind. Caravels such as those the Portuguese constructed were most used and also were best for the clandestine trade to which these ports were accustomed. From the Bay of Cádiz to Huelva there were communities of well-seasoned sailors and masters who knew the ways of the open ocean and knew them at different latitudes. They had experience of the quickening of the trades southward and knew that these winds flowed freely past the Canaries most of the time and continued southwest over the ocean. The Portuguese were accustomed to cross the trades on their African voyages. What if instead one followed downwind from the Canaries? Were the Canaries to remain the end of Spanish venture or to become a starting point for parts unknown and promising? The Moorish wars were nearly over and the last of the Guanches would soon be subdued. Portugal controlled the African coast and also the Azores. Between south and west, however, wind, current, and genial skies invited exploration. There was no hazard about return. Those whose sailed to the Canaries knew how to quarter northward across the trades to pick up westerly winds which would carry them home.

II

THE DISCOVERY

•

THE ANDALUSIAN BASE

As the war in Granada neared its end, there was greater interest in the Canaries and what lay beyond them. This was the case particularly in Spanish ports on the Atlantic coast of Andalusia. Navarrete summed up the situation thus: "The ship masters and pilots of the coast of Sevilla and Cádiz, especially those of Palos, Huelva, and Lepe, long accustomed to navigate to the Canaries and the African coast and trained in seamanship and cosmography, were inclined to try new discoveries." [1] The staging area was along the coast that swings from Cape Trafalgar to the Río Guadiana at the boundary with Portugal (fig. 2). The Río Guadalquivir discharges about midway of this stretch through wide marshes, known as Las Marismas. To the west of its mouth is a long belt of coastal dunes, the Arenas Gordas, harborless and almost unpeopled. Access from interior Andalusia to the Atlantic is thus limited to four portals. The easternmost is the Bay of Cádiz with Puerto de Santa María on its landward side, a road skirting the Marismas leading to Sevilla. Next is the mouth of the Guadalquivir, with the port of Sanlúcar de Barrameda linked by a navigable channel to Sevilla. Beyond the dune coast to the west is the estuary formed by the Tinto and Odiel rivers, with the towns of Palos, Moguer, and Huelva. Toward the Portuguese border is the harbor town of Lepe. These were the places that carried on communication with the Canaries and parts south and these were also to be the ports for the New World.

When Columbus failed to interest Portugal in his plans he came to this coast. The Franciscans of the convent of La Rábida gave him lodging and food. They also helped him present his case at court. From the convent he visited the neighboring townsmen of Palos and Moguer to talk about his project, to find understanding and support, and to learn about the Canaries. From here he went on to Puerto de Santa María, which belonged to the Duke of Medinaceli. The Duke took Columbus into his home and was almost persuaded to support the venture himself, but decided to recommend man and project to his kinswoman the Queen as a business proper to be undertaken by Castile. By good fortune or good sense

---

[1] Navarrate, I, xlvi–xlvii.

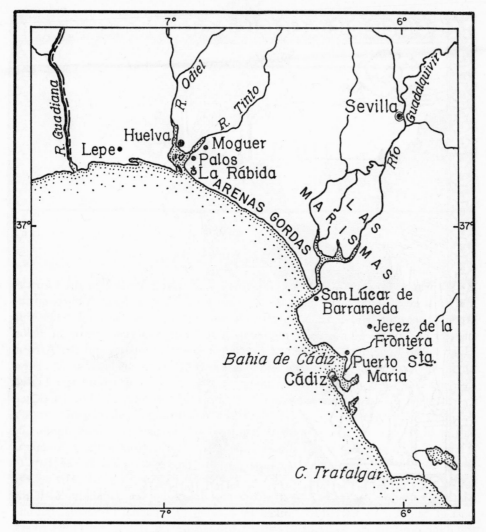

Fig. 2. The Atlantic coast of Andalusia.

Columbus transferred his campaign to the one Spanish area that was in the proper
position of geography and experience to help him.

THE AUTHORIZATION SECURED BY COLUMBUS

In view of the growing Portuguese success overseas, Spain would soon have to
face up to the strategic position of the Canaries. Columbus came along to supply
the push, proposing a bold venture out to sea in contrast to the step-by-step
advance of the Portuguese. By what means of appeal, imagery, and argument
he won approval remains unknown. His power of persuasion was such that his
qualifications are of little concern. He offered a vision and a theory, not a record
of accomplishment or status or means. A Genoese of humble birth and small

schooling, he had had only uncertain employment in lesser jobs, some of which had allowed him to travel to the eastern Mediterranean, northwestern Europe, and the Guinea coast, and to live on Madeira and in Lisbon. He had read eclectically in works of travel, natural history, and theology. He had picked up tales of mariners and had taken note of strange bits of flotsam cast up on Atlantic shores. As self-made cosmographer, he was in no way in advance of or abreast of the learning of the time. It is not known that he had ever been in command of a ship or of men or that he had experience as a navigator.

His objective remains obscure, perhaps because it was neither clear nor single of purpose. He argued the feasibility of crossing the ocean to the Far East by a westward course, which was granted by men of learning, if the distance were not too great. That this was his major purpose is not certain. As introduction to the Haklyut Society edition of the *Voyages of Columbus*, Cecil Jane wrote a monograph which he called "The Objective of Columbus," concluding that this was undefined and confused. Columbus claimed secret knowledge that gave him assurance of success. "He invited the sovereigns to embrace an enterprise, the exact nature of which he refused to define," partly because of secretiveness, partly because he did not know. . . . "Throughout his life his mental processes were somewhat confused, . . . those of an uneducated man of active mind. . . . It may perhaps be suggested with some confidence that Columbus himself was without any clear conception of that which he hoped to discover and gain, that his objective was altogether vague and that his purpose, when he set out on his first voyage, was not to reach any very definite point. It was to perform a mission, the precise nature of which he did not know, although he might suspect that which would in due course be made known to him." Thus, Jane thought, Columbus considered himself a chosen vessel elected to be "the missioner of God." Jane gave serious thought to the workings of this complex and puzzling mind. Mystic or mystifier, Columbus transferred readily from reality to make-believe, sure that he had secret knowledge at which he hinted, not saying whether it was by revelation or information.

The most explicit statement of the purpose and direction of the voyage is in the prologue to the Columbus Journal: "By reason of the information I had given to your Highnesses about the lands of India and of a Prince who is called the Great Khan, which in our Romance speech means King of Kings, he and his predecessors having sent many times to Rome to ask for teachers learned in our holy faith . . . your Highnesses . . . thought to send me Christopher Columbus to the said parts of the Indies to see the said princes and the peoples and lands and their nature and all, and the manner by which they might be converted to our holy faith; and ordered that I should not go by land to the East as is the custom to go but by the route of the West, by which until today we do not know for certain that anyone has passed." Thus he proceeded by way of the Canaries to sail until he reached the Indies "to give the embassy of your Highnesses to those princes and comply with what I had been commanded." The prologue was written after the return to Spain and its authenticity is suspect, for its Spanish is excellent as that of Columbus was not. Perhaps it was rewritten from his words. The claim that he had given the information about the Khan and the Far East to the Sovereigns is presumptuous, for the voyage had been under discussion at court by men who were better informed than he was. If the prologue was in fact presented to the Crown with the Journal, it declared a specific objective after the act.

The patent given to Columbus on April 30, 1492, stated no such geographical objective: "You, Christopher Columbus, are going by our orders to discover and gain, with certain light ships (*fustas*) of ours and with our men, certain Islands and Mainland in the Ocean Sea, and it is hoped that with the aid of God there shall be gained some of the said Islands and Mainland in the Ocean Sea by your hand and industry." He was instructed not to enter into any lands the Portuguese had found. Credentials were supplied that commended the party to friendly princes, in case they should get across the sea. These, however, do not prove that such was the purpose of the expedition. No one was sent to do the proper honors; there was no present of value from one sovereign to another, no emissary of the church. Nor were the ships supplied for trade with the Orient by goods, specie, or clerks. When the flotilla sailed it carried threescore seamen, a lesser number of jailbirds, and a small lot of cheap beads and trinkets.

The ships lacked fighting men and were not armed. The Portuguese looked well to their security at sea and on African shores, for armed Arab ships plied the Indian Ocean and beyond as intermediaries in the spice trade to Europe. Columbus sailed without the means to repel an ordinary corsair. Obviously he was expecting no harassment nor prepared for an attack. The only lands he might discover and gain with his handful of civilians would be uninhabited or occupied by simple and harmless savages. Such is the apparent explanation of the slender personnel and fitting out of the expedition. The Spanish Crown perhaps was thinking how Portugal had acquired vacant Madeira and the Cape Verde Islands. The Orient was neither undiscovered nor could there be thought of gaining any part of it by the means provided.

When the Queen and King accepted the demands of Columbus they did so without considering the consequences. The terms in their entirety were drawn up by Columbus and incorporated into his patent (*título*). "You the said Christopher Columbus, after you shall have discovered and gained the said Islands and Tierra Firme in the said Ocean Sea, or any part thereof, shall be our Admiral of the said Islands and Tierra Firme which you thus may have discovered and gained; and shall be our Admiral and Viceroy and Governor of them, and thereafter may call and entitle yourself Don Christopher Columbus and so may your sons and successors in the said office and charge entitle and call themselves Don and Admiral and Viceroy and Governor of these [lands]." Further, these rights should pass "from successor to successor forever and always." He was to have a tenth of the net proceeds of all products, pearls, precious stones, gold, silver, spices, and whatever would be bought, traded, discovered, or obtained there. Finally, he should have an eighth of the profits of its commerce by investing a similar share.[2]

How he managed to get these incredibly bold terms accepted has remained unexplained. He asked for hereditary title, entry into the gentility, and a share of the profits, all of which might not mean much if the enterprise resulted in little.

---

[2] Navarrete, II, Docs. 5 and 6.

Isabela was carried away by his presentation and confidence, and Ferdinand added his signature because it was her undertaking.

The patent demanded by Columbus gave a preview of dominant traits of his character, soon to become apparent: personal aggrandizement, absolute authority, unwillingness to consider the interests of others, and grasping for wealth. He would establish his name through his descendants "forever and always." A temperate and sensible person would have asked for less and would have asked for other things, nor would he have taken advantage of a lapse of foresight on the part of the Queen. The contract brought him into continuing conflict with the interest of the Crown, the colony he governed, and Spain. Fernández Duro observed that King Ferdinand never subscribed with good will to the capitulations because they placed in perpetuity into the hands of one family the government, administration of justice, and, in effect, the sovereignty of the Islands and Tierra Firme.[3] Antagonism between Columbus and royal officials was immediate and inevitable. Except for the support of the Queen he became more and more exposed and isolated from all except his own family. The *título* troubled the affairs of the New World for years. After his death his heirs brought suit for its full recognition, claiming that their perpetual rights extended to the whole of the Spanish New World.[4] A settlement was made in 1536, but some of the claims were not settled until 1564. For years they were a major impediment to the reform of colonial government.

PREPARATION FOR THE VOYAGE

Columbus was penniless and the Crown risked no funds of the public treasury or of its private means, contrary to the popular story of the Queen's jewels. A major part of the moneys seems to have been secured by Luis de Santángel, keeper of accounts of the royal household, borrowing from the funds of the Santa Hermandad, the secret police of the time. It was to Santángel that Columbus addressed the first communication of the success of the voyage, to become known as the First Letter, widely circulated in Europe in many printings. It is thought that Italian factors resident in Sevilla advanced funds, and also participating shipmasters, such as the Pinzón family of Palos. Even under the poor financial conditions then prevailing in Spain, the expedition was made ready at low cost.

Three ships were to undertake the voyage, which was scheduled to start from Palos, where Columbus knew many of the citizens. The caravels, *Pinta* and *Niña*, were owned and manned at Palos and Moguer. The larger ship, the *Santa María*, was brought around from Puerto de Santa María by its owner, Juan de la Cosa, a Biscayan who had been operating out of there. It was chartered for the voyage, with Cosa going along as master.[5] On the same date that Columbus got his *título*

---

[3] Cesáreo Fernández Duro, "Colón y Pinzón," *Memorias de la Real academia de la historia*, X (Madrid, 1883), 177.
[4] *Ibid.*, pp. 180–186.
[5] It has been maintained that two different persons by the name of Juan de la Cosa took part in the early events of the New World. Antonio Ballesteros y Beretta, who had accepted this view in his *Historia de América y de los pueblos americanos* (Barcelona, 1936 and later), finally concluded that there was only one, as set forth in his posthumous book, *La marina cántabra y Juan de la Cosa* (Santander, 1954).

the citizens of Palos were notified of a fine imposed on them "for some things done and committed," and therefore were ordered to equip the two caravels at their own expense and to provide the crews. The fine may have been for smuggling. The only suggestion why Palos was singled out is that its participation was needed and some sort of pressure was available. This was not necessary and probably would not have worked. Ships might be confiscated but Columbus would have small chance of success with an unwilling crew and officers under duress.

A crew was gotten together for the *Santa María* by offering suspension of sentence to persons held in various jails. This was done at the request of Columbus and provided a motley, inexperienced, and fainthearted lot. The *Pinta* and *Niña* on the other hand were manned by stout and competent seamen from Palos and Moguer, who joined voluntarily. These men knew Columbus and his plans from the time when he lived with the Franciscans at La Rábida. The leading citizen of Palos, Martín Alonso Pinzón, according to later testimony had convinced himself of the feasibility of such a voyage by studying charts in the Vatican Library in Rome. At any rate, he and two brothers agreed to go, and provided the *Pinta*. In adjacent Moguer the shipowning family Niño supplied the *Niña*. Such leadership assured, seamen from both towns signed up with a will. The *Pinta* and *Niña* were a community enterprise, strong in the bonds of shared experience and confidence. Crew and officers were neighbors and kinsmen. They had sailed together and would take their chances together in a greater venture. Martín Alonso Pinzón became captain of the *Pinta*, his brother Vicente Yáñez of the *Niña*, and a third brother went in a minor capacity.[6] Three of the Niño family took part: Juan as master of the *Niña*, Peralonso as pilot of the *Santa María*, a third as grummet or apprentice officer.

The three ships carried a complement of about ninety men, sufficient to work the ships, though most of the personnel of the *Santa María* lacked experience. The Biscayan, Juan de la Cosa, was a skilled pilot well established at Puerto de Santa María and had become wealthy, probably by trading to the African islands and mainland. The Pinzón and Niño brothers were seasoned navigators and old associates. Columbus had chosen well. The names Cosa, Pinzón, and Niño were to be writ large in the annals of New World exploration.

THE RECORD OF THE VOYAGE

The account of the voyage is based on a few sources, the First Letter of Columbus, his so-called Journal, the interviews Peter Martyr and the priest Andrés Bernáldez had after the voyage, the histories of Las Casas, Oviedo, and Gómara, and, of least dependability, what his son Ferdinand wrote in the history of his illustrious father. Interpretation, critique, and surmise have piled up into a vast body of Columbian literature.

The Journal is the source of a major part of what is known of the discovery, the only record of its calendar and geography. The original may have been a confidential report to King and Queen intended to remain a classified document.

---

[6] The studies of Fernández Duro on Palos and the Pinzón family have been summarized by Ballesteros y Beretta, *Historia de América*, especially vol. IV, 517–554.

Las Casas found a copy which he said was less than perfect, and copied this in his own hand. Parts of it Las Casas introduced into his *Historia*, which provided Herrera with the account of the discovery. The Lascasian copy of the Journal was rediscovered by Navarrete, who published it as the first item in his *Colección*.[7] The version is a daily record from the start of the voyage on August 3, 1492, to its end on March 15, 1493, except for the time in the Canaries between August 10 and September 5 and five days spent in a Cuban harbor. The account in part is in the third, in part in the first person. Such a change of person is found, for instance, in the entry for September 16: "Here they began to see many drifts of very green plants which appeared to have been newly detached from the land, for which reason all judged that there was an island near by, but not the mainland according to the Admiral, who says *because I judge the mainland to lie farther on*." The parts that seemed less important, Las Casas abstracted or paraphrased; for the more significant ones he quoted Columbus verbatim, usually with quotation marks. From the discovery of land on October 12 to October 24, for example, the Journal is in the first person and in quotation marks. Las Casas added comments of his own as glosses in the margins. The Journal, known only through its copy and abstract by Las Casas, has impressed most students as faithfully done, and is consistent with whatever else is known of the voyage.[8]

THE OCEAN CROSSING

It took eight days from Palos to the Canaries, where four weeks were spent seeing to it that the ships were in good repair, in loading water, wood, and meat, and in waiting to make sure that no Portuguese ships were at sea to intercept them. On the night of September 8 the flotilla set out into the west, having a brisk northeast wind. A due west course was kept for two weeks, thereafter falling off somewhat to the southwest. The maps of the time placed Cipango (Japan) and the Canaries in the same latitudes and showed the Japanese islands as lying more than a thousand miles to the east of Cathay (China). The shortest crossing, therefore, was indicated by keeping to the latitude of the Canaries (about 28° N.). Maps showed islands in the western sea such as Antillia, Brazil, and St. Brendan's. Watch was kept for them and sightings were reported but proved false. On October 7 "a great multitude of birds passed out of the North going to the Southwest by which it was believed that these were going to sleep on land or perhaps were fleeing winter, which was approaching in the lands from which they came, for the Admiral knew that most of the islands held by the Portuguese were discovered by birds." (This in fact was immemorial knowledge of seafaring men.) The ships at the time were south of the Bermudas, and were crossing one of the

---

[7] Navarrete's introduction to the first volume, especially pp. lviii–lxxvii, is still an important evaluation of the sources.
[8] Cecil Jane excluded it from his Hakluyt Society collection of *The Voyages of Christopher Columbus* (Series II, vols. LXV and LXX), although he made a competent translation, edited posthumously (New York, 1960) by L. A. Vigneras, the latter adding an informed introduction and notes. Jane was strongly prejudiced against Las Casas, as is all too apparent in the introduction to his second Hakluyt volume. This was published in the incompleted form in which it was left at his death. Had he lived to finish it he might, it is hoped, have come to a fairer judgment.

main routes of bird migration. Signs that land was near increased, and two hours after midnight, on October 12, land was sighted at a distance. In the morning they took possession of the island and named it San Salvador. There is still disagreement which of the Bahama group was first discovered, a matter that is not of present concern. The ocean had been crossed in thirty-three days. For the first several days the ships were still in waters frequented by the Portuguese. For several days prior to the landfall they knew that land was near.

The crossing had been made without mishap. The weather had been fine. There was no lack of water or food, and the diet was varied by taking fish. The men were all in excellent health. The traditional story that only the steadfastness of the Admiral kept the ships from turning about and running for home is a libel on Spanish seamen. Columbus made the voyage on the *Santa María*, whose crew was mainly made up of men who had been released from jail and who were unaccustomed to the sea. It may be for these that he began to falsify the sailing record at the outset (September 9), "deciding to count less distance than was run so that if the voyage should be long the men would not be frightened or dismayed." Each pilot, of course, kept his own and true record. There is no reason to think that the men of the *Pinta* and *Niña*, neighbors and kinsmen, both crew and officers, did not know how the voyage was progressing or that they would have taken satisfaction in such deception. On September 22 the Journal entry recorded head winds: "This contrary wind was very necessary to me, for my people were greatly encouraged, having thought that these seas did not blow winds by which to return to Spain." Spanish seamen, accustomed to go to the Canaries and Portuguese islands, who knew only how to sail before the wind? How then, when the ships left Española for the homeward voyage, did they head northeastward promptly and steadily until they got into the latitudes of westerly winds that took them past the Azores and home to Iberian shores? During part of the day of September 23 "the sea was calm and the men complained that there being no high sea it would never blow to return to Spain." Seamen well accustomed to calms in the passage between Spain and the Canaries who lost heart because of a brief calm? On October 10, two days after they had begun to see flights of birds going south, "the men could endure no longer, complaining of the long voyage, but the Admiral encouraged them as best he could giving them good hope of the profit they should have." Columbus, being on the *Santa María* heard the whining of landlubbers which he dramatized to contrast with his own courage. The seasoned seamen, the men of Palos and Moguer, led by their own capable navigators, had no cause to be dismayed by a prosperous voyage that may have been somewhat longer than any they had been on, but from which they were confident that they would know how to return. Columbus had originated and promoted the idea of the voyage; Spanish seamen made it possible and carried it through.

The Course of the Discovery

A number of Bahaman islands were reconnoitered from the landfall of October 13 to October 27. The eastern part of the Cuban north shore was then run out to December 5; the north coast of Haiti, promptly named Española by Columbus, from December 6 to January 16, when the return voyage began. The precise route and stops are not under consideration here, except for the last three weeks in Española.[9]

One week after the first landfall, the Journal entry (October 19) stated: "I wish to see and discover as much as I can in order to return to your Highnesses, if it please our Lord, in April. However, should I find where there is gold or spices in quantity I shall delay until I may have as much of these as possible." The ships were in good condition, the crews at full strength and in high spirits, and provisions and supplies had been taken for a year; yet an early return was planned when he had seen only a few sandy islands and their simple natives. The finding of gold or spices might extend the voyage. There was no mention of Eastern lands or their princes.

On October 21, while still in the Bahamas, he added to the account of the day that he would go to see another very great island, which, according to signs given by the Indians, he thought must be Cipango, called Cuba by them, "in which they say are ships and mariners, many and very great . . . Moreover I am still determined to go to the mainland and to the city of Quinsay, and give the letters of your Highnesses to the Great Khan and ask for an answer and come with it." On the 24th he had confirmation that Cuba was Japan and a land of great commerce. In the fortnight spent cruising about the Bahamas, Columbus showed no interest in continuing west but began to turn to the south.

Arriving in Cuba on the 28th, "the Admiral understood that ships of the Great Khan came there, and large ones, and that from there to the mainland was a journey of ten days." The following day the ships started "West to get to the city where it seemed to him that the Indians said its King was," and sailed west for three days. Navarrete placed the farthest point at Nuevitas; Morison, at Puerto Padre. Having gone briefly and leisurely on the proper track toward China, Columbus turned about abruptly and thereafter always went in the opposite direction. "It is certain, says the Admiral, that this is the mainland and that I am, says he, about a hundred leagues from Zayton and Quinsay." (These were the two great seaports of China that Marco Polo had visited: Quinsay on the bay of Hangchow and Zayton in the Strait of Formosa.) The wind had changed to a blow out of the north, the sky was stormy, it was getting colder, the coast had taken a trend to north-northwest, and, if the text was not corrupt, Las Casas stated, the Admiral thought himself at latitude 42° North. Perhaps the coast took on a northerly trend for a few miles; perhaps a cool air mass was moving across from Florida. These were poor excuses for turning back from the hundred leagues that he thought lay between him and the great ports of China.

The ships remained in port from November 1 to 12 (according to Morison, this was the port of Gibara). While here Columbus sent a converted Jew who knew some Arabic, a Spaniard, and two Indians to seek the king of that country, for whom the Admiral had letters and a present and whose friendship he wished. They returned in six days, having gone twelve leagues and found a village of fifty houses. Here the Admiral took the latitude by quadrant and found it to be 42°. The entry for November 12 concluded with the remark that it was

---

[9] Samuel E. Morison, *Admiral of the Ocean Sea* (Boston, 1942), has retraced the route by actual sail following the entries of the Journal.

somewhat cold and that hence it was not advisable to navigate northward in winter; Las Casas added in a marginal gloss that they might have discovered Florida in two days by going on. This was the last mention of Oriental destinations in the Journal.

The Letter of Columbus, written during the return voyage, sums up the decision to reverse directions: "When I got to Juana [Cuba] I followed its coast West and found it so great that I thought it mainland, the Province of Cathay; and since I did not find towns and settlements on the seacoast, except small ones, with whose people I was unable to have speech because they all ran away, I went ahead on the same route, thinking I could not miss large cities and towns; and at the end of many leagues seeing there was nothing new, and that the coast carried me to the North whereas my desire was to the contrary, because winter was already marked (*encarnado*) I determined to go South."

Columbus made too many excuses for not continuing to the land of the Great Khan, whose seaports lay at ten days' sail or at a hundred leagues. Coastline, wind, and current all led west. A purely local change of coast to the north was construed into a continuing change of direction. The passage of cool northern air for several days he interpreted as the arrival of winter cold, although he wrote at the same time about his delight in the tropical verdure. A brief change in wind became the adversity of head winds out of the north. Being at that time about at latitude 21° North he doubled it. It would seem that he knew he was expected to seek new lands to the west, that he did not wish to go in that direction, that his imagination lent itself to easy distortion of the facts, and thought that his own confused geographic knowledge might be accepted by those who knew even less. He persisted in believing that Cuba was China, although he knew the description by Marco Polo.

Columbus admitted that his desire was to go south. From the Bahamas to Cuba he had dropped perhaps three degrees in latitude and in the rest of the voyage would add only another degree and a half. Nineteen days passed between the discovery of land in the Bahamas and the aboutface in Cuba. Thereafter for eleven weeks the course was south of east until the voyage home began; the easting amounted to about eight degrees. The progress was slow, both because of numerous stops and because they were sailing against wind and current. All along the Cuban and Haitian coasts they were going into the trade wind, at times tacking out to sea as far as forty miles, at times lying in port when the wind was strongly out of the east. The stubbornness of the upwind passage is good proof of the quality of his pilots and seamen.

The Windward Passage was crossed on December 5; the north coast of Haiti was run out from harbor to harbor until Christmas Eve, when the *Santa María* sank, grounding on a reef to the east of Cap Haïtien. The eastward voyage was resumed on January 4, 1493, during the final week (January 10 to 16) at a much increased pace.

Three occasions to continue west were passed up: the first in the Bahamas, the second when he turned back in Cuba, and the last when he did not enter the Windward Passage. Columbus believed and continued to believe to the end that he had reached the Far East, yet neither at this time nor later did he prove it, as by seeking any of its great centers. What he had seen was quite unlike what Polo and other travelers to the Orient had described. He felt that some explanation was expected of him for changing the direction of his exploration and he gave answers that are not credible.

Jane had the important insight that from the beginning Columbus was interested in going south and that his ultimate objective lay in that direction.[10] Columbus expressed that desire after he got to Cuba; also in his letter he told that he had heard of an island to the south of Española which was called Matinino (Martinique) and that this was the first island on the way to the Indies from Spain. This is a puzzling passage. It is true that Martinique is so located for sailing from Spain to the West Indies, but Columbus at the time had not sailed within five hundred miles of the island. In his second voyage he made straight for that more southerly gateway to the New World.

The geography in the mind of Columbus was a mixture of fact, fancy, and credulity. Cipango would be the nearest part of the Far East and was identified at first with Cuba. Soon Cuba became an outlying part of Cathay or adjoined it. When he first heard of Haiti he misunderstood *bohío*, native name for house, for the name of the island. When he got there and heard the word *cibao*, meaning "stony mountains," he identified it with Cipango. There he also heard of a strange people who came to raid, by the name of *caniba*. This, he said, is "nothing else than the people of the Great Khan, who must be very close by and will have ships to capture persons, and since these do not return it is believed they have been eaten." Khan, cannibal, and Carib were given the same etymology. Cathay and Cipango were placed by him in the lands he had discovered. Other parts of the Far East that were known by name were added in his later voyages.

Columbus also reported by hearsay of fabulous places and peoples, having read the imaginary travels of Mandeville. In Cuba (Journal, November 4) "he understood also that far away there were one-eyed people and others with dog faces who ate people." In his Letter he told of an unseen Cuban province where the people are born with tails. Matinino (Martinique) was inhabited only by women, exercised in the use of bow and arrow and "protected by plates of *arambre* [copper or bronze], of which they have a great deal." Thus was the Amazon legend transferred to the New World. "In another island which they assure me is greater than Española the people have no hair at all. In this there is gold beyond counting, and from this one [!] and the others I am bringing Indians as proof." Peter Martyr, having heard the story of the Amazons, added dryly, "thus they tell me and thus I am telling it to you." [11] Places Columbus saw were relocated by him into the Far East without regard to the differences of their nature. Places he heard about vaguely he invested with the fabled qualities of romances of the Middle Ages.

THE SEARCH FOR GOLD

From the first landing to the end of his days gold obsessed Columbus, directed his explorations, and dominated his conduct. In his mind gold was associated with hot climates, an old view that gold was engendered by heat (and silver by cold)

---

[10] Cecil Jane, pp. cxv–cxviii of the first volume of *The Voyages of Christopher Columbus*.
[11] Peter Martyr, Decade I, Bk. 1.

which continued to have currency in the early mining days of the New World. It was stated in the Journal (November 21) for the Cuban coast: "Because of the heat which the Admiral says that he suffered there, he argues that in these Indies and where he was then, there was certain to be much gold." He had read about the Golden Chersonese (Malaya) at the southeast of Asia. He had been to Portuguese trading posts on the African Gold Coast. (In Cuba he compared its pleasant streams with the pestilential rivers of Guinea.) The inclination to the south that was evident on all four of his voyages, it may be suggested, rested on his belief that gold was to be sought under a tropical sun.

The search for gold began immediately on landing. The entry for October 13 said, "I was bent upon finding out if there was gold and saw that some wore a bit of it suspended from a hole pierced in the nose and by signs I learned that going to the South or making a turn about the island to the South there was a king who had large jars of it and possessed a lot." The deflection of his course from west to south was thus indicated at once. In the same entry he was sure that the gold was of local origin. He landed at the second island on October 15, having been told by signs that there was "very much gold and that they wear it as bracelets, anklets, earrings, nose rings, and breastplates," but, he added, "I do not wish to tarry, in order to reach and visit many islands so as to find gold." Daily reports of gold were heard, but on the 19th he admitted that the natives "are so poor in gold any little bit seems much to them." On the 22d a few nose pendants were traded, "but so little that it is nothing." On the 23d he decided to go on to Cuba "because I see that there is no gold mine here," giving up the search for gold mines in the coral islands of the Bahamas.

After four days in Cuba he had seen no gold worn by anyone, but had noted a nose ring of worked silver which he took as indication of silver to be found there. (If correct, it is one of the few notes of aboriginal contact with Mexico.) On November 4 he was told that the people of Bohío (Española) wore an infinite amount of gold on the neck, ears, arms, and legs. On the 12th he heard of an island to the east called Babeque (which Morison has identified as Great Inagua Island), "where as they indicated by signs the people collect gold on the beach at night by candlelight, and thereupon beat it into bars (*vergas*) with hammers." Mulling over the Babeque story, he added, "without doubt there are in these lands very great quantities of gold, which the Indians I am taking along say, not without cause, that there are in these islands places where they dig the gold and wear it about the neck, on the ears and arms and legs, and these are very heavy bracelets"—identifications which the natives could not have given because they did not know such things.

The means of communicating with the natives were obviously poor, and Columbus supplied what he did not understand from his imagination. He had seen no unworked gold and only an occasional bit of gold adornment hung from the nose. His continuing inquiries about gold directed him to the south, his desired objective. His persistence is remarkable. The trail had grown no warmer as he sailed from the Bahamas along the coast of Cuba. In seven weeks of search he had found only trifling ornaments here and there. These were said to be of southern origin and this much he could perhaps learn from the natives. They may have humored him by agreeing, as far as they could understand, with his eager questions.

Because of inclement weather Columbus did not go out to find the fabulous island of Babeque but crossed over to Haiti on December 6. On the 12th a woman was seen with a small piece of gold in her nose and on the 17th a cacique was wearing a piece the size of a hand (gold foil?). The following day at a festival in honor of the visitors an elder dignitary told of many islands at a hundred leagues and beyond where there was much native gold, one island that was all gold and others where it was gathered and sifted, smelted, made into bars, and worked into a thousand objects—procedures unknown to the natives.

In the province of Marien (the Plaine du Nord about Cap Haïtien) the party was festively entertained (December 21–January 2) by Guacanagari, the first high chief and the only one met on this voyage. In scenes reminiscent of Captain Cook in the South Seas the natives swarmed in to trade, especially to get articles of bronze or iron. Here for the first time gold was less than very rare, though it was not abundant. Guacanagari presented Columbus with a ceremonial girdle into which gold had been worked. The subchiefs wore "crowns," partly of gold, which had been beaten into very thin sheets, glued, and combined with other finery. One belt carried a mask which had two large ears of hammered gold, also a tongue and a nose of gold (December 22). Columbus thought there must be much gold in the area "because in the three days they had been in that port he had secured good pieces of gold and he could not believe that it was brought from another country" (December 23). To inquiries as to "where the gold was produced they named among other places Cipango, which they call Civao, and there they affirm there is great quantity of gold, and its Cacique carries banners of hammered gold; however, it is far away to the East." Guacanagari assured Columbus that there was so much of it in Cibao that it was held in small account. He placed some jewels of gold on the Admiral's head and chest, and a large mask with pieces of gold in the ears, eyes, and other parts (December 26). Cibao and four other islands to the east were named as having infinite gold (December 29)—all of them actually districts of Española. The Admiral heard of another large island, Jamaica, where there was much more gold than in Española, in pieces larger than broad beans (*habas*), whereas in Española they were like grains of wheat (January 6). No gold was found later in Jamaica, nor is there any record that he saw any unworked gold in Haiti at the time.

Throughout the voyage Columbus noted any gold object worn. Also he showed samples to the natives to see whether they would direct him where to find it. The answer he got, or construed, was always that it was to be found somewhere to the east or south. Thus he went from island to island and port to port. Gold was associated in his mind with islands. He kept hearing of islands rich in gold, even of some that were gold. Different districts of Haiti he interpreted as separate gold-rich islands, including the stony mountains of the interior, the Cibao. Also he heard of an "island" of Guanin, unaware that this was a native term for gold alloy, in distinction from pure gold, *caona*.

That there was a distinction between native gold and *guañín*, an alloy of copper and gold, was recognized dimly and late by Columbus, just before he

25

left Española. The account (January 13) concerns a native on Samaná Bay, the easternmost and last place entered. This area was occupied by a people known as Ciguayos, of different speech and ways. An informant said that there was very much gold and, pointing to the poop cabin of the caravel, that there were pieces that great. He called gold *tuob* and did not know it as caona, as it was called in the major part of the island, nor as *nozay*, as it was named in San Salvador and the other (Bahama) islands. Of the island of Matinino the Indian said, "it was all peopled by women without men, and that on it there is a great deal of tuob, which is gold or bronze . . . Also he spoke of the island of Goanin, where there is much tuob." Las Casas added marginal glosses: "*Caona* was the name for gold in the greater part of Española Island, but there were two or three languages." Las Casas added, "This Goanin was not an island, as I believe, but the base gold, which according to the Indians of Española had an odor for which they prized it greatly and this they called Goanin." The use of the term tuob for guañín apparently was restricted to the Ciguayos. The eagerness of the natives to acquire *cascabeles*, copper hawk bells carried as trade items, probably meant that they thought these to be of guanín. The Journal of December 26 said the natives were on the point of going crazy for cascabeles. Gold they beat into flat shapes, guanín they knew only by trade out of a distant and obscure south, nor did they know that it contained gold.[12]

On January 8 a boat was sent into the Río Yaque del Norte to take on water. It found that the sand of the river mouth was "all full of gold, to such an extent that it was a marvel, although very small. He says that in a short space he found many grains as large as lentils, but of the fine grains he said there was great quantity." Therefore the Admiral gave the name Río del Oro to the river. The gloss of Las Casas commented, "I believe that much of this must have been margarite, of which there is a lot there, and that perhaps the Admiral thought that all was gold that glistened." Las Casas was right. The Yaque carries flakes of mica into its lower course in its alluvial deposits, but not particles of heavy gold. Columbus found no golden sands there, on the beaches of the Bahamas, or anywhere else. He remained wholly innocent of the manner of occurrence of placer gold and therefore did not go inland to prospect mountain streams. It is doubtful that he got out of sight of the sea at any time.

Peter Martyr, present at court at the return of Columbus, had some relevant comments. He told that it was learned how gold was collected with small labor, from stream sands that had been washed down from the high mountains. This knowledge can have come only from the truant party of the caravel *Pinta*, which alone had seen how this was done. Columbus told Peter Martyr that he had found the island of Ophir (again an island in the mind of Columbus), but the writer sensibly inferred that it must have been the Antilles, suspecting thus early that the expedition had not reached the Far East. Peter Martyr thought the islanders held gold in some esteem, since they beat it into very thin sheets for ornamental wear, but that their skill at working it was limited. In recounting what he heard about the discovery Peter Martyr gave minor attention to its

---

[12] Las Casas, vol. I, ch. 57 for a discussion of *guanín*. Also Friederici; further, Sven Lovén, *Origins of the Tainan Culture, West Indies* (Gothenburg, 1936), pp. 463–473.

promise of gold. Good reporter that he was, he listened also to other members of the party.

THE DISCOVERY OF GOLD

The discovery of placer gold was made in the mountainous interior of Haiti, in the region later called the Cibao, and was due to Martín Alonzo Pinzón and the crew of the caravel *Pinta*. The elder Pinzón has been given a bad name in history because he absented himself without leave by Columbus. This happened November 21 when the three ships were off the northeast shore of Cuba; according to the Journal entry, Martín carried an Indian on board to help him acquire gold, and took off to the east for the island of Babeque, reputed to be rich in gold.

The matter was aired at length in the suit of the Columbus heirs against the Crown. Numerous depositions were taken in 1515 at Palos from friends and kinsmen of the Pinzón family, supporting the conduct of the elder Pinzón.[13] Columbus resented the dereliction bitterly and feared that Martín might have gone home "to inform the Sovereigns by lies" in order to escape the penalty he merited (Journal, January 3). Fernández Duro, after long and critical study of the participation of the brothers Pinzón in the discovery, suggested that the *Pinta* was in advance of the others on the Cuban coast and missed the signal from the flagship to turn back. This scholar did establish the major role of the elder Pinzón in making the expedition possible and in carrying it through, thus refuting many of the charges made against the conduct of the captain of the *Pinta*.[14]

Columbus spent six weeks on the coasts of the Bahamas and Cuba hunting gold, seeing only an occasional trifle worn, and entering vague hearsay of its sources in the Journal, fantastically embellished. An experienced old seadog such as Martín Alonso can hardly have been impressed. He did leave to do exploring on his own. The absence was extended, but it was not desertion for, having found a source of the gold that Columbus had been looking for in vain, he turned back to rejoin and report to Columbus. This act clears the elder Pinzón of the charge that he was intending to reach Spain first. Having the best sailing ship and a selected crew, he could readily have done so and kept from Columbus the knowledge of the discovery of gold. This was the conduct of a partner who had grown impatient of lying about in harbors, not that of one who would steal the glory from the commander.

The *Pinta* took off from Cuba into the east, supposedly to find the island of Babeque. At any event it came to Española from the north whereas the *Santa María* and the *Pinta* did so from the west. The first word the Admiral had of

---

[13] CDU, VIII, especially pp. 169–234.

[14] Cesáreo Fernández Duro published a first inquiry as "Colón y Pinzón," *op. cit.* (see n. 3 above), followed by other articles, a number of which have been collected by Luis Peñafiel in *Los hermanos Pinzón en el descubrimiento de América* (Buenos Aires, 1944). Fernández Duro, like Navarrete, had been a naval officer who devoted himself to Spanish history while at sea. His competence was recognized in the positions he held as Perpetual Secretary of the Real Academia de Historia and as President of the Real Sociedad dos Geografía. His conclusion that without Martín Alonso's support and participation Columbus would have lacked crew, pilots, and ships is an important reassessment of the discovery.

the truant ship was on December 27, after the sinking of the *Santa María*, when it was reported that the *Pinta* was in a river toward the far side of the island. At the time Columbus had come a third of the way along the north shore of Española and the *Pinta* was another third farther on. News of the *Pinta* was brought to the cacique Guacanagari, who passed it on immediately to Columbus. The *Pinta* therefore had not followed the coast of Española eastward, where it would have been noted by the natives and information given to Columbus. Columbus discovered the north coast of what is now the Republic of Haiti; Pinzón, that of the Dominican Republic. It is probable also that Pinzón preceded Columbus in landing on the island.

The information is scanty—the Journal entries for January 6 and 10, and testimony taken twenty-three years later, mostly from persons who could only say that this was public knowledge.[15] Columbus, who had become bitterly hostile toward Pinzón, and the friendly witnesses for Pinzón agreed that the *Pinta* had discovered and entered the inlet of the modern town of Luperón. This is the most northerly harbor of the island, a minor port, connected with the interior by a fair road south. Columbus noted it as "a good port, well enclosed, except for the fact that it has much *broma* [shipworm], from which the *Pinta* was in very bad shape." After the reunion on January 6 it was necessary to take time out there to calk the *Pinta*. This is the first notice of damage from boring mollusks to which ships later were subject on the Spanish Main. It also indicates that the *Pinta* was at rest in that harbor for some time. Pinzón had named the harbor and river after himself; Columbus renamed it Gracia. Both names were used; the eastern point of land is still called Punta de Gracia.

The Journal reported that Martín Alonso "stayed there trading for sixteen days, where they traded much gold." Again, "the Admiral says that the caravel traded in much gold, that for a belt end they got good pieces of gold of the size of two fingers and even of a hand." For the first time, not worked bits of ornaments but gold nuggets were in hand and in some amount. There is no nearby source of gold, the closest being to the south in the mountains of the Cibao, fifty miles or more away. Native gold was not an object of trade among the natives, as became apparent when the island was occupied. Even the great chiefs did not amass it. This harbor was only a place of small fishermen and small fields. The acquisition of native gold in quantity by trade was not in the pattern of native ways, and was out of the question for a minor fishing settlement.

The inquiry (*probanza*) of 1515 asked a leading question whether in the seven weeks (the period of absence of the *Pinta*) Martín Alonso had entered the interior of the island to the seats of three major named caciques and there found gold. Some respondents said they did not know, some that this was generally known, and some that they had been along and found gold, but did not mention time, distance, or names of caciques. Martín Alonso did not spend the sixteen days of which Columbus had heard sitting in the harbor. Sixteen days were more than enough to make the trip to the Cibao placers, and he may have been inland for a longer time during the seven weeks of his absence. There was only one area to go to for gold, the Cibao; they had come to the part of

---

[15] Las Casas, vol. I, chs. 65 and 66, is an elaboration of the Journal and a critique of the testimony.

the north coast nearest and most convenient to it; and their route is indicated by relief and modern roads about as shown on figure 3. When Columbus returned on the second voyage, one of the first things that he did was to send a party to the Cibao over about the same route taken by the men of the *Pinta*. He had the necessary information from them.

Off Montecristi the *Pinta* rejoined the *Niña* on January 6 with the news and a sample of nuggets. Two more days were spent plugging the leaks on the *Pinta* and loading water and wood. On the 9th day they anchored for a few hours at the entry to Martín Alonso's port, noted by Columbus as good, and then hurried on to the east. Before daybreak of the 16th the ships left the Bay of Samaná, the farthest point reached, for home. In a week Columbus had covered the farther half of Haiti's north coast, the first half of which had taken a month. With the proof given him of gold deposits he considered his mission accomplished and hurried to get back to Spain. The ships parted company on February 14 in a storm off the Azores, not to meet again until March 15, when both got to Palos on the same day, Martín Alonso dying on arrival.

TROPICAL IDYLL

The beauty of the islands moved Columbus greatly. He was in high spirits during the whole three months. The trade-wind shores he found as tropical nature at its best, and he reveled in praise of their charm and bounty. The perfume of trees and flowers, he said, was carried out to the ships at sea. The islands were lands of perpetual spring. Birds of many forms and colors sang sweetly in a vast garden of innocent nature, inhabited by the gentlest and kindest natives. To the Spanish humanist Ramón Iglesia, Columbus seemed to be writing the promotion literature of a tourist bureau,[16] which he did with Italian exuberance. The more he wrote the more he praised. Beneath his superlatives there was, however, appreciation of nature and natives and quite a bit of discerning observation.

From one island to the next the wonders increased. The first Bahaman island was very green and fertile, the next was better, of the third he wrote "may your Highnesses believe that this land is the best and most fertile and temperate and level and excellent that is in the world." On October 21 he said, "if the other islands are very beautiful and green and fertile this one is much more so and of great and very green groves. Here there are some large lagoons, and on and about them marvelous groves; here and on the whole island all is green, and the vegetation as in April in Andalusia; and the singing of the birds such that a man might never wish to leave here, and flocks of parrots that obscure the sun; and birds large and small of so many kinds and so different from ours that it is a marvel; and also there are trees of a thousand kinds; all bearing fruit according to their kind, and all marvelously scented."

Arrived at Cuba (October 28), he "never saw anything so beautiful, full of trees surrounding the river, handsome and green and different from ours, with flowers and fruit each in its manner. Many birds and little birds, that sang very sweetly. There was a great number of palms of another kind than those of

---

[16] Ramón Iglesia, *El hombre Colón y otros ensayos* (Mexico, 1944).

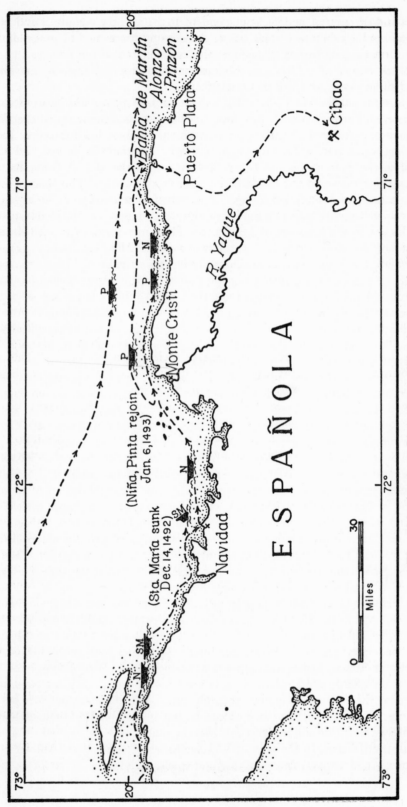

Fig. 3. Martín Alonso Pinzon's expedition in search of gold.

Guinea and of ours, of middle height and their trunks bare and the leaves very large, with which they roof their houses," and so on for a page of praise. In the Cuban Oriente, pine forests were first seen and admired. From one stop to the next the excellence of the harbors, the fertility of the country and the marvels of the vegetation were set forth in superlatives.

Having crossed over to Haiti a still higher pitch of praise was demanded. As they entered Tortue Channel, "the best lands of Castile cannot be compared as to beauty or fertility with these . . . nor did the plain of Córdoba equal them, the difference as great as between night and day." Again, "the air was like April in Castile, the nightingale and other birds sang as they did in Spain in that month, which they said was the sweetest thing in the world." The valley (Trois Rivières) he named Valle del Paraíso. The inland mountains were so high that the Pico de Tenerife was nothing in comparison. There was little left to say when he got to the province of Marien, the Plaine du Nord, in French days to come to be the most productive and valuable of all plantation lands.

The benign climate he appreciated gratefully. As yet there had been no experience of hurricanes. Of the fertility of the soil he knew little more than he did of the occurrence of gold. The Bahamas then seem still to have had a largely pristine vegetation, but no one with rural experience could have failed to notice their meager and thin soil. The Cuban shores he visited, except in the vicinity of Baracoa, were among the least fertile of that island. Everywhere he went the country was wonderfully rich or "marvelous," his favorite word.

His observations on the inhabitants are important, partly because they were the earliest. Although he called the natives Indians, he made no attempt to identify what he saw of them and their ways with the real Indies. Wild as was the hearsay that he set down, what he saw himself usually makes sense after it has been trimmed of the exaggeration that came so naturally to his temperament. The particulars of native life he noted will be considered under the native economy.

Columbus started the distinction between good and bad Indians. The latter, for whom he introduced both the names Carib and Cannibal, he heard of only as living in islands to the south, from which they were said to come to raid the northern islands. When he wrote his Letter during the return voyage, the Caribs entered into his calculations as a potential source of profit as slaves. When he got to court he had more bad things to say about them, causing Peter Martyr to write about cannibals as very horrible people. Columbus at the time had never seen a Carib and it is not known what he actually heard.

The only contact with a people differing from the rest (later known as Ciguayos) was in the last days, on the Bay of Samaná. Columbus mistook them at first for Caribs because they had good weapons, especially bows and arrows, which had not been seen before, and their appearance was more formidable. The visit at Samaná began and ended in amicable fashion. The Admiral had put his men on guard; taking alarm at a fancied hostile mien, they attacked with damage to the Indians. Columbus thought that, since these might turn out to be Caribs, it was proper that they should be put in fear of the Christians, being a people without fear and not cowards like the others.

From the Bahamas to the land of Guacanagari the natives were known as of one speech and temperament, amiable and open, inclined to be timorous until assured of the good intentions of the visitors. After the wreck of the *Santa María* the Indians turned to with a will to rescue everything. Columbus then wrote this tribute: "They are affectionate people and without covetousness and apt for anything, which I certify to your Highnesses that I believe there is no better people or land in the world. They love their neighbors as themselves and have the sweetest speech in the world and gentle, and are always smiling" (December 25). The island idyll he applied also to its people, but Columbus also began to think how he could use their tractability for his own ends.

START OF THE COLONIAL PLAN

The Crown had not looked ahead beyond this voyage or it would not have signed the capitulation. The voyage had been set up as exploration of an unknown west and was provided with competent mariners. There were no other persons of special competence or duty, no military, civil, or church officials, no one experienced in commerce or crafts. What would come of the voyage was left undefined except for the titles and prerogatives of Columbus. He was on the lookout for the spices, gums, resins, and medicinals of the Orient and he thought repeatedly that he had found them, but his identifications were wrong, and there was no one to set him straight. Mainly, however, he was looking for gold mines, about which he knew nothing, nor was there any miner or assayer in the party.

As governor-to-be of whatever he discovered and gained, his attention turned at once to the natives who would be his subjects. He sized them up thus on the day of his first landing: "They will make good servants of good understanding, as I see that they repeat promptly what is said to them and I think that they will easily become Christians." Soon (October 14) he thought of taking them as slaves: "When your Highnesses may so order, all can be carried to Castile or they can be held as captives on the same island." On December 16 in the Valle del Paraíso he repeated his estimate of the gentle natives, adding: "May you believe that this island and all the others are your own as is Castile, that here it is only needed to make a settlement and order them to do what one wishes, for with the men I have, and they are not many, I could go about all these islands without hindrance, for I have seen three mariners go on shore and cause a whole multitude of these Indians to flee, without offering harm to them. They are without arms, all naked, and without skill at arms and great cowards, a thousand running away from three, and thus they are good to be ordered about, to be made to work, plant, and do whatever is wanted, to build towns and be taught to go clothed and accept our customs." In the Letter he again spoke of the timidity and peaceable character of the natives. Referring to the cacique Guacanagari and the Spaniards left at Navidad, he wrote that he had formed "great friendship with the King of that land who took pride in calling me brother and considered me to be such: and even though they should change their mind, neither he nor his people know what arms are, and go naked as I have said, and are the most timorous people of the world. So that the men left there are sufficient to destroy all that country, without danger to their persons if they know how to rule." The need for labor would be met by requiring the natives to do the work.

Columbus also began at once to look for suitable locations to occupy and fortify, not for protection against the natives but to control access by sea. The mouth of the Río Mares in Cuba (Puerto Gibara according to Morison) seemed to him a good place to build a fort (November 12) and even more so the harbor later known as Baracoa. Of it he wrote (November 27), "I say that your Highnesses must not consent that any foreigner other than Catholic Christians shall trade here nor set foot, since this was the end and beginning of the undertaking." Was he thinking of trading factories along the coast such as the Portuguese were building along African shores? Three days after reaching Haiti he decided to call it Española, the Spanish Island. The inspection of suitability for ships and settlement continued from harbor to harbor.

Columbus had been sent to discover and take possession, but thus far had only taken ceremonial possession for Spain. There had been discussion about leaving some of the men, Columbus saying that many had asked him for permission to remain. The decision was taken out of his hands by the unexpected loss of the *Santa María* at midnight of Christmas Eve, grounding on a reef on a windless night and calm sea. Thus "he knew that our Lord had caused the ship to run aground there in order that a settlement be made there" (entry of December 26). The natives wept at the loss to their friends, but Columbus had been given the providential sign that he should build a town here, which he would call Navidad. By native canoes and eager native help, everything that could be removed was taken to the adjacent shore, where no time was lost in starting construction. The site was no more than an open roadstead by a river (Grande Rivière du Nord), but in addition to divine intervention it had the advantage of being a league and a half from the town of the ever-faithful "king" Guacanagari (in the vicinity of Cap Haïtien).

The entry of the 26th said: "Today I have ordered that a tower and fort be built, both very well, and a large moat, not because I think this is necessary for the men, for I have said that these men I have could subjugate the entire island, which I believe is greater than Portugal and has twice as many people; moreover they [the natives] are naked and without arms and are incurable cowards." A fort was the proper way to build according to his mind and he continued to build them in later years. His *fortalezas* were dramatic rather than functional, and did not set a pattern for later Spanish foundings.

The number of men left at Navidad has been given as thirty-nine, mostly from the *Santa María*. Everything aboard the ship having been saved, they were well found with provisions, Columbus said for more than a year, and with all sorts of gear. "On the return from Castile which he expected to make, he hoped to find that those he was obliged to leave would have acquired a barrel of gold and that they would have found the mine of gold and the spices." This was planned before news had come of the *Pinta*. The settlement at Navidad would reconnoiter the island and its resources, especially the source of gold. It would lack nothing, having ample supplies from the *Santa María*, a very fertile country, and an Indian population as cowardly as it was friendly. Columbus identified only four men as having manual skills, delegated authority hastily, and left without concern about how they would get along with each other or with the natives.

During the return voyage Columbus had leisure to review the results, to prepare the Letter to send from the first port reached, and to work on his Journal. The latter was the detailed report of the discovery, the Letter a brief summary. Both represented the plan of colonization as it took form in his mind and as he would propose it to the Queen and King. He would stress the wealth he promised to bring, which they would use for holy purposes. This (Journal, December 26) would be in such amount that the Sovereigns in less than three years could undertake and be prepared to go on the conquest of the Holy Sepulcher "which I did thus aver to your Highnesses that all the gains from this my enterprise should be spent in the conquest of Jerusalem." These were words to stir the heart of the devout Queen and to impress Ferdinand, who had very different needs for income. The Letter ends in a peroration calling on all Christendom to rejoice in the "turning of so many people to our holy faith and thereafter in the temporal benefits because not Spain alone but all Christians shall have here comfort and gain." In actuality Columbus was wholly concerned with temporal benefits.

The prospectus he drew in the Letter was brief and assured: "To speak only of what has been done on this voyage, which was carried out thus in haste, Your Highnesses can see that I shall give them gold as much as may need, with very little aid that Your Highnesses will give me; also spices and cotton as much Your Highnesses shall order, and mastic which until now has not been found except in Greece in the island of Chios and which the Seignory may sell as it wishes, and linaloe as much as they shall order to be loaded, and as many slaves as they order to be shipped, and these shall be of the idolators; and I believe to have found rhubarb and cinnamon, and a thousand other things of value I shall find, which the men I have left there will have discovered."

Columbus had taken off on the wings of his imagination. The Spanish treasury was bare. He promised that it should have all the gold it wanted. All that he had to go on were the placers the men of the *Pinta* had seen and the nuggets they had brought back. The tales he thought he heard of distant golden islands were fulfillments of his own wishes. He promised to provide cargoes of aromatics, spices, and drugs of Orient without limit. The Journal held reports from time to time of the finding of one or another such plant, and all were wrong. If bark or gum smelled or tasted somewhat like an item of Eastern trade it was considered to be such. The West Indies have a great number of aromatic trees, especially in the drier parts and in the secondary vegetation about clearings. Conspicuous among these are torchwoods (*Bursera, Elaphrium*), some of which are still popularly known on both islands and mainland as *almacigo* (mastic) or *linaloe;* both names were transferred from botanically remote plants of the Old World by Columbus and have been handed down from those days. They gave the Spanish name for cinnamon, *canella,* to a native tree because of the flavor of its bark. It has passed into taxonomy as the genus *Canella* of the family of Canellaceae. Columbus imagined that he had discovered the true items of the spice trade. The Oriental products being well established in European demands, their possible substitutes from the New World were never seriously tried or accepted. Columbus paid no attention to the introduction of spices (such as capsicum) or dyes in native use.

Spun cotton had been seen among the natives in all the islands, and the abundance of such plants was noted. Columbus included it among available sources of revenue, but did not think of it or anything else as a plantation crop. Some years later his brother Bartholomew introduced the payment of tribute in cotton in a part of western Española as a minor and temporary source of revenue.

From the beginning Columbus had the slave trade in mind. At the journey's end he proposed that these should be taken from among the idolators. By this he meant Caribs, for he had come to the conclusion that the Indians with whom he had been (the Island Arawaks) were innocent of idolatry and other reprehensible practices. He had never seen a Carib, but what he had heard about them was bad and so it would be proper and profitable to capture them to be shipped to Spain as slaves.

The design of the future was pretty well set in his mind as he returned to present himself to the Sovereigns. He would be governor and viceroy of a new and great colonial venture, differing from the Portuguese pattern. He was not concerned with plantations of sugar cane or other tropical products, or with trading factories; nor did he say anything about discovering the rest of the way to the great kingdoms of the East. He had discovered and gained Española and made a settlement there. It would be the future seat of his operations. Its gentle and timorous natives would be made to do the labor. It would yield the gold which had been the object of his search. From it other gold regions would be discovered and taken, and a trade in Carib slaves was to be developed. Spices and the like would also be available. He had found his goal in Española, which in the following years absorbed most of his attention.

THE DISCOVERY ANNOUNCED

Columbus entered the port of Lisbon on March 4, 1493. Both ships reached Palos on March 15, whence they had sailed six months earlier. It is thought that Columbus sent word of his success from Lisbon to the court, at the time in Barcelona. On March 19 the Duke of Medinaceli petitioned that he be given the right to send ships to trade in the lands Columbus had discovered; the reason given being that he had given aid to Columbus in the time of adversity. The news spread fast. On March 30 the King and Queen sent a letter to Columbus, addressing him by the titles he had been promised and urging him to come quickly and to take preliminary steps for a return voyage. In the state reception at Barcelona in April, the Admiral, now properly so called, presented a number of natives, samples of gold, and some native products, including Indian corn. Peter Martyr, who was watching the show, wrote that a certain Christopher Columbus, a Ligurian, had returned from the Antipodes, bringing news of many precious things but in particular of gold, which those regions generate by their nature.[17] The Columbus Letter was printed that spring, was quickly translated into various languages, and was the publishing sensation of the time.

At Rome, Pope Alexander VI, at Spanish request, issued a series of bulls during May, acknowledging the Spanish discovery and possession across the ocean, accepting their proposal as Catholic princes to reduce the inhabitants to the Catholic faith, and drawing the first famous line of demarcation between Spanish and Portuguese rights, a hundred leagues to the west of the Azores and the Cape Verde Islands. These bulls stressed not only the discovery by Columbus of re-

---

[17] Peter Martyr, *Opus Epistolarum*, no. 130 (Paris, 1670 [1st ed., 1530]).

mote and hitherto unknown islands and mainland but also the fact that "Columbus caused a strong tower to be constructed and placed in guard thereof certain Christians of those who had gone with him so that from there they would seek other islands and mainlands." The Apostolic power recognized the validity of possession as supported in the founding of Navidad.

III

ABORIGINAL CONDITION
OF THE ISLANDS

•

ARAWAK ISLANDS OF THE NORTH

The northern islands of the West Indies were populated, with minor exceptions, by natives speaking one language, gaining their livelihood in similar manner, living in houses of similar form, having the same organization of society, and being mostly of the same stock. One kind of people and culture occupied the Greater Antilles, which are Cuba, Haiti, Puerto Rico, and Jamaica, and also the Bahama Islands, known in Spanish days as Islas Lucayas. They were the first people to be called Indians, and this was the only name by which they were known to the Spaniards, evidence of their common qualities. They were the northernmost Arawaks, separated from their South American kindred by the Caribs of the Lesser Antilles. In anthropological usage they have come to be called Taino, a term introduced in the present century and taken casually from the name for a single social class.[1] I am therefore using the preferable designation Island Arawaks for the natives of this northern cluster of islands.

THE SPANISH INFORMANTS

The Journal of Columbus has the earliest observations on native life, some of which are repeated in his First Letter. Next to his descriptions of the coastal waters and their shores these are the fullest and best items of his reporting. His own account of the second voyage has not come down to us. Thereafter he was absorbed in other matters.

For the second voyage there are reports from several participants. The most familiar is the letter of Dr. Chanca, first of the men of medicine who were to add so much to the knowledge of far parts of the world. Gentlemen tourists went along to see the sights and two of them, the Aragonese Coma and the Genoese

---

[1] Sven Lovén, *Origins of the Tainan Culture, West Indies* (Gothenburg, 1935), accepted the term for his comparative study of Arawak ethnography and archaeology.

Michele Cuneo, wrote letters.[2] A friar, Román Pane, was assigned by the Admiral to give an account of native beliefs, which he did with limited insight.[3] The *Historia de los Reyes Católicos* by the priest Andrés Bernáldez is of interest because he included what he learned from Columbus and others about the discovery of Jamaica and the south shore of Cuba in 1494.

The greater part of what we know of aboriginal conditions is due to the three remarkable chroniclers: Peter Martyr, Las Casas, and Oviedo.[4] Peter Martyr d'Anghiera, Italian cleric and confidant of pope and high clergy, lived at the Spanish court as tutor to the royal princes, and wrote letters commenting on the political situation of the time, collected as *Opus Epistolarum*. With the discovery of Columbus his interest turned to the New World, which he was one of the first to recognize as such. Man of the Renaissance, rational, skeptical, and curious, he learned what he could about the new lands and their strange inhabitants by interviewing those who returned from overseas. The resulting letters were collected into his famous *Decades*, a running account of the discoveries and qualities of the New World from 1493 almost to the time of his death in 1526. Although he never saw the New World, he composed a good picture of its nature and natives.

Fernández de Oviedo y Valdés came somewhat late, arriving at Darién in 1514 as an official with the party of Pedrarias Dávila. His *Sumario de la Natural Historia de las Indias*, printed in 1526, consisted mainly of observations made on Tierra Firme with only brief experience of Española. He lived in Santo Domingo most of the time from 1532 to 1546, during which he began his major work, the *Historia Natural y General de las Indias*. He came to Tierra Firme when native life and ways were still in existence. Española he knew briefly at a time of advanced decline, and later reconstructed its early condition from what he was told by old settlers. Oviedo had a strong interest in natural history, which he observed attentively and in large part well. He described native plants and animals in greatest number and their uses by the natives. Oviedo and Las Casas met and clashed at court in disputes about Indian policy. This conflict of opinion in which Las Casas was the more aggressive was reflected in the writings of the latter.

Las Casas as polemicist has overshadowed Las Casas the historian and geographer. No one knew the country and its natives so well and so long. His father and uncle had come with Columbus in 1493. The uncle stayed three years as a captain at arms in central Española; the father stayed until 1498 and returned to Spain with an Arawak slave, the first Indian acquaintance of young Bartolomé.

---

[2] The Chanca letter was first published by Navarrete, I, 198–224. The Coma letter is known in a florid Latin version done by Niccolo Scillacio in December, 1494, reproduced in the *Raccolta*, pt. III, vol. II, pp. 83–94; also in J. B. Thacher, *Christopher Columbus*, vol. II (New York and London, 1904), with an English translation. The letter of Cuneo under date of October, 1495, at Savona is in *Raccolta*, pt. II, vol. II, pp. 94–107.

[3] It is included in the *Historie* of Ferdinand Columbus, originally published in Italian (Venice, 1678).

[4] Alberto Salas, *Tres cronistas de Indias* (Mexico, 1958), a balanced comparison. José Miranda has contributed a well-considered introduction to Oviedo's *Sumario de la Natural Historia de las Indias* (Mexico, 1950). There is current revival of interest in Las Casas, as in the Millares Carlo edition of the *Historia*, with the foreword by Lewis Hanke (Mexico, 1951) and in the Las Casas volumes of Giménez Fernández, in process of publication.

Las Casas came with Nicolás de Ovando in 1502, was sent on the campaign against the Indians of southeastern Española, and was given Indians to produce food and wash gold in the Cibao. After ten years in Española, he was invited to take part in the occupation of Cuba, marched with Pánfilo de Narváez through the length of that island, and was one of its first *encomenderos*. Years later, when he had become a Dominican friar, he began writing his history in the convent at Puerto Plata on the north coast of Española. He knew the two main islands from end to end earlier and better than anyone.

Las Casas was an attentive and acute observer. He had known Española during the years when its native condition was being broken down. To Cuba he had come as a pioneer. He took careful notice of differences in fertility, of vegetation and animal life, of native food production by tillage, fishing, and hunting. He had been a successful man of affairs, the only such informant who made his living in having charge of natives. A person of high intelligence, he described clearly, discriminating in the identifications he made, and taking care to locate what he described. His contribution to human and physical geography is large.

The historical talents of Las Casas also were unusual. Decades after the event and away from the scene he could recall in detail what had happened. He had a good memory for order of events and participants. He was a proper craftsman in his writing, saying whether he was paraphrasing, condensing, or quoting a source. He was aware that he was living in a major period of history and felt an obligation to keep the record straight for posterity. Therefore he collected documents, originals where he could have them, otherwise copies by his own or another hand, the Journal of Columbus being one of many illustrations. We should be much less informed if Las Casas had not gathered documents wherever he found them. His history took a long time to write, begun in the convent at Puerto Plata and finished decades later in Chiapas. As he moved about, his chests of manuscripts and books went with him.

His two histories are large and leisurely tomes that he worked at during an unusually long lifetime. They remained in manuscript, but were used by historians. His short and bitter indictment of the Spanish colonial system, the *Breve Relación de la Destrucción de las Indias*, written when the great reform of the New Laws was in process, was not printed until a decade after these had been put into effect. This hardhitting tract was concise and biting as were the various memorials he presented from time to time to the authorities. His histories had polemical passages, interspersed with homilies, but returned always to the sequence of events and changing scene. His prejudices he wore openly; his concern with data was meticulous. It took him about forty years to write the history of the Spanish New World to 1520, the proper terminus of its formative first stage. Giving himself ample space to be discursive while keeping the thread of his discourse in hand, he introduced many otherwise unnoted facts that throw light on the early years of the islands. No one was as much interested in their Indians or knew their ways so well.

GEOGRAPHICAL NAMES AND DIVISIONS

Columbus, as is the right of the discoverer, was the main giver of names to the islands. He would hear an Indian name, such as Guanahaní, the island of the landfall, which he renamed San Salvador. Cuba became Juana, in honor of the heiress to the throne. For the supposed name of Bohío he substituted Española. Finding a third great island on his second voyage called Boriquén, he named it San Juan (Puerto Rico). The name Santiago was tried for Jamaica, but was not adopted. "Cuba" also prevailed over "Juana," and Boriquén continued to be a name for Puerto Rico as well as San Juan. The first voyage discovered the Atlantic shores from San Salvador in the Bahamas to the Bay of Samaná of the Dominican Republic, which Columbus called Golfo de las Flechas. He was uncertain whether Cuba was a great island or part of a mainland. To an island ahead which he heard of as Bohío he gave the name Isla Española within three days of coming to it, when he had seen only about thirty miles of its coast, accepting the signs from Cuban natives that it was a very great island. Except for his doubts about Cuba, Columbus thought that he had started on the discovery of a chain of islands which would lead him east and south to places that were fabulously rich in gold. Thus as late as December 29 the Journal reported six golden islands lying ahead to the east, called Guarionex, Macorix, Mayonic (Maguana?), Fuma, (Yuna?), Cibao, and Coroay (Cotuí?), to which Las Casas added the gloss, "These were not islands, but provinces of the Isla Española." Three of the names are clear; the other three may have been heard inexactly by Columbus for districts and rivers that had some gold.

The only map that may be attributed to Columbus with some confidence is a rude sketch of the northwest coast of Española (fig. 4), with the names San

Fig. 4. Northwest coast of Española (sketch attributed to Columbus).

Nicolás, Tortuga, Natividad, and Montecristi, given by him on the first voyage. Cibao is the lone interior locality entered, more or less in its proper position. Cibao thus had lost its prior identification in his mind as an island and was moved into the stony mountain part of central Haiti, indicating that he made the sketch after his views had been corrected by the return of the *Pinta*. In his subsequent operations in Española, Columbus gained little additional knowledge of the native divisions of the island and their meaning except how far the authority of a particular cacique extended.

In 1508 Governor Nicolás de Ovando sent two parties to make geographic surveys. The better known to history was the circumnavigation of Cuba by Sebastián de Ocampo, not, as has been inferred, to find out whether Cuba was an island but to run out its shorelines preparatory to colonization. The other and more difficult job was given to Andrés de Morales, to make a survey of Española, both of coast and interior.

Morales has not had recognition as the first geographer to make a map and description from field observation of any part of the New World. No compiler of sailing charts or collector of information from records and conversation, he set out to map and describe the whole island. That he has been nearly forgotten is explained by the fact that his report and map became separated and the map has been attributed to the wrong parties. Neither is known in the original, which is true also of the Journal and letters of Columbus and of many of the most important early documents. Copies of the map have been recovered only recently. Peter Martyr saw the importance of the Morales survey, having both the report and map in his hands and having conferred with Morales at length. Three books of the third *Decade* were given over to what he thus learned and hold all we know of the report. In transmitting the text of this decade to Pope Leo X, Peter Martyr wrote, "I shall see to it that some day I shall send Your Holiness this particular map of Española," adding that before the time of this map the island had always been shown as having the shape of a chestnut leaf but that Morales had drawn it with large bights at each extremity. The text of Peter Martyr is not meaningful unless compared with its map, and the latter has not been available until lately. One of the two known copies of the map may have been the one that was promised to the Pope.

The Morales map was first rediscovered in the library of the University of Bologna, and published in 1929 by its librarian, Carlo Frati, as *El Mapa más Antiguo de la Isla de Santo Domingo (1516)*, reproduced from a colored manuscript on parchment. The map is unsigned and undated; the date in the printed title means only that it was bound into a copy of the 1516 Alcalá edition of the *Decades* done in a binding that is thought to have been of that time. Frati was of the opinion that Peter Martyr may have supervised the drafting of the map and had it bound with the book as a presentation copy. Frati did not attribute the map to Morales or to anyone else, but favored the idea that the volume may have been a copy given to Cardinal Cisneros while Regent of Spain. The excellent colored reproduction by Frati is here given in black and white (fig. 5). The Bologna map is in detailed agreement with the data Peter Martyr took down from Morales and should be credited to such authorship.[5]

Another copy of the Morales map appeared as the first plate in the facsimile atlas *Mapas Españoles* in 1951 (fig. 6). It is there credited to Andrés Morales.

---

[5] The Jane–Vigneras edition of *The Journal of Christopher Columbus* has a reduced color reproduction of the Bologna map (opposite p. 96), with the erroneous notation "perhaps by Bartholomew Columbus." Neither Columbus is known to have had cartographic or surveying skill. Neither knew parts of the island that are shown here in good outline and topographic detail.

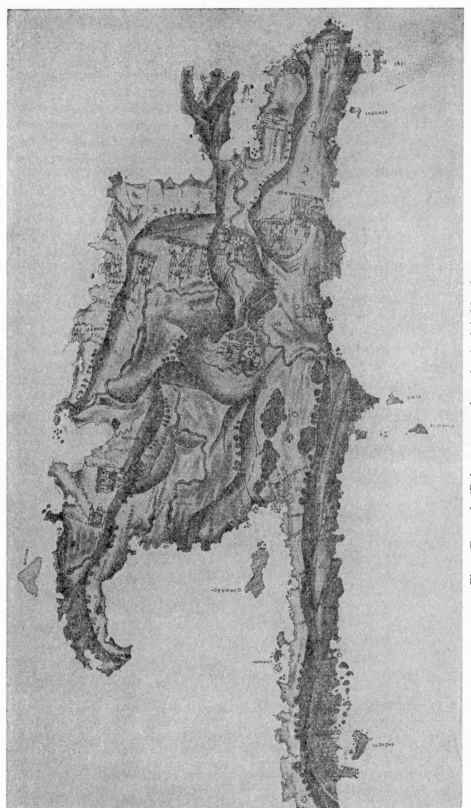

Fig. 5. Española (Bologna copy of map by Andrés Morales, 1508).

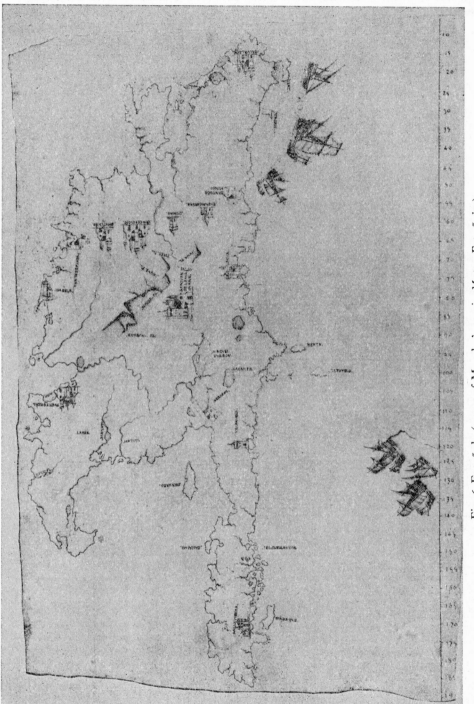

Fig. 6. Española (copy of Morales' map in *Mapas Españolas*).

The map has faded to a pale sepia, and shows fewer details of relief and drainage and fewer place names. Orientation and outlines are identical with the Bologna map. The Bologna copy is the more elaborate and carries native regional terms. The two maps were copied from the same source, as shown by an identical base and location of places. They were done by different draftsmen, as the technique and differences in spelling indicate.

The Morales survey having been made in 1508, his original map may be assigned that date as to content. The two known copies do not have any other and later data. They are far superior to anything that was done in the New World at the time or for years thereafter. The directions were determined by compass, the form of the island is very good, mountain ranges and rivers are well placed, and so is the toponymy. By inference the map was made from coast surveys and from traverses into the interior.[6]

Morales delineated Española as to form, coastal outline, hydrography, relief, and position of the villas. Also he made a reconstruction of its native territorial divisions at the coming of the Europeans. This was a most unusual interest for which I know no parallel elsewhere in the New World until much later. In spelling I have compromised between Peter Martyr and the Bologna map. Peter Martyr heard in Italian and wrote in Latin; the copyists at times were inattentive as they took down names that were meaningless to them.

Morales oriented the physical geography of Española about the four great rivers that rise in the same part of the central mountains and follow the four cardinal directions to the sea: the Yuna to the east, the Atibunico (Artibonite) to the west, the Yaque (Yaque del Norte) to the north, and the Neiba (Neiba with Yaque del Sur) to the south.[7] He described the high central mountains as experiencing all four seasons. In the cold season trees shed their leaves and the meadows turned white. In the highlands he knew plants like those of Spain—ferns, blackberries, and nettles. He recognized the parallel relief, a central cordillera running the length of the island from northwest to southeast, a great lowland paralleling it on the north, called the Valle de Magua, a somewhat lesser one on the south, the Valle de Maguana. Beyond the latter another parallel cordillera flanks a third elongated lowland then called Caiouani (the modern Cul de Sac of French Haiti). This arid basin was well described as to its great salt lake (now

---

[6] Andrés de Morales was one of the most experienced Spanish pilots, as the officers in charge of navigation were called. He served as such in the third voyage of Columbus and again with Bastidas and Juan de la Cosa in the discovery of the Gulf of Urabá. Peter Martyr reported that on the latter voyage he traded in a large diamond on the coast of Cumaná. (This was the first and long the only record of diamonds in the New World, suggesting aboriginal trade with Venezuelan Guayana, where diamonds are now found commercially.) Peter Martyr knew him as a pilot who was engaged in sailing between Spain and Tierra Firme, as a noted maker of charts, and as the author of a theory of ocean currents, close to modern views of oceanic circulation. Late in life he was named cartographer–pilot to the Casa de Contratación and was serving in that capacity at the time of his death. The archives at Sevilla therefore might yield further knowledge of this undeservedly neglected participant in the early affairs of the Spanish Main.

[7] This hydrographic diagram of the island was used before the time of Morales. Peter Martyr in a letter of May, 1500, mentions having heard of these four rivers as dividing Española into four equal parts. At that time the Spaniards lacked such knowledge by observation of their own, and therefore it may be considered as having been by native usage.

Lago Enriquillo) and five smaller lakes, ranging from saline to fresh, and all abounding in fish and aquatic fowl. Fishermen lived about the large lake and on an island in it, their life made somewhat hazardous by voracious sharks. (Evaporation has since lowered lake level and increased its salinity. A study of the changes in these lakes is one of many things waiting to be done.) For the southeastern peninsula he described land forms sufficiently well to be recognized as karst features, and told how at the southwest side of the Bay of Samaná he had entered a great cave by boat. The physical geography is properly and soberly set forth.

Peter Martyr wrote: "This pilot brings me a new description that was generally used by the natives and divided the island into five parts, each with the ancient names of its subdivisions." The Bologna map has these five major provinces, without boundary lines, and a fair number of their subdivisions. The text of the *Decades* lists a large series of divisions for the five provinces. Figure 7 is an attempt to reconstruct the materials; the boundaries are rude approximations of my own that assume confines set by terrain. Peter Martyr was told that the nobles (*nitainos*) were by no means inept cosmographers of their native land, but took care to know the limits of the states. The implication is that at the time of the survey there were still enough members of the former upper class to provide Morales with information about the native territorial divisions.

Peter Martyr heard that there was a native name for the island as a whole, Quizquella (Quisqueya), meaning "a thing than which there is nothing greater." Its division into five provinces began with the southeastern peninsula as Caizcimu, *cimu* meaning "front or beginning." That this should have been considered the front of the island is of interest, since it was here that the Arawaks first entered. Of its ten named subdivisions, presumably *cacicazgos* under a greater chief, only Higüey and Macorix remain in use. Its western limit was stated as passing from a very rough and wild montane country called Haiti, situated to the south of the lower Yuna valley, to the Río Ozama, and so down to the south coast in the vicinity of the city of Santo Domingo. Haiti thus meant rough hill country; an extensive and almost uninhabited area in the watershed of the Ozama drainage is still known as Montes Haitises. The first appearance of the name Haiti is through Morales, and was applied to this one area: "rough highlands which in particular are called Haiti because they are so frightful." The Caizcimu of Morales is about the same as the province of Higüey of Spanish usage, a limestone peninsula, dropping off to the Caribbean by a series of marine terraces. (Higüey was the seat of the most important cacique of the region, succeeded by a cacica, who may have had authority over the whole peninsula.)

The second "province," Huhabo, extended along the north coast from Samaná Bay to the Río Yasica; its interior limits were in the watershed of the range now called Sierra de Quitaespuela. Morales had least to say about it, and it was little mentioned in the colonial records. It was neither populous nor of much interest to the Spaniards, lacking mineral wealth, rich soil, good fishing, and good harbors, except for a part of Samaná peninsula. Columbus named the bay of that name the "gulf of the arrows" from his first encounter there with bowmen. These wore their hair long. They differed in speech and adornment, nor is it known that they were organized into the social classes of the Arawaks. Huhabo, therefore,

45

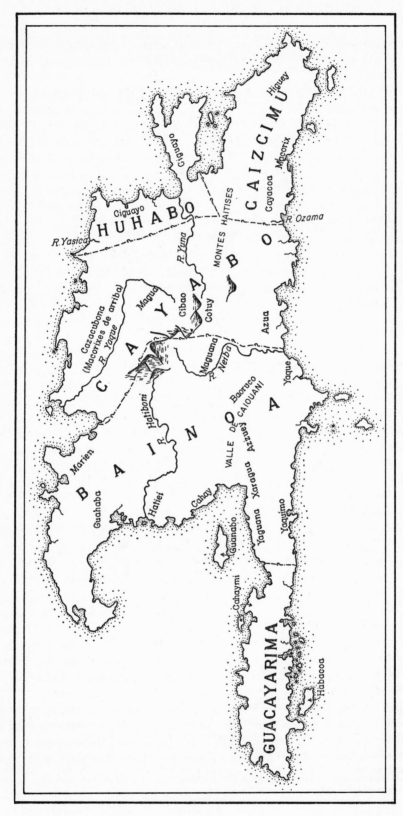

Fig. 7. Native provinces and subdivisions of Española according to Morales and Peter Martyr.

may not have been a province in the political sense of the others of Morales; possibly it was not Arawak but inhabited by a different ethnic group of lesser interest and numbers.

The third province, Cayabo, was the midsection of the island, extending from north to south coast, according both to description and map of Morales. On the north coast it reached from the Río Yasica to include the present political provinces of Puerto Plata and Montecristi. On the southern coast it extended from the site of Santo Domingo west to Ocoa Bay. Its most productive and most populous part was the great basin of Magua, renamed Vega Real by Columbus, which drains to the northwest by the Río Yaque del Norte and to the southeast by the Río Camú. Cayabo appropriated the whole drainage of the Yaque del Norte and thus included the northern flank of the central cordillera of which Cibao was a part and also Cotuy farther south in the mountains. (Later the name Cotuí was transferred to its present eastern location.) On the Caribbean side it included the area about San Cristóbal, later known for its gold and the fertility of its alluvial and terrace lands. Morales counted a dozen districts of Cayabo, including three that were of differing speech, toward the east and in the cordillera along the northeast coast. The northernmost was called Cazacubona, according to Morales "of very different idiom and called Macoryzes." Macorix is thought to have meant "foreign speech" and Ciguayo "long hair." These names were probably used for the same people. Northeastern Española was ethnically different; the Huhabo part was independent, and the rest from Puerto Plata southeastward through the hill country flanking the Vega Real was attached to Cayabo.[8] The manner in which Columbus occupied central Española supports the extent of Cayabo outlined by Morales as a native state. Its great chief or king (*rey*) had Magua or the Vega Real as his direct cacicazgo and his seat near and to the north of Concepción de la Vega. He was called Guarionex, perhaps title rather than name, as suggested by Peter Martyr in the remark that *gua* is the definite article applied especially to "kings."

The fourth province of Morales, Bainoa, included the Republic of Haiti except the southwestern peninsula. It also extended into the southwest of the Dominican Republic to the Bay of Neiba and over the interior basin of Maguana. Morales listed twenty-four divisions for this greatest of the island realms. Between the bays of Port-au-Prince and Neiba lay the cacicazgos of Xaragua, Azzuey (on the Etang Saumâtre), and across the Dominican border Baoruco, Neibamam, and Yaque. Yaquimo (Jacmel) was on the Caribbean shore south of Xaragua. About the Haitian Gulf, Yaguana (Léogane) to the west and Cahay (Arcahaie) to the north were important. On the north coast Cahini (Ile de la Tortue) and Marien (Plaine du Nord) were included, and in the interior the intermontane basin of Maguana (San Juan). The validity of this large extension of the province of Bainoa will be considered below.

The fifth and last province of Morales was Guacayarima, the name interpreted as meaning the posterior or anus of the island. It is nearly identical with the present Département du Sud of Haiti. Of the eleven divisions enumerated, Habacoa (Ile-à-Vache) and Cahaymi (Cayemites) have retained French modi-

---

[8] The town San Francisco de Macorís, at the southeast end of what was once the realm of Cayabo, retains the old name.

fications of the aboriginal names. There is no indication that the parts of this long and mountainous peninsula formed a political unit.

Morales undertook to make a dual regional division of Española, physical and political. Las Casas devoted the first eight chapters of his *Apologética Historia* to his own subdivision of the island, arriving at twenty-seven provinces by mixed criteria. These do not account for the whole of the island, but deal mainly with the more populous areas and their decline or abandonment. They include local descriptions of differing fertility of soil, vegetation, and land forms, such as his observations on the karst lands of Higüey. He made good observations on changes in vegetation as Indian plantings were replaced by pastures of livestock and on evidences of former Indian occupation. His regional descriptions will be of value for field studies that need to be made, but his mixed and incomplete regions do not serve for divisions of territory as do those of Morales.

The last, least satisfactory, and most copied division of Indian Haiti was made by Father Charlevoix in his *Histoire de St. Domingue*, with map by Sieur d'Anville (fig. 8). He subdivided the island among five great caciques: Cayacoa at the east, Behechio at the west, Goacanagaric (Guacanagari) in the northwest, Guarionex in the northeast, and Caonabo in the center and south, the latter as of Carib nationality. By supplying geographical for personal names, these become the Spanish regions, in the order above, of Higüey, Xaragua, Marien, Magua or Vega Real, and San Juan de Maguana. The five kingdoms were at most three, they did not comprise the entire island, and the boundaries as drawn were grossly in error.

MISCELLANEOUS PEOPLES OF THE ISLANDS

The exceptions to the general Arawak pattern are in geographically interesting locations. At the westernmost end of Cuba a primitive people was found, knowing no agriculture, living by collecting and fishing, and having very rude habitations. They were known as Guanahacabibes, and will be considered for that island. Morales added a report from the far end of the southwestern peninsula of Española in the territory of Sabana (Cayes) of strange people who lived in caves, did no planting, and fled like deer when they caught sight of strangers. Oviedo later heard of these cave dwellers as the rudest found in the Indies. Unlike those on Cuba, they did not live by the sea. Alonso de Santa Cruz noted that "at the beginning of the conquest of the island there were found in the province of Savanna de Guacayarima some wild people whom the Indians call Cenavas, fleet as deer, none of whom the Christians were able to capture." Their situation is similar in both islands: at the westernmost extremity and in a meager environment. The Arawaks came out of the east. Their predecessors retreated into the farthest corner, where some of them survived in a habitat that did not attract the Arawaks. In anthropological usage in the United States the name Ciboney has been given improperly to these pre-Arawak inhabitants of the West Indies, as will be noted later.

The long-haired Ciguayo and the Macorix of strange speech perhaps were alternative names for one ethnic group on the northeastern side of Española. Columbus thought they might be Caribs because they appeared warlike. Also

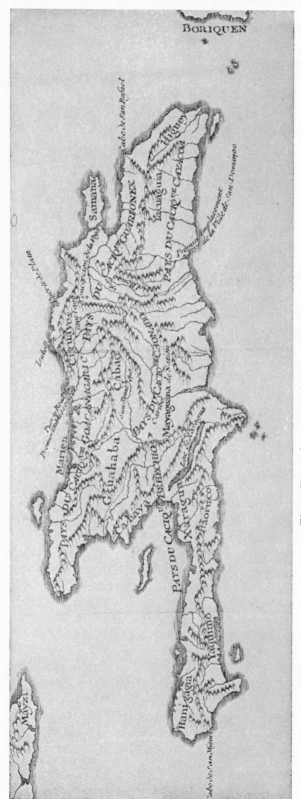

Fig. 8. Española as subdivided by Charlevoix.

they used bows and arrows, as was not the case in the northern islands elsewhere. Some who lived within the confines of Cayabo, as drawn by Morales, put up resistance later to the Spanish advance. Loven noted Carib traits in the meager data available, but preferred an Arawak affiliation. Possibly they were a mixture. They were soon swept aside or enslaved. Their land was of little interest to the Spaniards.

SOCIAL STRUCTURE

The aristocratic character of native society was evident from the first contact. According to the Columbus Journal, on December 16 the first meeting took place with a youthful "king" who was treated with reverence by the natives and to whom Columbus "did the honors owed him." The next day the Admiral for the first time used the term cacique to apply to the governor of that province (in Tortue Channel). On the 18th "there came with the King more than two hundred men, four of whom carried him in a litter." Moving on to Cap Haïtien, Columbus met another cacique (Guacanagari, though not as yet thus identified), again considered a king. "Until then the Admiral had not been able to understand whether he was named such as King or as Governor. Also they use another name for a great person, Nitayno, which he did not know whether it meant Hidalgo, or Governor, or Judge."

The society of the Island Arawaks was strongly stratified. At the top were the caciques, who were hereditary rulers, probably by matrilineal descent. The great caciques were at times referred to as kings. Caciques of the second rank were chiefs of districts. Below these were the nitainos, or nobles, by Spanish interpretation, then the commoners, and finally the unfree *naborías*. The social structure resembled that of Spain sufficiently so that European class terms were fairly applicable. Status appears to have been determined by birth, at least in the highest and lowest ranks. The information is mostly from Española, but Puerto Rico and Jamaica were similarly organized, and Cuba was largely so.

The five divisions of Española listed by Morales were retrospective, for they had ceased to exist at the time of his survey. He used native geographic terms for them, of which only Guacayarima appears in other accounts, and he does not mention caciques, who had disappeared by his time. Guacayarima consisted of many small independent cacicazgos. The organization of Huhabo, occupied by Ciguayos, is unknown, but it was independent of control from other parts. Caizcimu of the southeast was a sort of state under control of the cacique of Higüey, as indicated by the manner in which it was taken over by Ovando. That Cayabo was in fact a major state under the authority of the great cacique of Magua, Guarionex, is well supported by the events of the Columbus administration. Guarionex was the only sovereign cacique with whom Columbus came into contact. The cacique of Cibao was identified as a vassal of Guarionex.[9]

The western half of Española was the province of Bainoa, with Xaragua in key position. Morales included in it Marien on the north coast and Maguana in the interior. If Morales was right, Guacanagari of Marien was upgraded in historical accounts to an importance that he did not have. The same is true of Caonabo as cacique of Maguana. Both are seen in history through the eyes of

---

[9] Las Casas, *Apologética*, ch. 197.

Columbus, who was not informed of the island hierarchy. When Caonabo was eliminated, his widow, the famous Anacaona, went to live at Xaragua with her brother, "king" Behechio, to join in the rule of the west and later to succeed her brother. The suzerainty of Xaragua over a large area is shown by the fact that Behechio called in three hundred caciques, it was said, in order to do honor to Governor Ovando. Las Casas thought that Xaragua was the court for the whole island, its head the most respected, its people most polished in manner and speech, its *nobleza* the most ordered and numerous.

The translation of the native social order into European feudal terms worked well enough in the allotment of Indian communities to Spanish *vecinos*. Even the present administrative divisions reflect to some extent the political geography of Arawak days.

PLANTING AND CULTIVATION

The Arawaks, it may be inferred, brought with them from South America the plants of their cultivation and the accustomed ways of growing them. Their inventory of plants is only slightly smaller than on Tierra Firma, as is also the manner and range of their uses. Perhaps the most important difference—and it is one that has passed unnoticed—is that the islanders drank no alcoholic beverages. There is no account of alcoholic festivals or of any such indulgence. Coma noted with surprise that the only libation in their feasts was water. I shall suggest below that thereby their interest in growing grains and fruits may have been reduced. Elsewhere in South and Central America all agricultural peoples made fermented drinks, used them freely on ceremonial occasions, and grew certain plants for that purpose. In the absence of alcohol the Island Arawaks were like the Indians of Anglo-America, an unexplained and perhaps coincidental parallel. The Florida Straits, one of the most strongly marked cultural boundaries in the New World, was such also as to cultivated plants. Florida Indians grew seed crops that derived from Mexico. The Lucayo Indians of the Bahama Islands on the other hand were the northern outpost of South American root agriculture.

Preparation of the ground for planting began in the manner common to most of America, by the clearing of woods. It is not stated whether this was done by girdling or by felling trees. The former being much the easier, and the stone and shell tools of the islands being quite indifferent axes, it may be inferred that felling was not usual procedure. The dead stuff was disposed of by fire. Digging was done by a pointed and flattened heavy stick, the usual primitive spade.

The next step, and it is the first that attracted Spanish attention, was heaping the earth into mounds (*montones*). Descriptions of various heights and dimensions indicate that the earth was piled about as high as the mounds would stand and the depth of the soil permitted. Some were knee-high and several feet wide. They were more or less round, and provided a loose and well-aerated soil to grow root crops. Different plants, of upright, scandent, and climbing habit could be placed together in the same mound. These made an effective ground cover against soil erosion, and the clusters of mounds served also as balks to sheetwash. Such planted tracts were known as *conucos*, a name still used in the Spanish islands.

This manner of tillage was remarkably indifferent to slope. Poorly drained lowlands, such as those of the lower Yuna basin, seem to have been avoided. Most of the hill and mountain slopes of sufficiently deep soils were under cultivation. Las Casas said of the cordillera on the northern flank of the Vega Real that it was "as fertile on its crests as on its middle and lower slopes." [10] Oviedo wrote that the natives were concentrated along the coast, along riverbanks, in high places, on plains, and in valleys, which seems to include most of the country.[11] Today, as in early days, such conucos support people in number in rugged hill and mountain country, not only in the overcrowded Republic of Haiti and in Jamaica but in parts of the Dominican Republic, as in the hill country between the Río Haina and the Río Yaque del Sur. Where root crops are now grown along with bananas, coffee, and cacao, the mixed plantings of conucos still make free use of steep and irregular surfaces.

When the Spaniards commanded tribute in food from the natives, this was calculated by the number of mounds they were required to plant, usually to yuca or also to sweet potatoes. The plow being unknown to the natives, fields were not rectangular, and therefore there was no direct measure of area.

Shifting cultivation, often considered a common trait of primitive tillage, especially in the tropics, is not indicated in the record. It took a lot of labor to make the montones, in the course of which the roots of woody plants were removed. Once constructed, it was easier to maintain them than to start new clearings. The root crops removed very little mineral fertility from the soil, and their leaves and stems returned organic matter and potash to it. In this climate the growing season was continuous as was the harvest, and the ground was never bare of plant cover. Weeding was done by hand and may not have been much needed.[12] Tilled land may have been lost to invading grasses. I do not know that there were aggressive perennial grasses native to the islands. Sprouts and seeds of woody plants did press into the fields, especially when the Indian population died out. Las Casas in later years observed former conucos, their mounds still present and more or less intact, occupied by brush and woods. As long as the native population was numerous and vigorous it could cope with competing plants.

The *macana* was an important agricultural tool on the islands, more significant here as such than as a weapon, for which the peaceable islanders had little need. The name originated here and became widely adopted in Spanish usage elsewhere for similar instruments.[13] It was a sort of wooden broadsword, made of very hard and heavy wood, with a cutting edge on one or both sides, and mainly used on the islands as a sort of machete, serving as a brush knife and also for digging.

In the humid parts of Española the fertility and productivity of the Vega Real or Magua, the basin of Maguana, the north coastal plain of Marien, and the limestone lands of Higüey supported a teeming native population which could

---

[10] *Ibid.*, ch. 8.
[11] Oviedo, *Historia*, Bk. VI, ch. 1.
[12] Coma noted as the only conspicuous weed in the islands the innocuous purslane (*Portulaca inoxia*). This is less than specific identification, but the common purslane (*Portulaca oleracea*) is today indeed common in the islands, and this may be the first reference to its occurrence in the New World.
[13] Friederici.

and did provide food for the Spaniards. In the arid southwestern part, irrigation was carried on intensively, centering in the cacicazgo of Xaragua. Morales noted that in Xaragua and about the lakes it rained rarely and irrigation was practiced: "in all these parts there are ancient ditches by which the water is led to irrigate fields with no less art than do the inhabitants of Cartagena and Murcia." [14] The statement is terse and clear. This was no casual diversion of water but an extensive system of canals considered equal to those built by the Moors in Spain, and known as of ancient construction. Unfortunately, Morales did not explain. Las Casas also spoke of them in chapter 5 of his *Apologética:* "In the whole island of Española because of its high and general fertility there was no need to take water from rivers nor to divert it from springs in order to irrigate land, save only in the province and kingdom of Xaragua, which is very dry country though excellent, for which reason its artful inhabitants (*gentes pulidas*) diverted the river passing through there which was called Camín [*Rivière Blanche?*] . . . and made many and fine irrigation ditches that were needed to water their conucos or properties in all the surroundings of their city, which lies in a great plain." The most advanced culture, the greatest state, and the ruler of highest authority were in the irrigated lands of Xaragua. It is a pity that when this area was destroyed no one recorded anything but the slaughter of its assembled nobles. Nor do I know of any inquiry that has been made into the archaeology of the region. There is no record of irrigation in any other part of the islands or elsewhere in the Caribbean except behind Santa Marta in Colombia.

Conuco Crops

Mainly the fields were planted to root crops to supply starch to the native diet. All were reproduced vegetatively, mostly by stem cuttings as in the case of yuca and sweet potatoes. All were cultigens that depended on man for propagation. Most of the information is from Española. The first notices are from the Journal of Columbus and as such are of special importance. Having been on the Guinea coast of Africa and having seen there roots of similar use and not knowing the plants that grew them, he called them yams (*niames* and other spellings), as the true yams (*Dioscoreas*) were known to him from Africa. Mostly he was speaking of yuca under the name of yam, but he confused it also with the sweet potato. Thus the entry of December 21 had "bread which they make of niames, which they call ajes" (*age*, starchy sweet potato).

The great staple of the islands was the bitter yuca. Both the bitter and sweet forms of manioc are known throughout Spanish America by that name, first heard in the islands, which therefore is preferable to the Tupí-Portuguese name *mandioca*, Anglicized to manioc. Stem cuttings planted in the conuco mound provided tubers within a year, but commonly they were allowed to grow for two or more years for repeated partial harvestings. Las Casas described how several cuttings were placed in each mound; a first crop of tubers being available in a year, the best after a year and a half; the plants might be allowed to produce for three years.[15] A planting once in production could be used at any season of the year.

---

[14] Peter Martyr, Decade III, Bk. 9.
[15] Las Casas, *Apologética*, ch. 10.

Yuca is unexcelled and perhaps unequalled in its yield of starch. Las Casas, who had been in the business of growing it, said that in many cases a thousand montones (two acres or less of cultivated land) would yield a hundred fifty to a hundred seventy five *cargas* of cassava bread, each carga being two *arrobas* (the arroba 25 pounds), and that a carga provided food for one person for a month.[16] The poisonous roots were grated, drained of their juice, and baked into unleavened flat bread (cassava) in a procedure common to the American tropics. This bread is both tasty and nutritious and keeps without deterioration for months, even in humid and warm weather. The sweet or nonpoisonous forms were prepared directly by boiling, less commonly by baking. Both sorts are still widely grown. The plant is indifferent both to acid and somewhat alkaline soils, and some forms of it are remarkably tolerant of drought. It still shares first place with plantains in providing food about much of the Caribbean and in other parts of the American tropics. Modern commerce, organized for mass harvest, storage, and processing, has passed it by.

The sweet potato was second in importance. Lower in yield than yuca, it has the advantages of producing a crop in four months, covering the ground by its spreading and leafy vines, differing in taste from yuca, and supplying a green pot herb "like spinach," in Las Casas' term. The sugary races were called *batata;* those that were not sweet, *age (axe, aje, asse)*. The Spaniards soon came to prize the batatas for their sweetness, making them into conserves, as is still done. There has been needlessly long dispute about what ages are. They were described as less tasty than batatas, as a coarser food, and as being turnip-shaped or globular. Botanically they are races of sweet potatoes (*Ipomoea batatas*), low in sugar and with more or less globe-shaped tubers. The old name is forgotten, but the starchy, turnip-shaped tubers are still grown, especially in the Dominican Republic. They may have been more common in Indian times than the sweet batatas, but the Spaniards preferred the latter and took these into the kitchens and gardens. The ages have not disappeared, as is often stated, but their distribution and their taxonomic relation to the sweet potato have not been studied.

Lesser plants grown for their starchy roots were described by Oviedo and have been cited often in modern literature. They are all still to be seen here and there in minor cultivation. Yautía (*Xanthosoma*) continues to be popular in Puerto Rico. Araurú, or arrowroot (*Maranta*), llerén (*Calathea allouia*), yampee (*Dioscorea trifida*), and the edible-rooted canna are found commonly in household gardens today. The peanut (*maní*) became first known to Europeans in the islands, and formed part of the conuco assemblage.

Another complex of cultivated plants, maize, beans, and squashes, grown from seed and thought to have originated in Mesoamerica, also found a place in the island conucos. These probably came late, by roundabout route south through Central America, east across Tierra Firme, and thence north into the islands.

Columbus, although somewhat confused as to what the "roots" were, knew the manner of their planting and preparation as food, including the making of cassava bread, which he first mentioned by name. These roots, he said, were "their life" (December 13). Indian corn he noted only once (December 6), by

[16] *Ibid.*, ch. 11.

the name *panizo*, and this was in Cuba. He did bring a sample back to Spain, which Peter Martyr heard was called *maiz*. The latter planted some of the seed and from them gave our first description of the plant. A generation later Oviedo wrote the oft-cited account that the islanders grew maize to be used only as roasting ears and for parching the dry seeds. It was not a major foodstuff of the islands, but it was to some extent a bread grain; Oviedo came too late to learn this. Peter Martyr began his account by saying that "they make bread from a certain grain," and noted that this grain was snow-white inside.

Coma confirmed and expanded the statement of Peter Martyr. Coma had gone on the second voyage of Columbus and returned from Española in February, 1494; the letter describing his experiences was written later in that year and is known only in the Latin version Scillacio made in December, 1494. The part of the letter that describes the plants of cultivation is introduced into the passage on the Carib islands, which were the first lands he saw. Two stops were made there, a week on Guadelupe and several hours in a skirmish with the Caribs of St. Croix. The Guadelupe landing took a week, occupied with locating a party that had gotten lost. There was no contact with Caribs there, who had all fled into the woods. What Coma wrote about the use of ages (*asses* in the letter, an Arawak and not a Carib word) and maize (for which he gave no name) was information which he gained later in Española. The plants he may have first seen growing in Guadelupe, and this probably suggested telling about them in that connection. Of maize he wrote: "it is a grain of very high yield, of the size of the lupine [referring to the cultivated white lupine of the Mediterranean], of the roundness of the chick-pea (*cicer*), and yields a meal (*farina*) ground to a very fine powder (*effracto tenuissimo polline*); it is ground as is wheat (*frumentum*) and yields a bread of very good taste; many chew the seeds when in need of nourishment." The last statement may refer to parched corn, as did Oviedo's comment. Coma described a large and round-seeded maize that was ground into fine meal and baked into bread. This indicates a flour corn, as does Peter Martyr's snowy white endosperm. Their accounts agree on a kind of maize that was used for grinding and baking.

The beans and cucurbits that are usually grown with maize were mentioned only as being present. Columbus noted *faxones y favas* in Cuba (November 4 and 6) as "very different from ours," perhaps a reference both to kidney and lima beans. The mention of beans, as *frijol*, *haba*, and *judía* in variant spellings, is casual. Apparently they were not an important food. In the Spanish vernacular of the New World, squashes (*Cucurbita*) and bottle gourd (*Lagenaria*) were called *calabazas*, as were the tree gourds (*Crescentia*). Gourd containers were much used by the islanders, probably mostly of *Crescentia*. The most likely squash to have been present (*Cucurbita moschata*) has an Arawak name, *auyama*, which however was first added to the Spanish vernacular in Tierra Firme.[17]

---

[17] The ancient Romance word *calabaza* J. Corominas (*Diccionario Crítico Etimológico de la Lengua Castellana*) thought as having about the same meaning as gourd in the wider sense, a hard-rinded, large, hollow fruit. *Lagenaria* is the familiar example. What else the name may have been applied to in the Mediterranean is not known. Las Casas compared the vines of ages and batatas with those of the calabazas of Spain, finding the former "more delicate and lacking the little spines that the plant of the calabaza has" (*Apologética*, ch. 10). This is one

A Miscellany of Yard Plants

Parrots, cotton thread in balls, and spears were given as presents at the landing of October 12. Columbus made repeated reference to cotton in the Bahamas, Cuba, and Española. In Cuba the two men who had been sent inland to find the Great Khan told of having seen more than five hundred arrobas of spun and worked cotton in a single (multifamily) house. On the last day in Samaná Bay Columbus reported "much cotton and very fine and long."

Cruising through the Bahamas (October 15) they picked up a lone paddler in a canoe who carried some of the native bread, "and a calabash of water and a piece of red earth made into powder and then kneaded, and some dry leaves which must be something greatly appreciated among them for already in San Salvador they had brought me presents of them." Thus soon were *bixa* and tobacco encountered. Bixa yielded the reddish body paint that possibly gave rise to the term "red Indians."

Cotton, bixa, and tobacco were not planted in the mounds of the conuco. There are no descriptions of where or how they were grown. It is not even known whether the tobacco that was first seen being smoked there was *Nicotiana tabacum*, for which Cuba later was famous, or *N. rustica*, which was grown in Indian cultivation from Chile to Quebec. The production of either required specially prepared beds, planted only to tobacco.

The island cotton was referred to as a small tree, which is the habit of the variety of *Gossypium barbadense* proper to the West Indies, a South American cultigen of ancient introduction. The difference between it and the silk cotton of bombacaceous trees was recognized, Dr. Chanca for instance distinguishing between cotton trees of the size of peach trees and other spiny trees that gave vegetable wool. Cotton, important in all parts, was cultivated most extensively in the province of Xaragua and in Jamaica. It was repeatedly mentioned as growing wild, which would appear to mean that it escaped from cultivation.

Bixa is a handsome shrub, still seen in variant forms in the rural districts about houses. Because of the prized coloring matter about the seed capsules, it was carried widely about the American tropics and was thus introduced into the islands.

A black vegetable color used for body painting was extracted from the edible fruit of the jagua (*Genipa*), a handsome hardwood tree, still common about habitations. Peter Martyr thought it was cultivated, having heard that the color was from certain fruits resembling pears and that these were grown with great care in gardens.[18]

The calabash tree (*Crescentia cujete, hibuero, higüero*) is still seen in rural settlements in extraordinarily large fruited forms, in these gigantic dimensions certainly a cultigen. Cohoba (*Piptadenia peregrina*), used as a narcotic snuff, mixed with tobacco, was probably introduced from South America. Of island fruit trees the one most likely to have been brought by man from Tierra Firma is the mamey (*Mammea americana*), which Las Casas said was found at first

---

of the distinctive qualities of the common pumpkin (*Cucurbita pepo*) and is lacking in *Lagenaria*. Linné thought that *C. pepo* was a native of the Old World, whereas the whole genus is of the New World. Something other than *Lagenaria* was known to Las Casas as calabaza in Spain.

[18] Peter Martyr, Decade I, Bk. 7.

only at the extremity of the Guacayarima peninsula. (The town of Abricots there bears the French Haitian name for mamey.)[19]

The strangest item is that of *manzanillas*, a nondescript Latin American name in current popular use for a variety of plants that are unrelated and whose fruits may have no resemblance to little apples. Las Casas said that "they planted small trees of manzanillas for purgative use adjacent to their houses, as something they esteemed greatly." These grew to one and a half times the height of a man, "of few branches and small girth; the leaf is very handsome, almost like that of the yuca from which cazabí bread is made, like a great hand with the fingers spread apart; the fruit is like that of hazelnuts and similarly white, and called *ben* by physicians, the sap white and milky." Oviedo had a similar description of manzanilla, a name he thought inappropriate, and added that the seeds were enclosed in a burr (*capullo*).[20] The descriptions indicate a plant of the Spurge family (Euphorbiaceae), to which yuca belongs. They do not fit the native American physicnut (*Jatropha*), but apply to the castor bean (*Ricinus*) of African origin, now found growing spontaneously in many parts of tropical and subtropical America. Vavilov and his team of Russian geneticists were puzzled by the diversity of *Ricinus* in their tropical American collections.

Las Casas said flatly that, in contrast to Tierra Firme, there were no *huertas* in Española, meaning fruit or kitchen gardens. Even the pineapple, he thought, had been brought by Spaniards from Puerto Rico. Oviedo, on the contrary, said the natives had groves of fruit trees in their villages. Las Casas may have oversimplified; the uncertainty, perhaps, is what he considered a huerta. Pine-apples were grown by the Carib islanders in gardens and for making wine, which was not used in the north. Capsicum peppers were common seasoning; two kinds were described by Las Casas as domestic, and a third as wild. One cultivated pepper was red, long, and finger-shaped; the second was round like a cherry and more pungent, the wild one having small fruits. There were wild fruits in diversity to be eaten out of hand, but if fruit was not needed in quantity to make alcoholic drinks the incentive to plant such may well have been lacking.[21]

For the numerous plants of cultivation that did not fit into the mounding practice of the conucos other locations were required. Tobacco must have been grown in special beds. Trees and shrubs were cared for near the houses; these I am calling yard plants for want of a better name. The villages were loose and formless clusters except for a central open space. In the Dominican Republic they still have this appearance, and there one may still find assemblages of the economic plants of which Oviedo and Las Casas wrote. Although the Indians

---

[19] Oviedo is the main reference on plants in native use. Las Casas, *Apologética*, chs. 10 to 12; cf. also Friederici, and Lovén, *op. cit.* (see n. 1 above).

[20] Las Casas, *Apologética*, ch. 12; Oviedo, *Historia*, Bk. X, ch. 4.

[21] The hypothesis is offered that the domestication of tropical fruits may have connection with their vinous attractiveness. Those of the New World that were taken most under native care and thus ameliorated by selection are rich in sugars, some cloyingly sweet. The pineapple was altered most greatly from its ancestral form by selection in vegetative reproduction as to size, sweetness, and juice. The tree fruits are available over a short season; the pineapple is planted for continuing yield. It was a major source of wine in the lands south of the Caribbean and was thus grown in native plantations (huertas) from Guadelupe Island to Panama and beyond. Spanish familiarity with it began in the Carib islands. It was so much appreciated that some were taken to King Ferdinand, who "conceded it the palm" among fruits (Peter Martyr, Decade III, Bk. 9).

died out very early, their plants have survived in number. Such are the great-fruited calabash trees, bixa bushes, woody cottons, and mamey trees.

The yard plants of village settlements are a neglected record of past cultural conditions and connections.

FISH, FLESH, AND FOWL

Plants provided the starch and sugar of native diet; animals supplied the protein and fat in admirable balance. It was an economy of growing roots for carbohydrate food and of getting most of the rest of the diet from the water, both salt and fresh.

The Journal of Columbus took immediate notice of the native boats (October 13) "made of the trunk of a tree like a long boat and all of one piece and fashioned with great skill, holding from one to forty-five people, propelled by a shovel like that of a baker, and bailed by calabashes." He soon heard the name as *canoa*, thereafter standard Spanish usage for dugout boats. The first notice of fishing gear was in Cuba (October 28 and 29) of "nets of palm fiber [?] and cords, a fishhook of horn [turtleshell], and harpoons of bone and other apparatus for fishing."

The sea, on and offshore, estuaries, streams, and lakes were all harvested for shellfish, fish, turtles, marine mammals, and waterfowl, listed and described at length by Oviedo. The abundance of sea food and the skill at taking it impressed the newcomers. When Columbus on the second voyage landed his twelve hundred hungry men at Isabela, the fishermen of the small village supplied fresh fish in abundance. Fishing at sea was carried on by nets and hook and line, and also by using suckerfish, or remoras, which attached themselves to large fish, turtles, and manatees. Fishing by hook and line was done by long lines that were cast (*volantines*) and also, according to Oviedo, by poles as in Spain. On the south shore of Cuba fish were kept in pens in large numbers. Freshwater fish were also taken by the use of *barbasco*, a general name for fish stupefacients. The eggs of sea turtles were harvested on beaches and turtles were taken there and at sea. Cuneo reported these as "infinitíssime, grandíssime," and as ranging from two to fifteen hundredweight. Nets were strong and large enough to take turtles and manatees, the latter also being taken by harpoon according to Oviedo. These large seacows pastured freely on plants of the estuaries and were an important source of food until they were decimated by the Christians, who were permitted to eat them on fast days. Waterfowl were abundant in winter. A convenient way to take them was to float large calabashes, in some of which native swimmers were concealed who would pull birds under water without disturbing the flock.

Pigeons, doves, and parrots were very abundant; parrots were taken easily by knocking them from the roosting trees in which they congregated. Large iguanas, permitted on fast days, were a food item that the Spaniards learned to appreciate. The only land mammals other than bats were hystricomorph rodents, especially the large and tasty *hutias*. The majority were ground-living and, according to Las Casas, "lived and reproduced in herbaceous vegetation (*yerba*) and not in the woods, not in burrows and caves, but at the surface of the ground and of them there was an infinite number." [22] Enciso thought that Jamaica especially abounded in hutias. Such coneys and hares, as the Spaniards called them, were hunted by fire drives, with one group setting fire to the savannas and the others waiting to knock over the fleeing creatures.

Serious depletion of wild life followed soon upon the settlement by Europeans, mainly because of the animals brought with them, especially dogs, which soon ran wild, and hogs that ranged freely and increased rapidly. The light predation by Indians, birds of prey, and constrictor snakes was succeeded by the ravages of these new carnivores and omnivores that ranged from mountain to seashore in fast-increasing numbers, not merely of large appetite but greatly disturbing the breeding and feeding habitat of the native animals.

Domestic animals were of very minor significance. The Muscovy duck was kept by the island Caribs, but I know of no record that it was found among the islanders to the north. The case for keeping guinea pigs (*cori*) rests mainly on Oviedo. It is certain that he had the domestic cavy in mind, for he spoke of pure white, black, and particolored animals found in the houses. Las Casas said nothing to that effect. A Spanish introduction before the time of Oviedo is possible but unlikely, since they were not of known interest to Spanish households.[23] Their remains have been reported in the archaeology of the Lesser Antilles, presumably from Arawak horizons there. Perhaps Las Casas overlooked this item of native culture.

Dogs that did not bark were noted by Columbus. These were found throughout the islands, and later around the Caribbean and beyond. They were small, Las Casas said, of the size of a lap dog, and were eaten,—indeed, were kept to be eaten. Oviedo thought they were used in hunting, an unconfirmed statement of marginal probability. In the starving time of 1494 the Spaniards ate them up, it was said, which could have been true only of the northern district at the time. At any rate, they became extinct on the islands before the Indians did, an early loss in a culture yielding to pressure. At a guess, this dog was both family pet and entrée served up at festivals, as it was in Mexico.

The food economy of conucos and of aquatic exploitation has some resemblance to that of Indonesia; yuca and other starchy roots were supplemented by the products of fishing, as rice and fish formed the basic diet in the East Indian islands. In productivity the West Indian native economy cannot be rated as inferior.

HANDICRAFTS

The native arts are known almost only from observations during the years of contact. The artisans worked mainly in perishable materials, wood, fibers, and cane. The illustrations in the volumes of Oviedo, Benzoni, and others are of no value, for they were done by draftsmen in Europe who had not seen the originals.

Woodworking was the craft in which the islanders were equal and perhaps superior to natives in any part of the New World. Their canoes and paddles were

---

[22] Las Casas, *Apologética*, ch. 10.
[23] Oviedo, *Historia*, Bk. XII, ch. 4. The reference may not mean much. He said that "at present there are many here [in Española] and in many other islands and in Tierra Firme" but gave no further localization in the chapter on coris.

admired by all observers as to functional design and elegance. There is no adequate description of them, and only a few remains of paddles have been recovered. In the Baracoa region of Cuba, Columbus saw "a canoe made of one tree as large as a *fusta* [small ship] of ten or twelve thwarts, very beautiful, beached beneath a shed or *ramada* made of wood and covered with large palm leaves in such manner that neither sun nor water could damage it" (November 27); on November 30 a very fine canoe 95 palms long in which he thought a hundred and fifty persons could find place; and on December 3 five very great canoes finely ornamented, and another like a fusta of seventeen thwarts, sheltered under a boathouse. Similar accounts of very large canoes, some with carved and painted prows, and stored in special boathouses, were given from the other large islands. These were hardly fishing, trading, or war canoes, but prestige conveyances for special occasions. For the largest craft, trunks of the giant Ceiba trees were said to have been used, perhaps the only kind that grew to such size. Ceiba wood is porous and would seem to have required a varnish. Superior wood for canoes was available and used in tropical cedar (*Cedrela*), mahogany (*caoba, Swietenia*), and *Calophyllum*. The shaping of dugout boats for speed, balance, and maneuverability indicates a competence of similar order to that of the Polynesian boatbuilders and those of the northwest coast of America.

Ceremonial seats of wood, elaborately carved and highly polished, were greatly esteemed. These were the *duhos*, mark and prerogative of rank in a society that observed much protocol. Oviedo, in describing the game of ball played on ceremonial occasions in the central court of a village, wrote: "around it they had seats of stone and for the cacique and principal persons they placed some small wooden benches, very well worked of fine wood and with many figures both in relief and depressed, engraved and sculptured thereon, and these benches or low seats they call *duho*."[24] When Bartholomew Columbus made the first entry to Xaragua, Queen Anacaona honored him with a gift of fourteen duhos, some of which were shipped to Spain. Peter Martyr saw these and was impressed. Knowledgeable in art, he found them worked with wonderful skill, engraved with lifelike countenances of specters that were said to appear at night, such as serpents and human beings. An expert present gave the judgment that they were made of ebony. These ceremonial seats were status symbols in the Arawak islands and appeared also among them on Tierra Firme, where a landing party of the third Columbus voyage in the Gulf of Paria was taken to a plaza to which seats of very black wood, elaborately carved, were brought in honor of the visitors.[25] An ebony wood may have been used. *Diospyros ebenaster*, a true ebony, is found in Haiti and in other parts of central America. There are other trees of the ebony family, as of the genus *Maba*.

Anacaona had a warehouse stocked with duhos, dishes, basins, and other containers made of highly polished black wood, the workshops being on the island of Guahaba (Gonave), according to Peter Martyr. Finely finished bowls of very dark and hard wood were traded widely and were prized presents, as were tubes for the taking of snuff, according to Las Casas.[26]

---

[24] Oviedo, *Historia*, Bk. VI, ch. 2.
[25] Peter Martyr, Decade I, Bk. 6.
[26] Las Casas, *Apologética*, ch. 197.

To the observations of spun cotton in balls that Columbus saw in the Bahamas and Cuba, he added "cloths of cotton like mantillas" (Bahamas, October 16). Married women wore short skirts of woven cotton called *naguas*, an island name that the Spaniards introduced widely on the continent. Xaragua and Jamaica excelled in weaving, and in the latter hammocks were made of woven cotton.[27] Other fiber plants, some perhaps planted, were used in fishing gear and for netted hammocks. These included kinds of Agave and Furcraea under the names of *henequen* and *cabuya*, and also *maguey* and *pita*, again words that passed into mainland use from Mexico to Chile.[28] Oviedo described the manner in which the fleshy leaves were retted for the extraction of henequen and cabuya fiber.[29] The fiber of hibiscus (*mahoe, mahagua, damahagua,* apparently *H. tiliaceus*) was prized for cordage and nets. The fishing gear was as diverse and competent as anywhere in the New World.

Gold was the only metal procured and worked, casually and in small amount. The islanders were neither miners nor metallurgists. They distinguished between native gold and alloyed gold objects, knowing the latter only by trade and tradition, and having very little of either. Alloyed pieces, called guañín, were known as having been brought out of the south; they were not prized as gold but as rare and attractive ornaments. Dr. Chanca knew that they made nothing of gold "as wealth, but only for good appearance."

A little native gold was fashioned to be hung from the nose or ear. The persistent search of Columbus recorded how few there were of such ornaments. A more important use was in ceremonial belts and masks into which gold was introduced as very thin pieces. Chanca told how it was made to adhere to masks by the use of pitch (*betún*). Coma described the belts, which were badges of distinction, as cotton fabrics into which thin sheets of gold had been worked, adding that the use of gold was slight and primarily for the pleasure it gave in headdress and bands, especially to the women. Native metal or imported artifact, it was not the gold that was valued but the artifice. Coma also told how gold nuggets were hammered by round stones into very thin sheets, a tedious process by which the desired gold foil was prepared.

The Indians were familiar with the localities where native gold could be found when they wanted it, which was not often nor in large amount. As they had done for the party from the *Pinta*, they guided the two expeditions Columbus sent out in January, 1494, to gold placers. Neither reward nor duress was needed; if the Spaniards wanted to get the yellow stuff, the Indians were agreeable to take them to the right places. All the Spanish discoveries of gold in Española and Puerto Rico seem to have been made thus. Arrived at such a place the guides scrabbled for nuggets in stream bars with their fingers.[30] They knew where the heavy gold would be found among the gravel in certain parts of a stream course and could be picked out by hand. There is no evidence that they used any more systematic means of recovery or that there was a regular search. They did not sort out fine bits of "gold dust" nor could they make use of lumps too large to be

---

[27] *Ibid.*
[28] Friederici.
[29] Oviedo, *Historia,* Bk. VII, ch. 10.
[30] Peter Martyr, Decade I, Bk. 2.

beaten into desired shape. The island natives did not wash for gold, nor did they dig for it.

When Columbus took control in the Vega Real he ordered the caciques to collect a definite per capita tribute in gold. Guarionex told him that his people could not do this because they did not know how, but that if they were released from this demand he would plant, as tribute, a conuco extending from Isabela on the north coast to Santo Domingo on the south—a confirmation, incidentally, of the extent of Cayabo given by Morales. Guarionex knew that Columbus was demanding the impossible, whether there was much gold or little. Columbus did not realize that the natives knew even less about producing gold than he did.

Attracted by an Indian account of gold on the south side of the island, Bartholomew Columbus in 1496 took native guides who led him to the second major gold field, later known as the mines of San Cristóbal. "There they encountered deep wells [or pits] excavated in times of the ancients. The Admiral claims that Solomon King of Jerusalem secured from there the immense treasures of which the Old Testament speaks. Whether this is truth or not is not for me to judge, but it seems to me to be far from such." Thus wrote Peter Martyr in his first *Decade*. The specific locality of the pits thereafter was known as Minas Viejas.

HABITATION

The first reference to houses was in the Bahamas: "inside well swept and clean, and their beds and furnishings of things like cotton nets [gloss by Las Casas: *hamacas*] these houses are all like *alfaneques* and very tall and with good chimneys, but among many settlements I have seen none of more than twelve to fifteen houses." [31] In Cuba the houses were still better and bigger: "They were made in the manner of alfaneques, very large, and gave the appearance of tents in encampment without order of streets, but one here and another there, inside well swept and clean, and their adornments in good order. All are of very attractive palm branches" (October 29). Later Cuban notes added that all houses had two doors, that many persons lived in one house, and that the inhabitants "must be related and descended from a single person" (November 29). Alfaneque was a round Moorish tent, such as persons of high rank occupied at falconry and in war. Las Casas commented on the chimneys: "These chimneys are not outlets for smoke, but a sort of crown at the peak of the Indian houses, for which reason he thus says, they leave an opening high for the smoke to get out."

The summary statement of Las Casas is that the villages (*pueblos*) had been very numerous but not very large, ranging from two hundred to five hundred householders (*vecinos*), "or I should say that in each house ten to fifteen vecinos lived with their wives and children. In a single house of thatch, which will will be thirty to forty feet across and circular and lacks separate rooms, ten to fifteen vecinos may live happily." [32] The ordinary village then would have held from a thousand to two thousand inhabitants in twenty to fifty multifamily houses, a size that conucos could have supported within a convenient distance. The space per person was sufficient, since the houses were used mainly for sleeping quarters.

The most detailed description of a house is a little-noted passage of Las Casas:

[31] Columbus' *Journal*, October 17.
[32] Las Casas, *Apologética*, ch. 46.

The inhabitants of this island of Española and of the neighboring islands and of part of Tierra Firme around the shores of Paria and elsewhere built their houses of wood and thatch in the form of a bell. These were very high and roomy so that in each there might be ten or more households (vecinos). Posts as thick as a man's leg or thigh were set round about to a depth of half a man's height. Above they were joined by lashings of woody vines. Over such a frame they placed many other pieces of thin wood crosswise, also very well tied by vines. On the inside designs and symbols and patterns like paintings were fashioned by using wood and bark that had been dyed black along with other wood peeled so as to stay white, thus appearing as though made of some other attractive painted stuff. Others they adorned with very white stripped reeds that are a kind of thin and delicate cane. Of these they made graceful figures and designs that gave the interior of the houses the appearance of having been painted. On the outside the houses were covered with a fine and sweet-smelling grass. I knew one such house which a Spaniard sold to another for six hundred castellanos or gold pesos.[33]

The Arawak house then would have had these features: It was circular in outline and bellshaped in profile. This would indicate that roof and sides were one, not a conical roof that rested on a separate wall. The large size required the setting of upright posts and poles at short intervals, the longer ones converging in a peak, formed and held by lashings of strong, supple woody vines (*bejucos*), which are still thus used. The tip of the roof was protected by what Columbus called a chimney, and Las Casas called a *coronilla*, perhaps a pottery vessel. The cross members of the frame were thin pieces of wood, according to Las Casas; in Oviedo's terms, laths (*latas*). At present there is much use of hollow palm trunks, split into narrow strips and used as sheathing in roofs and as battens or siding on walls, perhaps a carryover from aboriginal days. The preferred thatch was of grass, the sweet-smelling grass of Las Casas, the long and thin grass of Oviedo, or fronds of fan palms. Inferior roofing was provided by the tough leaves of bihai (*Heliconia*) or the leaves of pinnate palms. The high roof provided storage room in depth, including a place to keep the remains of ancestors. There is agreement that the houses were occupied by a group of related families, probably maternally so; but nothing was said about the internal living accommodations.

Bohío was the name the Spaniards heard for the native house in the islands. As such it probably should be reserved for the round house occupied by an extended family. The great house of the caciques, of the same form but larger and serving for ceremonial meetings (*caney*) was often recorded as bohío. When Tierra Firme was occupied, the island terms continued to be used for Indian houses of different sorts. Peter Martyr had a report of a chief's house (near Cap *Haïtien*) as thirty-two long steps in diameter, surrounded by thirty ordinary houses; the chief's house covered with reeds and canes in various colors and interwoven with marvelous art.[34]

Each village apparently had its local head, or cacique. The houses formed a random and loose cluster, in the middle of which was an open space on which the great house of the cacique fronted. This open area, usually rectangular, was a place of assemblies and festivities. Here the Indians held their *areitos*, dances

[33] *Ibid.*, ch. 43. The more familiar description of Oviedo is given by Lovén, *op. cit.*, pp. 344–345 (see n. 1 above).
[34] Peter Martyr, Decade I, Bk. 2.

accompanied by musical instruments and songs of their past and their customs. Here also they held their ball games which were a principal spectacle and entertainment. The Spaniards called the game *pelota;* its native name was *batey,* and this was applied also to the ballground and thus to the central courtyard, which was flanked in some cases by stone seats. Large settlements may have had two or three such courts. In the Dominican Republic, villages may still be seen in which the houses are grouped about an open, grassy rectangle, not a Spanish plaza, and perhaps of the more ancient pattern. The name "batey" has now been transferred to the villages of field hands on sugar plantations.

NON-ARAWAK REMAINS

A primitive and ancient occupation of the islands is attested by the widespread archaeologic remains of a shell culture in coastal locations, which has been inferred as surviving to Spanish days in the primitive folk who have been misnamed Ciboneys.

There is evidence also of an earlier presence of people of advanced culture that differed from that of the Arawaks. The first such indication is the elaborate irrigation works that were seen in and about the region of Xaragua in arid southwestern Española. These were in native use at the Spanish coming, but were considered as of ancient construction. A second is the Minas Viejas of the San Cristóbal mining district in which Columbus thought he recognized the mines of Solomon. The Arawaks did not know how to dig for gold, as Guarionex pointed out, nor any other way of procuring it except by picking up nuggets. Nor was their culture oriented toward the possession of gold.

In 1851 Sir Robert Schomburgk visited the Cibao Mountains, as they were then still properly called, entering by way of Jarabacoa to the Valle de Constanza.[35] In the basin of Constanza he found large aboriginal earthworks, several hundred feet of walls up to six feet high, and what he considered to be grave tumuli to the number of more than a thousand. Also there were many pieces of greenstone, alien to the region. Twenty years later, William Gabb made the first and still virtually the only geological survey of the Cordillera Central, saying of Constanza: "From the remains still existing, it is evidently on the site of a former aboriginal village of no small importance. Earthworks several hundred feet in extent, similar to those found in the Mississippi Valley, are still visible, in a good state of preservation, overgrown in places by trees two feet in diameter." [36] Gabb had known the Indian mounds in the Mississippi Valley. Both men were observers of merit. The earthworks, unfortunately, were not more closely described nor were the "tumuli." The scanty accounts do not suggest any characteristics of Arawak villages. That the tumuli may have been the mounds of a large conuco is made unlikely by the abundance on them of greenstone foreign to the area—a stone which has been widely prized and carried, appearing in archae-

---

[35] Robert Schomburgk, "Visit to the Valley of Constanza," *Athenaeum* (London, 1852), pp. 797–799.
[36] William M. Gabb, "On the Topography and Geology of Santo Domingo," *Transactions of the American Philosophical Society*, XV, new series (1881), 56.

ologic horizons in different parts of the New World. If they were indeed tumuli, they differed from known Arawak burial customs.[37]

Schomburgk continued across the central cordillera to the basin of Maguana. Near the town of San Juan de la Maguana he went to the Cercado de los Indios, which he measured as having a circumference of 2,270 feet, situated in a savanna and formed of granite boulders weighing from thirty to fifty pounds. These had been piled up to give the appearance of a road 21 feet wide. The boulders, he thought, had been carried in from a nearby stream. The great stone ring, in his opinion, was not likely to have been made by the Indians whom the Spaniards encountered, nor is such an enclosure identified elsewhere with Arawak settlements.

The irrigation system, mining pits, earthworks, circumvallation of stone, and presumed necropolis with tumuli point to the presence of folk other than Arawaks and were thus interpreted by the natives. The matter awaits study.

SIZE OF THE NATIVE POPULATION

Without exception those who knew the islands at the time of their discovery were strongly impressed by their large population. This was especially true of Española, the island most intimately observed, and least so for Cuba.

It remained for scholars of the present century to assert that the islands had been sparsely inhabited. Kroeber, whose estimates were accepted by Julian Steward in the *Handbook of South America Indians*, and Angel Rosenblat concluded that Haiti had no more than a hundred thousand natives at the time of European entry and that the rest of the Arawak islands may have added a like number. The discrepancy between early and modern estimates of native numbers is irreconcilable. Of the modern students, Rosenblat alone was familiar with the documents of the time, but concluded that they did not merit attention as to numbers because the discoverers, conquerors, and missionaries magnified their own deeds by exaggerating the number of natives.[38] In the islands, however, there was no prowess at arms or success at mass conversion to boast of, had such been the inclination. There was no conquest. When the amicable natives turned to resistance in their extremity, no Spaniard had the bad grace to speak of his valor. There was no missionary effort until the coming of the Dominicans, at which time the natives were a dying race. There was neither reason of vanity nor of practical ends to inflate the native numbers.

The commonest early version was that Española had in excess of a million inhabitants. The Licenciado Zuazo was sent over in 1517 by the Regent, Cardinal Cisneros, to examine the state of the colonies under plenary judicial powers. His report to King Charles was made at the beginning of 1518, and stated that there had been a million one hundred and thirty thousand at the beginning of coloniza-

---

[37] Lovén, *op. cit.*, p. 544: "Never has a particular necropolis been found nor any mound over an excavated grave," referring to Arawak burial practices in general.

[38] Angel Rosenblat, *La población indígena y el mestizaje en América*, vol. I (Buenos Aires, 1954), especially pp. 102–107. He held a theory of demographic progress in which population growth continued while Indian numbers declined.

tion.[39] A round figure of more than a million appeared in Oviedo, López de Gómara, López de Velasco, and others. Gómara gave the number as derived from an act of Columbus, who "repartió la tierra y más de un millión de Indios," called hombres in a later passage.[40]

Gómara was right. There had been an allotment of Indians that has escaped demographic attention. Under date of December 4, 1519, fourteen Dominican friars of Española sent a long account to King Charles: "with regard to the early days they had been informed that the number of persons it had been possible to count amounted to one million, one hundred thousand . . . these were counted by the Adelantado himself [Bartholomew Columbus] on orders from the Admiral once upon a time when it was planned to collect tribute." [41] The letter continued that some years earlier a religious had given the same number, doing so at court in the presence of Bishop Fonseca; the friar, however, thought that there were not that many, but rather six hundred thousand, of whom there remained at that time only forty thousand. The Dominicans added, "perhaps there were six hundred thousand, perhaps there were more than two million as many others have affirmed of those who came at the beginning and have said that the entire island was as populous as the land of Sevilla." Las Casas heard from Archbishop Deza of Sevilla that Columbus had given him a figure of a million one hundred thousand.[42]

The oft-repeated figure was not taken out of thin air. An attempt had been made to count the Indians for the purpose of drawing up a list of tributaries. After the "pacification" of 1495 Columbus decreed that the Indians should pay a per capita tribute in gold to be collected through their caciques. The Admiral returned to Spain in the spring of 1496, leaving to his brother the Adelantado the government and the organization of the tribute. The only time when the tribute rolls could have been drawn up was in the spring and summer of 1496. Later in the year Bartholomew was busy starting up mining in the San Cristóbal area and building of the town of Santo Domingo. In 1497 and thereafter he was occupied in trying to suppress a revolt; the system of Indian tribute had broken down. There is no other year than 1496 available for setting up the rolls.

This population number was known both in Spain and in Española. The Dominicans must have heard it also in Santo Domingo from the Adelantado, who had taken the rolls and had returned to the island to live there.

Believing that the natives would do whatever they were told, Columbus ordered each person, both male and female, between the ages of fourteen and seventy to pay a fixed quantity of gold. It was to that end that the count of natives was made by the Adelantado. It could have been done only through the caciques, who were to be the collectors. To have exaggerated the number of their people would have put the caciques in jeopardy. The purpose being a census of available labor, the number of children was not of concern.

In the summer of 1494 a good many natives in the Cibao and the Vega abandoned their conucos and fled to the wilds, to such an extent that this became the

---

[39] CDI, I, 307–310.
[40] López de Gómara, *Historia general de Indias* (Antwerp, 1554), pp. 26, 32.
[41] CDI, VII, 399–401.
[42] Las Casas, Bk. II, ch. 18.

"starving time" for the Spaniards, considered by them as a conspiracy. It was recorded as a time of high mortality among the natives. The ensuing "pacification" of 1495 was hard on the natives. The population available for enumeration in 1496 therefore was not at full aboriginal strength.

A tribute list of 1496 could have covered only the "province of Cayabo," which was subject to Guarionex, and the district of Marien, under Guacanagari. These were the only parts under Spanish control at that time, and they formed a scant half of the island. The western and eastern parts of the island had not been occupied nor even seen except along the northern and southern coasts.

The smaller islands lying around Española give additional information about aboriginal population. Columbus noted the island of Tortuga (Tortue) as "very beautiful and very populous, like Española Island, and the land similarly all planted, so that it appears like the *campiña* of Córdoba" (Journal, December 14). It was soon depopulated and later served as a base for freebooters.

Returning from Jamaica in 1494, Columbus was forced by stormy weather to take refuge for a number of days in a harbor of Isla Saona, at the southeastern end of Española. During this time Saona was reconnoitered and named. Columbus called it Bella Saona in honor of Michele Cuneo of Savona, who was along as the guest of his countryman. The Admiral made the gesture of presenting the island to Cuneo—the first, though ineffective, land grant of the New World. Cuneo wrote in his letter: "It was well named the beautiful, for it has about 37 villages with at least 30 thousand souls"—a reasonable estimate for such a number of villages. The island later was an important source of cassava for ships and the town of Santo Domingo until it was ruined by Ovando. It is now uninhabited and overgrown with woods and brush.

The island of Mona, between Puerto Rico and Haiti, has a similar history. Ships took on cassava and other provisions there, and it was selected by Bartholomew Columbus as his *repartimiento*. It too is now uninhabited except for a small resort. Guahaba (Gonave) has been mentioned as the center of fine woodcraft at the time of Anacaona. It has been repopulated by Haitian Negroes, but is one of the most destitute of the West Indies.

Some of the mountain country is too cold for the crops of conucos, but little of it lacks sufficient soil. There is almost no reference in early Spanish days to the high mountains, for the gold was found at lower elevations, and there were fewer Indians there. Morales did report highland settlements about Cotuí "in the clouds and surrounded by high mountain crests, with many inhabitants." This was the original Cotuí, a high basin in the southern part of the Cordillera Central, perhaps the modern Valle de los Cerros to the southeast of Constanza. The archaeologic site at Constanza, now a place where wheat is grown, is another record of mountain dwelling, though not attributable to Arawaks. Steepness of slope, if soil was sufficient, was no deterrent to native occupation. It is only by chance report, such as that of Morales, that Indian presence at higher elevation is indicated.

During the government of Ovando (1502–1509) there were fifteen Spanish towns (see fig. 20, chap. vii). The native population was then in an advanced state of decline, but there were still enough left to give indication of their distribution. Except for the city of Santo Domingo and the mining villa of Buenaventura, the towns were located for the most convenient access to native labor. The villa was supported by the Indians in the adjacent area who were subject to its vecinos. The natives of the island were thus parceled out among the fifteen towns. Their location in Ovando's time is a fair guide to where Indians were in sufficient number to support the donees. The full complement of villas was in existence when the Morales map was made (1508—see fig. 6).

Almost nothing is known of the location or number of Indian villages. They were built of wood, cane, and thatch that soon decayed. In the more humid parts, forest, and in the drier ones, scrub, repossessed their sites and the conucos about them. The southeastern peninsula is at present the most active frontier of land clearing. Here settlement is advancing into a forest that appears primeval but has retaken a country that was once well settled and notably productive.

Las Casas wrote his *Apologética Historia* mostly in the second quarter of the sixteenth century and told of once populous areas that he had seen changed to livestock ranges or abandoned to wild regrowth. The former conucos could still be seen under the wild vegetation. "The fields they had were in mounds of earth which are not readily removed by water or wind; in all the island you will not find a corner without such mounds, in clear evidence of its former tillage and of an innumerable population." [43] Las Casas was of the opinion that Española had held a native population of more than three million, that Jamaica and Puerto Rico had been of similarly dense population, but Cuba such only in parts. The people, he said, lived in order and peace, which was true and demographically significant. He continued, they were healthy and lived to a good age. The women had three to five children. "Where there is no war nor hunger nor pestilence there are always more people growing up than die."

The physical and cultural conditions were highly favorable. The climate that Columbus compared to May in Andalusia found expression in French and English times in opulent and populous plantations which had no advantage of crops, tillage, or management over the islands in their native status. The major hazard of weather is from hurricanes, which do least damage to root crops; a minor hazard is drought, to which these crops are least sensitive. The white man never fully appreciated the excellent combination of plants that were grown in conucos. The mixed planting system gave the greatest range of terrain usable without regard to steepness or regularity of slope. The plants grown were neither demanding nor exhaustive of soil fertility, and were relatively indifferent to soil acidity. They needed no special means of storage, had no critical time of harvest, and were in production at all seasons.

It would have been a competent agricultural system without yuca. With this great staple it was productive as were few parts of the world. According to Las Casas, who had been a commercial grower, "twenty persons working six hours a day for one month will make a planting of such conucos that will provide bread for three hundred persons for two years." [44] The main labor was in setting out the cuttings and caring for the plants until they were well established. The Hieronymite friars in charge of the colony from 1517 to 1518 reported to King Charles that they had set out eight hundred thousand montones of yuca, which

---

[43] Las Casas, *Apologética*, ch. 20.
[44] *Ibid.*, ch. 11.

would feed more than seven thousand Indians for a year.[45] This would amount to the provision of bread for more than three persons from one acre. Europe knew no food plants of comparable yield until the American Solanum potato was introduced. Conuco planting gave highest returns of food in continuous supply by simplest methods and moderate labor. Seasons and crop plants being as they are, there was no urgency at any time about work in the fields.

The economy worked because production of the land was in balance with food taken from the water, and the bounty of the waters also was great. Fish and shellfish exist in the same kinds and in similar numbers as then, but the manatee and green turtle have disappeared, and waterfowl are greatly diminished. Nor does the present population have the water skills of their Indian predecessors.

The tropical idyll of the accounts of Columbus and Peter Martyr was largely true. The people suffered no want. They took care of their plantings, were dexterous at fishing and bold canoeists and swimmers. They designed attractive houses and kept them clean. They found aesthetic expression in woodworking. They had leisure to enjoy diversion in ballgames, dances, and music. They lived in peace and amity.

---

[45] Documents of the friars are in CDI, I, 247–411.

IV

ESPAÑOLA UNDER COLUMBUS

•

THE CONTRACT IN FORCE

When Columbus came back from the discovery, his contract went into effect. It gave him and his heirs perpetual government of what he had found and a division of future proceeds with the Crown. It made no provision for a colony in which there would be rights to settle, hold land, engage in private enterprise, or form communities that governed themselves. It said nothing of the status of the natives and their government. As Columbus had wished it, and now had it under seal, all authority was in his hands, virtually without direction or limit. In fact, this was the first of the India companies, to be owned by the Crown and himself in permanent partnership and sharing of gains. As Céspedes del Castillo has characterized the political economy, it was a monopoly held by the Crown and Columbus, in which others were engaged only as employees on fixed pay (*sueldo*).[1] Its charter was the capitulations Columbus had secured before the voyage of discovery.

Trouble was built into the enterprise from the start. The authority given to Columbus was not limited and he had no intention of yielding any part of it, nor the inclination or ability to organize a staff that could manage it. His plan was simple. He would concentrate on the exploitation of Española for the production of gold by levying tribute on the natives, holding the chiefs responsible for its collection. The plan depended on his conclusion that the natives were timorous and would work as ordered, and on his conviction that there was a great deal of gold. A small number of Spaniards would be sufficient to maintain control by arms and would obey his orders.

The news of the discovery spread quickly through Spain from court and castle to waterfront and marketplace. Preparations were rushed to send a numerous fleet to occupy Española. The reconquest of Spain had been completed. There was peace, boredom, lack of employment, poor harvests, and hard times. Many common soldiers and young gentlemen who had been to the wars were idle. Many wanted to go on the overseas venture. Room was found for around eleven hundred, without asking whether they were needed or what they

---

[1] Jaime Vicens-Vives (ed.), *Historia social y económica de España y América*, II (Barcelona, 1959), 517 ff., especially 530.

would be used for. There was little selection for special abilities and no subsequent training. It was a random lot that enrolled and there were far too many of them. They joined up lightheartedly as salaried employees, nor did they know the temper of their governor.

When the novelty of the adventure wore thin and was followed by hardships, sickness, and hunger, when pay was in arrears and the men found that they were not free agents, the island would become a prison. Columbus failed to reckon that he would have a lot of men he did not need nor knew how to employ. He lacked the quality of leadership that bound men to him in loyalty and affection. His alienation from his men was early and increased. They were not sharing in a common effort and their management was confused and capricious. His talents were not those of an administrator and governor.

Juan Rodríguez de Fonseca, at the time Archdeacon of Sevilla, was in charge of preparations of the new voyage for the Crown, and thus began the fateful antagonism between the two. The excessive right of title, its monopolistic character, and the intransigence and administrative inability of Columbus cast the first shadows ahead.

THE SECOND VOYAGE

The fleet of seventeen ships left Cádiz on September 23, 1493, with fifteen hundred men, supplies, livestock, and a diverse store of seeds and plants for field and garden. There were no women aboard. More provisions and animals were taken on in the Canary Islands. When the fleet cleared the island of Ferro on October 13, the decks were filled with horses, cows and calves, swine, sheep, and goats. Spanish ways of living were to be established. Columbus expected seed wheat and grape cuttings shortly to provide the accustomed bread and wine. Only a scattering of persons understood husbandry and hardly any of them thought of themselves as emigrants who would found new homes.

The crossing was made in twenty days; Dr. Chanca said they would have done it in six less had the flagship been a better sailor. The landfall was at the islands Marie Galante and Dominica on November 3, both so named then. Columbus had heard of islands to the south of Española and let the ships run before the wind. Thereafter the trade-wind route from the Canary Islands to a passage between the Leeward and Windward Islands was the standard track of sail from Spain to the New World. Chanco wrote, "by the grace of God and the good knowledge of the Admiral we came as straight as though we were following a known and established route."

Before they turned north for Española a landing was made on Turuquia (Guadelupe, French Guadeloupe). There was a week's delay because a party got lost in the wooded mountains. The Caribs ran away, but there was opportunity to examine villages and fields, to find proof of cannibalism and note the importance of cotton growing and the excellence of its woven cloth.[2] The

---

[2] Letter of Chanca (Navarrete, I, 198-224). He gave the first record of the domestic Muscovy duck: "There were ducks in the houses, most of them white as snow and some of them black, very handsome, with naked crests, larger than those back home and smaller than geese." The lack of any such reference from the Arawak islands suggests that this important domestic fowl of South America had not been carried to the northern West Indies.

fleet continued north along the lee side of the islands, which Columbus named as they passed by. A stop was made at Santa Cruz (St. Croix), where a sharp fight confirmed the valor of the Caribs. In the years following, this was the regular route for ships going to Española. Ships would land on one of the Carib islands to get water and wood, perhaps to capture a few natives, and then continue north. The islands remained unoccupied, not because of fear of the Caribs but because there was nothing in them of value to the Spaniards.

Arawak women who were freed from Carib captivity showed the direct way, along the south side of Puerto Rico, through the Mona Passage, and to Cape Samaná, where the coast was familiar to Columbus. If their confidence in directing the ships is correctly reported, these women had good knowledge of island geography. On November 28 the fleet dropped anchor off Navidad, which Columbus had left eleven months before. A little more than two months out of Cádiz, a month and a half from the Canaries, the ships had been about a month under sail. There had been no misadventure, straying from course, or delay except to find the party that had lost its way. The voyage was made to deliver a large number of people and cargo to Navidad, not for exploration. The discovery of the Leeward Islands, Puerto Rico, and the eastern tip of Española was incidental and because Columbus had prior expectation that the direct or fastest crossing of the ocean was by sailing all the way before the trade wind.

THE FOUNDING OF ISABELA

Navidad was found in ruins and the men who had been left there were dead. Suspicion fell on the cacique Guacanagari and his people who had been so generous of help when the *Santa María* was lost and had given aid to build Navidad. The natives greeted the return of Columbus with apprehension. The incident is relevant because in clearing themselves of blame the local Indians placed it on a cacique of the interior, called Caonabo, first heard of in this connection.

What had happened at Navidad was about what should have been expected. The men who elected to stay were mostly riffraff that had been picked up to man the *Santa María*. Columbus left them with orders to acquire gold and discover its source. He expressed confidence that the cowardly natives would submit to whatever the Spaniards willed. The men at Navidad were free to roam about and behave as they willed instead of being put under discipline and held to account for their conduct. Oviedo summed up what happened thus: "The natives could not endure the excesses, for they [the Spaniards] took their women and used them as they wished and committed other violences and offenses, being persons without a leader and without order," also saying that the Spaniards fell to fighting among themselves. Further Oviedo thought that it might be inferred from the fulminant outbreak of syphilis in Europe following the return of the men of the first voyage that those left behind also were thus ravaged.[3]

Columbus had taken the sinking of the *Santa María* as a divine sign to found a town at that unlikely site. Navidad having been destroyed, he looked else-

[3] Oviedo, *Historia*, Bk. II, ch. 8.

where for a proper port to discharge men, animals, and cargo and to serve as a permanent town. He had seen the length of the north coast and its harbors. Immediately to the west of Navidad is one of the best harbors of the island, Puerto Real of the Spanish, Cap François of the French, Cap Haïtien today. This was the seat of Guacanagari, cacique of populous Marien and ever faithful to Columbus. Columbus, however, was no longer interested in anything to the west.

"The Admiral decided that we should turn back up the coast by which we had come from Castile because the news of gold was from that direction. We had contrary weather so that it was more trouble for us to go back thirty leagues then to come from Castile. With the adverse weather and the length of the way, three months had passed when we [finally] landed" (Chanca). The fullest account is from Las Casas, who had a lost manuscript of Columbus. The Admiral examined the coast about Montecristi "to see whether it had the qualities he sought for a settlement, but his inclination was chiefly to the Monte Plata because he thought, as he said, that it was closer to the province of Cibao where he had understood, on the first voyage, that the rich gold mines were." [4] Both Montecristi and Monte Plata had been named by him on the first voyage. Montecristi would have been a fair location for a port town and is such at present. Its harbor is well under the lee of the high headland of El Morro and is adjacent to and above the Yaque floodplain. The news of gold had been brought by the *Pinta*, a year earlier, from farther east, and in that direction Columbus would seek a harbor nearer to the gold fields. He knew the harbor from which Martín Alonso had gone to the gold district. To have made it the site of his new town would have been to acknowledge the judgment and services of the elder Pinzón. The alternative was to choose the next harbor beyond, Puerto Plata (fig. 9).

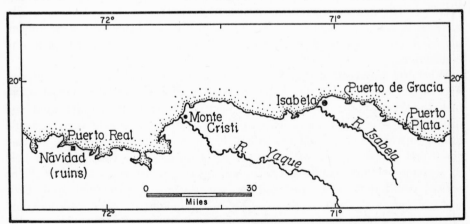

Fig. 9. Columbus' return to northern coast of Española.

The fleet took its course east, working tediously upwind as far as the harbor of Pinzón, renamed Gracia by the Admiral. He doubted that the place had enough drinking water or productive land, a judgment contradicted by the present settlement there. Thus the ships stood out to sea again, met strong head

---

[4] Las Casas, Bk. I, ch. 88.

winds and turned back, to round Cape Isabela and anchor in its lee at the mouth of the Río Bajabonico.

A strange episode, this search for the site of the new town. The fleet, composed mainly of nimble caravels, took longer to make the thirty leagues east from Navidad than it had taken to sail from the Canaries to the Dominica Passage. There was no bad weather, only the strong head winds common along that coast. Arrived at Puerto de Gracia, they could have debarked men and animals to rest and refresh themselves, to confer with the natives who had guided the Pinzón party into the interior, and to send out men by longboat and canoe or on foot to explore alternative harbors. It was only twenty miles by land and about the same by sea to Puerto Plata, with three intermediate bays worth looking into. It was ten miles west to the Río Bajabonico, which he would name the Río Isabela. The sensible thing to have done in so important a matter was to inspect that coast with care. In a day's time men could have rowed or paddled or walked in reconnaissance of the country to a sufficient distance to secure information of eligible places. Nothing of the sort was done, not even for the bay in which they were anchored. Columbus took the fleet out to sea to swing back around Cape Isabela, anchor in its lee at the mouth of the Río Bajabonico, and that was the journey's end. Later, as will be noted, he claimed that by miraculous intervention the ships were obliged to stay there, being unable either to go on or turn back.

The place at which Isabela was built may have been seen in passing, but it had not been examined. The fleet came to anchor at an unknown spot that offered few advantages. The harbor is little more than a roadstead, sheltered by Cape Isabela to the east but open to the west and north (fig. 10). A bench of

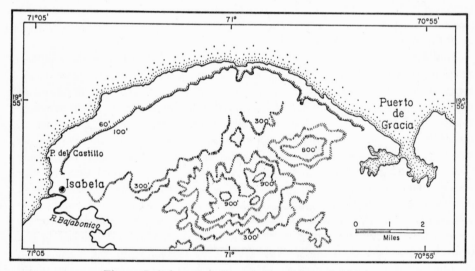

Fig. 10. Isabela and environs (adapted from A.M.S.).

higher land looks out to sea and over an alluvial plain to the south through which the river flows into a tidal flat. Clay was available at the site to make tiles and also stone for building and for burning lime. Also there was a small fishing village. No account was taken of the fact that in turning from the windward side of the coast range (the Monte Plata of Columbus) to its lee a well-watered and productive country was left for one of scant rain, scrub vegetation, and small population. The geologist William Gabb, visiting the site in 1870, sized it up in these words:

> Standing on the table-land at the mouth of the Isabela River, the site of the first settlement of Columbus on the island, the view is cheerless in the extreme. As far as the eye can reach, nothing is visible but a succession of dry yellow hills, parched and barren. No green things are to be seen in the distance, except a rare mangrove swamp, suggestive of mud and quicksand. To heighten the effect, the spectator sees a similar growth at his feet, reeking with foul odors, and around him is nothing but thorn-bushes and cactus. It is difficult to imagine what could have induced the great discoverer to have pitched on such a spot as this, when the coast of Hayti to the west, and the entire coast of Santo Domingo, to the east of Isabella, offered so many more inducements—equally good and better harbors, more accessible and better water, rich vegetation instead of a desert, and, in one word, all the conditions for the safe establishment of a weak colony in a strange and hostile country. There are a few fragments of roughly-built stone walls still standing, barely more than a foot high; and the owner, who acted as my guide, expressed his perfect willingness to sell site, ruins, landing, cactus, mangrove swamp —all, for a hundred dollars.[5]

Prudence would have indicated a temporary camp until something was known of the locality, the surrounding country, and the route to the desired gold fields. Disembarkation took place on January 1, 1494, and work was begun immediately to lay out the town, which Columbus named Isabela in honor of his patron the Queen. This was to be the capital of his viceregal domain. It was the first serious mistake he made as governor. With the stubbornness that was one of his dominant traits he insisted to the end of his life that Isabela had the best location in all Española.

The plan Columbus carried in his mind was of a fortified town in the medieval Spanish manner. According to Las Casas, "he was in greatest haste and used extreme diligence in building at once quarters for the food and the munitions of the fleet, a church and hospital, and for himself a strong house . . . and allocated solares [the large lots for the principal persons] and ordered each one to build his house." Streets and plaza were laid out. The public buildings were of stone, the rest of wood and thatch. Las Casas knew the ruins in later years when they were overgrown with brush and trees.[6] Peter Martyr noted that the city was surrounded by moats and parapets.[7] The site was surveyed in 1891 by an American naval party that plotted the identifiable foundations and enclosures.[8]

The colonists were hardly in condition for the physical labor required to build a town. Many had never done such work and none had labored in the tropics. They had been under way for eleven weeks from the Canaries in cramped quarters, about ninety to a ship, along with the livestock that required

---

[5] William M. Gabb, "On the Topography and Geology of Santo Domingo," *Transactions of the American Philosophical Society,* XV, new series (1881), 66.
[6] Las Casas, Bk. I, ch. 88.
[7] Peter Martyr, Decade I, Bk. 3.
[8] Report and map reproduced in J. B. Thacher, *Christopher Columbus,* II (New York and London, 1904).

much of the deck space. Food, especially meat, was in short supply. The kindly natives flocked in to provide fresh fish and ages, both of which Dr. Chanca judged to be excellent. He also reported that within four or five days a third of the people fell sick. The illness continued for several months and affected the greater part of the newcomers. Las Casas said that hardly a man escaped the terrible fevers, many died, and the mood was one of anxiety and sadness at being so far from home and in such circumstances. The long voyage in close quarters must have been favorable to the spread of intestinal infection, further aided by their close congregation in building the town.

Columbus composed a long and rambling Memorial at the end of the first month.[9] The general sickness had slowed the progress of settlement, but the Admiral was of good cheer as to the future. He regretted that he could send only the samples of gold that Hojeda and Gorbalán (of whom more below) had found, but this business would shortly be prospering. Improvement of the road to the interior had begun and he would build a fort inland to protect the operation. Construction was going ahead at Isabela and the gardens that had been set out were doing well. Wheat fields and vineyards, cattle and hogs and draft animals were needed so that the colony could live in the Spanish manner. There was no mention of native foodstuffs.

The next order of business was to get the gold production going. Columbus asked the Crown to excuse him from going on another discovery that year: "As has already been written by letters, for the present year I do not think it will be possible to go on discoveries until this matter of the gold-bearing rivers that have been found be put into proper order. [Although he had not yet seen any part of the interior he had by this time some idea of the occurrence of native gold.] It is certain that the gold is not engendered in the rivers but in the ground, the water running against the mines [the gold-bearing ground] carrying it along with the sands; and it has been found in many rivers, along with some rather large ones, in others so small as to be founts rather than rivers, carrying only two fingers of water, from which its source may be traced. Therefore not only gold panners (*lavadores*) will be useful to collect it in the sand, but others to dig it from the ground, which will be the best and in greatest quantity; and therefore it will be well if your Highnesses send washers of gold and some of those who work in the mines at Almadén so that in the one way and the other the business be carried on." The latter probably were not rock miners of gold-bearing quartz veins, but workers with pick and shovel for digging terrace gravels. At any rate Columbus had the benefit of observations as to how gold was to be found in the island.

The Memorial also sounded out the prospects for transporting natives to Spain. "There are being sent in these ships some Cannibals, men and women, boys and girls, which Your Highnesses can order placed in charge of persons from whom they may be able better to learn the language while being employed in forms of service, gradually ordering that greater care be given them than to other slaves." Thinking the Cannibal islands to be the largest and most populous it seemed "that to take males and females from them and send them to Castile will be

---

[9] Given to Antonio de Torres, captain of the fleet that returned February 2, and the only document from the hand of Columbus concerning the second voyage.

advantageous, losing their inhuman custom of eating people and, learning the language in Castile, they will more readily receive baptism and secure the welfare of their souls." Who were these "cannibals," considering that in Guadelupe the Caribs had all fled, and there had been only a brief skirmish in St. Croix? "The welfare of the souls of the said Cannibals and also of those here has raised the thought that the more that may be sent over the better it will be." Spanish livestock would be traded for cannibals, who were recommended as better than any other slaves. This was a direct proposal of a slave trade in Caribs and also a discreet feeler about sending over Indians from Española. The saving of heathen souls would be one gain; for another, the Crown would have proceeds from slaves.

GOLD IN THE CIBAO

Within the week of landing at Isabela, Columbus sent out parties to the gold region of Cibao. Cuneo, who gave the earliest account, said that the Admiral sent two captains with about forty men in good order, with two Indians as guides to a place called Cibao. They crossed a river greater than that of Sevilla [Yaque], finding many Indian habitations and being well received. They were detained at another river which they dared not cross; here the Indians not only assured them of the large quantity of gold in Cibao but presented them with nuggets, one of which was of eight, one of fifteen, and one of twenty-two *castellanos*, the latter with a piece of rock adhering. On their return the Admiral wrote the King that soon he hoped to give him as much gold as the mines of Vizcaya yielded iron. The two captains were Alonso de Hojeda, who was to be one of the principal figures of the Spanish Main, and Gorbalán. There is disagreement whether they stayed together. One returned to Isabela after twenty days, the other a day later. Columbus in the Memorial said that they went in different directions, that they found many rivers so rich in gold that he was hesitant to repeat it, but that Hojeda found most, in each of which he reported that there was an incredible amount.

On March 12 Columbus was ready to set out himself for the gold country, the first time in either voyage that he had left the seashore. Some gentlemen went ahead with a gang of laborers to clear the way over the first low range south of the Isabela River, the pass known to the present as the Puerto de los Hidalgos. From it Columbus had his first view over the great basin of the Río Yaque, aptly named by him the Vega Real (fig. 11). The river was reached five leagues beyond, and the second night was spent on its banks (fig. 12). The march by foot and on horseback continued, banners flying, trumpets sounding, and the occasional boom of guns, all of which the natives enjoyed as they trotted along to watch the parade. A league and a half farther on they came to a large village on a second river and at a short distance from a sierra. Las Casas thought this was the Río Moa, which would place the Indian town about where the present town of Valverde is. They followed still another river they named the Río Verde, probably the present Río Amina, passing through large settlements, and made their fourth camp at the Puerto de Cibao, eleven leagues from the Puerto de los Hidalgos, having thus crossed the basin of the Yaque. Distance and

77

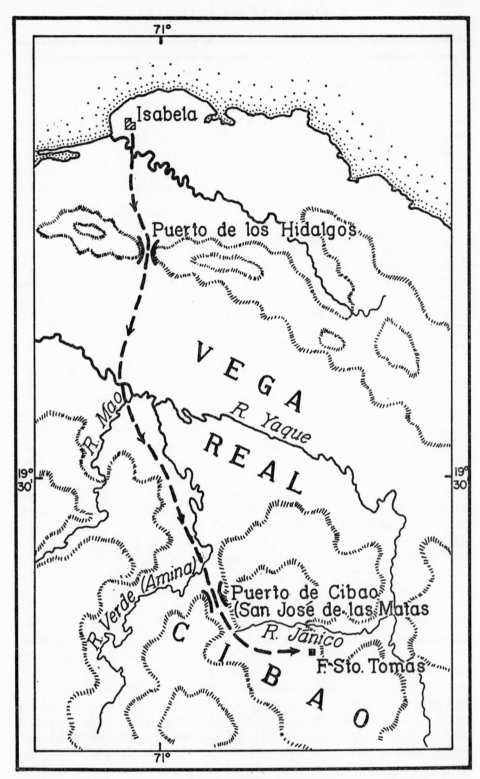

Fig. 11. Route to the Cibao gold field.

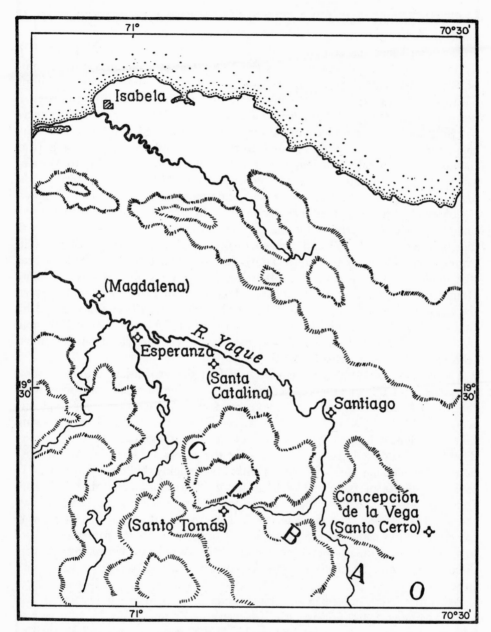

Fig. 12. Forts guarding the Cibao.

direction indicate that this camp was made near San José de las Matas. On the 16th they went over the pass, looking back over the Vega and ahead into the Cibao: "a very rugged country of stones great and small, an infinite number of arroyos, of short grass and many very tall pine trees spaced as olive trees are in the groves of Sevilla" (Las Casas). This is a good description of the granite area on the northern flank of the central cordillera, with boulders shaped like woolsacks, steep ravines, and open pine forests. They had reached the gold country

79

and were met by natives bringing nuggets collected in anticipation of the coming of the great white chief.

The term Cibao has since been altered in meaning and location. Today it is by local usage the lowland that was the Vega Real of Columbus, the meaning of "stony mountains" now forgotten. At the time of Gabb and Schomburgk, Cibao Mountains was the name of the central cordillera. In original usage it was one part of the northern flank of that sierra, approximately the southern half of the present province of Santiago, well described by Las Casas. This rugged montane country drains north to the Yaque and its only ingress is from the north. Aboriginally it belonged to the state of Cayabo, according to Morales. Las Casas, agreeing, attached it as a dependency to Guarionex, the lord of the plain of Magua (Vega). The matter is of importance to events later in that year.

Columbus planned another *fortaleza* in the gold country. He decided promptly on the site, a hill encircled by the Río Jánico. The artisans he brought with him built a fort of wood and tamped earth (*tapia*) and dug a moat about its exposed side. He named it Santo Tomás in answer to those who had doubted that gold would be found. The place is shown on the official map of Santo Domingo of 1952 as Fortaleza de Santo Tomás, about three miles southwest of the town of Jánico. Las Casas later had a plantation at its base and engaged his Indians there at placer mining. The long account of the expedition of Columbus by Las Casas which I have followed may have been derived from his uncle, who was a captain at arms at the time.[10]

The account by Cuneo, who participated in the expedition, differs in some particulars and fills in others. According to him, five hundred men went with the Admiral and were gone for four weeks of very bad weather, poor food, and worse drink. Going and returning they crossed two very large rivers by swimming and those who could not swim were helped across, each by two Indians. The Indians took all the equipment over the rivers by carrying it on their heads. The wooden fort of Santo Tomás was quickly built at about twenty-seven leagues from Isabela. The hunt for gold was unsuccessful, but Indians from ten leagues around came in bringing gold to trade, to the value of two thousand castellanos. The nuggets weighed up to 24 castellanos and some were like *tibar*, an old name for refined gold [v. Corominas]. Some Spaniards engaged in secret trade to the extent of another thousand castellanos, but almost all were discovered. "Some had their ears cut off, others the nose, so that it was a pity to see."

Pedro Margarite, nobleman of Aragón and confidant of King Ferdinand, was left in charge at Santo Tomás with fifty men to stay among the friendly natives, who continued to bring in food and gold. The white men were still an exciting novelty to the natives and there had been no trouble. Columbus started back on March 21, and reached Isabela near the end of the month.

The occurrence of gold in Haiti was explained by William Gabb in his geologic survey of 1869–1871. He is still the best source of information on the central cordillera, which he interpreted as a long attenuated anticline or arch, a mass of igneous rock (dioritic) that was intruded (batholith) into sedimentary rock (Cretaceous). The sedimentary beds were strongly altered (metamorphosed)

[10] Las Casas, Bk. I, ch. 90.

by heat, distortion, and dislocation. Erosion has removed most of the covering beds except along the flanks of the range where metamorphic rocks overlie the granitic base. His interpretation of the native gold was that "almost everywhere the metamorphosed slates carry quartz veins, sometimes barren, sometimes aurif-erous . . . true veins of segregation. They are most numerous in the vicinity of the injected masses of crystalline rock . . . Those nearest to the intrusive rocks are always gold-bearing; and those at a distance from them are invariably barren . . . every stream running through the metamorphic rocks in the immediate neighborhood of masses of syenite carries gold in its sands, while all those run-ning exclusively in the syenites, or at a great distance from them are without the precious metal." By way of illustration he cited the lack of gold in the upper stream courses (above the original Cibao country), whereas "immediately on entering the slates they and all their tributaries are gold-producing." [11]

The Indians in the Cibao on occasion picked up nuggets in the gravel of mountain streams, washed down in the erosion of quartz veins in the meta-morphic rocks. The Cibao area was the only part of the north flank of the great sierra in which there was significant concentration of placer gold. When the Spaniards on the north coast asked for gold, the natives there knew about this area in the middle of the island and led Pinzón, then Hojeda, and finally Columbus to the proper places. Thus the first gold rush of the New World started.

DIGRESSION TO JAMAICA AND CUBA

Columbus, having founded his town at Isabela and a fort in the Cibao, returned to the coast confident of success. He could reconsider what he had written in the Memorial, that it would take all that year to establish the colony. The Crown had instructed him to renew discovery by sea. He recalled the story of the golden riches of Jamaica of which he had heard on the first voyage. He would leave the affairs of the colony in the hands of his brother Diego, assisted by a council. He had also sent for his other brother, Bartholomew, who was expected in the next fleet. There were ships lying idle at Isabela. The interval was op-portune to go on the requested exploration.

On April 24 Columbus set out with three caravels to find out what might lie to the west. The accounts are from Peter Martyr, one that the priest Bemáldez heard from Columbus, and that of Cuneo, who went on the voyage. Morison retraced the course of the voyage and gives a lively description of the shores seen. The course was through the Windward Channel, along the south coast of Cuba to Cabo Cruz, south to Jamaica, back to the cape, and on west, at times along the Cuban south coast, at others picking their way through low keys, which Columbus called the Jardín de la Reina. The farthest point reached was near the west end of Cuba. It was a long and tedious voyage carried out with care and competence.

The inquiries Columbus made whether Cuba was island or mainland gave him assurance that it was part of Tierra Firme. Midway of the Cuban south coast he heard of a province with a name resembling Polo's Mangi or Mango, which

<hr>

[11] Gabb, *op. cit.*, p. 89.

was southern China. At the farther end the coast turned somewhat to the south and this, he thought, meant that they were on course for the Golden Chersonese (Malaya). The long exploration reconfirmed his notions of the geography of the Far Orient.

Before turning back he sent a notary to get all his men to sign a deposition certifying that they had reached the mainland of the Orient. It stated that in continuing along this shore the Admiral "had recognized many times and so pronounced that this was Tierra Firme, in particular the province of Mangi." Bizarre penalties were promised if any should change their minds later. Everyone signed. The men were tired and bored and weary of eating fish, conchs, and oysters to eke out their stores. They had been seeing the same low islands and marshes, running aground occasionally on mudflats, and visiting a few Indian settlements. If the Admiral insisted that they were on an eastern shore, of which few of them had ever heard, he could have their agreement, after which they would go back to Española.

The attitude of Columbus was the same as on the first voyage. He wanted to claim that he had reached the Oriental mainland, but he had no desire to test his belief. When they returned to Española, according to Cuneo, a learned priest of Lucena maintained that they had not reached the Far East but were on a very large island, "to which statement, considering the manner of our navigation, the greater part of us were agreed, and for this reason the Admiral has not allowed the priest to return to Spain with us, lest, commanded to appear before His Majesty, he might by such response cause the King to abandon the enterprise." The Crown was interested in finding a way to Cathay; Columbus was determined on exploiting islands for gold. He had obeyed royal orders in sailing a notable distance to the west. The sworn deposition affirmed that Cuba was "Tierra Firme at the beginning of the Indies." Thus the Admiral had satisfied orders and was free to return to his real objective, Española.

The Cuban waters offered little of interest other than their varied and abundant marine life and native fishermen. The shoal waters had a rich fauna, surface and bottom; in one part the ships were delayed in passing through a sea covered with turtles. The main account of fishing by remoras is from here and also of the drying of fish over fires. The largest villages seen were midway, at the base of mountains (Trinidad to Cienfuegos). Inquiry for gold here and along the seacoast of the Sierra Maestra received negative answers.

After leaving Cuba, Columbus took another look at Jamaica, this time taking time to reconnoiter at leisure its west and south coasts. On the prior landing on the north shore they had been met by a large number of canoes, and many Indians came from the interior, Cuneo saying about sixty thousand, to see the strange visitors. Bernáldez had it from the Admiral that the gardens of Valencia were nothing in comparison to those of this coast, that the canoes were the largest and finest, each cacique having his own, finely decorated fore and aft with painted patterns; the Admiral having measured one that was 96 feet long and 6 feet wide. On the south coast they were received in state by a cacique, his family, and retinue who came out in canoes. The dignitaries wore elaborate feather headdresses and cloaks. Again there was mention of finely worked black wood, this time as trumpets. Peter Martyr understood that the Jamaicans were of more acute genius and skills than the other islanders. Persuaded that the gold of Jamaica was a fiction, Columbus had no further interest in the island.

More than a month was spent in discovering the south coast of Española, including the stop at Saona, as described by Cuneo. On September 29 the caravels got back to Isabela, ending a five-month voyage.

FIRST DISORDERS AND TIME OF FAMINE (1494)

Trouble began before Columbus left for Cuba and grew worse in his absence. He wished a capital befitting his new station and ordered the building of an unneeded town in a wrong location by inexperienced and unaccustomed labor. The local area produced little food from conucos and nothing more was heard about natives supplying fish or about Spanish fishing. The supplies which the ships had been able to leave soon ran low. Rationing of food was necessary and became more severe. The hardtack was used up and the flour was about at an end. Columbus decided to grind the wheat that had been brought for planting and to build a water mill, a dam to be constructed across the river. To keep this and other public works going, such as building houses and a road, he ordered that all who were not sick must labor or have their rations cut off. Supplies needed for the fort at Santo Tomás and the three caravels that went to Cuba reduced the food available at Isabela still further.

The first task, the production of food, was neglected in favor of objectives which should have been deferred or not undertaken at all. As hunger became famine, everything edible, including the animals that had been brought from Spain, was eaten up.

In his Memorial, Columbus mentioned that more than two hundred persons were not on wages, many of whom he would like to put into his service because of their ability and prestige, and to this end he asked money of the Crown. This was written before the pinch began. These were gentry, clergy, ships' officers, persons attached to the court, who were free to come and go and were not under orders from Columbus. His order that whoever did not labor should not eat was felt to be degrading. This command to "hidalgos and men of the court or of the black mantle was the origin of his being defamed before the Crown and all Spain as cruel and odious . . . and from this seed there came his fall." [12] According to Las Casas, Isabela was already in a state of famine, its men gaunt and weak, when Columbus returned from the Cibao at the end of March. Las Casas told that in later years the ruins of Isabela were thought to be haunted by the ghosts of gentlemen who had died of starvation.

Disaffection was repressed by punishment. The royal comptroller, Bernal de Pisa,[13] became embroiled with Columbus, tried to take ship for Spain, was caught and jailed. Thus the first conflict between the Admiral and royal officials.[14] Columbus demanded total obedience from everyone. Those who were sent by the Crown were responsible to it and in the discharge of their duties

---

[12] Las Casas, Bk. I, chs. 92, 93.
[13] CDI, XXI, 365–366 gives the terms of his appointment as agent of the Crown.
[14] Las Casas, Bk. I, ch. 90.

did not accept an overriding authority of Columbus. The rift was present from the beginning and grew deeper.

The good relations with the Indians also began to break down in the spring of 1494. The trouble started at the crossing of the Río Yaque. Alonso de Hojeda left Isabela on April 9 with a party to reinforce Santo Tomás. At the river he seized the local cacique, his brother, his nephew, and a vassal, lopping off the vassal's ears in the "plaza" of the pueblo, the charge being that some local Indians had made off with clothes of Spaniards while helping these across the river. The alleged offense had been committed on an earlier occasion. The prisoners were sent in chains to the Admiral at Isabela, who ordered their hands cut off, but then yielded to the pleas of a cacique "from the other side of the river," one who had given aid both to the Admiral and Hojeda in their previous entries to the Cibao. The river crossing, a critical link between Isabela and Santo Tomás, was thus foolishly broken by Hojeda. Thereafter that locality was insecure and hostile. Las Casas commented that Hojeda, ignorant of the language, could not have known what the guilt was nor who was guilty.[15] Thieving was no part of island ways, Columbus having testified earlier to their lack of covetousness. The act of Hojeda was the first of a long series of outrages by him upon the natives of islands and mainland.

There was also the cacique Caonabo to reckon with, first heard of at the ruin of Navidad as hostile. In his Memorial, Columbus warned of him as a danger to those who went inland, "a very bad and bold man." Cuneo, going with the Admiral to the fort of Santo Tomás, heard that Caonabo (Cuneo wrote Guacaonabo) was in control of the gold and was only two leagues from the fort, that they did not go to seek him because of scarcity of bread, also that the chief could put fifty thousand men in the field. At the same time, however, Cuneo told of natives flocking to Santo Tomás from ten leagues around to offer nuggets.

Peter Martyr had a report about this lord Caonabo, whose name or title meant "King of the Golden House." [16] In the uncertain Spanish rendering of the island speech, "Guacaonabo" was the Golden House, a splendiferous title which the Spaniards interpreted as a great store of gold or the control of its source. Blame for the Navidad disaster made him an enemy, and his title was thought to mean that he was rich. The indicated step was to get rid of him and gain control of his gold. Columbus proceeded to act without further inquiry. Caonabo was the cacique of Maguana, the basin on the far side of the Cordillera Central, beyond its highest and most impassable part. His country was not gold-bearing, nor had he anything to do with the Cibao.

Hojeda took a letter of instruction from Columbus to Margarite in command at Santo Tomás, dated April 9, 1494.[17] Hojeda was bringing sixteen horsemen, two hundred fifty crossbowmen and shield bearers, a hundred ten musketeers, and twenty officials to be put under the charge of Margarite. "You shall go with all these men all over the island to reconnoiter its provinces and people and land and what is in them," most particularly the province of Cibao. He was instructed to "take good care of the Indians, that there be no evil or hurt done

---

[15] *Ibid.*, ch. 93.
[16] Peter Martyr, Decade I, Bk. 2.
[17] Navarrete, vol. II, doc. 72.

to them nor shall they be taken against their will." However, referring to the affair at the crossing of the Yaque, "since it happened that on the road I built to Cibao a certain Indian stole something, if it should be found that any of them do steal, they also shall have their noses and ears cut off as punishment, because these are members that cannot be hidden, for by such means there will be assured the *rescate*[18] of the people of the whole island, giving them to understand that what was done to other Indians was because of the theft they did and that those who are good shall be treated very well and the bad ones shall be castigated." It would be necessary to secure food as they went along and "if by chance food could not be purchased" it was to be taken as honestly as possible. Thus the first instructions to Margarite were to make a general *entrada* and impose the peace Columbus offered.

The Admiral went on to consider how best to lay hands on Caonabo, a matter he greatly desired. An official was to be sent with ten men to the seat of the cacique, bearing gifts to show the chief "that I have great desire of his friendship and that I shall send him more things and that he shall send us gold," not neglecting to let him know "that we have an infinite number of men and that every day many more will come, and that always I shall be sending him things which will be brought from Castile. Treat him thus with words until you have his friendship, in order the better to seize him." Margarite was instructed to repeat such missions until Caonabo felt assured of the friendship of the Christians. In case Margarite had no plan of his own to capture Caonabo the Admiral proposed one. When the cacique had been persuaded to visit Margarite, he would come naked as was the custom. He should then be dressed in Spanish clothes so that he could not slip through their hands and escape. His brothers should be captured at the same time. The whole tenor of these instructions from Columbus refutes the oft-repeated story that Margarite had called for help in order to repel a supposedly impending attack on Santo Tomás by Caonabo and that the additional troops were sent for that reason. The cacique was at his home far from the Cibao on the other side of the cordillera. A small party was to go there confident of being secure. There was no Caonabo menace.

Margarite neither marched out of Santo Tomás with his troops to go about the still mainly unknown island, and take possession of it nor did he bait the trap for Caonabo. Oviedo, who knew and liked Margarite, said, "he was a man who neither did nor consented to violence or offense to the Indians," and related how he stayed at Santo Tomás to share with his men the hunger they suffered.[19] The fleet bringing supplies and Bartholomew Columbus reached Isabela on June 24. Some time thereafter Margarite, Fray Buil, and others who disapproved of what was taking place, sailed for Spain. The men whom Margarite had left at Santo Tomás scattered by twos and threes into Indian communities, abandoning the fort, which thus faded from the scene. Margarite and Buil returned to the court, where they were well received and remained. It is thought that they gave adverse information on Columbus and the state of the colony.[20]

---

[18] To my knowledge the first use of this term in the New World. It had the meaning of trade under some pressure and often meant that goods were commandeered.

[19] Oviedo, *Historia*, Bk. II, ch. 13.

[20] Both have been severely censured by later writers as derelict in their obligations to Columbus on the assumption that they were under his orders. Fray Buil (Bernal Boyl in Rob. Streit,

The condition of the colony continued to deteriorate. Isabela was in serious straits, Santo Tomás was abandoned, and Spaniards were roaming about living off the natives. Oviedo later heard that half of the Spaniards at Isabela and Santo Tomás died of hunger and disease. Oviedo again blamed the ravages of syphilis (*mal de las buas*) "because the origin thereof is the *Indias*, and I say properly Indias, both because of the land where this sickness is native and because of the Indian women of these parts," who communicated it to the Spaniards. He thought that syphilis had been introduced into Europe by men of the first voyage, from whom it spread through Spain into Italy and beyond, and that those of the second also suffered heavily.[21] Las Casas agreed: "All Spaniards who lacked the virtue of chastity were contaminated on the island, the Indians, male or female, being little affected." [22] An ancient disease of this part of the New World and of little damage to the natives, it gave savage punishment to Europeans.

The year 1494 was a far worse time for the Indians. Las Casas, always taking a sympathetic view of the Indians, had it that at the return of the Admiral from Cuba "the country was all upset, frightened, and in a state of horror and hate and in arms against the Christians." He put the original blame of Hojeda and the scare thrown into the natives at the river crossing, and on the conduct of Spaniards who drifted about the Vega, indulging in sensuality. The Indians satisfied their frugal wants with small labor of planting, hunting, and fishing. The Spaniards who squatted on them required more in a day than a native needs for a month, Las Casas thought, in exaggeration of such parasitism. The newcomers bullied and mistreated the Indians, both commoners and nobles, who thus were taught to abhor the society of Christians. Moreover, they took Indian women, "wives and daughters by force without respect or consideration of

---

Bibliotheca Missionum, II [Aachen, 1924], 4–6, in biographic and bibliographic data) went as representative of Pope and Crown (Navarrete, vol. II, docs. 52 and 73) and was charged with keeping the sovereigns well informed. He had been sent previously by King Ferdinand on a diplomatic mission to France, whence he had returned to establish the Minim order in Spain and be its vicar general. In Española he was the ranking religious and came into sharp conflict with Columbus. The special trust placed in him by the crown is indicated by instructions to the Admiral that he and the friar should select the person to replace the royal comptroller Pisa (Navarrete, vol. II, doc. 73).

Margarite also was a free agent, as was recognized by Columbus in his Memorial: "Mosén Pedro [Margarite] and Gaspar and Beltrán and others who have remained here were captains of caravels that now have gone back, and do not have benefit of salaries; but they are such persons as should be placed in affairs of importance and confidence. A salary not having been determined for them that shall be different from the rest you shall ask their Highnesses for me to determine what each of them is to be given by year or month, as may serve best." At the time Columbus was especially impressed by Margarite: "Because Mosén Pedro Margarite, *criado* of your Highnesses, has served well and I expect will do so in the future in the matters that may be entrusted to him, I have been pleased that he has stayed on here." The Admiral therefore hoped that Margarite would be given an encomienda in the Order of Santiago to which he belonged, to support his family in Spain. Margarite was perhaps the most distinguished of the Spanish gentry. He had not been engaged on salary at the time of the Memorial requesting such provision. Peter Martyr knew him as a nobleman of Aragon and an old intimate of the King. Veteran officer in the Moorish wars, Margarite was trained in handling men at arms. Did his acceptance of command at Santo Tomás, with or without salary, obligate him to carry out the further and distasteful orders of Columbus? He considered himself free to leave and did so. The Council that governed in the absence of the Admiral took no steps to stop him.

[21] Oviedo, *Historia,* Bk. II, ch. 13.
[22] Las Casas, *Apologética,* ch. 20.

person, dignity, state, or marital condition." The natives, and especially the caciques, took to hiding out and soon began to avenge themselves on stray Spaniards.[23]

Oviedo blamed the Indians as entering into a conspiracy to get rid of the Spaniards by agreeing not to plant crops, ceasing to serve the Spaniards, and running away. He said that the number that died was beyond counting. Peter Martyr at the time still viewed the overseas enterprise with benevolence, but had heard that "there was such hunger about the island that more than fifty thousand have died, which it was known happened to them because of their malice. Seeing that our men intended to settle in the island they thought to get rid of them by withholding the provisions of the island and so they determined to refrain from sowing and planting and also that each should destroy and root out on his land both kinds of the breadstuffs they cultivated. This was done especially in the Cibao or Cipango mountains since they knew that the gold abounding in that province was the main reason that kept our people on the island." [24]

TAKING CAPTIVES (1494-1495)

The calendar of the latter part of 1494 is obscure. The caravels got back from the Cuban exploration at the end of September; the Admiral was gravely ill and the conduct of affairs passed to Bartholomew Columbus, who had arrived in late June. According to Cuneo, many were found sick and food was lacking at Isabela. "Seeing which the Lord Admiral ordered about four hundred men to forage through the island, but in a few days, as it pleased God, there came four caravels from Spain bringing food, from which the company took great comfort."

Columbus again took up the plan of catching Caonabo that Margarite had ignored and Hojeda accepted the mission. According to Las Casas, Hojeda took nine men, he alone being on horseback, crossed the central mountains, and visited Caonabo at his seat near San Juan de la Maguana. Caonabo was invited to come to Isabela to see the great white chief, and was presented with a finely made set of handcuffs and foot shackles of brass to simulate the prized turey or guanín. He was given a lesson in riding horseback in the savanna near his seat, and while thus diverted was gradually removed from the sight of his companions and captured. Fettered and brought back to Isabela, he was put on display in the house of the Admiral.[25] Thus the first of the caciques was eliminated.

The first Indian uprising took place late in 1494. To protect the dangerous Yaque river crossing, a fort was built, called Magdalena (fig. 12), at the place where Hojeda had stirred up trouble the previous spring. This was Macorix ter-

[23] Las Casas, Bk. I, ch. 100.
[24] Peter Martyr, Decade I, Bk. 4.
[25] Las Casas, Bk. I, ch. 102. Las Casas heard this version when he got to Española and maintained it as the true account as against the Ferdinand Columbus version of capture by conquest. Las Casas thought Caonabo was lost when a storm sank a ship in the harbor of Isabela, at the time six hundred slaves were being loaded for Castile, his notes not telling what happened to the cargo of slaves. I suspect that he confused the February, 1495, consignment of slaves, which left without mishap, with another event. Caonabo at any rate did not get to Spain.

ritory and these Indians seem to have been less docile than the rest. The fort was attacked, perhaps burned, by the cacique of a nearby pueblo and ten Spaniards were killed. An expeditionary force from Isabela trounced the rebels, took numerous prisoners, and drove the chief into hiding.

This punitive expedition in Macorix country began slave raids in Española. Las Casas stated briefly that many prisoners were taken of the men of the cacique Guatigara because he had killed the ten Christians. Five hundred of these were sent as slaves, to be sold in Castile, in the four ships of Antonio de Torres that sailed on February 24, 1495.[26] Cuneo returned home on this fleet, and gave a fuller account:

> Obliged to depart for Spain our caravels, on which I wished to go back home, had collected into the town [Isabela] sixteen hundred men and women of the said Indians, of whom, male and female, we loaded the said caravels with five hundred fifty of the best on February 17, 1495. [This may have been about the capacity of the four caravels, on which there also went passengers, including Diego Columbus.] As to the remainder there was given an order that whoever wished might take whatever he liked; and it was thus done. And when everyone was thus provided there were left over about four hundred who were turned loose to go wherever they wished, among whom were many women with babes at the breast. Such, in order the better to escape and fearing lest we might again seize them, abandoned their children indiscriminately and took flight, as persons in desperation, and fled so far as to remove themselves from our town of Isabela by as much as seven or eight days across the largest mountains and rivers, so that it would be impossible to have them again. Among the captured persons there was taken also one of their kings with two subalterns, whom it had been resolved to kill the next day and they were confined to that end but during the night they gnawed through their fetters and escaped . . . When we got into Spanish waters there died on our hands about two hundred of the said Indians, whom we threw into the sea, the cause I believe to be the unaccustomed cold . . . We landed all the slaves at Cádiz, half of them sick. They are not people suited to hard work, they suffer from the cold, and they do not have a long life.

Cuneo was a generally cheerful observer; this was his one somber passage.

Ships had been making the circuit between Cádiz and Isabela to bring supplies, mostly food for the colony, but with no cargo to take back. The enterprise was getting more and more into debt for food, even fish being transported across the ocean.[27] Nothing was being produced, not even gold. The slave trade was a partial solution, and the punitive expedition into Macorix country offered the immediate opportunity. The captives that were not shipped to Spain were parceled out among Spaniards. The Indians were given the proof that the Christians were not harmless guests with an odd hankering for yellow nuggets. Thereafter, Columbus engaged in shipping slaves from the island of the erstwhile friendliest people.

PACIFICATION AND TRIBUTE (1495–1496)

The Admiral, having recovered from his illness, undertook the occupation of the interior by force of arms. A party headed by the Admiral and his brother Bar-

---

[26] *Ibid.*

[27] Navarrete, vol. II, doc. 85, cédula of April 9, 1495, lists the cargo to be sent in the next sailing from Spain as including wheat, barley, pulses, sugar, biscuit, wine, oil, vinegar, dried figs, bacon, and salt fish.

tholomew, called the Adelantado, set out from Isabela on March 24, 1495. It consisted of two hundred of the best footsoldiers, twenty horsemen, and twenty dogs trained to attack, and was accompanied by the ever-faithful cacique Guacanagari of Marien and his men. In the words of his son Ferdinand, the Admiral went *a punto de guerra* to subjugate the island, admitting that "the greater part of the Christians had been committing a thousand excesses for which the Indians held them in mortal horror and refused to render obedience." [28] On entering the Vega of the Yaque they were met by a large number of Indians who were quickly dispersed "like flights of birds" or were captured.[29] Until then Columbus had seen only the Indian settlements along the road between Isabela and Santo Tomás. Now the Vega Real and the Cibao were overrun, the northern two-thirds of the realm of Cayabo over which Guarionex was lord. He and the greater part of the subordinate cacique submitted, almost without resistance. This was no proud conquest, nor was it called such. The easy submission was entitled "pacification." Son Ferdinand said that by means of the expedition the island "was brought to such obedience and quiet that a solitary Christian could go in security anywhere in the island, the Indians carrying him wherever he wished to go on their shoulders as though they were post horses." He continued, "Divine Majesty permitted that there was such great want of food and grave sickness as to reduce them to a third part of what they had been before so that it might be seen that these things proceeded from his High Hand."

The march of possession led to building a new fort in the center of the island, Concepción de la Vega. The cacique of the Vega, Guarionex, had authority as far as the north coast and the Cibao, and was anxious to keep the peace. It made sense to establish a base close to the seat of the cacique in order to control the interior and have the benefit of the conucos of that fertile region. The site chosen for the fort was a conspicuous hill overlooking the seat of Guarionex. A substantial structure of tapia was surrounded with battlements. The hill, about ten miles north of the present site of the city of La Vega, is now known as Santo Cerro, and has an old church that is a national shrine. Concepción replaced the abandoned Santo Tomás for control of the interior, both Vega and Cibao.

Magdalena, guarding the crossing of the Yaque to the south of Isabela, appears to have been lost in the Indian uprising and was replaced farther upstream by the fort of Esperanza, somewhere in the vicinity of the present town of that name. If Las Casas remembered rightly, it was on the side toward the Cibao, which would have been south of the river. Between Concepción and Esperanza the intermediate forts of Santiago and Santa Catalina were constructed (fig. 12). Isabela was still the only Spanish town and port, but most of its men had been removed to guard the interior forts. Concepción was a center of activity that foreshadowed a nascent town.

Having gained the easy submission of the natives of the interior, Columbus thought of a simple way to assure the profitable conduct of his government. The Indians were to pay tribute and their chiefs were to collect it. The Spaniards in his employ would be the armed means of enforcing the collection. According to Peter Martyr, "the Admiral called many chiefs together under promise that the

---

[28] Ferdinand Columbus, *Historie* (Venice, 1678), ch. 60.
[29] Las Casas, Bk. I, chs. 104, 105.

Admiral would not permit his men to roam about the island, where under pretext of finding gold and other things they had left nothing intact or undamaged. All promised that each person between the ages of fourteen and seventy would render to the Admiral the desired products of their locality. Those of Cibao would deliver to the city every three months a certain quantity of gold. Those who lived where there were spices or cotton would tribute the quantity assigned per person." [30]

Las Casas gave this version: "The Admiral imposed on all inhabitants of the Cibao, the Vega Real, and others living near the mines that each one fourteen years old or more, should pay gold of the measure of a Flemish hawksbell every three months . . . those not living near mines each to contribute an arroba of cotton." Each native was to wear a disk about his neck to show that he was paying tribute. [31]

There is no evidence that any of the tribute demanded was provided then in spices or cotton. Columbus wanted immediate returns, which he thought he could exact in gold. Guarionex pleaded their ignorance of gold recovery and the famous offer to plant a conuco extending from north to south coast for the benefit of the Christians if his people were released from tribute of gold. Peter Martyr thought the plan collapsed because of the upset of the native economy: "The bitter hunger rescinded these things for they had scarcely the strength to get food . . . The majority of the chiefs in these necessitous straits gave part of the tribute promised, asking the Admiral humbly that he should take pity on their misery and condone it until such time as the island might be restored to its earlier condition, Cibao being in the worst state."

The assessment made it necessary to find out how many persons of working age of both sexes each cacique had at his disposal. This so-called census could not have been undertaken until the "pacification" was ended and the caciques were called together and given their orders. The resultant figure of 1,130,000 was secured after a sensible reduction in native numbers had taken place. As noted before it cannot be assigned a date earlier than the latter part of 1495 or later than the early part of 1496. The reduction of native numbers by two-thirds from 1494 to 1496, on which Las Casas and Ferdinand Columbus agree, was an excessive estimate and does not apply to the greater, still unreduced part of the island.

Española was in poor condition as the year 1496 began. From Isabela to the Cibao and the Vega the natives were in distress, and diminished in numbers. Many had taken flight. The tribute, although reduced, was beyond their means of compliance. The shipping of slaves to Spain was beginning to give offense at home; the receipt of gold was slight. The Crown was under continuing expense at sending over food, naval stores, and other supplies. The Spaniards remaining in the island lacked skills and inclination to make the things needed, to engage in husbandry, or even to mine. [32] Those who had returned to Spain brought complaints about the conduct of affairs in the island and the necessitous state of the colonists, if such those may be called who had no intention of settling nor could have done so had they wished. In March, 1496, Columbus took ship for Spain in

---

[30] Peter Martyr, Decade I, Bk. 4.
[31] Las Casas, Bk. I, ch. 105.
[32] Navarrete, vol. II, doc. 85 for a list of the things required.

two caravels with two hundred twenty Spaniards who were abandoning the island and with thirty Indians.[33] The purpose was to reassure the Crown and to ask for patience and more support. No triumphal return this: he presented himself before the Sovereigns in the humble garb of a Franciscan friar.

ADMINISTRATION OF THE
ADELANTADO (1496–1498)

Before the Admiral left, word had come of another gold region across the mountains to the south of the Vega. One story had it that a Spaniard living in a distant Indian village was informed of it by his native woman. Las Casas thought that Guarionex, wearying of the importunity of the Spaniards, thought to get them off his back by telling about another gold region. Indian guides led a party from the Vega (Concepción) to the new district. It returned confirming the report. Columbus chose the name San Cristóbal for the prospective mining district in honor of his patron saint.

The Adelantado gave his attention during 1496 to the new gold field, building stations on the way to it, and a port on the south coast. He built the fort of Bonao at a day's travel south from Concepción de la Vega in a wide and attractive basin of the upper Yuna drainage, "on the road to Santo Domingo and on the banks of the Río Yuna below the sierra that faces the rising sun" (Las Casas). The site, now the town of Monseñor Noel, was well chosen. An easy and direct road leads to La Vega. A few miles to the south a gradual ascent begins to the watershed between the Atlantic drainage of the Río Yuna and streams that flow south into the Caribbean. The present main highway of the Dominican Republic follows the same route that the Spaniards took from La Vega through Bonao to the southern gold fields. This only direct and easy road between the north and south coasts is indicated by its topographic advantages and the successive forts that were built following the ancient Indian route across the island, midway of which, Guarionex, last overlord of Cayabo, had his seat.

A short distance south of the pass (La Cumbre on the highway) the arroyos that form the Río Haina were found to be gold-bearing, the beginning of the San Cristóbal placer country. The first locality known was to the west of the Río Haina, the Minas Viejas, referring to the ancient pits that Columbus thought had been worked by Solomon. Placers on the east bank of the Haina were called Minas Nuevas (New Mines). A fort was begun, which Peter Martyr said was known as the Fort of Gold because the earth used in making its walls carried gold. He added that it was not finished because a famine set in.[34] In the long run this southern placer area probably was the most productive one of the islands. Nuggets of good size were found, but nothing is said of systematic exploitation at this time. Most of the Spaniards still knew no more of placer mining than did the Indians. Experienced washers of gold had been asked for but perhaps had not come. The silence of the record suggests that the search for gold was still a matter of hunting for nuggets. The discovery area lay on both sides of the upper Río Haina. Later a placer locality thereabouts was known as Arbol Gordo from a tree

---

[33] Las Casas, Bk. I, ch. 111.
[34] Peter Martyr, Decade I, Bk. 5.

which, by its dimensions, was probably a ceiba. There is still a place by that name.

Two years earlier, as the Admiral was returning from Jamaica along the south coast, he looked for a harbor that would be suitable for a second town, and liked the mouth of the Río Haina. It was probably from there that he sent messengers across the island to Isabela to announce his return. Bartholomew went on from the new gold area to the coast to find a suitable harbor. He took soundings and decided on the mouth of the Río Ozama, ten miles to the east of that of the Haina. Here he began building Santo Domingo in August, 1496. Its harbor is a ría, a drowned river course, narrowly cut into a marine terrace, a high and well-drained bench suited for a town site on either side of the river. The east side was chosen. The new gold region lay eight to ten leagues inland, without any difficult terrain to cross. In contrast to that of Isabela, the countryside here was productive and well peopled, having adequate rain and fertile valleys and coastal terraces. The approach from Spain by the Dominica Passage was shortened and downwind all the way. The new town soon proved to be in good position from which to cross the Caribbean west and southwest to Tierra Firme. The site of Santo Domingo was very well chosen, better than could be known at the time.

When the building of Santo Domingo was well under way, Bartholomew marched west to make the first entry into Xaragua. Up to this time Spanish activities had been confined to Cayabo, of which Guarionex was the great chief. The meeting with the great cacique of the west, Behechio, throws further light on the aboriginal domains of Cayabo and Bainoa. Bartholomew met the hosts of Behechio drawn up at the Río Yaque del Sur and thought them there to give battle. Instead the Spaniards were received with ceremony and conducted to Xaragua. It seems that Behechio, knowing of the approach of Bartholomew, sent an honor guard to the frontier where the Spaniards would enter his domain. The land route west has little option of terrain and must have followed mainly the line of the present highway from Santo Domingo to Port-au-Prince. The meeting at the river took place at the western boundary of the present Provincia de Azua. Beyond this point the provinces of Maguana, Baoruco, and Barahona pertained to Bainoa and thus to the domain of Behechio, as Morales assigned them.

At Xaragua, Bartholomew and his men were given an elaborate reception in the "palace" (the great *caney*) of the "king," Las Casas supplying information on the court ceremonial.[35] Anacaona, widow of Caonabo, had moved down from Maguana to live with her brother Behechio. Both did the honors for the Adelantado. At the end of the festivities Behechio asked how he should give tribute, "since in all my kingdom gold neither originates nor is collected, nor do my people know what it is." (At a later date a little gold was found in the Massif du Nord.) The matter was resolved amicably by agreement to provide cotton and other fibers and to supply cassava bread. The year following, Behechio and Anacaona sent word to the Adelantado that the tribute of cotton and cassava was ready for delivery, cotton in both raw and spun form having been supplied by thirty-two caciques. A ship was ordered down from Isabela to load the supplies.[36] Bartholomew also sent men to the brazilwood country of Jacmel on the southwest coast

[35] Las Casas, Bk. I, ch. 114.
[36] *Ibid.*, ch. 116.

to cut and store dyewood to be shipped by sea.[37] By these steps the Adelantado initiated the pacific attachment of the as yet undisturbed western "kingdom." Events elsewhere put an early end to this, promising extension of Spanish control.

Bartholomew had his headquarters at Santo Domingo and was in process of removing the men from Isabela, which he judged rightly to be unneeded, lacking local resources and in an area already despoiled of its natives. In the Vega, Guarionex was still trying to meet the demands of tribute the Admiral had imposed, but was unable to restrain his subordinate caciques, who were chafing under the forced tribute and various indignities. A revolt broke out which Bartholomew, moving up from Santo Domingo, quickly suppressed with heavy native losses. Guarionex was captured, but was released to make another forlorn attempt to keep peace with the alien regime.

At this juncture, in the year 1497, a new and worse danger arose in a Spanish revolt, led by Francisco Roldán, mayordomo to the Admiral who had remained as alcalde mayor at Isabela. Bartholomew had begun to dismantle Isabela; the Indians to the south in the Vega were sullen after their defeat; and the Spaniards were restive in their status as employees. The Admiral had gone to Spain and had passed the authority into the hands of his brother. There was resentment among the Spaniards that their control should pass from one Italian to another. Roldán judged the moment opportune to advance his own fortunes and break the rule of Columbus, and in large measure he succeeded. Roldán took the arms still stored at Isabela, sent word to the Indians that he would liberate them from tribute, and started south. The two forces confronted each other at Concepción. Neither risked the issue to a test at arms. After some palaver, Roldán and his followers moved over to Xaragua, with which Bartholomew had nothing more to do thereafter. There, in the words of Las Casas, "they found the supplies and paradise, the freedom and impunity they were seeking." [38] Peter Martyr heard charges and countercharges as told at court.[39]

The situation had gotten beyond the control of the Adelantado. Roldán and his men were left alone to do as they wished in the west. The disaffected Spaniards drifted to that side of the island. The natives, in particular of the north and in the Vega, were harried by both partisan groups. Roldán had stirred them up to futile hopes and then apparently used them as badly as did the Spaniards who remained with Columbus. Guarionex fled north to take refuge with Mayobanex, chief of the mountain Macorix. The Adelantado ravaged the northern mountains, captured both caciques, and took many Indians whom he shipped out as slaves. Mayobanex died a prisoner; Guarionex was kept in jail until 1502, at which time he was sent in chains to Spain and was lost at sea in the fleet that went down in the famous hurricane. Thus ended the last native rule in Cayabo.

In his two and a half years of government, Bartholomew completed and maintained a string of forts from Isabela to Santo Domingo (fig. 13). Roldán and his partisans left Isabela to live independently in the western parts of the island; others moved into the Vega; and others went to Santo Domingo, the seat of government and trade. The Indians in the central part of the island were subdued

---

[37] Peter Martyr, Decade I, Bk. 5.
[38] Las Casas, Bk. I, ch. 119; also chs. 117 and 118.
[39] Peter Martyr, Decade I, Bk. 7.

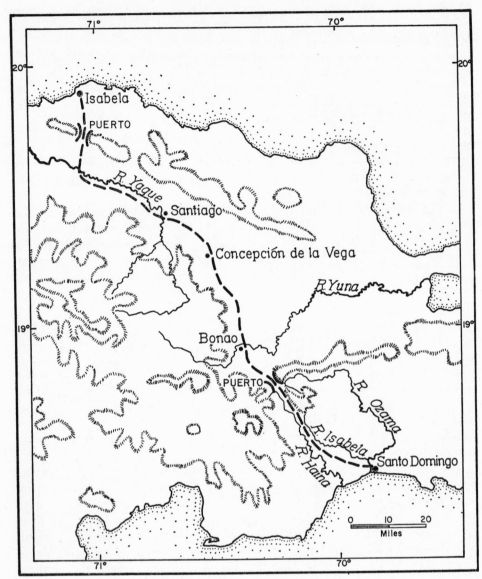

Fig. 13. Route across Española established by Bartholomew Columbus.

and leaderless, and had suffered serious losses. The Adelantado tried to enforce the tribute system the Admiral had imposed, permitting however the substitution of cotton and cassava for gold. It worked briefly in Xaragua until Roldán moved in. Something of the sort was tried in the central part of the island, but did not succeed, for the caciques who would have been the collectors had been liquidated, lost their authority, or fled.

The Admiral's plan could have worked only by preserving the social structure of native life, and this was destroyed. The Spaniards were military or civil employees, supposedly on salaries, and these were paid irregularly and sometimes not at all. They had not been selected or trained in the tradition of military or civil service. Many went home in the caravels of March, 1496. Perhaps half of those who stayed joined Roldán. Even before the revolt of Roldán, individual Spaniards had been squatting on Indian communities and diverting their labor and products to themselves. What was happening to gold production is obscure, but apparently very little was received in Spain.

Bartholomew tried to continue the system his brother had ordered. In the central part of the island he secured a peace of submission at the price of native life, hope, and dignity. The new and possibly better start he had begun in the west he was forced to surrender to the partisans of Roldán. These were in open opposition to the monopoly that Columbus had founded, foreshadowing its end.

THE ADMIRAL IN SPAIN (1496–1498)

Columbus needed to get back to court to answer complaints and to persuade the Crown that soon the colony would become profitable. The expectation of gold, spices, and precious woods had not been met. The fabled East he said he had found existed only in his own mind. There was a lot of explaining to do.

From Isabela he could have taken the usual course northward and so come speedily to Spain. Instead he chose the tedious way of going east and south against trade wind and current in order to have another look at the Carib island of Guadelupe. Here conucos were raided for yuca, and time was taken for the Indians he had on board to prepare a store of cassava before the ship turned northward. Several inferences may be made: the superior quality of cassava as ship bread was now appreciated; Isabela was unable to furnish supplies; there was no fear of the Caribs, who were chased into the woods after a brief skirmish. Again Columbus was drawn to the south, the direction that always attracted him.

The reception at court was favorable. Columbus presented the royal pair with "a good sample of gold and many *guaycas* or masks with their eyes and ears of gold and also with many parrots." [40] These masks probably were trophies taken from caciques in the "pacification" of the prior year.

There followed a year of conferences concerning the future of the colony preserved in a series of documents, dated April to July, 1497, which continued all the rights and privileges of the Admiral.[41] The conduct of island affairs was approved, and Bartholomew was officially named Adelantado, a title and position he had held previously only from his brother. By royal orders the natives should be attracted peaceably and quietly to serve the Crown, "in benign subjection and principally that they should be converted to our Holy Catholic Faith" (*cédula* of April 23, 1497). This affirmation was not put into effect; missionary labors began only in later years. There was provision for the building of a second town "on the other coast and convenient to the gold mines," an *ex post facto* approval of Santo Domingo. Dog tags were approved for the natives to keep track of their tribute of gold, and it was recommended that a mint be established.

Salaried personnel was to be contracted to the number of three hundred thirty, forty of them to be of officer grade (*escuderos*), a hundred forty foot soldiers

---

[40] Las Casas, Bk. I, ch. 112.
[41] Navarrete, vol. II, docs. 103–126.

and of other services, thirty mariners and thirty grummets, twenty washers of gold, fifty agricultural workers, ten gardeners, twenty civil officials, and thirty women (the first provision for the other sex). The agriculturists were to be settled near the Spanish towns in order to sow fields of grain and raise stock, and were to be provided with seed wheat and with work stock on credit. Wheat was the breadstuff to be produced. There was no mention of the native economy. The provision of June 15, 1497, added seed barley, and specified the tools to be provided: spades, mattocks, picks, mauls, crowbars, and millstones, but plow points were not included. (Since the work stock was to be used in cultivating fields, the inference may be that unshod wooden plows were to be used.) The list of personnel added priests, a physician, a druggist, and a herbalist. Also there were to be musical instruments for pastime. The bureaucrats at the conference drew detailed plans to people the island with Spaniards of specified if somewhat strange skills. These were still to be engaged on salary, the military personnel outnumbering all the rest.

Orders of June 22, 1497, designated that certain kinds of delinquents should be deported to Española, these to be collected from various parts of Spain and sent to Sevilla, there to await embarkation. How they were to be used was not stated.

Native rights still were not acknowledged or considered; the Indians were to be held in "benign subjection." Private ownership of land was authorized for the first time. On July 22, 1497, Columbus was given letters patent for the distribution (*repartimiento*) of lands to individuals "in which they can sow wheat (*pan*) and other seeds and plant gardens (*huertas*) and fields of cotton and flax and vines and trees and fields of sugar cane and other plants and build and erect houses and gristmills and sugar mills (*ingenios*)." The conveyance of such lands was specified: the donee could sell, give, exchange, or otherwise alienate such property, "such persons obligating themselves to have and maintain residence (*vecindad*), occupying their house in the Island of Española for four years following the date of assignment." These proprietary rights were to be limited to "what had been fenced in to the height of one tapia, all the rest that remained unenclosed, its fruits and produce having been harvested, to be common pasture and commons (*baldíos*) for all." Brazilwood and all metal-producing lands were reserved to the Crown. Such was the first design of a land policy that looked to permanent establishment of Spanish settlers in Española.

Most of the provisions remained schemes on paper. The giving of homesteads to small freeholders was not carried out. The repartimiento that the Admiral was soon forced to introduce was of native communities given to Spaniards, not of small farms worked by Spanish labor. European grains proved unsuited to the tropical island yet they were still planned as the food staples. The salaried status of the Spaniards continued. The Crown held the rights to minerals and dyewoods. The colony was to receive deported criminals, and thirty women were to begin providing homes. Columbus received additional guaranties for himself and his heirs. The native population and the administration of colonial affairs, the two most important matters, were disregarded. The deportees were sent, and few others.

It took more than a year to get from conferences to orders, patents, and privileges, and almost as long thereafter to find funds and participants. Many had returned from the island indigent and in poor health. According to Oviedo, those who got back to Spain were of the color of gold but not of its sheen, and, he added, they soon died. Gómara said, "their color changed to yellow like saffron." [42] The climate of the island was considered pleasant and healthful, but there was much sickness on the island and of invalidism afterward. Unlike the previous voyage, there was no rush of persons to go overseas. It took time to find and persuade volunteers and to collect deportees.

THE THIRD VOYAGE (1498)

At the end of May, 1498, a modest fleet of six ships was ready to sail on what is known as the third voyage of Columbus. Two caravels under Hernández Coronel had been dispatched some months earlier and arrived at Santo Domingo before the main party left Spain. At Gomera, then the usual island of the Canaries from which to start the crossing of the Atlantic, Columbus divided his fleet. Three ships were to go directly by way of the Dominica Passage. He took the remaining three on an unscheduled detour. Nothing had been said of a voyage of exploration, but, being again at sea and having provided, as he thought, for the colony by five ships bearing men and supplies, he took the opportunity to go into unknown waters, dropping down to the Portuguese Cape Verde Islands and thence by slow passage of the doldrums arriving at the island of Trinidad and the Gulf of Paria. Again, as in his previous voyages, he was drawn to find out what lay farther south.

About two weeks were spent sailing about the Gulf of Paria, this being the discovery of the southern continent. Columbus was suffering from inflammation of the eyes and is thought not to have left shipboard. The crew were well entertained in native villages and secured many ornaments of guanín and strings of pearls, neither of local origin.

The physical geography of the gulf perplexed Columbus. The northern margin of the Orinoco delta, not recognized as such, the fresh water of the western side of the gulf, the mountains of the Paria peninsula to the north, exaggerated in distance and elevation by the humid tropical air, became to his imagination the proscenium behind which lay the Earthly Paradise, known as being at the end of the Earth. He concluded that he had found another world (*otro mundo*) at the end of the world continent, of which Cuba was one promontory and this another and the most easterly extension.

The cargo was beginning to spoil in the moist heat, and so in mid-August he left the gulf to sail west in sight of the mountainous peninsula of Paria and to pass east of Margarita Island, which he named from afar for the royal princess, not for the pearls soon to be found there. And so north to Santo Domingo, which was entered on the last day of August.

The three ships he had sent ahead from the Canaries to take the direct passage to Santo Domingo had lost their course. When they did make port, it was in Xaragua, with most of their cargo spoiled. The two ships that had been dispatched in February had arrived with their cargo and ninety workmen, in part

[42] Oviedo, *Historia,* Bk. II, ch. 13; Gómara, *Historia general de Indias* (Antwerp, 1554), ch. 22.

deported criminals. The latter party is the only one about which there is specific information. According to Las Casas, they were "under pact and agreement to labor in all work of the mines and to cut brazilwood, of which at the time there was thought to be a great deal, and thus the Admiral wrote to the Adelantado his brother, and I saw the letter, that if there should be found some one of those already over here who knew the mines he should be provided with a gang of these workmen, each to be assigned a daily quantity of gold to produce, and what they might produce beyond such amount was to be their own. Fourteen of the laborers were designated to cultivate and work land and to sow wheat and other things." [43] Columbus later complained bitterly about the worthless and criminal element introduced at this time.

FINAL ATTEMPTS TO REORGANIZE
THE ECONOMY (1498–1499)

Columbus still held to operating with salaried employees. Their work was to be stimulated by sharing profits, as shown in the letter cited above. A little free enterprise was in the interest of management and of the honesty of the employee.

The system of native tribute collected through the chiefs had broken down irrevocably with the destruction of the social structure of the central part of the island. Columbus thought it would have succeeded had he not been delayed so long in Spain, and he still thought he would be able to restore it; he did not say how.[44] He expressed satisfaction that the Spaniards had learned to appreciate the cassava bread, that the Indians were planting "for us the bread and the ajes [ages] and all other food supplies of theirs." The Indians were, in fact, feeding the Spaniards and providing personal services under a sort of squatter sovereignty that had followed the "pacification" of 1495.

The business of producing gold was not working. In his letter to the Sovereigns of May, 1499, Columbus considered what had "been the cause why God Our Lord has concealed the gold from us," concluding that it had been on account of the inordinate greed of the people who came to make a quick fortune, disregarding his warnings. A likelier answer is that the easily found pockets of nuggets had been cleaned out, that the Indians knew of no other places to which to take the Spaniards, and that these still knew nothing of placer mining. The supposedly experienced miners brought over in 1498 seem not to have had much success, since the gold remained "concealed."

Although it would take time to reëstablish the Indian tribute and the productivity of the gold fields, Columbus had in mind two immediately available sources of revenue. These he outlined in a letter that went with the ships of October, 1498; Las Casas quoted from the letter in his possession, which he said was in the hand of the Admiral.[45] The first source of profit was to be by cutting brazilwood, which would bring in twenty million maravedis a year. One such shipment is of record, for the ships that returned in October. Peter Martyr knew of their bringing three thousand pounds of dyewood, called *verzinum* by the Italians and

---

[43] Las Casas, Bk. I, ch. 119.
[44] *Ibid.*, chs. 156–163.
[45] *Ibid.*, chs. 150, 154 and 155, with a number of verbatim passages.

brasilium by the Spaniards. A letter in Italian by one Simone Verde identified the dyewood as *verzino*.[46] It may be inferred that this was the brazilwood which Bartholomew had ordered cut at Jacmel when he went to visit Xaragua. In later times some such wood was cut near Jacmel, but not much of it nor for long.[47] On such slight basis Columbus calculated half the annual income needed to put the colony on a paying basis.

The other promise of quick gain was by the slave trade. Columbus was quoted as saying, "In Castile, Portugal, Aragón, Italy, Sicily, the islands of Portugal [Madeira and Cape Verde] and Aragón [Balearic Islands] and the Canaries many slaves are required and fewer are now coming from Guinea." He continued that, although many of the slaves taken in Española at that time soon died, this would not continue, for the same thing had been true at first of the Negroes and the Canary Island natives who had been brought as slaves. Las Casas, who had been quoting from the letter, regretted that "a man good by nature and of good intentions should have been so blind in so clear a matter" as to wish to base the royal revenues and the prospering of his own affairs on "the cargoes of innocent Indians made slaves and shipped as so many pieces (*piezas*) as he called them."

The October fleet added slaves to its cargo of dyewood. In the north a cacique and his people who had run away were hunted down to be loaded aboard the ships, in somewhat the same area and manner that Cuneo had described three years before. The shipmasters agreed to a moderate charge per head, including feeding, and were to take their pay out of the proceeds of their sale in Spain. There was no more pretense of going to the cannibal islands to catch slaves. A plentiful supply of rebels or fugitives would be available in Española. Shipowners, Columbus thought, would come to seek these cargoes as the profits of the trade became known. Four thousand slaves a year, he estimated, would bring twenty million maravedis, the same as the brazilwood. To get this income of forty million a year an outlay of only six would be needed.

Columbus summed up his revised economic program thus: "Here there are these slaves and brazilwood, which appears to be a living thing, and even gold, should it please Him who gave it and will give it again in time." Columbus remarked that the number of natives was somewhat reduced, but he considered it a reservoir that would supply labor for the island and slaves for European markets. The brazilwood as "a living thing" perhaps meant that it was expected to regrow after cutting. Gold production would be resumed whenever God so willed.

His mood at the return was buoyant. Finding that many of the old residents were disillusioned or disaffected, he announced on September 12 that all who wished to return home could do so and would have free passage and board on the returning fleet.[48] Some three hundred availed themselves of the offer, including the father of Las Casas. The colonists who had come five years before were thus reduced by three-fourths, but he was confident a new group would soon give a new start. In the letter that went back with the fleet he contemplated a continuing flow of immigrants to share the ease of those already enjoying the island

---

[46] Data collated by A. Ballesteros y Beretta, *Historia de América* (Barcelona, 1936 and later), V, 358.
[47] A coastal scrub *Caesalpinia?* The dyewoods of the Antilles are in need of study.
[48] Las Casas, Bk. I, ch. 150.

life: "Soon there will be settlers (vecinos) here, for this land abounds in every-thing, especially in bread and meat. There is so much Indian bread here that it is a marvel, by which our people enjoy better health than from wheaten bread, and for meat there are pigs and chickens beyond number (*infinitíssimos*) and there are small animals like rabbits but better as to flesh and of these there are so many all over the island that an Indian lad accompanied by a dog will bring in fifteen to twenty of them daily to his master. There is no lack of anything except wine and clothing. For the most part it is a land of the laziest people in the world; of our people here, be they good or bad, each has two or three Indians to serve him and dogs to hunt for him and, though perhaps it should not be said, women so handsome as to be a wonder!" In another letter he wrote that the increase of pigs had come from eight he had bought in Gomera at the start of the second voyage.[49] The Letters Patent and the other plans drawn up in Spain merged into a rosy and hazy picture of a life of ease in a bounteous land, supported by will-ing Indians of both sexes.

FAILURE

The immediate problem that confronted Columbus was the revolt of Roldán. This had been going on for a year and had divided control of the island between Roldán in the west and the Adelantado in the center. The latter had the seat of government at Santo Domingo, both gold fields, the Vega Real, and the country around Isabela—roughly Cayabo, the former realm of Guarionex, who was then still in jail as hostage for the conduct of his former subjects. Roldán with about half the Spaniards had withdrawn into Bainoa; Roldán himself lived in Xaragua, where Behechio was still the cacique and exercised some control over his wider realm. The excesses of Roldán's men as charged by Las Casas may have been true, but it must also be noted that Bainoa retained the native political structure and its population and ways well beyond the time of the Admiral and the Adelan-tado, whereas the central part of the island did not. At the time of the return of the Admiral the situation was at a stalemate, with neither the Adelantado nor Roldán making any decisive moves.

Roldán probably had the stouter adherents. Bartholomew had been unable to take the offensive with the men who had remained loyal, nor did the Admiral risk battle. Instead of venturing an uncertain issue at arms, Columbus undertook nego-tiations with Roldán. The latter played his hand skillfully and daringly and won. The price of his renewed allegiance to the Admiral was that he and his men should be given rights of *vecindad*, that is, agreement to settle where they wished in possession of native communities of their choice. Their original demand was to do so in and around Xaragua, which would have meant the concentration of potential troublemakers in one area distant from Santo Domingo. They were satisfied, however, to accept allotments of Indians in various parts, around Bonao, Concepción de la Vega, Santiago, and other choice locations. This was the begin-ning of the change from forts to civilian communities, later to become villas. Roldán was given what he wanted for himself, the control of Xaragua. The agreements with the erstwhile rebels were reached in 1499. It then became neces-

---

[49] *Ibid.*, ch. 162.

sary to reward similarly the men who had remained loyal. The original central administration of all Indian communities under direct tribute was dead.

The Letters Patent of 1497 had provided for the allotment (*repartimiento*) of land to bona fide settlers; the intent was to get small farmers to take up land and cultivate it. Small freeholdings were contemplated, but it is not known that such repartimientos were made. When Columbus was cornered by Roldán he allocated Indian communities, also to be known as repartimientos, to individual claimants. These had been in rebellion against the authority of the Adelantado and had refused to return to that of Columbus, viceroy of the Crown, except at such price. This was the origin of the actual system of repartimiento, later called *encomiendas*. These were subsequently given, at least nominally, in reward of merits and services. They began as extortion from a governor too weak to deny the demands. Neither Columbus nor Roldán knew that they were starting an institution that was to dominate the Spanish Indies for centuries.

The conveyance of a repartimiento was in terms of a stated chief and his people, both assigned to serve a particular Spaniard. Las Casas paraphrased it as giving a certain Spaniard charge of a named cacique to care for so many thousand mounds.[50] The conveyance was not of land but of native communities, identified by their chiefs, not by name of place or by territorial limits. The assigned communities were at the disposal of the beneficiary to plant conucos, have personal services, provide labor in the mines, or for anything else, without limit of benefit or tenure.

At the discovery of Paria the Admiral had thought to send Bartholomew to establish a fort and settlement on the mainland, but his waning hold on Española made it impossible for him to divide his forces.

In May, 1499, when his troubles were many and his spirits low, Columbus sent a long letter to the King and Queen, aptly named by Las Casas the epilogue of the Admiral. In it he placed the blame for his difficulties on others, especially on Roldán, who he said had been a nobody and whom he had raised to high estate. He imagined also subversion of his authority by unnamed *conversos*. Untrue reports were being circulated about him, and he asked that an investigator be sent to examine the true conditions. There are strange passages in the letter that must have given pause to the Sovereigns and their counselors: "God Our Lord who knows well my intention and the truth of everything will save me as He has done until now, because until this day there is no person of malice toward me whom He has not castigated." He envisioned a great populace about to come over to settle. "Its seat shall be in Isabela, where the beginning was, for it is the most proper site and better than any other in the land, as should be believed, for Our Lord brought me there miraculously. I was unable [there] either to go back or ahead with the ships, but only to unload and make the settlement." He dwelt on the fertility and attractions of Isabela (well known at the time as a poor site from which Bartholomew had removed what could be moved), again saying that it had been designated by God through a miracle.[51] The letter hurt his case. It was decided to send over a referee, one may well believe not only to examine the state of government but also that of the Admiral.

---

[50] *Ibid.*, ch. 160.
[51] *Ibid.*, ch. 162.

A year later (May, 1500), no such inspector having yet come and his old confidence restored, Columbus wrote in a very different vein. As Las Casas paraphrased the letter:

> . . . in this year of 1500 he had brought the people of this island of Española, who were, he said, without number, by divine grace, to be under royal rule and obedience, to such a degree that a single Christian could go over the whole island, which, he said, is larger than all Spain, and could order the greatest cacique in the land about and be obeyed; and he said moreover that in this same year of 1500 he had ordered the Indian pueblos to be joined into large ones, and that all should become Christians and serve Their Highnesses as do their vassals in Castile, in such a manner that without detriment to them and without undue levies but with very great moderation, they would pay each year sixty million (*maravedis*), and that by the year 1503 the Crown shall have of rent in gold a hundred twenty thousand pesos, and that he takes oath to hold this to be certain.

What Columbus declared and promised in the last letter he was to write as governor was far removed from the reality of which the court was by no means uninformed. The repartimientos had made an end of direct tribute. There was and would be no aggregation of natives into large communities, nor conversion to Christianity. The promise of handsome revenues had been made too often with negative result. He was still seeing the island as though five years of disintegration had not happened. He was at the end of his road, unaware that it was such.

Peter Martyr gave the terse summary of the end of the regime: The Sovereigns, "wearied by so many complaints on all sides and principally because by reason of the discords and seditions of such abundance of gold and other things so little was brought, named a new Governor to look into all these matters and pass justice." [52]

The Crown had decided to intervene a year earlier when Columbus had asked for an examining justice (*juez pesquisidor*), and had named Francisco de Bobadilla, Commander of the Order of Calatrava, of long and distinguished services. Public affairs in Spain delayed his departure until June, 1500. Meanwhile the situation of Columbus had been improved by the compact with Roldán, as shown in the buoyant letter cited above. He no longer needed, and probably no longer expected, such a judicial visit.

However, when three hundred repatriates returned to Spain at the end of 1498, each with a slave from Española, the Queen knew that she had been misinformed. "What power of mine does the Admiral hold to give my vassals to anyone?" She ordered that these should be freed and returned to their homes with Bobadilla. The account is from Las Casas, whose father thus surrendered the slave he brought back.[53]

When Bobadilla sailed late in June, 1500, he went not only as judge with plenary powers but also carried a commission to remove Columbus from the position of governor and to take over the office, the replacement however to be announced after he had determined the state of affairs. If Española was to be kept, a new government was required. In the seven years of his control the Admiral had failed to make good on his promises. His own men were out of hand and

---

[52] Peter Martyr, Decade I, Bk. 7.
[53] Las Casas, Bk. I, ch. 176.

the majority had abandoned the island. The benign rule of the natives was now evident as abject subjection. His own letters gave reason to question whether he was of sound mind. It had become necessary to replace him, but the demission was to be done gently.

Meanwhile, another revolt of Spaniards against Columbus broke out in various parts of the island, unknown as yet in Spain. When Bobadilla entered the harbor of Santo Domingo, his first sight was of two gallows, one on each side of the river, a Spaniard hanging from each. Five more, it was learned, had been hanged within the week and five more were awaiting execution. The mildest of the Columbus brothers, Diego, was in charge at Santo Domingo; the Admiral was reported hunting down rebels about Concepción, the Adelantado doing the same in Xaragua. Bobadilla forgot his instructions to proceed slowly and, moving in with the full authority that he commanded, sent the three brothers back to Spain in chains. This angry and demeaning act is what he is remembered for in history. Thus ended, ignobly for all concerned, the first Spanish government in the New World.

V

CHANGE OF GOVERNMENT LICENSE
TO DISCOVER
(1499–1502)

•

TIME FOR A CHANGE

The contemporary perspective on Columbus was informed and fair. The chroniclers took pride in his discovery that gave Spain title to a new world but they saw also his limitations and failures. It was his son, Ferdinand, who first drew his image as a paragon of vision and virtue who was brought low by his enemies.

The seven years of Columbus' government were a continuing and growing series of disappointments and deficits. The extravagant prospectuses of promised wealth went on but revenues did not materialize. When gold was not forthcoming, Columbus attributed it to a temporary withholding of divine favor and would bridge the interval by the easy and sure profits of dyewood and slaves, for which he presented wholly imaginary figures. As he continued to hold to an illusory geography undisturbed by every evidence that he was wrong, so he invented riches that did not exist. It was well apparent that he was a chronic, compulsive romancer who lived in a world of wishful thinking.

Nor did Columbus know how to govern men. He failed signally in getting men to follow him faithfully. The majority returned to Spain when it was possible for them to leave, making their grievances widely known. Roldán led the stoutest part of the remainder in successful revolt. A further revolt was in progress when Bobadilla arrived. There had been no time of peace and goodwill. The initial friendliness of the natives became compliance through fear or escape by flight. Columbus lacked ability and inclination to adapt himself and to learn from changing circumstances. He had secured an excessive title to which he clung. These were his Indies over which his rule would be absolute and which he would pass on to his heirs. The conflict with representatives of the Crown began at the founding of Isabela. It may be that the regard of the Queen protected him in office while the condition of Española continued to deteriorate to the crisis in which he asked for a judge of inquiry. He was still as sure as ever that he was right, that others bore the blame, and that these would be confounded. Instead, Fonseca and Ferdinand used the opening for his removal, having decided that if the affairs of the Indies were to be rescued Columbus would have to go.

The attempt to rehabilitate the Indies began in 1499 with two measures: the appointment of Bobadilla as governor, and the licensing of independent expeditions to go out from Spain to trade and explore. Both steps were taken at the same time and for the same reason. Fonseca stepped into the open as arbiter of the affairs of the Indies.

INTERREGNUM OF BOBADILLA

Francisco de Bobadilla was named Governor and Judge "of all the islands and mainland of the Indies" on May 21, 1499. On the same date a Royal Provision was directed to Columbus, addressing him only as Admiral, to his brothers, and to other persons having in their power the forts, houses, ships, arms, and so forth belonging to the Crown, ordering all to be turned over to Bobadilla at once. On this date the Crown thus resumed freedom of action overseas. Columbus and the men in Española, however, were not informed of the new order until Bobadilla arrived in Santo Domingo in August, 1500. The new governor was sent to remove Columbus; it was only the precipitateness and severity of his action that displeased the Sovereigns.

All minerals were declared the property of the Crown, thus providing for mining by license and royalty. Bobadilla revived interest in gold mining by giving the vecinos freedom to mine without requiring them to pay "any part for a certain time" to the Crown, to its displeasure.[1] Whatever the incentive he offered, the Crown benefited. Las Casas, arrived in Santo Domingo in June, 1502, said that the returning ships carried a hundred thousand castellanos in gold for the Sovereigns and an equal amount in private hands, suggesting a royalty of one-half. Gómara had it that "Bobadilla placed on those ships more than a hundred thousand pesos of gold for the King and others, and that this was the first large wealth known to have been collected there. One nugget worth 3,300 castellanos was sent to the Queen.[2] A figure of 276 kilos has been estimated for the gold produced in 1501, a substantial amount divided between Crown and vecinos.[3]

The estimates of gold vary, but Gómara was right in thinking it was the first proof that the island could produce gold in quantity. The major source apparently was the San Cristóbal district and especially the Minas Nuevas.[4] The gold which Columbus had said God had concealed was quickly revealed when the vecinos were free to exploit it.

The new regime brought better times to the Spaniards, of whom about three

[1] Navarrete, vol. II, doc. 141.
[2] Gómara, *Historia general de Indias* (Antwerp, 1554), ch. 32.
[3] Guillermo Céspedes del Castillo in Vicens-Vives (ed.), *Historia social y económica de España y América*, II (Barcelona, 1959), 532.
[4] The famous great nugget was said by Las Casas (Bk. II, ch. 3) to have been found in the time of Bobadilla when Francisco de Garay and Miguel Díaz de Aux in partnership were working gangs in the New Mines, on the banks of the Río Haina. An Indian woman, resting for lunch, discovered it on the side of a small stream. It weighed 35 pounds, a lump of gold mixed with stone (quartz?). Garay became one of the richest men of the island. He and Díaz de Aux took part in later events in New Spain.

hundred had remained. Apparently no more men were leaving for Spain, nor were new ones arriving. No disaffection or disturbance took place during Bobadilla's tenure. There were three Spanish pueblos at the time, Santo Domingo, Concepción, and either Bonao or Santiago.[5] No new settlements were made, nor does control appear to have been extended over additional Indian communities.

Bobadilla returned to the island a number of freed Indians who had been slaves of the Spaniards repatriated in 1498. A royal cédula of June 20, 1500 declared that the Indians of the island were to be free vassals of the Crown of Castile.[6] There were no more roundups of Indians, uprisings, or reprisals. Indians were no longer a marketable commodity and their condition was alleviated to that extent. However, there is no indication that the Spaniards who held repartimientos of Indians released any. An upsurge of mining was underway, perhaps the beginning of mining as against the collecting of gold. The mines were worked by Indian labor and were supplied by Indian porters with food from Indian conucos. The more mining, the greater the pressure on and dislocation of native life. It is inferred that in the south-central part of the island the decrease in native population continued.

The two years during which Bobadilla was caretaker of Española were prosperous for the Spaniards, and perhaps somewhat less onerous for the natives.

Bobadilla's indeterminate tenure was ended when he was recalled to Spain, possibly because he had finished the job in Española, possibly because he allowed the colonists too large a share of the proceeds of gold. As the fleet was leaving for Spain, Bobadilla, the records of inquiry into his administration, and the gold he had collected, were all lost in the hurricane of July, 1502, which sank most of the ships.

FONSECA ISSUES LICENSES TO TRADE, DISCOVER, AND GOVERN

It was the custom of the court to move about from place to place. The affairs of the Indies, however, were managed from the beginning at Sevilla. Ships and crews might be readied in any port of Andalusia from the Condado of the Río Tinto to the Bay of Cádiz, but the business of the Indies was done at Sevilla. When the second voyage to the Indies was prepared, the then archdeacon of the cathedral of Sevilla, Juan Rodríguez de Fonseca, was assigned to look to its equipment and personnel. Later he rose in the church hierarchy from one bishopric to a greater one, but always his main responsibility was the Indies and their profit to the Crown. Fonseca was the untitled minister of colonies, more powerful than most ministers, competent and unscrupulous. He served his sovereigns well on the whole, to no neglect of his own profit or that of his protégés. He is considered to have been the center of a cabal about the Crown which was unchallenged until after the death of Ferdinand.[7] Appointments and orders were made or approved by him. He set up a taut organization, formalized in 1503 as the Casa de Contratación at Sevilla, controlling the business and the administra-

---

[5] CDI, I, 428. Testimony taken in 1520.
[6] José María Ots Capdequí, *El estado español en las Indias*, 2d ed. (Mexico, 1946), p. 34.
[7] Manuel Giménez Fernández, *Bartolomé de las Casas*, I (Sevilla, 1953), especially pp. 10–12.

tion of the Indies. Its purpose was to increase the revenues from overseas. His own interest in spiritual matters was slight, and none of it extended to the welfare of the bodies or souls of the Indians.

Fonseca and Columbus were unevenly matched: the one calculating, efficient, and patient; the other visionary, disorganized, and impetuous. As Columbus became more and more enmeshed in his own mistakes, Fonseca managed "to reduce almost to nothing the enormous prerogatives" Columbus has been given.[8] When the fall came, Fonseca was ready to take swift action.

Bobadilla was to be titular governor of both the islands and Tierra Firme, but was concerned in fact only with Española. The Admiral had blocked attempts of others to have access to the Indies. His own expectation to found an establishment at Paria on Tierra Firme had been thwarted by the revolt of Roldán. Paria promised revenue from pearls and would be a strategic area to detach from claim of possession by Columbus. Men had landed in the Gulf of Paria in the third voyage and had found the natives rich in pearls and willing to trade. On that occasion the Admiral had stayed on board ship, no act of possession had been carried out, and beyond the Gulf of Paria land was sighted only from a distance as the fleet turned north to Santo Domingo. The Gulf of Paria was indicated as a new base from which to carry on exploration and trade.

Mariners experienced in the waters of the Indies were available, such as Juan de la Cosa and the Pinzón and Niño brothers. Alonso de Hojeda had abandoned Columbus, had attached himself to Fonseca, and was looking for profitable adventure. Bankers and merchants in Sevilla were ready to advance funds against a share in the proceeds of trading voyages. Fonseca set about issuing licenses in the spring of 1499 to go on expeditions of trade and exploration, at the same time that the new government was authorized for the Indies.

The contracts (*capitulaciones*) were signed by Fonseca, acting for the Crown, and by an individual who represented other unnamed partners.[9] The signer as party of the second part led the voyage; his silent partners were men of means, living mainly in Sevilla, and included Italian and Spanish factors. The license was a matter of record, not so where the expedition went or what it accomplished. Navarrete collected the documents on these minor voyages, as he called them, in his third volume and wrote an introduction that is still one of the best synopses. The interviews of Peter Martyr ended in 1501 when he left Spain for a lengthy absence. Las Casas relied mainly on Peter Martyr. The *Pleitos de Colón*, transcribed by Fernández Duro, add numerous geographic data.[10]

All the capitulations carried instructions to keep away from shores that pertained to the King of Portugal and not to trespass on any land that had been discovered by Columbus. Fonseca provided at least some of the parties with charts made by or for Columbus. All the expeditions pivoted about the Gulf of Paria, which had been discovered by Columbus, from which it may be inferred that they were told to disregard this part of the instructions. Although the removal of Columbus as governor had been decreed, still unknown to him, the

---

[8] Céspedes del Castillo in Vicens-Vives (ed.), *op. cit.*, II, 523.
[9] *Ibid.*, p. 527.
[10] CDU, VII and VIII. More depositions in CDI, XXXIX.

larger question of his rights by discovery had not been raised. Fonseca in licensing the "minor voyages" was opening another attack on the contract of 1492. The long and bitter contest of later years between the heirs of Columbus and the Crown hinged upon what Columbus had discovered, what constituted discovery, and how far such rights extended beyond the locale of discovery. Fonseca selected the Gulf of Paria as the most promising point of attack. Perhaps he thought that Columbus was already eliminated; perhaps he saw that this was the best place at which to block off the claims of Columbus. Fonseca expressed himself in action, not in letters or memoirs.

Four voyages are known to have been licensed and undertaken in 1499: those of Alonso de Hojeda, Peralonso Niño, Vicente Yáñez Pinzón, and Diego de Lepe. The latter two ran out the coast of Guayana and Brazil about to Cape San Agustín, but did not enter the Caribbean and therefore are not considered here. Maps of the time, such as the one made by Juan de la Cosa in 1500, have led to conjectures of other voyages or perhaps only chance strayings off course. The voyage that has been attributed to Vespucci in 1497 is apocryphal, in my opinion a clumsy fabrication for which Vespucci is not responsible.[11]

DISCOVERY OF THE PEARL COAST AND VENEZUELA (1499)

Both the Hojeda and Niño parties sailed from Spain in the latter part of May, a few days apart. Both took their course to the Gulf of Paria, Hojeda with a fleet, Niño with a single ship. Their tracks crossed at times but they did not meet. For both, route and schedule are incompletely known.

Peralonso Niño had been with Columbus on the first and second voyages. Some witnesses in the *Pleitos* thought he had also been on the third voyage, which was denied by others. It appears that Fonseca prudently selected men who had not been to Paria with Columbus, but supplied them with charts of that voyage. Peralonso, an experienced pilot in the Indies, lacked funds to procure and fit out ship and crew. The backing was supplied by the Guerra brothers of Triana (Sevilla), Cristóbal going as captain of the ship with thirty-three men.[12]

The caravel of Niño and Guerra went directly to the Gulf of Paria and followed the north shore of Paria peninsula west from the Dragon's Mouth. This long and narrow mountainous strip, a luxuriant rain forest in its eastern part, becomes arid scrub country to the west, the latter now known as the peninsula of Araya. Here they landed to cut and load brazilwood and thus chanced on the beginning of the Pearl Coast, in the strait between the mainland and Margarita Island and southwestward beyond Cumaná. They knew nothing of the peculiar ecology of pearl oysters—the salinity, temperature, and sea bottom that made this a major pearl ground of the New World—but they soon found that the natives here had a lot of pearls and were ready to trade them. A very profitable trade continued for six or seven months, as they proceeded westward from place to place along the mainland. What thereafter was known as the Pearl Coast was

---

[11] Briefly considered in my "Terra Firma: Orbis Novus," *Hermann von Wissmann-Festschrift* (Tübingen, 1962).
[12] L. H. Vigneras has made clear the activities of the Guerras, with new documentation, in *Añuario de estudios americanos,* XIV (Sevilla, 1957), 333–348.

much larger than the extent of rich pearl beds, of which they may have remained unaware. Peter Martyr was told that they brought back 96 pounds (@ 8 oz.) of pearls, some as large as hazelnuts, very clear and beautiful, though poorly strung.[13] Las Casas raised the figure to more than a hundred and fifty pounds, which may have been exaggeration or may have taken into account the undeclared or smuggled amount for which the Crown instituted suit of recovery after the return. The trading voyage, first of its kind, was very successful and without mishap. Its purpose and the small crew may have kept it innocent of violent encounter with the natives.

Peter Martyr queried Niño on the return about what he had seen. In Paria there was a region called Haraia (Araya) notable for its great salines (the salt pans that later were for a time one of the major resources of the Caribbean) (fig. 14). Beyond they came to the regions of Cumaná and Maracapana (Barcelona) and then to that of Curiana, which had a harbor like Cádiz (perhaps Puerto Píritu). (The long curving coast between Barcelona and Cabo Codera does resemble the Gulf of Cádiz.) Peter Martyr heard about their exploration as extending more than a hundred and twenty leagues west of the Dragon's Mouth, which is about right for the western limit of the low smooth coast ending at Cabo Codera and the rock out to sea then called Farallón, now Centinela. Peter Martyr found the determination of the geography not clear, since some said that Niño did not get that far, because Curiana did not produce pearls but these were found only in the small regions of Cumaná and Maracapana. Niño, however, said only that they had great success in trading for pearls in Curiana. Vinas testified in the Pleitos that the ship left the Dragon's Mouth and "they went discovering down the coast until they got to the pearls, which will be a hundred and thirty leagues more or less along the coast and there they traded in pearls and from there they returned to Castile." [14] Again the distance would indicate that they followed the low coast to its far end. The Farallón was thereafter the dividing point between the land of the pearl trade and the territory assigned to Hojeda. The Niño-Guerra discoveries thus ran from Araya by way of Cumaná and Maracapana the length of the Curiana coast as far as Cabo Codera, all of which became known as the Pearl Coast because of the initial success of trading for pearls not because of the location of pearl beds.[15]

The other expedition of 1499 into the Caribbean was licensed to Hojeda by special favor of Fonseca. Juan de la Cosa went as chief pilot and, being a person of means, which Hojeda was not, is thought to have undertaken part of the costs. Amerigo Vespucci, the third notable who participated, represented Medici interests in Sevilla and managed his part in the venture somewhat independently of the others, apparently having two ships at his disposal.

The course of the voyage is given in two versions, one by Vespucci, the other relating to the main party. The only consecutive account is the letter of Vespucci to Lorenzo Pier de Medici of July 18, 1500, written in the first person as though

---

[13] Peter Martyr, Decade I, Bk. 8.

[14] CDU, VII, 309.

[15] Navarrete, vol. III, n. 4 on p. 13, correctly stated that the Curiana coast extended west to the Farallón and that historians had confused it with another region to the west that was named Coriana. The latter is the land about Coro. From Las Casas to the present Carib Curiana and Arawak Coriana have been thus confounded.

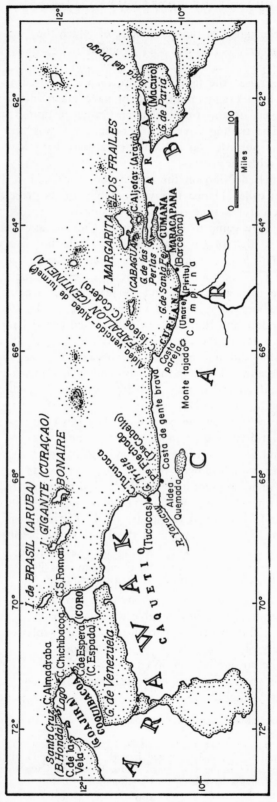

Fig. 14. The Pearl Coast of Venezuela.

he alone had been in charge. Some of its dates are in conflict with those of the others. It may be that Vespucci left the others during the outbound crossing of the Atlantic and was not with them on Terra Firme.[16] The matter has not been resolved.

The ships started together from Spain, probably on May 18 and certainly not earlier.[17] Two stops were made on the coast of Africa and at least four in the Canaries, where the provisioning was completed, as was the custom. They could not have left the Canaries before some date in June. It is probable that Vespucci took off shortly to make a reconnaissance of the coast of Brazil. The main party made their landfall well down the coast of Guayana, toward the end of June. Hojeda and Cosa then turned up that coast into the Gulf of Paria; Hojeda testifying in the Pleitos that they went thus for about two hundred leagues. From the gulf they entered the Caribbean by the Dragon's Mouth, which must have been early in July.

From the Dragon's Mouth they sailed straight downwind to land on Margarita Island, where Hojeda testified that he went about on foot, the point being that the island had only been sighted by Columbus but that the actual discovery belonged to Hojeda. Other testimony in the Pleitos supported him.

From Margarita the ships made contact with Tierra Firme, perhaps in the vicinity of Barcelona and Puerto Unare. The pilot Andrés de Morales testified that Hojeda and Cosa had gone from Margarita to Maracapana (Barcelona) and along the coast to the seat of a certain cacique, with whom Cristóbal Guerra had been previously, and continued thence along the coast.[18] Morales had heard this from both men and later verified it on his own voyages. Niño and Guerra had previously made a visit to a cacique on the Curiana coast, near the harbor that reminded them of Cádiz. Morales was one of the best-informed pilots of the Spanish Main, not a partisan, and is dependable. When Cosa made his map the following year his entries for this long low stretch of coast were *costa pareja*, *campina*, and *monte tajado*, all properly descriptive of that terrain. Perhaps because the other party had preceded them, they passed by here quickly.

Beyond the low coast an Andean spur juts out to sea to form Cabo Codera, with Centinela Island in front. The island was known as Farallón at the time and is thus entered into instructions given in Spain for later operations. From here to the westward the Spaniards had trouble with the natives. An *aldea vencida* was so named because the place was taken by force, also Puerto Flechado with an *aldea quemada* nearby, where a village of about a hundred fifty houses was burned; and the mountain-backed coastline was known as the "costa de gente brava." They had gotten into a hornet's nest of Caribs.

The most important locality was Puerto Flechado, appearing first on the Cosa map and determined as to location in the rutter of Enciso. Enciso gave the distance from cape and gulf of Aljofar (Araya) to Cape Tucuraca (Tucacas) as eighty leagues, both in the same latitude, a fair approximation of distance and position. Cabo de Isleos (Codera) he placed midway, and Puerto Flechado

---

[16] F. J. Pohl, *Amerigo Vespucci—Pilot Major* (New York, 1944), has thus argued.
[17] Antonio Ballesteros y Beretta, *La marina cántabra y Juan de la Cosa* (Santander, 1954), chs. 11-15, has put together the known sequence.
[18] CDU, VII, 202.

between the capes of Isleos and Tucacas, with numerous small islands in front. This location applies to the later Puerto Cabello and only there. Either that town or one of the bays immediately to the east must have been the Puerto Flechado, so called because a Spanish party took time out there to recover from the wounds of Carib arrows. Vespucci described the incident, in which he took part, and said that they remained there for twenty days, which is too long to fit the Hojeda-Cosa calendar.

A short distance beyond Puerto Flechado, they entered Arawak country and followed its coast until they were fifteen leagues south of the Isla de Gigantes (known by that name until it became Curaçao). Vespucci supplied the tale of the good-natured giants. From it they sailed ten leagues west to the island of brazilwood (Aruba), where, according to Vespucci, a large population lived in houses built with ingenuity out into the water, as in Venice. By this version the name Venezuela originated outside the gulf that is thus called. On Aruba, Vespucci saw houses full of fine cotton; while they were helping themselves, they also took house beams of brazilwood. Because of the tight schedule on which they were proceeding, they could hardly have discovered either island unguided.

After Aruba the ships turned south to the mainland at Cape San Román, then so named, which, as Ballesteros pointed out, fixes that date as August 9. In the scant three weeks remaining, they coasted the Gulf of Venezuela and the Goajira peninsula. Details are few. The Cosa map shows to the south of the Gulf of Venezuela another bay that receives a large river from the southern interior. The resemblance to Lake Maracaibo and the Río Zulia is striking. There was no time for such observations, which may have been given by natives. The name Coquibacoa appears for an Indian town, later extended to the peninsula now named Goajira. The tip of this peninsula had special attention, as shown by the seven place entries on the Cosa map, of which only Cabo de la Vela has continued in use. The names tell of an arid land and of fishing. The discovery continued beyond Cabo de la Vela, as shown in two entries by Cosa, then turned back to sail north from that cape to Española, which was reached on September 5, the ships leaking and needing repairs.

The pace had been hurried and sustained, with little attention given to trade and not much time for looting. The information secured would prove useful in a later voyage, but meanwhile a pay load was needed. Hojeda landed at Yaquimo (Jacmel), where Bartholomew Columbus had been cutting brazilwood, and robbed what he could load. This landing also gave Hojeda opportunity to stir up another revolt against Columbus. Unfortunately for him, Roldán at the time was supporting Columbus and warned Columbus of the trespass. Hojeda then sailed around the Guacayarima peninsula to the Indian district of Cahay (Arcahaie), north of Xaragua, where the ships were provisioned with cassava bread. Finally the Bahamas were harried for slaves; Vespucci said that 232 were loaded and that the entire profit of the voyage amounted only to five hundred ducats. The return to Spain was in the spring of 1500.

Almost a thousand miles of Tierra Firme had been discovered to the west of the Dragon's Mouth, and also the important offshore islands of Margarita, Curaçao, and Aruba. In Atlantic waters Hojeda and Cosa had followed the coast of Guayana, and Vespucci had been to the north coast of Brazil, as had Yáñez Pinzón and Lepe by separate voyages. From the shoulder of Brazil at Cape San Agustín to Cabo de la Vela the existence of another continent had been demonstrated by these "minor" voyages of 1499.

RETURN VOYAGES TO THE PEARL
AND VENEZUELAN COASTS (1500–1501)

All the expeditions were back by summer of 1500; none had had a really bad time, and the Niño-Guerra voyage had paid off handsomely, probably the first venture in the Indies that did so. The Guerras were onto a good thing and had no more need of Niño.[19] The Pearl Coast became their reserve for some years, and other licensees were warned to keep off.[20]

A second voyage was made ready promptly and paid well, this time in more diversified commodities. It was contracted to Cristóbal Guerra, who disembarked in the province of Cumaná and there secured many pearls and baroque pearls (aljófar) from the natives, also loaded twenty pipes of Cassia fistula and "from another island they got a lot of brazilwood and slaves," all of which was reported to Bishop Fonseca.[21] Enciso knew a port of Cañafistola in the western part of the Curiana coast, referring to the pods of some native Cassia that was tried as substitute for the Far Eastern Cassia fistula. The island where brazilwood and slaves were taken is identified in a document of December 2, 1501: "Cristóbal Guerra went at our Orders to the land of Canarias [misprint for Curiana], where the pearls of the Ocean Sea are . . . and by his orders took and killed certain Indian men and women in the island of Bonayre and those whom he took alive he brought and sold many of them in the cities of Sevilla and Cádiz and Xeres and Cordoba and other places," for which he was brought to account.[22] Trade had become raid. Passing beyond the Pearl Coast and out of bounds for his license, Cristóbal Guerra started slaving on the island of Bonaire, thus first of record. The action taken for bringing slaves must have been ineffective, for in the ensuing years the Guerras were thus engaged as far west as Cartagena.

The Guerra interest was not directed to exploration or colonization. It was rescate that turned him from trade to pillage and slave hunting, ranging the coasts of Tierra Firme at will without let or hindrance and with the knowledge of Fonseca.

Hojeda was given his asiento for a return voyage,[23] but the departure was delayed for more than a year while he sought new backers and participants. Juan de la Cosa meantime had joined Rodrigo de Bastidas for still another ex-

---

[19] Vigneras, loc. cit., has traced the role of the three brothers of Triana in five overseas voyages.
[20] Thus the capitulation with Hojeda of July 28, 1500 (Navarrete, III, 86): "You shall not touch on the land of the pearl trade of this part of Paria, from the place of Los Frailes [islands] and the bay before Margarita to the other side as far as the Farallón, and on all that land which is called Curiana you shall not touch."
[21] CDU, Juan de Noya in VII, 255.
[22] CDI, XXXI, 104 ff.
[23] The instrument was of July 28, 1500 (Navarrete, III, 85–88).

ploration, and Amerigo Vespucci had gone into the service of the King of Portugal to discover the coast of Brazil and beyond. The second voyage of Hojeda was again a private venture of which the Crown was to receive a fifth. It was to engage in further discovery and to establish a government on Tierra Firme under Hojeda.

The new government was called that of "the Island of Coquibacoa" and its eastern limit was set at the Farallón. No limit was drawn to the west and Hojeda was told to continue from his previous discovery "toward the part where it is known that the English were engaged in discoveries," to set up markers in token of Spanish possession, and thus contain the English advance. The reference was to advice from the Spanish embassy in London that John Cabot and men of Bristol were pushing south along a northern mainland coast, an adumbration, as was shown also on the map of Cosa, that the western shores were a continuous land body of great extent. Fonseca, who drew up the contract, planned an advance base at the western limit of the known Tierra Firme from which exploration and possession would be carried on.

Hojeda was told to follow up information secured on his prior voyage, to wit, of green stones of which he had brought a sample from Coquibacoa, of another place of pearl trade, and "you shall seek the mines of gold of the existence of which you say that you have news that such exist." The green stones would have led to the emerald mines of interior Colombia. The new pearl district would have been the coast about Río de la Hacha; the gold mines, the mountains behind the Gulf of Darién. Coquibacoa (Goajira) had given proper leads to look for new sources of wealth.

Hojeda lacked the qualities needed to be explorer or administrator and paid little attention to his instructions. He neither followed the coast west nor did he go inland. He did build a token base toward the tip of the Goajira peninsula, probably at Bahía Honda, and named it Santa Cruz. It was in a barren country, served no purpose, and was a casual gesture. Instead, he took his ships to range east along the proscribed coasts of Margarita, Cumaná, and Curiana, trading and raiding. The partners fell out and the other two conspired to put him in jail temporarily at Santo Domingo. The venture was wholly disorganized; there was no settlement made, no government established, no discovery undertaken. From the end of 1500 into 1502 the shores of Tierra Firme were ravaged by both Cristóbal Guerra and Hojeda. Thereafter there is almost no mention of these parts for some years; the raids ran into more resistance and brought less revenue, and attention was turned to discoveries farther west on Tierra Firme.

The strategy of Fonseca had been to eliminate the claims of Columbus on Tierra Firme and to limit those of Portugal and England. East of the Gulf of Paria, Yáñez Pinzón was to be Captain General and Governor of the mainland as far as Spanish authority could be maintained against Portugal. Little of profit was found among the forest Indians of Guayana and Brazil and no establishment was made.[24] In the middle, the Pearl Coast was reserved to the operations of Guerra, without provision of government. West of the Farallón, Hojeda was to govern, explore, and hold back the English. It was a proper plan, on paper.

---

[24] CDI, XXII, 300 ff., and XXX, 535 ff.

NATIVE CULTURES OF THE COAST
OF TIERRA FIRME

The men who discovered the Caribbean mainland had little interest in the natives and how they lived other than what profit could be had from them. There are few parts of the New World of which we know so little at the time of first European contacts.

The best account is by Peter Martyr, who asked Peralonso Niño what he had seen on the Pearl Coast, in particular in Curiana.[25] He was told that women took care of the crops and made bread from roots and also from corn. The men engaged in hunting and were excellent bowmen who could bring down any bird or four-footed animal. There was abundance of game: deer, *jabalí*, hares, pigeons and doves, dark-colored *pavos* (curassow), and pheasants (guan?). The canoes were smaller and less finely made than in Española or among the island cannibals. Ducks and geese (Muscovy ducks) were raised by the women in the houses. The natives were accustomed to keep a certain herb in their mouths almost continuously (first mention of chewing coca). Salt was produced at Araya, made into bricks, and traded.

Niño gave the first notice of organized trade, which seems not to have been known to the natives of Española. The manner of bartering was described as being like the haggling between women and vendors in Spanish markets. "They hold markets (*ferias*) of their own to which each brings the products of his region," such as pottery brought in from other parts. Salt bricks were traded into the interior. Strings of pearls were traded to the west, in return for which they got "little birds and many other small animals beautifully made of gold" and of the fineness of German florins. When asked whence these things came the people of Curiana answered that they came from Cauchieto (Caquetío) six days' journey to the west. The Niño party had picked up the trail of cast gold objects, first and only occasionally seen in Española. The Curiana people got such gold from the Caquetío to the west, who were not identified as miners or metallurgists but as traders of gold jewelry for pearls. (The Spaniards had come upon the trade route by which gold objects were carried from the Gulf of Darién to Paria.) There was also trade between coast and interior, in addition to salt bricks and the dried and salt fish that was taken inland.[26]

By the Niño account the visitors were received with hospitality at Curiana and continued to be thus treated. This was in the heart of the Carib coast. Caribs were not named as such, nor was there mention of cannibals, except for a party seen at the Dragon's Mouth. The Caquetío with whom the Curiana folk traded customarily were Arawak. It would seem that the mainland natives, both of the Pearl Coast and of the *costa brava*, were not identified at that time as Caribs and that they were not preying upon the Arawak Caquetío.

---

[25] Peter Martyr, Decade I, Bk. 8.

[26] Gómara, *op. cit.*, p. 80 (see n. 3, above), gave at a later date an account of fishing on the Pearl Coast by hooks, nets, arrow, fire, and drives. Canoes went out at night carrying torches to attract the fish, which were then harpooned or shot by bow and arrow. Also a line of swimmers would form behind a school of fish and drive them toward shore. Among the salt and dried fish traded were eels and congers. Gómara also gave a description of the preparation of arrow poison.

Jahn has established the distribution of Arawak and Carib from later sources.[27] These mainland Arawak were peaceable, hospitable, and generous and were thus celebrated in the verses of Castellanos. Enciso knew them as "of good disposition, the women more genteel (*gentil*) than in other regions," their weapons lances up to twenty-five palms long and also dart throwers, whereas their neighbors to the east used longbows with arrows an arm's span in length. This distinction in weapons held widely for mainland as well as the islands: the Caribs were bowmen and the Arawaks used lances and dart throwers. Jahn drew the boundary between Carib and Arawak west of Puerto Cabello, following the Río Yaracui. The Caquetío occupied all the country about the Gulf of Venezuela, the peninsula of Goajira (Coquibacoa), the Dutch islands, and inland across the Andes. Pile villages were associated with the Caquetío by the name Venezuela, some such having been seen earlier on the north coast of Cuba.

THE DISCOVERY OF URABÁ

The expeditions brought news of a tropical world across the Ocean Sea, a Tierra Firme that stretched an unimagined distance west and east. Sevilla and Cádiz heard a new geography of capes, gulfs, rivers, and islands at the far side of the trade winds, with promise of gain and adventure. The captains were busy seeking renewals of licenses to follow up their discoveries. Hojeda and Juan de la Cosa had decided to go their separate ways. While the former dallied in acting on the large privileges he was given by Fonseca, Cosa formed a partnership with Rodrigo de Bastidas, who, like the Guerras, was a businessman of Triana, across the river from Sevilla. The most experienced pilot of the Indies and the merchant who had never been overseas lost no time in joining forces. The license was given on June 8 to Bastidas, in the usual manner that designated a single party; Cosa was probably an equal partner.

That Bastidas and Cosa were in a hurry is shown by the fact that they agreed to pay the Crown a fourth of the proceeds instead of the customary fifth. Cosa knew everything that had been heard in Coquibacoa of gold, pearls, and gems in the unseen country beyond. They settled for the right to trade in that direction while Hojeda was discussing the government in Tierra Firme that was to be his. Hojeda planned an armada of ten ships; the new partners furnished two caravels. While these were being prepared, Cosa found time to complete his world map at Puerto de Santa María.[28] The other pilot secured was Andrés de Morales, here first appearing of record in affairs of the Indies.

The caravels started their voyage in October, 1500. Las Casas, newly come to Española, saw the return of the Bastidas party to Santo Domingo in the summer of 1502, and gave its account in these words, which I have abridged somewhat:

In this year of 1500 the news of gold and pearls on Tierra Firme was increasing day by day, those who went to that coast having profited well by trading trinkets of small value. Little as the gains may have been, they were considered a great deal at that time when Spain was poor in money. Thus the desire to grow rich in-

[27] Alfredo Jahn, *Aborígines del occidente de Venezuela* (Caracas, 1927), fig. 1.
[28] Ballesteros y Beretta, *op. cit.*, chs. 16 and 17 for this voyage.

creased among our people and also the fear of sailing distant seas diminished, especially among the citizens of Triana, who are seamen for the most part. One Rodrigo de Bastidas, a citizen of Triana and a man of honor, good understanding, and property determined to fit out two ships and to go to discover and trade for gold and pearls, which was the aim of all. He came to an agreement with several persons, in particular with Juan de la Cosa, then the best pilot in those seas. Having secured the license from the Sovereigns, or rather from Bishop Fonseca, who managed everything at the time, they left Cádiz, with Bastidas named Captain. They sailed to Tierra Firme by the direction and route that the Admiral had discovered until they reached land, which they followed, trading as they went. Arrived at the gulf and province of Coquibacoa which today we call Venezuela, they sailed on down the coast past what is now Santa Marta and Cartagena and on as far as the reëntrant of the sea that is the Gulf of Urabá with the province of Darién, which was very famous for some years. Leaving that gulf they continued down the coast to the West until they got to the port of Retrete, where the city of Nombre de Dios now is. Having traded a lot of gold and pearls they left there and came to the Gulf of Xaragua, where they lost the ships and then went by land to Santo Domingo where I saw them at the time and also part of the gold they had secured. It was told that they brought two or three chests of gold objects, which were then held to be greater riches than anything theretofore imagined. They also brought some Indians. I do not know whether these had been taken by force or came of their own will. These walked about the city of Santo Domingo in their bare skins as they were accustomed in their own land, their genitals enclosed in tubes of fine gold shaped like funnels.[29]

The Pleitos add further information. The instructions, as usual, were to keep away from the Pearl Coast. The pilots, experienced in crossing the Atlantic, set a course somewhat to the north of Tierra Firme. The first land reported was a "green island," which may have been Grenada. I know no mention of other islands or of the mainland short of Coquibacoa, other than the vague statement by Las Casas that they traded along the coast. Hojeda testified that, while he was preparing to start on his second voyage, Bastidas and Cosa "went to the coast of Tierra Firme where this witness had ended his discoveries on the first voyage and discovered along the Tierra Firme coast from Coquibacoa on." The caravels may have made their way directly to the Goajira peninsula.

The ships took their careful and leisurely course down the coast of Colombia (fig. 15). This was a voyage conducted by competent mariners and we may infer that the coast was well charted. The harbor that resembled Cartagena was so named then, and numerous other features of the Colombian coast became known to subsequent voyagers by names probably given at this time. Pilots of the last voyage of Columbus knew, from the charts they carried, when they reached the coast that had been discovered by Bastidas. The new coast beyond Cabo de la Vela perhaps is what Las Casas had in mind when he said that they traded as they went along the coast.

Andrés Bernáldez probably was in Sevilla when the party returned and heard their account.[30] According to him, they found many and large settlements including a large city where they landed by invitation of the cacique and found and traded objects of metal, the ships finding harbor in a river of no great volume. (The description fits the Río Sinú and the Sinú people.) Thereupon they went

---

[29] Las Casas, Bk. II, ch. 2.
[30] Ballesteros y Beretta, *op. cit.*, pp. 272–274.

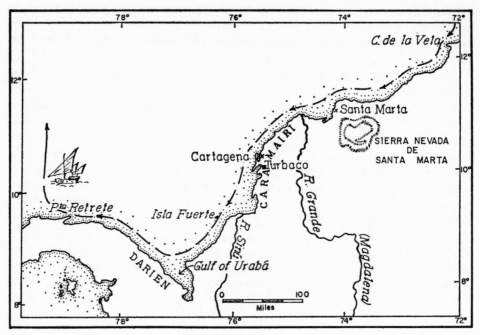

Fig. 15. Bastidas follows the Colombian coast to the Isthmus.

on to a land from which they obtained much gold, Bernáldez learned. Cosa steered the ships to the land of gold, following the hearsay in Coquibacoa of the previous year, and this land thereafter was known as Urabá. How far they penetrated the Gulf of Urabá and how long they stayed is not known, but they left with a cargo of treasure, caravels in bad condition from the borings of ship-worms. Urabá was their great discovery, which opened a new center of attraction for Spanish exploitation.

From Urabá they followed the Panamanian coast to the snug harbor of Retrete. Thence by hard work and good seamanship they made a northeasterly crossing of the Caribbean, stopping in Jamaica and also on a small island off south-western Española (Navassa?) before the worm-riddled ships foundered in the bay of Xaragua. From here they made their way overland with their treasure and Indians to Santo Domingo, there to be harassed by charges of Governor Bobadilla. They secured passage in July in the fleet that was lost in the great hurricane, but were among the survivors along with their treasure. They arrived in Spain in September, 1502, after an absence of twenty-three months. Most of the year 1501 had been spent in the discovery of the coast between Cabo de la Vela and Retrete, an addition of about two hundred leagues to the known coast of Tierra Firme, a new land of golden promise.

Bastidas and Cosa had followed the trail of manufactured gold almost to its source. Niño and Guerra had found that such articles were traded into the Pearl Coast from the Caquetío to the west. Cosa, while piloting the first Hojeda voyage, heard in Coquibacoa of gold as being found farther to the west. In the Sinú and Urabá, Bastidas and Cosa came upon gold pieces in native possession in hitherto unknown abundance. They found no gold mines and did no prospecting. They may have known nothing of the occurrence of gold in nature or of its metallurgy. This was a trading venture. As the natives of the Pearl Coast traded strings of pearls for Spanish trinkets and needles, so these of the west exchanged their gold jewelry for European items of little value.

Some of the stuff traded was fine gold. More of it was cast in diverse alloys, called guañín by the island name, or base gold. The natives did not value the objects according to the gold they contained; the Spaniards were interested in nothing else. Bernáldez heard that at the native city, which I have surmised was Sinú, "they saw things of brass (latón) and copper and of what they brought as gold." Afterward "the Indians repented and demanded their gold back and returned the jewelry and things they had received, and Bastidas, in order not to arouse them, gave them back their gold." In the land from which he brought much gold (Urabá), "the gold is of low grade, like Florins, and is infinite in amount." The chests full of gold were later mentioned in the services Bastidas had rendered the Crown; the inquiry asking whether he had brought the Sovereigns "a great sample and quantity of rich pieces of gold in the form of necklaces, canoes, trumpets, drums, and many other pieces of gold." [31] Gold animal figurines had been noted previously on the Pearl Coast. Modern museum collections show that these were common also in Colombia. More unusual items mentioned in the questionnaire tell of other more unusual forms of Indian bijouterie.

With this voyage Bastidas established himself as a man of property and public office in Española, and Cosa added wealth and prestige for his future engagements on Tierra Firme. The Gulf of Urabá opened a new focus and phase of Spanish exploitation.

At this first contact with the Colombian coast the natives were peaceable and friendly, as those of the Pearl Coast had been. The Spaniards landed at will and stayed at their leisure. Las Casas, always critical of the conduct of his countrymen, gave Bastidas a good character, which he kept in later years in Española and in the colonization of Santa Marta. The untroubled course of this voyage of discovery is in contrast to later events on this coast. Subsequent large and well-armed parties met stout resistance and defeat at the hands of the same natives who had received the men of Bastidas amicably.

---

[31] CDI, II, 369.

VI
VERAGUA, LAST VENTURE OF COLUMBUS
(1502–1504)

•

THE ADMIRAL TAKES ONCE MORE TO THE OCEAN SEA

The prospects of the Indies had improved in the three years since the spring of 1499 when Fonseca gave the first contracts to private parties for trade and exploration. These voyages were not costing the Crown anything, and the one to the Pearl Coast had paid good revenue. The new discoveries gave Spain title to a southern Tierra Firme of great extent. Private capital was ready to exploit the new lands. Bobadilla had opened the gold fields of Española to profitable enterprise. His successor, Nicolás de Ovando, had begun an ordered colonial administration.

Columbus had been retired to Spain, deprived of authority, but he was still the Admiral of the Ocean Sea. Again he offered his services, claimed his rights, and used his powers of persuasion. He still had the sympathy of the Queen and was on her conscience. He would not govern Española again; the rights to Tierra Firme that rested on his discovery of Paria had been transferred to others; but again he was heard by her and was placed in command of a fleet to go out on discovery. The authorization was given on March 14, 1502, and the cost was borne by the Crown, for ships, men, and supplies, implicit acknowledgment that Spain owed him an unpaid obligation.

The adversities of the past overcome, Columbus would now achieve his great objective. He wrote a letter to the Pope in February, 1502, in a mood of exaltation: In his second voyage he had gained fourteen hundred islands and three hundred and thirty-three leagues of the mainland of Asia [by which he meant Cuba], in addition to other most famous, great, and many islands to the east of Española. The latter he had circumnavigated in eight hundred leagues, had reduced its entire very great population to be tributaries to his Sovereigns, and had settled it. This island he held to be Tarsis, Cethia, Ophir, Ophaz, and Cipango, rich in all metals, but especially in gold and copper. It produced brazilwood, sandalwood, linaloe, and many other spices. (There followed an extreme miscalculation of how far west he had gone.) In the third voyage, which was to the south, he had found endless lands and a sea of sweet water (the discharge of the

120

Orinoco into the Gulf of Paria), in which region he believed the terrestrial Paradise to lie, and he found there a very great pearl fishery (an incorrect claim). For the voyage he was about to undertake he asked His Holiness to supply religious who would spread the Christian faith. This was his purpose in writing to the Pope. (As Ballesteros y Beretta pointed out, it was improper for Columbus thus to try to bypass the Crown. The request was ignored. Columbus at no time showed any interest in Christianizing natives.) The letter concluded by recounting that he had promised the King and Queen that he would give them all the revenue they needed to equip an army of horse and foot soldiers to reconquer the Holy Sepulcher. In the present year he would have given them a hundred twenty quintals (hundredweights) of gold and the certainty of as much more in five years to come, had not Satan interfered to prevent it, by malice of which enemy this holy end had not been realized.[1]

In April he wrote the magistrates of San Giorgio at Genoa: "Our Lord has given me the greatest favor he has shown to anyone since David . . . The affairs of my undertaking are glowing and will give great light if they are not darkened by those who govern . . . I am returning to the Indies to carry on in the name of the Holy Trinity." He signed himself "first admiral of the ocean sea and viceroy and governor general of the islands and mainland of Asia, the Indies of the king and queen my sovereigns, and their captain general of the Sea and of their council."[2] Some of these titles he had lost, and some he had never had; only one remained his, that of Admiral of the Ocean Sea.

In the instructions from the Crown of March 14, 1502, Columbus was addressed only as "our Admiral of the Islands and Tierra Firme that are in the Ocean Sea on the side of the Indies." He was told to go promptly, to take possession in the royal name of whatever he might discover, and to prepare a comprehensive account of all such lands, people, and their resources. He was to relate everything before an official notary provided by the Crown. Everything of value was to be registered and placed in the care of this royal official. No slaves were to be taken; if any chanced to come voluntarily to serve as interpreters, this was permitted on the understanding that they would be returned. The instrument carried no appointment to govern, but did authorize leaving Spaniards in the new discoveries. It was a commission to discover and trade without indicating direction or destination.[3]

ROUTE OF THE VOYAGE

The four ships sailed from Cádiz on May 11, 1502, with the usual stop for provisions in the Canaries, and arrived at the island of Martinique on June 15.[4]

---

[1] Navarrete, II, 280–282.
[2] *Raccolta*, Part I, vol. II, p. 171
[3] Navarrete, I, 279–281.
[4] The terse itinerary kept by the notary Diego de Porras is the most reliable account. It, the letter by Columbus written in Jamaica in July, 1503, and the Relación of Diego Méndez were published in Navarrete, vol. I, and have been variously reprinted. The most explicit account of the events of the voyage is in the *Historie* of Ferdinand Columbus, who accompanied his father as a teenager, and recalled vividly this greatest adventure of his life. (Spanish version and notes by Ramón Iglesia in Hernando Colón, *Vida del Almirante don Cristóbal Colón* [Mexico, 1947]).

Columbus was accompanied by his brother Bartholomew as second in command and also by his young son Ferdinand. According to the notary of the voyage, Diego de Porras, the Admiral first called the men together on Martinique to disclose the route he would pursue, which was by way of Española. Ferdinand said that the intention had been to go to the coast of Paria and thence to continue until he found the strait through Tierra Firme, but that this plan was dropped because one of the ships was in poor condition and it was hoped to exchange it for a better one in Santo Domingo.

This version is not acceptable. The crossing of the Atlantic had been made in very good time, indicating that the ships were doing very well. Had Columbus intended to follow the coast of Tierra Firme from Paria, he would have run on the more southerly course before the trade winds to that familiar landing. Instead he took the standard route to Española by way of the Dominica Passage. Here he landed at Martinique, where several days were spent at ease, unmolested by the native Caribs. Columbus in his letter later written in Jamaica said that he had intended to make Jamaica the starting point of his explorations and had so written while in the Dominica Passage, thus confirming that his original plan was to go by way of Española. The Admiral had been given express instructions not to go by way of Española—a sensible provision, since the recently arrived Governor Ovando might find the entry of Columbus embarrassing. The Admiral, looking to Jamaica as his base, disregarded these orders, tried to put in at Santo Domingo, was refused entry by the new governor, and loitered alongshore.

The large fleet that had brought Ovando was about ready to sail home carrying the former governor, Bobadilla, and the wealth of gold he had collected, the long-imprisoned cacique Guarionex, and the Bastidas party and their treasure from Urabá. It was thus that the pilots of Columbus had occasion to see the charts of the Bastidas exploration. Las Casas, newly arrived, witnessed the contact. Columbus, wise to Caribbean weather, warned that a hurricane was approaching. Ovando disregarded his advice and ordered the fleet to sail. Most of the ships, treasure, and men were lost early in July off the southeast shores of Española in the worst disaster of the time.

The four ships of Columbus fled westward to escape the hurricane that was approaching out of the east and scattered into the shelter of Ocoa Bay, where they reassembled as the storm subsided, in the protection of reef-fringed Puerto Viejo de Azua. From here they followed the coast west to the port of Yaquimo, known for its brazilwood. Still vexed by high seas, they struggled "on all fours" (*a gatas*) as Columbus wrote in his letter of a year later, to some cays off the eastern tip of Jamaica. The sea was not yet ready to yield its control, but here, he continued, "it changed from great waves to calm and to a strong current that carried me to the Jardin de la Reina without any sight of land." From Santo Domingo to Cayo Largo (?) off southern Cuba they were driven over seas he had first sailed eight summers before. By a whim of tropical storm he found himself at a point of departure into the unknown which he would not have selected.

Instead of being on Jamaica, Columbus was well to the north and west of where he wished to be, within a very short distance of the terminus of his voyage eight years earlier, at which time he mistook the Cuban coast for that of Mangi of southern China. "From this island, which had been discovered before, and adjoins the land of Cuba, he took his course to go to discover," leaving there on July 27 on a south-southwest course and crossing a gulf of a little more than ninety leagues to sight an island off the mainland three days later (Porras). This direct and fast passage from Cayo Largo (?) to the Bay Islands of Honduras was made at a season when the wind is briskly out of the east, across the course they took, as is also the drift of the sea. Perhaps they were aided by a temporary shift of wind in getting to southward, which, as at previous times, was the direction sought. It would have been easier to follow on to the west and thereby to discover Yucatán. Instead he pointed the ships south (fig. 16).

The high island to which they came was called Guanaja by the natives, the Admiral naming it the Island of Pines on account of many such trees there.[5] From it other high land appeared to the south at a distance of ten to twelve leagues. This mainland was reached at Cape Honduras, named Punta de Caxinas by Columbus, and here the ships turned east. "From this point he began to go discovering along the coast, and because of contrary winds he made slow headway: he never departed from the coast of this land by day, and every night he came to anchor next to the land: the coast is pretty hazardous, or appeared to be so in that very stormy year of much rain and tempestuous skies: he went on continuously in sight of land, as one may go from Cape S. Vicente to the Cape of Finisterre always seeing the coast: fifteen leagues beyond this point he took possession on a river that was coming in flood stage from the high country and is called Rio de la Possession" (Porras). This is the Río Negro, also called Río Sico, which has built a broad delta with the main channel at its extreme right. The lesser distance given by Porras suggests that the main distributary was then at the western margin of its delta.

Beyond the Río de la Possession the coast changed: "Passing on beyond here all the land was very low, of very savage people, and of very little account: almost at the end of the low country the land formed a cape. Up to here it had been most difficult to navigate and [therefore] he gave it the name of Cabo de Gracias a Dios." Porras gave the distance from the point of Caxinas to Gracias à Dios as 80 leagues, a fair estimate considering that they were tacking back and forth daily. It took a month to cover a lesser distance than they had made in three days from Cuba to the Bay Islands. The name Gracias à Dios commemorates to this day the stubborn determination of Columbus to head east against wind and current.

The next leg of the voyage was south from Gracias à Dios to Cariay, 137 leagues by the reckoning of Porras, and requiring less than two weeks. They were running out the length of the Mosquito Coast of Nicaragua and that of Costa Rica. This coastal plain held nothing of special interest. Porras entered a Río del Desastre at 70 leagues south of Gracias à Dios. The name was explained by Ferdinand as due to the loss of a longboat; its crew were drowned while getting water and wood. It may be identified with the Río Grande de Mosquitia. Twelve leagues farther on they came to Cabo de Roas, about right for Punta de

---

[5] Testimony of Noya in CDU, VII, 257.

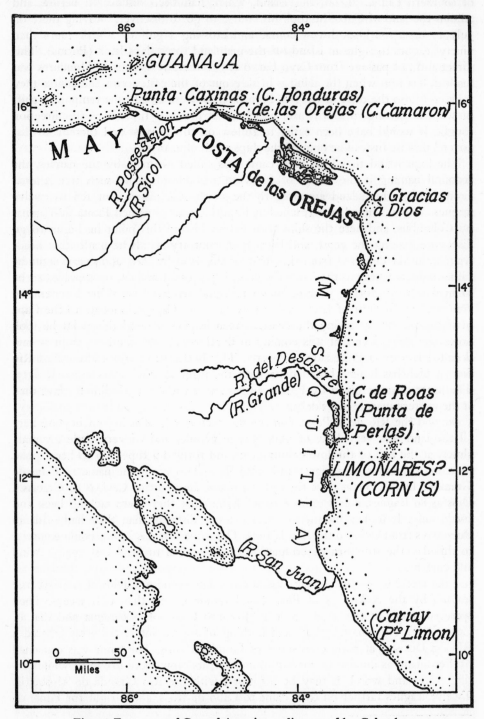

Fig. 16. East coast of Central America as discovered by Columbus.

Perlas and Pearl Cays.[6] From Roas to Cariay, Porras counted 55 leagues, the proper distance to Puerto Limón.

From Gracias à Dios they were sailing south day after day, always the direction of Columbus' desire. To starboard lay the coastal plain, here and there trimmed to a bluff face by waves, elsewhere forming long sand bars that enclose lagoons. To seaward were clusters of cays past which they picked their course.

Peter Martyr had in hand a lost account that adds information:[7] The first part of the mainland was a region called Quiriquetana, which the Admiral called Ciamba (Champa reverting to the imagined identification with Indochina). One part of this was the district of Maia (the first appearance of the name Maya). This was a fine country, full of live oaks and pines, with wild grapes and seven kinds of palms (the western part of the coast of Honduras). From here it took forty days to gain seventy leagues (to pass Cape Gracias à Dios). There were rivers of crystalline waters along which grew canes thicker than a man's arm (*Guadua?*, the giant bamboo-like grass of the New World tropics). Thereafter they came to another great river with four small islands forming a harbor (Río Grande de Mosquitia?). "To the east of these, at a distance of thirteen leagues, sailing always against the current, he found two small islands; because he saw a fruit growing on them that resembles our limes, he called them the Limonares." The two islands were between the great river and Cariay, well out to sea from the coastal cays. At a guess these may have been Great and Little Corn Islands, the larger one rising to an elevation of a hundred meters and visible to ships sailing close to the mainland. Such a swing eastward would explain why there is no mention of the largest river, the Río San Juan, outlet of Lake Nicaragua. If they sailed south from Great Corn Island they would have missed that river and shortly would have raised the high mountains of Costa Rica and come to Cariay, which was situated at their base.

Cariay was the first important stop. On September 25 "we anchored at a small island called Quiribiri and a pueblo on the mainland called Cariay, the best people, country, and site we had found until then. The land was high and of many rivers and abounded in very tall trees, the said island very leafy, full of groves of straight trees, palmitos, mirobalans (*Spondias*) and many other kinds, for which reason the Admiral named it 'la Huerta'" (Ferdinand Columbus). Island and town were a short league apart, with a river nearby. Cariay has been securely identified with Puerto Limón, the Caribbean port of Costa Rica.[8]

"From here he went on and as he was examining ports and bays, thinking to find the strait, he came to a very great bay: The name of this land is Cerebaro;

---

[6] Samuel E. Morison, *Admiral of the Ocean Sea* (Boston, 1942) has interpreted the "cabo de Roas" or Porras as Monkey Point because of its red cliffs, well to the south. But Porras wrote *roas* (stem of a ship), not *rojo* (red).

[7] Peter Martyr, Decade III, Bk. 4.

[8] On the 450th anniversary of the discovery, the Academia de Geografía y Historia de Costa Rica issued a commemorative volume, *Documentos para la historia de Costa Rica relativos al último viaje de Colón* (San José, 1952). In its latter part Bishop Thiel and Henri Pittier discussed the site of Cariay, especially its proximity to a river. Pittier, who knew the physical geography as well as he did botany, used a United Fruit Company survey to show that formerly the Río Matina discharged into the small bay of Moin adjacent to Puerto Limón. A final item of interest in the volume is the article by Jorge Lines on local archaeologic finds, in support of the mode of sepulture reported at the discovery.

here the first object of fine gold was had." "By information of Indians he went to another large bay called Aburema, where the land was very high and broken" (Porras). These are the bays of Almirante and Chiriquí, backed by the eleven thousand foot Volcán de Chiriquí. The distance from Cariay to Aburema as given by Porras is 42 leagues.

The second half of October was spent along the Caribbean coast beyond Laguna de Chiriquí, getting to the harbor of Portobelo on November 2 (fig. 17). The time was brief, the harbors that could be entered were few, and the coast was exposed and wave-swept. Porras summed it up: "This land along the shore of the sea is craggy, of very dense woods; there are no settlements on the coast but only at two or three leagues inland and one cannot go from sea to settlements by land but only by river and canoe." Nearly a score of rivers rise in the cloud-capped and rain-drenched serranía of the interior to make their steep descent through rain forest to the north coast. Wave-cut cliffs alternate with river mouths which are blocked at times by bars thrown up by waves and reopened by freshets out of the highlands. Since the land was reported to be rich in gold, short stops were attempted. Names of "provinces" were heard without identification of distance, from Cateba of the fire-scarred cacique, through Zobraba and Urira and thence seven leagues to Veragua and so to Cubiga, where the guide they had brought from Cariay said the gold-bearing land ended. This was at fifty leagues from Cerebaro (Almirante Bay) and may be placed at Río Palmilla and Punta Rincón. The guide was properly informed; this was the stretch in which streams course directly and rapidly from the mountains to the sea and carry gold. The name Veragua was soon extended to the larger region of the cliffed coast.

By the account of Ferdinand, Portobelo was entered on November 2, Puerto de Bastimentos (Nombre de Dios) on the 10th, and that of Retrete, about twenty miles farther east, on the 26th. Portobelo was so named by his father "because it is very large, beautiful, and populous, and has about it much cultivated land"; Bastimentos (provisions), "because all the surroundings and small islands were full of maize fields"; Retrete, "a secluded place in which there was room for no more than five or six ships." Retrete was the end of discovery; "on some sailing charts of some of the mariners, this land joined that which Hojeda and Bastidas had discovered" (Porras). In all, Columbus had discovered three hundred and fifty leagues of new coast.

When the Admiral left Spain the western limit of known Tierra Firme was at Cabo de la Vela. At Santo Domingo, charts of the Bastidas party showed an extension of the coast as far as Retrete on the Isthmus of Panama. In the last four months of 1502 the Admiral traced the west coast of the Caribbean from the Bay Islands of Honduras to the Gulf of San Blas. Both the Crowns of Spain and Portugal had been interested in finding out the position and extension of this new Tierra Firme. Was it India, or would there be a passageway through it or a way around it to continue westward to the Far East? Yáñez Pinzón, Diego de Lepe, Vespucci, perhaps Vélez de Mendoza, sailing under the flag of Castile, and Cabral and the second voyage of Vespucci under that of Portugal, had traced the eastern and a far southern extension of a new continent. Hojeda, Cosa, Bastidas, and now Columbus had found Tierra Firme to be continuous at the

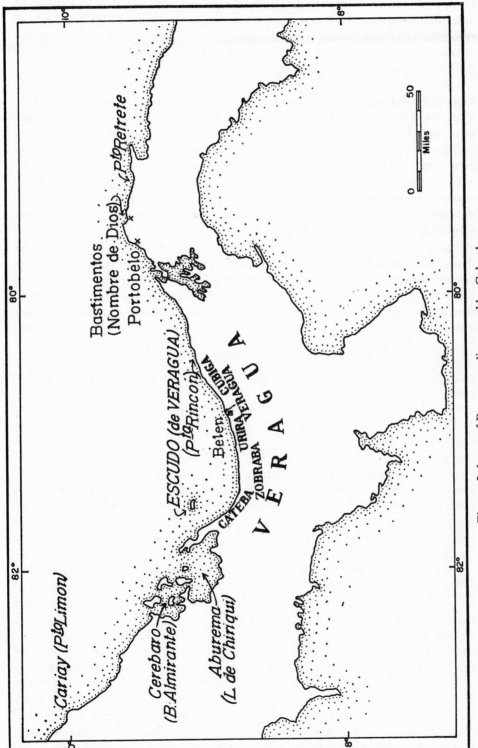

Fig. 17. Isthmus of Panama as discovered by Columbus.

north from the Gulf of Paria to that of Honduras. The Admiral had found no strait and, except for the Mosquito Coast, saw mountains all along the coast. The exploration ended, he would return to the search for gold.

FIRST OBSERVATIONS OF CENTRAL AMERICA

From the Bay Islands to Cape Gracias à Dios the ships headed into strong easterly wind; from that cape beyond Cariay (Puerto Limón) they were abeam of the wind. Only in the bays of Almirante and Chiriquí were they in quiet waters; in the farther Panamanian coast they were again exposed to strong waves. They came in the rainy season which may have been unusually stormy that year.

The coast of Honduras, first to be seen, was "all healthy, lovely, fortunate as to climate, yielding to none in the fertility of its land, in part a montane country and in part a noble plain of perpetual spring and autumn" (Peter Martyr). Its woods of live oaks and pines and wild grape vines were a first notice of the northern flora that extends into Central America. Little was seen or said of the Mosquito Coast. From Cariay through the Veraguan coast the mountains of the interior, seen through mist and clouds, appeared to be of very great height.

The landfall on Guanaja was among people differing greatly from those of the islands. As they lay off Guanaja they saw a great and impressive canoe coming from the west. Ferdinand remembered it well:

> The Adelantado being at that island with the desire to learn its secrets, it was his good fortune that there came at that time a canoe as great as a galley, eight feet wide, all of a single trunk, and made like the others, the which came loaded with merchandise from western parts, from the side of New Spain. [He wrote this years after the conquest of New Spain.] Amidships it had a canopy of palm leaves, like that of gondolas in Venice, which protected what was underneath in such a manner that neither rain nor waves could wet anything within. Under this canopy were the children, women, and all the baggage and merchandise. The crew of the canoe, although they were twenty-five, did not have the spirit to defend themselves against the batels sent in pursuit. The canoe thus taken by us without a fight was brought to the ships where the Admiral gave many thanks to God, seeing that in one moment, without effort or danger to his own men, he had been provided with a sample of all the things of that land. He then ordered that there should be taken from the canoe whatever appeared to be most attractive and valuable, such as cloths and sleeveless shirts of cotton that had been worked and dyed in different colors and designs, also pantaloons of the same workmanship with which they cover their private parts, also cloth in which the Indian women of the canoe were dressed, such as the Moorish women of Granada are accustomed to wear. Also long swords of wood with a groove along each edge, wherein stone knives were set by means of fiber and pitch, cutting like steel when used on naked people; also hatchets to cut wood, like those of stone used by other Indians, save for the fact that these were of good copper, of which metal they also had bells and crucibles for smelting. For food they carried roots and grain such as they eat in Española and a certain wine made of maize, like the beer of England, and they had many of those kernels which serve as money in New Spain, which it appeared that they valued highly.

In the earliest account, written by Peter Martyr, there were two canoes that belonged to a merchant returning from other lands and laden with goods to be sold at a fair, such fairs being customary in these parts. Among the wares were large and small knives (*novaculae, cultelli*) and cleavers (*secures*), made from a translucent yellow stone; some of these tools were hafted into hard wood. Also there were ceramic objects made with remarkable skill, items worked of wood, and some of marble.

The pillage of the trading canoe gave a preview of an extensive and elaborate native commerce, in this instance between central Mexico and the Gulf of Honduras. The cargo was being brought from the west and some of it came from distant parts. The cotton goods may have been from Yucatán. The tools and weapons of yellowish obsidian were from central Mexico, also the marble or alabaster, known as Mexican onyx. The copper bells and good copper axes indicate Michoacán as source. The kernels that served as coins were cacao beans, produced mainly on the Pacific coast.

This was the first contact with a merchant class which would later be found throughout New Spain and even farther, known mainly as trading on land. When Nuño de Guzmán came to the Pánuco coast at the northern end of the high native culture, a native merchant there gave the first account of the Pueblo peoples of New Mexico, a thousand mile journey to the north. In central and western Mexico there were towns of such traders, who in later years served as interpreters and guides in the conquest of New Spain.[9]

The use of cacao beans as money, the holding of fairs, the diverse stock of trade goods, and the merchant proprietor all told of a way of life very different from that of the Antilles, and more complex. The cargo was being taken east and its diversity suggests that it was a fair sample of articles imported from the west. The only hint of what might be traded in return is the mention of crucibles for smelting metal. Interior Honduras later became known to the Spaniards as a source of gold but not of copper or other metals, nor was it known for much else. Yucatán, on the western side of the Gulf of Honduras, had no metals and the volcanic highlands of central Mexico had very little. The gold treasure Cortés found in the Aztec state had been amassed from various outlying areas by tribute and trade. Mayan Yucatán also acquired its gold by commerce, and may have obtained some of it from interior Honduras, as suggested by the crucibles. What Columbus encountered in the Indian trading ship and did not recognize as to its significance was an elaborate and extensive native commerce that might have led him to the gold placers of Honduras or to the cities of Yucatán.

The landfall at Guanaja Island and the landing on the adjacent mainland were the first European contact with any of the high cultures of the New World, which later were found to extend north as far as the Río Pánuco. Possibly Columbus had a glimmering of such a culture when he identified the new coast with Champa of Indochina. He did not follow it up nor did he tarry here or have any inclination to return. The discovery was not appreciated at the time, and had no bearing on the later conquest of New Spain.

The Bay Islands and the adjacent mainland were parts of Maya country and were known by that name. Peter Martyr heard it thus. Bartholomew Columbus, in Rome in 1506, also knew it as such. In the Pleitos, which preceded the dis-

---

[9] The place names of Mexico and Guatemala in very many cases are Nahuan (Mexican) in parts where other Indian languages were spoken. The Spaniards learned from such guides a Nahuan toponymy as far as Arizona and New Mexico.

covery of Yucatán, the question was asked whether Columbus had discovered "a land called Maya, where there was and is a point of land that was named Cajinas and some islands, one of which is named Guanaja," the answers being affirmative.[10]

That the people were Mayans, participants of the culture known as Mesoamerican, is supported by information in addition to that of the trading canoe. Ferdinand remembered that they did not have the broad faces of the islanders. Peter Martyr heard of them as tall and well built, also that they grew maize and yuca, ages and batatas, mirobalan (*Spondias*) and cotton trees. Fowls resembling the peacocks of Europe in color, size, and savor were raised to eat. The people painted their bodies black or red with the juice of certain fruits [*Genipa* and *Bixa*] grown for that purpose in their gardens. When the Admiral held the ceremony of possession, Ferdinand recalled that the natives came "bearing fowls of the country which are better than ours, geese, dried fish, and red and white beans that are like frijoles." The people wore colored shirts and pantaloons and had corselets of quilted cotton. The so-called domestic "geese" were Muscovy ducks which the Spaniards took to be geese because of their large size and different appearance. The so-called peafowl or native chickens were domestic turkeys, here first seen and appreciated at once as food. Unlike on the islands, beans were a local staple food, Ferdinand remembering that there were red and white kinds and that they were like frijoles. It has never been determined what passed under the name of "frijol" in Spain before the discovery of the New World. The term soon came into general use for all kinds of kidney beans (*Phaseolus vulgaris*). Unlike those of the islands, these natives were well clothed in colored cotton fabrics. Dress, corselets, beans, and turkeys as well as the goods carried on the trading ship gave the first record of a new culture.

At the Río de la Possession Columbus left the land of Mayan ways. The guide who had been taken from the trading vessel was turned loose as of no further use. Porras noted that beyond this river the land was very low, the people very primitive (*salvaje*), and the country of little account. They were entering the Honduran part of the Mosquito Coast, still one of the least populated and known parts of Central America. Beyond the river a low, wet coastal plain widens to the east, with a series of lagoons along the coast. The nightly stops gave leisure to find that the coast was sparcely inhabited by a ruder sort of natives. Ferdinand remembered them as almost black, naked, and of very rustic ways. At the beginning of the low country a low cape (Cape Camarón) was named Cabo de las Orejas because the natives there had their ear lobes enlarged to the size of a hen's egg. After rounding Cape Gracias à Dios the Mosquito Coast having nothing of interest was passed rapidly without further report. It was and largely still is the least inhabited land along the Caribbean.

At Cariay (Puerto Limón) they came to a third kind of coast, country, and people. Ferdinand thought Cariay had the best people, land, and location they had seen. Porras, always terse and to the point, reported: "He came to a province called Cariay, with the land rising to a great height. The people were found to be very well disposed, very acute, and desirous to observe. They admired greatly

---

[10] CDI, XXXIX, 415.

whatever thing was shown them. Here some of the principal persons owned some guanín. They had woven cotton. All go naked along this coast except for their private parts, which the women and men cover with cloth they get from the inner bark of trees. They have their bodies and faces all painted like Berbers. Here we saw wild pigs and great cats which they brought to the ships. Some of the Indians were taken to serve as interpreters and the people were left somewhat scandalized." This is the original mention of the bark cloth of Caribbean Central America, prepared like the tapa cloth of the South Seas. Ferdinand told of the eagerness of the natives to engage in trade; they would swim out to the ships with articles they wished to barter: arms, mantas of cotton and shirts of the same material, and small eagles of guañín.

"The Admiral ordered the Adelantado to go inland with a party to reconnoiter the Indian town, their customs and nature, as well as the nature of the country. The most notable thing they saw was that inside of a large palace of wood and covered with canes there were sepulchers, in one of which there was a body, dry and embalmed, and in another two, without bad odor and wrapped in cotton cloths. Over the burials was a tablet on which animals were sculptured; on others was seen the figure of the deceased, adorned with many jewels, objects of guañín, beads, and whatever they esteemed most." Ferdinand was getting a first look at the mortuary customs of lower Central America and Colombia, which later were to support Spaniards by grave robbery, a business that has continued to the present.

Taking a guide from Cariay the fleet went on to Cerebaro (Almirante Bay) "where there were pulled up on land twenty canoes and the people on shore naked as they were born except for a mirror of gold at the neck and some with an eagle of guanín." One of the patens weighed fourteen ducats, an eagle twenty-two (Ferdinand). Peter Martyr heard of the fertility of the country about the lagoons, how the people went about naked but painted, and that they were very fond of garlands and crowns of flowers. Referring to Aburema (Laguna de Chiriquí) "here was found the first object of fine gold worn by an Indian as a paten upon the chest, and it was acquired; here Indians were taken to find out where this gold was and whence it was brought; from here he began to go trading all along the coast" (Porras).

When the Indians of Laguna de Chiriquí told of a gold coast farther on, the ships left the quiet waters of the bay to take their course eastward along that wild Caribbean shore. Where they were able to land at the mouth of a river, they traded for gold objects, especially the disks they called mirrors or patens, recorded as to number at several places. The extent of the coast of profitable rescate of gold was fifty leagues, according to Peter Martyr and Ferdinand; Porras noted that beyond Veragua there was less gold, also that Columbus while "outward bound passed along the whole coast of Veragua without learning the secret of the land." (The name Veragua, originally of one cacicazgo on the river of that name, was thus extended to a stretch of about fifty leagues between Chiriquí Lagoon and Punta Rincón). During the two weeks thus spent Ferdinand said, "the Admiral did not care to acquire more than samples of the things the land held," meaning its prospects of gold. Except for gold ornaments, the notes on the Indians are scanty. At the first river entered, Ferdinand saw Indians wading out, brandishing lances, blowing horns, beating on a drum, the while they chewed herbs. The wind instruments, according to Peter Martyr, were conch shells.[11]

From Cubiga, a day's sail beyond the seat of the cacique of Veragua, "the Admiral continued without stopping until he entered Portobelo." The region that lies about the port is not wild, but cultivated and full of houses, one distant from another by a stone's throw or a crossbow shot; it appears like a painted scene, the most beautiful there is." The next harbor was named Bastimentos because of its many fields of maize. At the harbor of Retrete, Ferdinand, whom I have been quoting, commented: "the people of this country were of the best appearance thus far found among Indians, for they were tall and spare, without distended bellies, and had handsome features. All the land was filled with small herbs and had few trees." The note of Porras was: "At the Port of Retrete the Indians only had earrings of base gold. Here there appeared many indications of the customs and usage of the Indians of the pearl country." The natives at Retrete at first came peacefully to trade, but "a thousand outrages" by the mariners soon took place and the Indians withdrew from further contact. This central part of the Isthmus lacked the cliffed coast and the high mountains of Veragua, was more populous and largely under cultivation, but it gave less promise of gold.

From Puerto Limón to San Blas exploration had proceeded through coasts of strong physical contrast but occupied by people of similar ways, whom Porras correctly recognized as of cultural affinity with those farther east.

As the ships turned west again to look further into the source of gold, more was learned of native life. As in Española, the political organization was under chiefs, called *quebí* in variant spellings; Peter Martyr gave *quivi* as kinglet; Columbus, Quibian as the name of the ruler of Veragua. Porras called him cacique; Peter Martyr agreed that cacique in Española had the same status as quebi on the Isthmus. The most important chief met on this voyage was at Veragua, which may have been his appellation rather than the name of his country. The name Veragua promptly passed into Spanish usage for the whole of the reputed gold coast.

The dispersed manner of settlement had been noted about Portobelo. At Veragua Ferdinand wrote of going to the pueblo of the Quibio, "and although I call it pueblo, it is to be noted that in that land there are no houses adjoining each other, for they live as in Vizcaya, the ones separated from the others." By the Diego Méndez account, the house of the chief was on a flat hilltop in a large plaza, surrounded by three hundred trophy skulls, suggesting a palisaded enclosure.

About Veragua, "their food is fish which they take with nets and fishhooks of bone which they make out of turtle shells, cutting them by means of cabuya fiber in the manner of one sawing." The lad Ferdinand was alert to the kinds of fish, the several ways of their taking, and their preservation: "and it is a marvelous

---

[11] Anchoring in the mouth of a large river called Cateba they again saw the use of horns and tambours for assembly. "Here was the first time that there was seen evidence in the Indies of an edifice, which was a large piece of masonry (*estuco*, in its older meaning), which appeared to be worked of stone and lime. Of which the Admiral ordered a piece to be taken, in memory of such an antiquity" (Ferdinand). This is the first archaeologic note for the mainland, far removed from parts where stone and mortar are known to have been used.

thing how many there are at the time when they enter those rivers, which they take in great quantity and preserve roasted for a long time."

Ferdinand continued:

> They have for their nourishment also much maize, which is a certain grain that grows like *miglio* [sorghum?], in a spike or ear, from which they make white and red wine, as beer is made in England, and they add spices to their taste by which it gets a good taste like sour wine. They make another wine from trees that look like palms, and I think are of that kind, although they are [not] smooth like other trees but have on their trunks spines as long as those of a porcupine. From the pith (*medula*) of these palms which are like palmettos they extract the juice by rasping and pressing, cooking it with water and their spices, and they consider it very good and prize it. Also they make another wine from the fruit we found in the island of Guadelupe, like a great pine cone; and the plant is grown in large fields from shoots that grow out of the same piña, as is done with the lechuga. This plant lasts for three or four years, always producing fruit. They make wine also from other kinds of fruits, especially from one that grows in very tall trees, as tall as cedars, and each fruit has one, two, or three stones, like nuts, though not round but like garlic or chestnuts. The skin of this fruit is like a pomegranate and looks like that when it is taken from the tree although it lacks the little crown. The flavor is like a peach or a very good pear. Some of these are better than others, as is true also of the other fruits. They are also found in the islands, called mameys by the Indians.

This is a rich store of memories from observations of a few weeks. Ferdinand was fourteen at the time and never again saw the New World. He remembered how turtleshell was sawed to the desired shape by cutting it with *cabuya* fiber. He had seen anadromous fish come upstream to spawn and watched the ways in which they were taken and prepared. Maize he knew as a staple food in Veragua, but he was more interested in the beer made from it, some colorless, some red. Palm wine was made from spiny palms by extracting their pith, which indicates the wine palm (*Acrocomia*), still thus used in Central America. Pineapples were planted on a large scale for making wine, in the manner still practiced. The sweet-fruited mamey (*Mammea*) yielded another wine. This part of Tierra Firme indulged in large diversity and consumption of alcoholic beverages.

Cassava bread was unknown to Central America; instead, maize was ground to bake into cakes. When the ship biscuit had been consumed, the Spaniards had to depend on maize, which here was amply available to them. In mid-February, 1503, the Adelantado marched inland from Veragua in search of the gold fields and "continued his journey with thirty men to Zobraba, where there were more than six leagues of maize fields, like fields of wheat" (Ferdinand). At the time the hills were cultivated and peopled where now there is almost unbroken rain forest, nearly empty of habitation.

When Columbus asked where he could find gold he was directed to the streams flowing from the higher mountains and was told where the coast began and ended that received such gold-bearing rivers. This was general knowledge. That he did not discover the secret of the coast on the outward voyage was due to the haste of the passage, which was limited to a few stops alongshore. He did find out that the river and cacique of Veragua offered the best prospects. The natives of the Isthmus valued gold as ornaments. They had objects of gold alloy which had been traded in from elsewhere, and also nose and ear pieces beaten out of fine gold that may have been made locally. Columbus obtained what jewelry he could get, but, unlike Bastidas and Cosa, who had preceded him to the east, not trade but "mines" were his objective. When he returned to Veragua looking for nuggets the cacique "with very good will so informed him and sent two of his sons along with the Christians to show us the mines" (Porras). These, at eight leagues inland from the port, were a large number of pits dug to a depth of about three feet. Peter Martyr was told that the gold was sought at certain seasons of the year; that the natives were well practiced in such operations, and that these were attended with ceremonies. He heard that the natives believed in a divinity presiding over the gold, which may have been a Spanish interpretation of the ritual observed, that they never sought gold without having purified themselves, abstaining from cohabitation with their women and from other pleasures, and using great restraint in eating and drinking. These prescriptions indicate magical or religious association.

THE RETURN TO VERAGUA AND
FOUNDING OF SANTA MARÍA DE BELÉN

"On December 5, the Admiral, seeing that the violence of the east and northeast winds did not cease and that he could not trade with those people [at Retrete], determined to turn back to assure himself of what the Indians had said of the mines of Veragua" (Ferdinand). Storms buffeted the ships for weeks; it was early in January, 1503, before they reached the mouth of the Río Veragua, to find it blocked by a wave-built bar. Turning back a league or so to the east, a perilous entry was found for the ships into another river. This being the day of Epiphany, its native name of Yebra was changed to Belén. The play of sea wave against river flood, alternately building and breaking bars across the river mouth, determined the landing in a river other than the intended one.[12] Having found shelter in the mouth of the Río Belén, they decided to make it the base of their search for gold mines. The site, determined by accident of an ephemeral change of coastline, was as unselected as Navidad and Isabela had been, and proved to be about as unsuited for settlement.

There was an exchange of civilities between the Spaniards camped on the Río Belén and the big chief of Veragua. This was followed by some trade in "mirrors" and other gold pieces; most important, the cacique told where the gold mines were and offered to send his sons as guides. The bad weather continuing, it was a month after their arrival when the exploring party set out. The Admiral being down with the gout, the Adelantado took sixty-eight men to see what they could find. Ferdinand gave the details: by longboat at sea to the Río Veragua, a league and a half up that river to the seat of the chief, where a day was spent. The next day they made four and a half leagues, sleeping by a river that they had

---

[12] The process was described by Diego Méndez, when some months later the ships were delayed in leaving: "The port of the Río Belén or Yebra where we were at the time had closed on us. This was by reason of the force of the tempests of the sea and of the winds that carried in sand and heaped it up in such quantity as to close the entry of the harbor." Ferdinand said that, the January rains having ceased, the mouth of that river was closed by sand and they remained trapped, praying for rain "for we knew that rain would raise the river and the mouth would be opened, as happens in those rivers." Their prayers were answered by a freshet and they were able to take their departure.

crossed forty-three times. Since all the rivers take a direct course down the flank of the sierra to the sea, this means that they were following upstream into the mountains. Going another league and a half, the guides brought them to the "mines" in a dense forest, the trees "reaching to the sky." Two hours were spent digging at the base of the trees with good results, considering that no mining tools had been brought and no one had any experience in securing gold. The journey had been made to get information about mines; all returned in high spirits. Porras, who went along, said they crossed the river thirty-nine times, that the country was difficult because of ridges and streams, that no gear was carried, that the gold was in small bits, and that there was no later return to the locality.

Several days after the return to Belén, the Adelantado, according to Ferdinand, started for the Río Urira, seven leagues west of the Río Belén, some going by land and some by boat. Bartholomew went on to Zobraba of the great maize fields and to Cateba of the fire-scarred cacique. They heard of caciques inland who had much gold, but no mention was made of seeing any placer. More mirrors and patens were traded, and the Spaniards were well received and well fed. It was noted that the principal men were addicted to chewing a dry herb, with which they mixed a certain powder (coca taken with lime). The reconnaissances undertaken were to the west and south of the Río Belén, in order to get a closer look at the country which, they had been told the previous fall, held the secret of gold. This coast of fifty leagues and the mountain streams that discharged into it constituted thereafter what the Spaniards called Veragua.

The Adelantado had found "on all that coast no port or river greater than that of Belén for settlement." As soon as he got back, "they began to build houses on the banks of the Río Belén at a lombard shot from its mouth, above a cove on the right-hand side as one enters the river." The houses were built of wood, their roofs thatched with palm leaves from trees on the beach (perhaps *Manicaria* palms of the coastal swamp, rather than of the beach as Ferdinand indicated). A large house was built to serve as storehouse and arsenal and was stocked with munitions and food. Fishing gear in variety was stored, because of the abundance of fish and the limited availability of land game. The Adelantado was designated to remain in charge of eighty men and one of the ships. Such was the founding of Santa María de Belén, the most ephemeral of the settlements made by Columbus, existing for less than two months from the start of its building.

The hospitality of the Indians turned to apprehension when they saw that the Spaniards were preparing to remain. The Spaniards were worried by the bar that shut off exit to the sea. Also they had become suspicious of the natives. Ferdinand in innocent candor entitled his 97th chapter: "As to how for greater security of the Christian settlement the Quibio was captured with many principal Indians." He explained: "At that time it was known through the interpreter that the Quibio or cacique of Veragua had decided to come secretly to burn the houses and kill the Christians because it weighed greatly on all the Indians that these should settle on that river. It appeared that to chastise him and as an example and to put dread into the neighboring people, it was desirable to take him with all his principal men and send them to Castile, and that his people should stay in the service of the Christians." The Adelantado went to the pueblo of Veragua, found the cacique waiting to do the honors as host, seized him by a ruse, captured the greater part of his numerous household, and hauled them off as prisoners. The Adelantado stayed behind to loot the gold in the residence of the Quibio. The booty was divided among the participants after the royal fifth had been set aside. The affair was described at length by Ferdinand. Porras reported that the Admiral ordered the seizure of the cacique "whereby much injury was done, as they burned his settlement, which was the best on that coast and of the best houses, of very good timber, all covered with palm thatch, and they took his children and have brought some of them here [to Spain] whereby all that country was scandalized." The action had its precedents in Española and on eastern Tierra Firme, and was a usual procedure.

The local breed was tougher than that of the islands. Some of the captives escaped by swimming a distance of a league to shore from the ship on which they had been confined. The cacique got away. The aroused natives forced the abandonment of Santa María in the space of two weeks. One ship was left there, riddled by shipworms. The other three sailed on April 16, and one of these was soon lost for the same reason. The remaining two lasted until they reached Jamaica. Thus ended the final attempt of Columbus to found a colony. Years later, when the claims of his heirs were settled, they were given the title of dukes of Veragua, a land their ancestor was unable to hold and which they never saw or had benefit of.

COLUMBUS' LETTER FROM JAMAICA

The comprehensive account that was ordered in the instructions to Columbus apparently was never written. Ferdinand had access to some journal that filled in dates between those of the terse *relación* of Porras, as Peter Martyr also may have had. The letter Columbus wrote in Jamaica in July, 1503, is his only known version of the voyage. Written while the party was stranded on that island after the loss of their ships, the letter was given to Diego Méndez as he set out by canoe to get help from Española. The tone of the letter reflects the mood of depression in which Columbus was at the time, being largely lamentations, complaints, and self-pity. As a record of the voyage it is hardly intelligible. Its omissions are numerous and perplexing, and the geographical confusion is vast. The letter of more than six thousand words is concerned only in minor part, and by disconnected passages, with places and people seen. Far more space is given to the weather, which turned bad as they got to the Dominica Passage, and most of the time thereafter was described as terrible beyond belief. Columbus cited Biblical and Apocryphal writ, and a trance in which a voice assured him that all his tribulations were inscribed in marble and that his Creator was testing him for the reward he would have. The information the Crown asked for of a geographic nature was given as bizarre cosmologic theory, hearsay, and least of all description.

In the middle of the letter Columbus confessed his confusion and blamed the weather for it:

> Of my voyage I say: that a hundred and fifty persons were with me, among them many who were capable pilots and mariners: no one can give certain account where I went or came, the reason being obvious. I departed from the above port

of Brazil [Yaquimo]: in Española the storm did not allow me to go by the route I wished, it being necessary to go where the wind wished. At that time I became very ill: no one had navigated to that part [he had done so]. After some days the wind and sea ceased and the storm changed into calm and great currents. I landed at an island called *de las Pozas* [a cay off Jamaica?] and from there went on to the Tierra Firme. No one can give a true account of this, there being no sufficient record, going with the current for so many days without seeing land for so many days. I followed the coast of Tierra Firme, and this was determined by compass and art.

The storm he said drove him to Jamaica and then a fast-running sea to the Jardín de la Reina. When he was able to do so, he sailed to Tierra Firme, where he met terrible contrary wind and current against which he struggled for sixty days to gain seventy leagues, during which time he was unable to enter any harbor, nor did the storm and rain and lightning cease, as though it were the end of the world. And so to Cabo Gracias à Dios.

Porras was a notary, not a navigator, and Ferdinand was a stripling on his first and only major voyage. Neither was confused as to where they were at any time, and they agreed on route and calendar. Porras, who had never been in those parts, knew when they sighted Jamaica and got to a low island "already previously discovered and bordering on the land of Cuba, from which the discovery began." Columbus had been the original discoverer; the island probably was Cayo Largo. It took a large lapse of memory on the Admiral's part to say that they did not know where they were until they turned Cape Gracias à Dios. Why the omission of the Bay Islands, the trading ship, the "river of possession," the people of the long ears? In an unconnected and confused passage in another part of the letter he seems to have had the Honduran coast in mind: "I found another people who eat humans, as the hideousness of their appearance shows. There they say that there are large copper mines. Axes thereof and other objects worked, smelted, and soldered I had and forges with all their apparatus for smithing including crucibles. There they go clothed and in that province I saw large sheets of cotton of very skilled embroidery and others subtly painted in colors by brush." The data can refer only to what he saw on the Mayan coast of Honduras, and its clothed and metal-trading people, whereas east of the "river of possession" were the wild natives who looked ugly enough to be cannibals.

The next places noted were Cariay, Cerebaro, and Veragua. Those of Cariay, he thought, were given to witchcraft; also he mentioned the sepulcher there. The voyage continued south on the trail of gold. "They named many places to me on the seacoast, where they said there were gold and mines, the farthest being Veragua, distant a matter of twenty-five leagues." Having arrived there he expected to send men to the mines, but when sea and wind increased he went on to the port of Bastimentos, which he was forced to enter because of the storm, and then on to Retrete, where he was detained by the cruel weather. On venturing out again he was held by a sea turned to blood, boiling like a caldron over a great fire. He described the fury of the weather as such that the people longed for death as release. They returned to Veragua, although he was not disposed to do so. Such was his explanation for ending the outbound discovery.

The events at Veragua were told by him more or less as in the other accounts, though less clearly. Indian guides took the Spanish party inland to the "mines" and to a high hill. There they were told that there was gold in all directions as far as the horizon, and that the mines extended for twenty days' journey to the west. "One thing I dare to say, for there are many witnesses, and it is that I saw in this land of Veragua greater indications of gold in the first two days than in four years in Española, and that the lands surrounding could not be more beautiful or better cultivated, or the people more cowardly, and a good port and beautiful river, defensible against the world." This despite the fact that in earlier passages he had written of the obstruction of the river by sand bar and the losses suffered by Indian attack.

The Admiral had seen no gold placers. His brother had come back from the interior with the news that there were such and had brought a few samples of gold, hastily picked up. This modest prospect was transformed in the imagination of Columbus into the Golden Chersonese, which Josephus had written was the source of the gold of Solomon. "If this were so, I say that those mines of the Aurea are one and the same as those of Veragua, which, as I have said, extend for twenty days' journey to the west and are at the same distance from the pole and from the equator." (They were at about 9° N.) It had been prophesied that Jerusalem and Zion were to be rebuilt by a Christian, and it had been said that he would come from Spain. His men would be bearing the best news ever brought to Spain.

This rambling and disconnected letter, which I have tried to put into some order, ended with a statement which is also epitaph: "Gold is most excellent; of gold there is formed treasure and with it whoever has it may do what he wishes in this world and come to bring souls into Paradise." These passages are reminiscent of the elation he had felt ten years earlier on the first voyage. At this time he was a castaway on the shores of Jamaica, not knowing how or whether he would get home but having a vision of a golden land in Veragua.

MISSED OPPORTUNITIES

On this last voyage Columbus might well have anticipated Cortés to Mexico and Balboa to the Pacific Ocean. That he did neither is consistent with his conduct and views of earlier years.

The hurricane and its aftermath determined that the voyage of discovery began from a cay off the southern coast of Cuba, known to Columbus from his voyage of eight years earlier. Its identification by Navarrete as Cayo Largo east of the Isle of Pines is acceptable. The storm having passed, the wind at that season should have been briskly from the east or northeast. The Yucatán Channel and the northern tip of Yucatán lie directly west of Cayo Largo. Columbus had previously been on that track nearly to the end of Cuba, at which time he had decided that it was the Mangi coast of southern China. Having no desire to repeat that western route, he turned the ships south into the Caribbean. Porras noted the course as south-southwest. Actually they fell off well to leeward, making Guanaja in the Bay Islands almost due southwest from Cayo Largo.

Here and on the adjacent mainland there was a remarkable opportunity to learn about Mayan civilization, conspicuously advertised by the trading canoe that was returning from the west. In his letter from Jamaica, Columbus identified no location short of Cape Gracias à Dios nor made mention of native ways along the Honduran coast except for the few notes cited above which make sense only if they referred to this area. If he was aware that he had come upon an important discovery he should have told the King and Queen about it. He was in a tight situation on Jamaica from which he was far from sure that he would escape. The letter reads like a last testament as well as a plea for the services he had rendered. Its tone is not one of holding back information but of protest. It would appear that he paid scant attention to what he was seeing, hurried the ships eastward along the Mayan coast without a look to the west, stopped at the river of its eastern limit for the ceremony of possession, and continued the tedious job of beating his way against wind and current to Cape Gracias à Dios. His interest was not in learning about that country but in getting out of it. The naming of the cape declared his relief at coming to the place where he could turn south.

Writing the life of his father after Spain had become a world empire and in support of the family claims to the New World, Ferdinand made this apology: "Although the Admiral had been made aware by that canoe of the great riches, polity, and skills of the people of the western parts of New Spain, nevertheless it seemed to him that since these lands lay to leeward he could sail to them whenever it would be convenient for him to do so and therefore did not wish to go to them; and he followed his intention to discover the strait of Tierra Firme in order to open the navigation of the south which he needed to do to discover the Spice Lands." The son rationalized the objective of his father in terms of insight and purpose that the father did not have. This was a last venture that had been granted Columbus, who at fifty-one was an old man in broken health. Whatever he would do to win another stake had to be gained on this voyage. The coast of Honduras was a chance landfall by accident of weather— his objective lay elsewhere. As in each of his earlier voyages, his interest was directed to the south, not to the west.

The other opportunity for a major discovery came at Cariay, the frontier of another high culture. "There I knew of the mines of gold of the province of Ciamba [Champa] which I was seeking," Columbus wrote. The natives at Puerto Limón owned gold ornaments and gave information that the metal came from elsewhere, in particular out of the south. Therefore Columbus took guides thence to Chiriquí Lagoon and so came to Veragua. While sailing down the coast he heard, perhaps from these same guides, of a

> . . . province of Ciguare which according to them is described as nine days' jour-ney overland to the west; there they say that there is gold in infinite amount and that they wear corals on their heads, heavy bracelets thereof on their feet and arms, and with it ornament and cover seats, chests, and tables. Also they said that the women there wear necklaces hanging from head to shoulders. In this that I am saying all the people of these places agree and say so much that I should be con-tent with the tenth part. Also all knew pimienta [black pepper]. In Ciguare they engage in fairs and merchandise: these people thus declare and they showed me the mode and form they practice in trade. They also say that these ships carry cannon, bows and arrows, swords and cutlasses, and that they go clothed and in

that land are horses, and they engage in war, and wear rich clothing, and they have good houses. Also they say that the sea surrounds Ciguare and that from there it is ten days to the river Ganges. It appears that these lands lie with regard to Veragua as Tortosa is to Fuenterrabia or Pisa to Venice.

Columbus as usual heard too much and used his preconceptions to fill in what he did not understand. Mingled with nonsense, however, are items that fit the Mesoamerican culture that extended from Mexico along the Pacific side of Central America through Costa Rica and well into Panama. Such were the fairs held in an organized manner of trade; the full-length clothing, some of which was sumptuous; body armor of quilted cotton; practice in warfare; and substantial houses. Such a culture did exist on the west side of the mountains, across from Puerto Limón and Almirante Bay. The natives on the Caribbean were well informed of the Pacific side of the Isthmus, as was shown some years later when Spaniards were occupying the Pacific coast. The longest crossing, from Puerto Limón to the Gulf of Nicoya, now followed by the railroad line, required no more than nine days of leisurely travel. A series of peninsulas, almost surrounded by sea, extended from Nicoya to Azuero, any one of which might have been the "province of Ciguare."

It would have been an easy matter to put the Ciguare story to proof. The crews were taking their ease at Puerto Limón and again on Chiriquí Lagoon. In both places the natives were friendly and provisions were ample. The ever-dependable Adelantado could lead a party on land as well as at sea. The Admiral thought enough of the story to elaborate it to King and Queen. He thought the other shore belonged to the Indian Ocean and even construed a sailing distance of ten days to the Ganges. He had indeed been given significant information about another people of artful ways living on the shore of another sea at no great distance. He had embellished the account with trappings of the Orient and the hearsay of infinite gold. And he took no steps to verify what he heard.

THE HARD WAY BACK

After the evacuation of Belén, two weeks were spent in getting to windward on the coast of Panama. One ship had been abandoned at Belén, a second at Portobelo, their bottoms rotted and riddled by shipworms. The remaining two were in little better condition; one of them was the caravel that had been thought unseaworthy at Santo Domingo. The easting course was maintained until the coast fell off southward beyond the Archipelago de las Mulatas, as presently named, with the object of getting as far east as possible before sailing north across the trade wind that would deflect their course to west of north. "We took the route to the north, with the wind and current out of the east, because we tried always to sail as close as possible to the wind" (Ferdinand).

They were carried to the west of Jamaica, first seeing land after ten days: "two very small and low islands, full of turtles so that all that sea appeared strewn with rocks, for which reason those islands were named Tortugas" (Ferdinand). This was the first sighting of the lesser Cayman Islands, at the season when sea turtles congregated there. On May 12, two days later and thirty leagues farther north, they made land at one of the cays of the Jardin de la Reina. By the account of Diego Méndez they continued to the south coast of Cuba, where the villa of Trinidad was later built. Their pilots had done quite well at keeping the wind abeam, having drifted less than two degrees west of their point of departure.

They were, however, little nearer to Santo Domingo than when they had left the Panamanian shore; the hardest part of the return lay ahead of them, upwind all the way. By the Porras account they worked their way to Cabo de Cruz, southernmost point of Cuba. On St. John's Day (June 24), pumping and bailing constantly, they made Puerto Bueno (Dry Harbor) on the north coast of Jamaica. Finding neither people nor drinking water, they went on the next day to Santa Gloria (St. Ann's Bay), where the ships were beached permanently. For the next fourteen months the party was marooned on Jamaica, supported with food and services by the natives. Columbus got back to Sevilla in November, 1504, only days before the death of Isabela.

Although the itinerary and calendar of the voyage are for the most part well established, the letter of Columbus veiled it in obscurity and error. Having said that no one could give a true account of how they got to Tierra Firme, he continued: "There is no one who can say under what part of the heavens or when I left there to come to Española. The pilots believed that the landfall would be made at the island of San Juan [Puerto Rico] and it was in the country of Mango four hundred leagues farther west than they said. Let them answer, if they know, where the location of Veragua is. I say that they can give no other reason or account than that they went to some lands where there is much gold and thus certify; they do not know the route by which to go back there; it would be necessary to discover it anew in order to get there. There is one sure way and means, by astrology; whoever understands this has the means. It is like prophetic vision." On account of the strong currents and wind, he said, ships were obliged to sail with the wind in the Indies, forgetting that in the preceding passage he had stated that the pilots thought they were headed for Puerto Rico, a long upwind passage beyond the possibility of sail at the time. He placed Veragua halfway between equator and pole and referred to Cuba as Mango (Mangi, south China).

The letter is that of man who had taken leave of his senses. Since the letter would pass through unknown hands, reticence about places discovered might be expected, but hardly the misinformation it contained. Diego Porras, in the *relación* he made as notary of the expedition, said that Columbus confiscated the charts that had been made: "The mariners no longer had sailing charts, the Admiral having taken them away from everyone." The statement might be dismissed as coming from one who was hostile to the Admiral, having been involved in the revolt in Jamaica. Pedro Mateos, who was called to testify in their behalf by the heirs of Columbus, deposed that "he wrote a book which contained all the sierras and rivers he had seen in the said province . . . and the Admiral afterward took it from him." [13] There could be no secret of Veragua with so many men. When some of these came again on later voyages the locations of Belén, Veragua, Portobelo, and others were recognized. The Lagoon of Cerebaro became the Bahía del Almirante, which it still is.

---

[13] CDI, XXXIX, 416.

THE SAME IMAGE AND OBJECTIVE

The last voyage retained the preconceptions of the first. Columbus had forgotten nothing and learned little. His letter adds almost no information about native ways. At Cariay he considered the people to be great wizards and noted in two lines the tomb his brother had visited, followed by fifteen lines about a fight between an Irish dog and some captured animals.

His knowledge of geographical position and celestial navigation had not improved.[14] He discoursed on the cosmography of Ptolemy and Marinus of Tyre, and reduced the ocean to a seventh of the earth's surface. Josephus was authority for the source of the wealth of Solomon and David. His image of the world experienced little rearrangement. The earth was of such size that the western shores he had found were the eastern shores of Asia. Latitudes were strangely arranged, such as a Caribbean place halfway between pole and equator. Cathay lay off to the north and west, remaining beyond his horizon as it did on the first voyage. Mangi, or South China, he had placed in Cuba and there it stayed, although Cosa and others had represented Cuba as an island. On this final voyage he made place for Champa of southern Indochina in Central America. The Malay Peninsula—Golden Chersonese, or Aurea, as he called it—was identified with Veragua.

The Asiatic identifications involved a strait to the south of the Malay Peninsula, named Catigara and thought to lie somewhat below the equator. That there was such a sea passage between India and China was generally known. Marco Polo had returned through it. Arab merchant ships met and traded goods with vessels of Indochina and China along a sea route around the southeast of Asia. Columbus knew of Catigara and had asked for persons who spoke Arabic to go on this voyage.

The search for such a strait had been one of the objectives of Spanish voyages for several years. If the new lands were in Asia, such a strait would be found not far from the equator. Each returning expedition, however, enlarged the known extent of a continuous Tierra Firme to the south. Facing on the Atlantic, this austral continent had become known from the Gulf of Paria around the shoulder of Brazil into South Temperate latitudes. Along the south shore of the Caribbean it had been run out west to the Gulf of Urabá. Vespucci had looked for the strait of Catigara well beyond the tropic along the south Atlantic coast and found none. This and his determinations of longitude decided Vespucci that Tierra Firme was part of a new world, a fact Peter Martyr appears to have suspected all along.

Columbus was in fact putting his grand assertion of the Indies to the crucial test by sailing south from Honduras. If there was no strait between Honduras and Urabá, where he was headed, he was not on an Asiatic shore. Columbus had geographic notions convenient to his world image, but he did not think of them as subject to proof or disproof. He carried no instructions to search for a strait, but we may accept that he did so as others had been doing. The statement

---

[14] E. G. R. Taylor in Cecil Jane, *The Voyages of Christopher Columbus*, II (London, 1930), lxxvi–lxxxiv.

of his son that his father was thus engaged can be discounted, for it was written well after the outline and position of the New World and the Pacific Ocean were known. It is supported, however, by the account Porras kept during the voyage, that Columbus went on from Cariay "and as he proceeded inquiring into ports and bays, thinking to find the strait he came to a very great bay," Cerebaro (Almirante). Also, Juan de Noya testified in the Pleitos that they returned along the coast from Portobelo "looking for the Spice Lands and never found them." Thus the search for the strait was concentrated on the coast between Puerto Limón and Portobelo, the lowest latitudes reached, and the region the Admiral thought to be the Golden Chersonese. He was looking in the proper sector if this was Asia.

Instead of a strait of the sea, Ferdinand said that his father found a strait of land, which was true, though it canceled out the imagined Asiatic geography. As they approached Cariay from the north they saw high mountains inland, which seemed even higher in the dim tropical air. From there along the coast of Veragua they sailed by the base of a continuous mountain range, gradually decreasing in height eastward into the hills of the Canal Zone. On the far side of the mountains they had been told that there was another sea from which Columbus thought it would be a clear and short voyage to the Ganges. The Golden Peninsula had become an isthmus. The strait did not exist where it must have been if this were Asia.

It was not to the end of discovering the strait that the voyage was undertaken nor did the proof of his error enter the mind of Columbus. He returned in the belief that he found the Golden Chersonese. As it had been from the first landing on the Bahamas, gold was what he wanted, the gold that admitted souls to Paradise. On this last occasion as on the first, south was the direction in which gold would be found. He found it in Veragua in ornaments obtained by trade and loot. His brother brought back a sample of native gold from a place inland to which the natives went to dig for it. This slight promise Columbus expanded into gold mines that extended for twenty days' journey. According to the register kept by Diego de Porras, two hundred twenty pieces of gold and twelve of guanín had been secured by trade, and various items of loot taken from the cacique Veragua. No raw gold was noted. The total amount was a little more than seventeen marks, or a hundred twenty ounces of gold and guanín objects. The expedition had cost a good deal and paid a trifling return.

EPILOGUE BY THE ADELANTADO

After the death of the Admiral in May, 1506, Bartholomew went to Rome, hoping to get support for an expedition of his own. Nothing came of it except a long-lost and somewhat indirect account. He gave a certain friar in the Lateran a sketch and description of what he had seen on the voyage to Veragua, the time of his visit being late in 1506 or in the following year. The friar passed the material on to a patrician of Venice, Alessandro Zorzi, or Strezzi, who was engaged in collecting accounts of voyages. When Bartholomew's description was incorporated into the Zorzi Codex is uncertain, but it was not later than

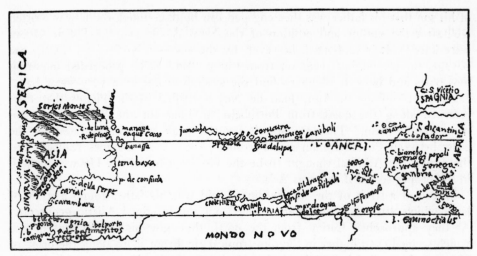

Fig. 18. Sketch map from the Zorzi Codex.

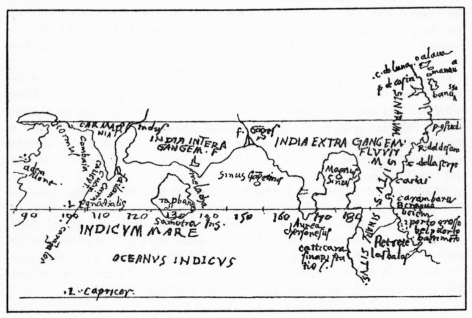

Fig. 19. Sketch map from the Zorzi Codex.

1525.[15] Neither the *Informatione* nor the sketch maps are unaltered copies of what Bartholomew gave to the friar. The text reverses the order of the journey, beginning on the coast of Panama and ending at the Bay Islands. The first and second sketch maps (figs. 18, 19) overlap and disagree in the orientation of the coast of Central America.

[15] The Italian text (*Informatione*) of Bartholomew was published in 1868 by Henry Harrisse in his *Bibliotheca americana vetustissima* (New York, 1866). The sketch maps that went with the text were reproduced by Fr. v. Wieser in 1893 (*Mitt. Inst. Österr. Geschichtsforschung*, Ergänzungsband IV). George W. Nunn wrote a critique, "The Three Maplets Attributed to Bartholomew Columbus," in *Imago Mundi*, IX (Stockholm, 1952), 12–22.

What we have is at third hand, but is the imperfectly recorded voice and hand of Bartholomew. Allowing for the reversal of the voyage, the information supports that of Ferdinand and Porras. It antedates by years the history by Ferdinand. The Porras *Relación* then and long after was an unknown document filed away in a Spanish archive. The *Informatione* of Bartholomew was not derived from either of these sources. Nor was it adapted from the Jamaica letter of the Admiral, first published in Italian in 1505 and known as *Lettera Raríssima*. The Admiral's letter named no place between Jardín de la Reina and Cape Gracias à Dios. The Bartholomew version has Bonassa (Bonacca, alternative name for the island of Guanaja), names for two other Bay Islands, Cape Caxinas, *terra baxa* for the low plain to the west of Gracias à Dios (here called p. de consuela, which has about the same meaning), and other places, the copyist of the maps having some language difficulty.

Of Cariay the text said that it is "inhabited by people of a good sort who live by their industry and engage in trade as is done in the province called Maia"; also, "we saw a sepulcher with its cubical vault above, on which were carved animals of diverse kinds." Bartholomew led this excursion and contributed an archaeologic note on the box-shaped stone cysts found in Costa Rica and Panama, later sought by grave robbers for their gold ornaments. At Bonacca (Guanaja) and on the adjacent mainland, "the sustenance is chiefly a certain white grain of the size of a *cesare* [Cicer, chiche, or chick-pea] and grows just as it does in the Balearic Islands, in ears (*panochie*), from which they make a superior bread." This adds another early reference to maize and a maize bread which was white and excellent, perhaps the first experience of the tasty maize tortillas. *Panochie* is Italian of the time for ears of maize, like the Spanish *panoja* and Catalan *panotxa*. The identification with a grain known in the Balearic Islands adds another bit to the evidence that maize was in familiar early cultivation in parts of the Mediterranean.

The text has an introductory statement by Zorzi that Bartholomew gave the friar "a design by his hand of the shores of such lands whereon were described and placed the conditions and nature and customs and habits of those people and the said friar Jerome being in their charity monastery in Venice, being a friend of mine, gave me the said design and also gave me in writing the conditions and peoples of those lands." The text that follows is in the third person. Both text and sketches thus were adaptations. Neither indicate revision to agree with later knowledge. Zorzi, like Peter Martyr before and Ramusio after him, was a compiler of travel accounts as received. The sketches he reproduced were of a geography that was no longer current; they and they alone represent the visionary map of Columbus as presented through the brother.

The sketch maps from the facsimile of Wieser (figs. 18, 19) are by different hands, the second the better informed. The first, with Italianized spelling and copyist's misspelling, construed a connection between the southern mainland (here labeled MONDO NOVO) and ASIA by an isthmus extending from Retrete, by way of Portobelo and Cerebaro to Cariay. Beyond the isthmus a land of the Chinese (SINARUM SITUS) extended northward to north China (SERICA), the mountains of which ran down as far as the Honduran coast. To the west of the isthmus was the great gulf (*sinus magnus*). The second sketch overlaps the western part of the first, and its orientation is better. It shows the isthmus as part of China, with Catigara on the west side, well below the equator as Ptolemy had it, the equator being wildly displaced on both maps. Beyond the Magnus Sinus is India. The width of the Magnus Sinus is ten degrees, which kept the sailing distance from the Pacific shore of the isthmus to India within the possibility of the ten days Columbus had inferred. The fantastic design of land and sea fits the ideas of Columbus. Bartholomew cannot have given description or sketch to the friar later than 1507, after which he was in Spain or Española. If the Adelantado deferred to his brother in matters of geography, this is about what he would have conveyed to the friar in the Lateran. A non- or post-Columbian map could hardly have been that bad. The part covering the discoveries of the fourth voyage carries only place names of that voyage, some of which were not known later. Such as it is, the sketch is the cartographic representation of that discovery as communicated by the alternate in command.

VII

ORGANIZATION OF THE INDIES

(1502–1509)

•

The prospect for the Indies had improved by 1502. Bobadilla had quieted the Spaniards on Española, had no Indian troubles, and had shown that the placers could yield good returns. There was a Pearl Coast on Tierra Firme where the natives had good pearls in abundance and engaged in trade with others to the west, exchanging pearls for objects of fabricated gold. Bastidas and Cosa had gone to discover whence this gold came. There was good brazilwood on the mainland and the promise of gems. Licenses were in demand for trading ventures which would share their profits with the Crown and defrayed their own costs. Only the title of Admiral was left to Columbus but he was permitted to sail once more to see what he might discover. Frey Nicolás de Ovando, Commander of the military order of Alcántara, proven in long and capable service, was named to succeed Bobadilla as Governor.

THE OVANDO GOVERNMENT (1502–1509)

Ovando arrived at Santo Domingo in mid-April, 1502, with about twenty-five hundred persons, some to serve in administration, some intended to be settlers, and again a good many at loose ends. At the time there were around three hundred Spaniards on the island, about the same number as when Columbus was removed two years before, a minor remnant of the total who had come in the decade since discovery.

Santo Domingo had port facilities, offices of administration, military personnel, and a number of vecinos and their Indian servants. Some Spaniards were living at Concepción de la Vega, others at Santiago, and a few at Bonao. Still others were scattered about in Indian communities, living where and as they pleased through the midsection of the island, and having access to the two mining districts.

The landing of the multitude of newcomers put an immediate strain on the island economy. Among them were soldiers who had been mustered out, impecunious young gentlemen, civil officials, artisans, and a few religious. A beginning

147

was made at bringing in families, and for the first time Española became a permanent home for some emigrant Spaniards instead of a tour of duty or a passing adventure. Times were again bad in Spain, apparently more so than usual, and people were ready to take their chances at bettering their fortunes overseas. Also the relaxed administration of Bobadilla had produced returns from the gold fields by freer access. Española was again thought of as a land of some promise. More people flocked to join Ovando than there was need of or provision for.

Many of the newcomers rushed promptly to the gold fields. Sickness broke out among the arrivals, and mortality was high. Las Casas, who was one of the newcomers, said that a thousand died and more became ill. The gold diggings had been taking heavy toll of natives, and were rated by Las Casas as a major cause of native deaths; according to his information, a fourth to a third of the work gangs died in each *demora*, the period of six to eight months they were forced to work in the mines. The diggings were of small extent and were in nearly continuous occupation by large numbers of laborers, who, according to Las Casas, were subject to fevers.[1] The crowding of workers without sanitation in humid tropical tracts gave excellent conditions to contaminate water and soil, breeding places for enteric disease. As Spaniards moved into these camps, they also sickened and many died. At a guess, there may have been about fifteen hundred Spaniards on the island at the end of 1502.

The fleet that brought the colonists had scarcely left when the notorious great hurricane sank most of the ships and razed the town of Santo Domingo. Ovando promptly set about rebuilding, and moved the town to the opposite side of the river where it now stands. The new town was laid out on a larger scale and in rectangular pattern, with masons, carpenters, and tile workers engaged to build it after the Spanish manner. The hurricane gave Ovando the opportunity to employ the skilled labor he had brought, resulting in an adequate and permanent town on a new planned site.

Ovando had been given elaborate and emphatic instructions on the good treatment of the natives, the Crown being informed of the abuses to which they had been subjected.[2] The instructions did not take into account what to do in the event of an uprising. Columbus had engaged in violent "pacification" and gotten into trouble back home because he used force to capture and sell slaves. Ovando avoided such a step, but soon found occasion to use violence, first by punitive reprisal and then by preventive action against what he construed as threat of uprising. Where Columbus had bungled, Ovando found the legitimizing terms in the suppression of revolt and the anticipation of treason. Commander of a military religious order, his vows laid no obligation of humanity upon him.

Wishing to find out where a port should be established on the north coast, Ovando sent a party to sail around the eastern end of the island. It stopped at the island of Saona, as was usual, in order to load cassava, which the natives there were accustomed to provide to ships. A local cacique was supervising the loading when one of the party in wanton mischief sicked a mastiff at him to see what would happen. (Columbus had introduced dogs trained to attack natives.) The dog killed the chief and an Indian revolt and flight developed. This gave Ovando

---

[1] Las Casas, Bk. II, ch. 40.
[2] CDI, XXXI, 13 ff.

the opportunity to march a contingent into the southeast, with young Las Casas as a member of the levy. In the "pacification" the island of Saona was wholly depopulated and has so remained ever since. Numerous captives were taken in the peninsula of Higüey, the "queen" of Higüey was slain, and her successor agreed to a treaty of peace, an unusual feature in Spanish-Indian relations. The terms were that Higüey in future was to supply cassava and other food on demand as required at shipboard. At the time the southeastern peninsula had not been placed under repartimiento. Perhaps the native hope was that provisioning ships would forestall such occupation. Ovando put veterans of Columbus in charge of this invasion and these taught the newcomers how to proceed against the natives.

In the autumn of 1503 Ovando marched into the western part of the island, ostensibly to visit Anacaona in Xaragua. Widow of Caonabo and sister of Behechio, who had since died, she was ruler of the west. She and her brother had received Bartholomew Columbus in proffer of friendship and voluntary tribute. Later a tolerable arrangement had been made with Roldán and continued without disruption of the native state. Ovando and his strong and fully equipped military force were welcomed and entertained lavishly by Anacaona and an assembly of subordinate caciques called in for the occasion. The latter numbered scores by one account, hundreds by another. In the midst of the festivities Ovando gave the signal for the massacre; those of higher rank in the regal bohío were burned with the bohío, and those of lesser rank outside were cut to pieces. The queen was reserved for a decent hanging. Diego Méndez, seeking help for the Columbus party that was then stranded in Jamaica, found Ovando at Xaragua and witnessed the act by which Ovando "caused to be burned and hanged eighty-four caciques, lords of vassals, and with them Anacaona, the first señora of the island, whom all obeyed and served." Oviedo, in apology for the crime, said that Ovando had expectation of a treasonable uprising. Thus ended the western state which for years had preserved itself, meeting the demands of the strangers. Diego Veláz-quez, one of the two captains in charge of the massacre, went on to ravage and subjugate the independent cacicazgos of the southwestern peninsula of Gua-cayarima and so to extend Spanish rule over all the west of the island. He re-mained in charge in the west as deputy of Ovando and later applied this experi-ence to destroy the native structure and people of Cuba.

The southeastern peninsula was wholly overrun in 1504 in the so-called war of Higüey. In it the last major cacique of the island was eliminated. The operation was led by Juan de Esquivel and Hernán Ponce de León, both veterans of Columbus. Esquivel later took Jamaica and destroyed it. Ponce de León did the same for Puerto Rico, but then tried it once too often on the tougher natives of Florida.

Ovando had executive ability and left his stamp upon the island. The principal effort and success of his first two years was to gain control of the entire island, which he did by breaking its native political structure. The major chiefs were liquidated along with many of the lesser ones, and the rest were reduced to the status of overseers. The repartimiento that Roldán had forced upon Columbus was developed into the general means of control of natives. Ovando named the beneficiaries and if these did not satisfy him the benefices were given to another.

As Commander of the Order of Alcántara he had administered encomiendas in Spain; he now became the principal architect of the encomienda system of the New World.[3]

The political economy was brutally simple. All the natives were given into the charge of individual Spaniards or assigned to the Crown, some for personal service, most to forced labor in field or mine. There were instructions and admonitions from Spain that the Indians were subjects of the Crown who had rights as well as duties, that they might be required to work but only under proper care and limitations, and at just wages. These prescriptions may have been given in good faith, but they meant nothing in the island. There was no check on the kind or extent of native subjection to their masters. Some Indians in the northwestern part fled to Cuba, which was still unreduced; others escaped into wilder parts of the mountains. Most were hopelessly trapped, to be used at whatever forced labor was required. There was no one to stay the hand of the governor nor did he temper the conduct of the Spanish vecinos.

In Spain the Queen was on her deathbed and died before the island was fully parceled out. The King had the grave problem of succession to the throne of Isabela. Also, his main interest in the Indies was to get revenue, as was that of Fonseca. Ovando was reminded repeatedly of the need for revenue and held it his principal duty to provide it.

Ovando organized the production of gold in such a manner that the Crown profited by honest accounting and the vecinos also prospered. The two gold districts of Cibao and San Cristóbal were brought into much larger production by increasing the incentive. This was done by reducing the royal share from one-half to one-fifth[4] and by awarding the licenses to mine to those who produced the most gold. All minerals were the property of the Crown; the right to exploit them was given by the governor.

The governor also controlled the apportionment of natives. To be a successful entrepreneur, one needed to be granted a sufficient number of Indians. Next, one obtained a license to mine or sublet one's Indians to someone who had a mining license. The grantee could send his Indians from anywhere in the island to work in the mines. The governor kept watch over the returns, rewarding the successful producer by allotting more Indians, and taking away from those who got less out of their natives.

This system of reward and denial unfortunately took no account of the conservation of the labor force, but subjected the native population to destructive exploitation. The fewer Indians there were, the more they were in demand, to be worked harder. The demora was instituted as a protective device, limiting to six or eight months a year the time a work gang could be employed in the mines. For the rest of the year they were returned to their own community to care for their conucos; the one-to-one or two-to-one ratio of mining to crop-growing time thought adequate to sustain the production of both gold and food.

Gold was almost the sole export of the island and sustained the internal commerce. Foodstuffs, especially cassava bread, were supplied to the mines in large

[3] Ursula Lamb, *Frey Nicolas de Ovando, governador de las Indias* (Madrid, 1956), has documented and evaluated Spanish polity of the time and its application by Ovando in Española.
[4] *Ibid.*, p. 167

amount and to provision ships. Santo Domingo grew to respectable size and wealth and became a market of importance. The repartimientos far from Santo Domingo or the mines might not be in a position to transport foodstuffs, but they could profit by sending work gangs to the mines. The system of demora thereby exposed all parts of the island to similar pressure on the natives.

THE FOUNDING OF VILLAS

In his original instructions (September 16, 1501) Ovando was told to found new towns: "It is necessary to establish some settlements and it being impossible to determine from here their proper form, you shall inspect the places and sites on said island and according to the quality of land, place, and people in addition to the present pueblos you shall undertake to establish others in the number that seems proper to you, in the places and locations that seem proper." The instruction continued: "Because it is our pleasure that the Christians living in said island or who may live there in the future shall not live dispersed and that none shall live outside of the places to be founded, anyone may be permitted to have on his property (heredad) a hut or small house in which to lodge when he goes to visit or work his property." [5]

This is the first outline of segregation of Spanish and Indian communities that was to be prescribed for Spanish America. Christians were not to live dispersed about the country. This rule was observed more or less throughout Spanish America. Soon the Spanish community became a villa, and the name "pueblo" was limited to an Indian settlement. The villa was an organized community governed by a council (cabildo) with officials holding office for a term. The vecino was a citizen of a particular villa at which he was expected to reside and in the affairs of which he participated. Commonly the villa governed its own affairs and elected its own officials. The villa also had control of surrounding territory. Ovando placed those who held repartimientos or encomiendas into villas; most of the island was divided among these villas except for the Crown reserves of mineral lands and the baldios of waste and uninhabited land.

The political geography before Ovando is obscure and was undefined. The securing of repartimientos and rights of vecindad that Roldán forced on Columbus did not involve setting up local government or living in villas. Ovando was instructed to found an adequate lot of towns and to concentrate the Christians within them. The subjugation of the western and eastern parts of the island gave opportunity to provide for many who had come with him. The previously occupied middle of the island he also thus reorganized. The results were ratified in 1508 by the royal designation of coats of arms for fifteen such corporations,[6] the greatest number reached in the history of Española. The location of these fifteen towns is shown in figure 20. The copy of the Morales map in the Duke of Alba collection depicts all fifteen embellished with imaginary towers and battlements of medieval Spain. However, it does place the villas in terms of the good cartographic knowledge of Morales. Since the location of a number of them is

---

[5] CDI, XXXI, 17, 18.
[6] CDI, I, 15 ff.

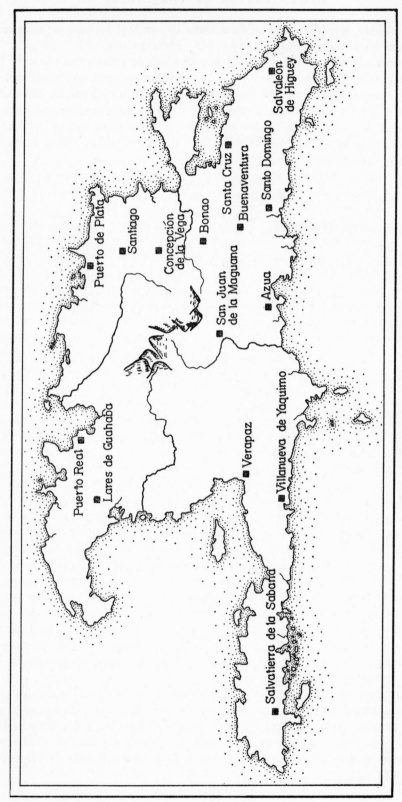

Fig. 20. The fifteen towns of Española.

unknown today, it is preferable to show them on the Morales base rather than to place them on a modern map.

The order of the establishment of the towns awaits antiquarian research. For the most part they were set up in 1504 and 1505, soon after the "pacification." The first town Ovando is known to have founded replaced Xaragua, the Indian capital of the west which he had destroyed. To it he gave the ironical name of Santa María de la Vera Paz. It was situated near the western end of the lake of Xaragua (Etang Saumâtre). So far as I know, neither the great Indian town nor its Spanish replacement has been rediscovered.

About midway between it and Santo Domingo, Ovando set up Azua de Compostela on the south coast, some ten miles to the southwest of the present town of Azua, on the sheltered bay of Puerto Viejo de Azua.

Villanueva de Yaquimo (Jacmel) was built at the harbor where the Adelantado and later Hojeda loaded cargoes of brazilwood. Far out on the southwestern peninsula of Guacayarima, Salvatierra de la Sabana was located on the Bay of Les Cayes. Peter Martyr reported it as a "colony with a port, called Zavana, located in a swampy plain good for cattle and horses, with a river overflowing the plain that brings quantities of eels which are stranded as the flood goes down. From these the holds of ships are filled and especially the settlers turn out their hogs to fatten thereon." [7] Salvatierra was the home of Balboa and of Diego Velázquez. The latter as lieutenant of Ovando in the west was his agent in founding villas there and settling vecinos. It was from Salvatierra that Velázquez set out, accompanied by its vecinos, to subjugate Cuba.

The new villas of the west were situated to gain control of the most populous Indian districts. Thus San Juan de la Maguana, the former seat of the cacique Caonabo, was in an attractive position, having a very fertile basin, an abundance of Indians, and access to the gold districts to the east. In the northern interior of the present Republic of Haiti the native province of Guahaba was reported to be very populous and had remained almost undisturbed. The villa founded there was named Lares de Guahaba, in honor of the governor's commandery in Extremadura. When López de Velasco compiled the official Geografía de las Indias in the 1570's, he knew the name but found no memory of where it had been. I know no other approximation than its position on the Morales map. On the northwest coast Puerto Real (Cap Haïtien) was built near the seat of Guacanagari, where Columbus had first been welcomed to the fertile plain of Marien.

The seven new villas founded by Ovando in the west represented the Spanish appropriation of the former realm of Bainoa and of the southwestern peninsula, in part previously undisturbed country, in part having been subject to lesser and passing exactions by the Adelantado, Roldán, and Hojeda. Ovando's massacre of the caciques assembled by Anacaona was prelude to the assignment of the natives of the west to the villas-to-be.

The appropriation of the southeast, henceforth known as Higüey, followed the same pattern. After the "war of Higüey" two villas were set up, both very uncertain as to their location, for they flourished briefly, while their Indians lasted. The map of Morales is the best guide. It places Santa Cruz de la Haniguayana in the vicinity of modern Sabana de la Mar, and Salvaleón de Higüey to

---

[7] Peter Martyr, Decade VII, Bk. 9.

the coastward of present Higüey, perhaps to the south. These two villas are of some interest because Juan de Esquivel and Ponce de León were their leading vecinos and left from them with their companions to seek greener fields in Puerto Rico and Jamaica.

A port on the north coast was needed to replace Isabela. Puerto Plata was the proper choice, although the Indian population in the back country had been depleted by raids of the time of Columbus. The remaining new foundation was that of Buenaventura of the upper Río Haina, where the San Cristóbal mines were producing well. A mint was established there to smelt, stamp, and account for the gold produced. For the Cibao gold region, Concepción de la Vega also was provided with a mint and given status as a villa, and the preëxisting Spanish centers of Santiago and Bonao were organized into villas.

The distribution of the fifteen Spanish towns outlines the economic geography of the island at its economic peak, from 1505 to 1508. Santo Domingo, confirmed as capital, was commodious of harborage, convenient for overseas and coastal shipping, at the terminus of the one good land route leading north across the island and passing near both gold fields, and also hub of the roads leading west to Xaragua and to Maguana. In Ovando's time it took on the appearance of the first city of the New World with rectangular blocks, public buildings, and houses of masonry. Buenaventura and Concepción were headquarters for the business of gold mining and storage places for the gold produced, which was smelted and stamped there twice a year and paid the Royal Fifth. The revival of the Cibao gold field, which supported Concepción, was due to the production of fine gold—so fine as to pour through a salt shaker. The inference is that experienced Spanish placer miners were reworking the crude diggings of earlier years for finely disseminated gold.

Concepción, Santiago, and Bonao had superior land for conucos and good pasture for increasing numbers of livestock. Puerto Plata was a minor port, but was needed as a safe shelter on the north coast for ships returning to Spain; the Mona Passage was used for the return voyage, and Puerto Plata was usually the last port of call before crossing the Atlantic.

The seven new villas of the west were profitable mainly as sources of labor for the mining districts. There was a brief flurry of mining in the mountain country behind Puerto Real, including discovery of copper. Yaquimo occasionally shipped brazilwood, which had been reserved to the Crown. Most of the western villas were too far from the mines and from Santo Domingo to carry food overland, and they were at the leeward end of the island, which made transport by ship tedious or impossible.

The two southeastern villas had the advantage of limestone lands prized for producing cassava, which was loaded on ships or carried overland to the capital and mines. From here, also, work gangs could be taken conveniently to the mines.

The effort to encourage families to settle seems to have had some success with artisans and tradesmen, to the benefit of Santo Domingo in particular. Las Casas pointed out that those who got out of line would find themselves placed on the next ships that were homeward bound or were warned that such would happen. Las Casas also agreed that, bad as the administration was for the Indians, it was competent in looking after the interests of the Crown and of the Spaniards. The three hundred whites at the arrival of Ovando were said to have increased to eight to ten thousand at the end of his administration. Española had become a place of opportunity where people found life overseas desirable.

Under Ovando the entrepreneur retained four-fifths of the gold; more competent methods of recovery had been introduced, and the demora was well organized. Except for the original Cotuí, a district high in the mountains to the southwest of Bonao, and a little activity behind Puerto Real, there was negligible discovery of new gold-bearing areas. Fortunes were also made by trade, the merchant Nicuesa having accumulated the wealth that gave him the means to undertake the colonization of Castilla del Oro in 1509. Litigation was active and profitable; the lawyer Enciso thus invested his gains at the same time in the Darién venture of Hojeda. Bastidas, discoverer of Urabá, transferred his residence from Sevilla to Santo Domingo and prospered in business to become rich and respected and keep his good name. Capital that had been accumulated on the island in this period of Spanish prosperity financed in the main the occupation of Tierra Firme.

ACCELERATED DECLINE OF NATIVE POPULATION

The administration of Columbus reduced the native population in part by ineptness, in part by violent, ill-considered measures. The Admiral had no Indian policy other than his unworkable tribute system. Also, his operations were limited mostly to the midsection of the island. Ovando, in contrast, put into effect an efficient organization step by step, subjugating the entire island, eliminating the caciques, and allocating all natives to encomenderos or the Crown. The system of demora kept the mines supplied with work gangs. The Spaniards were assembled into villas. Española was converted into a Spanish colony in which the vecinos prospered and from which the Crown had steady and good income.

The operation was maintained by treating the natives as expendable. After his return from Española to Spain at the end of 1504, Columbus petitioned the King for restoration of his rights. Las Casas quoted the Admiral as saying, "the Indians of this island of Española were and are its riches, for it is they who dig and produce the bread and other food for the Christians and get the gold from the mines for the latter, and perform all the services and labor of men and of draft animals. He says [Las Casas continued] that he is informed that six out of seven of its Indians have died since he left the island." [8] However exaggerated such loss of native population between 1500 and 1504, Columbus was shocked by the change since his last sight of the island, and he was right in saying that the fortunes of Española depended on its natives.

Las Casas was of the opinion that between 1494 and 1508 more than three million souls had perished on the island—slain in war, sent to Castile as slaves, or been consumed in the mines and other labors. "Who of those born in future centuries will believe this? I myself who am writing this and saw it and know most about it can hardly believe that such was possible." Whatever the validity of his estimate, Las Casas had come with Ovando, taken part in the subjugation, held a grant in the Cibao, and witnessed the native decline.

---

[8] Las Casas, Bk. II, ch. 37.

In anticipation of the recall of Ovando, Miguel de Pasamonte was sent as Royal Treasurer, arriving in November, 1508, to be for some years in fact if not by title in control. Las Casas reported him as "having counted all the *Indios* in this island as sixty thousand persons." [9] Since all the natives were in encomienda, an approximate count of their numbers was readily available and would have been those of an age suited for service, presumably, as Columbus had done. All fifteen Spanish villas were still in existence at the time, in fact had been given their coats of arms that year, as if they were expected to be enduring communities. Letters from the King to Pasamonte and Ovando in May, 1509, expressed concern about the scarcity of natives, the one to Ovando saying "all those over there write me that there are very few Indians in this island of Española." To remedy the shortage he authorized bringing in Indians from other islands.

By the end of Ovando's regime, fifteen years from the start at Isabela, it was apparent that Española was at a crisis. An administration of more than ordinary ability had lost sight of the longer perspective. The piety of Ovando had no quality of mercy for the natives, nor was he concerned with treating them as a permanent asset. The fatal weakness was that the governor requested the allotment of Indians for the purpose of keeping up the production of gold. Work gangs were taken into the mining districts from the farthest parts of the island. The time they were assigned to work in the mines, the demora, at first six months, was soon lengthened to eight, and eventually was without limit. The fewer the natives became, the more were they in demand. The gold placers, being of limited extent, required deeper digging and closer reworking, more units of work for each unit of return. Diminishing productivity of the placers had to be met by more labor as the labor supply grew shorter. The accelerating decline of the natives threatened disaster at the time of greatest prosperity of Española.

INCREASE OF LIVESTOCK

The livestock on Española were said to grow and reproduce better than in Europe and to need no attention. The growing season of pasture was year long. There were palatable grasses in the savannas, one of which, a fine thatch, Las Casas thought the stock destroyed. Other grasses and herbs were introduced accidentally by ships. As the natives declined, conucos were abandoned and became pastures. There were no native predators. The island was clean of stock diseases and parasites. Española was the earliest example, and an outstanding one, of the ease of stocking an island with grazing and browsing animals.

"In 1507 the King authorized the free use of the many pasture lands which he had been informed existed in Española" and at the same time Ovando stated that no more mares were needed for breeding.[10] The island was open range, populous with cattle, horses, and pigs. What Columbus had begun, Ovando made into the second business of the colony, which in contrast to the gold mines required little labor beyond marking the stock as to ownership and rounding it up from time to time to take what was wanted. The pattern of livestock ranching for the New World was formed here. The particular herd, called *hato*, usually of *ganado*

---

[9] *Ibid.,* ch. 42
[10] Lamb, *op. cit.,* pp. 171, 173, 183.

mayor, that is, cattle and horses, was private property; the grazing land at first was not. Owning a herd became enjoyment of grazing rights and these in turn became land titles. How hato changed its meaning from herd to landed property is in need of study. The term "rancho" was unknown in the islands. Parts of the free range were preëmpted by individual owners of herds and these became a new, perhaps the first, lot of landed proprietors.

The island was most congenial to the hardy range hogs introduced from the Canaries and Spain. They rooted out the plants in the conucos, wandered into the piny woods, and found sustenance from seashore to mountains. Because of their fecundity and ability to fend for themselves they soon became feral; licenses to hunt wild pigs were issued as early as 1508. William Gabb, in his geological reconnaissance of the interior mountains of 1870, wrote of encountering mountain folk who were hunters of wild pigs: "the noblest game is the long-legged, long-nosed, slabsided porker, who with ears and bristles erect, and the last kink taken from his corkscrew tail, makes his way with a rush and a grunt through the bushes." [11] The breed of such razorbacks is still common about the villages and reportedly still lives wild in the mountains.

There was no problem of sustenance for the Spaniards in Ovando's time. Beef and pork were in abundant supply, as they had not been in Spain, and were available to every villa. The byproducts lard, tallow, and hides, were in surplus and were shipped. Cassava bread had been accepted to replace wheat. The conucos that remained under care were adequate to provide all the breadstuffs needed.

Nothing is heard of a shift to the cultivation of maize, the yield of bitter yuca as cassava being much greater and having the advantage of keeping indefinitely. Garden vegetables, of Spanish introduction, were grown as desired by Indians in household service. The bounty of the land was great from the rapid increase of European livestock and the high productivity of native tillage. Perhaps the phenomenal increase in cattle, horses, and pigs somewhat obscured the fact that these were taking over a land from which the native population was fast disappearing.

ATTENTION TO NEIGHBORING ISLANDS

Ovando was Governor of the Islands and Mainland of the Ocean Sea, bearing the same title that had been given Columbus. Actually both governed only the island of Española. Fonseca had sent parties from Spain setting up token governments in South America. One such had been given to Yáñez Pinzó in 1505 to take charge of San Juan (Puerto Rico). This is somewhat more than an antiquarian trifle. The King took this action very shortly after the death of the Queen, naming Pinzón "mi Capitan y Corregidor de la isla de Sanct Xoan." Pinzón was obligated to pay his respects to Ovando, but was not under the latter's orders. Ferdinand had called a conference of experts on the Indies, the Junta de Toro, in which Vespucci and Pinzón proposed a new and desirable navigation. This may be the link to the grant to Pinzón and to the subsequent voyage of Pinzón and Solis, which will be considered later. Pinzón was to settle the island of San Juan; the

---

[11] William M. Gabb, "On the Topography and Geology of Santo Domingo, *Transactions of the American Philosophical Society*, IV, new series (1881), p. 125 and *passim*.

concession was to run for his lifetime and that of his heir.[12] He went briefly to the island, perhaps built a stockade, and left some livestock. It would seem, therefore, that the King and Fonseca were contemplating a base in Puerto Rico that would be independent of Española.

In 1508, near the end of his administration, Ovando turned his attention to the other islands. The obvious reasons were the shortage of native labor, the increase in the Spanish population, and the desire to find new gold districts. Also, unless he made good his authority over the outlying lands, governments independent of his were in prospect for such unappropriated territories. At the same time that he sent Morales to make the survey of Española, he dispatched Sebastián de Ocampo to make a reconnaissance of the coasts of Cuba, a circumnavigation that took eight months. This was not the first knowledge that Cuba was an island, as has been inferred, but a survey to provide information for its occupation.

Pinzón had gone on other navigational errands and left his title to San Juan in abeyance. Ponce de León was in charge at the villa of Salvaleón de Higüey, the easternmost Spanish town in Española and near to the Mona Passage. Through this strait ships bound for Spain took their way, stopping to take on cassava bread at the harbor of Higüey or at Isla Mona. The vecinos of Salvaleón made their living by the sale of foodstuffs and by leasing Indians to work in the mines. Curiously, the men of Salvaleón had not investigated what lay across the Mona Passage until some of their Indians told of gold in San Juan. Ponce de León got authorization from Ovando and set out with a party for San Juan in July, 1508. They were received in the friendliest fashion and led to the mountain streams that carried gold, in repetition of the manner in which the placers of Cibao and San Cristóbal had been shown to the Spaniards. Some of the chiefs offered in their innocence to plant additional conucos so that the Christians might have food when they returned to gather gold. Ponce de León reported the successful exploration to Ovando in May, 1509, one of the last events in that administration.[13]

The more productive and populous part of Puerto Rico was the south side. The gold was in streams of the cordillera that runs east-west through the middle of the island and was found in most abundance on the northeast flank, the geology being similar to that of central Española. The villa San Germán was founded convenient to the Mona Passage and placers of the western island. The more important villa was Puerto Rico de San Juan on the northeast coast, where an excellent harbor lay near the best auriferous streams. The exploitation of the island was a lesser but accelerated version of that of Española. The natives lived in cacicazgos which were apportioned to vecinos of the two villas. The Indians were forced to work in the gold placers, to grow food for the Spaniards, and to carry their burdens. They died under the oppression and also in a desperate rebellion in which they were aided by the Caribs of the neighboring island of St. Croix. Ponce de León soon became one of the principal and richest men of the Indies. (He is honored by a statue in the city of San Juan.) Vázquez de Espinosa, writing a century later, thought that the island had originally held a population of six hundred thousand without counting women and children. The figure is held to be grossly exaggerated, but is in line with the early estimates for Española;

---

[12] CDI, XXXI, 283, 285-287.
[13] CDI, XXXIV, 480 ff.; Las Casas, Bk. II, ch. 48; Oviedo, *Historia*, Bk. XVI.

the culture, climate, and soil being similar in the two islands. San Juan was de-populated in little more than a decade, and thereafter was mainly range for livestock.

The Lucayas Islands (the name Bahama Islands is of seventeenth-century English introduction) lay along the homeward course of ships that left the Caribbean either by Mona or Windward Passage. On occasion natives were snatched here to be taken to Spain, as by Hojeda and Vespucci. When the labor shortage became acute in the mining districts of Española, the nearby islands were thought of for replenishment. On January 29, 1509, Ferdinand advised Ovando that he had spoken with learned advisers about introducing slaves from other islands and that these found no conscientious objection; he had written about the matter previously.[14] The business therefore had been under earlier consideration, a formula of legitimation had been found, and the King used the bald designation of slaves. On May 3, having been assured that very few Indians were left in Española, the King ordered Ovando to import all the Indians that could be obtained from the neighboring islands "in the manner in which they have been brought on other occasions, so that those needed shall be placed in our enterprises and the others be given in allotment in the manner that has been used until now." [15] In other words, slave raiding of other islands had been going on and Ferdinand wanted to have the first choice of such captives for his Crown enterprises of mines, plantings, and livestock; the rest were to be handed over to private beneficiaries.

Puerto Rico had been placed under Ponce de León as lieutenant governor. He needed its Indians in the new mining districts of the island. Jamaica was known to be populous and productive, especially through the long involuntary stay of Columbus. Its size and tracts of difficult terrain, however, would have demanded well-organized expeditions to round up natives in number. Cuba, larger and less well known, would have required even more effort. The Lucayas on the other hand were a great lot of small islands, lacking refuges except by flight to another island and their people were known to be without guile; these would be the easiest to seize.

The harvest of the Lucayo natives began under Ovando and was extended under royal orders in the government of Diego Columbus. One of the first royal orders to the latter on August 14, 1509, concerned an offer by a group of partners to procure Indians at reduced cost and approved that these should be given such a contract (asiento), their share to be one fourth, the other three-fourths to go to the Crown. If the captives made no resistance they were to be given into service as naborías (that is life-long serfs, to approximate a European term); otherwise they were to be sold as slaves.[16] A dozen vecinos of Concepción formed the part-nership to fit out ships for the business of capturing Lucayans.

Puerto Plata and Puerto Real on the north coast were the ports of the slave operations. The loss of captives in transit was high, the ships making their slow and clumsy return against wind and current while the captives were confined closely below deck. Las Casas described the evil traffic. In his seventh *Decade,*

---

[14] CDI, XXXVI, 271.
[15] CDI, XXXI, 424 ff.
[16] *Ibid.,* pp. 438–439.

Peter Martyr put together what he could learn of these islands and what had happened to them—the first account of life in the New World in the past tense. He said that more than forty thousand persons of both sexes had been taken out of the Lucayas "for the unquenchable thirst for gold." Justification, where such was thought to be needed, varies in the documents of the time. The Indians were to be brought so that they might be instructed in the Christian faith, but there is little evidence of such interest until the Dominicans took their stand for human rights in 1512. The Lucayas were among the "useless" islands from which it was proper to ship natives to places where they would be employed. Most of the capture and transportation took place between 1509 and 1512, during which time the price per head went up from 5 to 150 gold pesos, which is also an indication of what was happening to the Indians on Española. The Lucayas Islands were the first part of the New World to become wholly depopulated, for which the date 1513 seems acceptable. The "discovery" of Florida by Ponce de León in 1513 was, in fact, an extension of slave hunting beyond the empty islands.

VIII
ATTEMPTS TO OCCUPY TIERRA FIRME
(1504–1509)

•

PRELIMINARIES

The year 1503 was one of expanded activity in the affairs of the Indies. The Casa de Contratación was in operation at Sevilla to control the trade with the Barbary Coast, the Canary Islands, and the Indies, making specific mention for the latter of the land discovered by Bastidas, the pearl "islands," and whatever Columbus might be in process of discovering on the voyage on which he was then absent. Also the new office was to take charge of "the first armada that by our orders is to go to the said land discovered by Bastidas." [1] This was to be privately financed and was to exploit the trade Bastidas had begun with profit. The tenor of the *ordenanzas* is commercial and concerned with Tierra Firme.

There was brisk competition for the contract. Bastidas made a bid, as did Juan de la Cosa. Cristóbal Guerra tried to form a partnership with Cosa, who would have none of it. That Cosa was the preferred person was apparent in his designation by the Queen (April, 1503), to be "Alguacil mayor of the Governor who by my orders will go to reside in the said gulf of Urabá." [2] The appointment declared the intention at this early date to found a government on Tierra Firme at Urabá.

During this time of projects and preparations for trade on Tierra Firme, the Queen was persuaded to issue, on October 30, 1503, an astonishing order, the notorious provision to permit the capture of rebellious "Cannibals." After proscribing capture or injury for any Indians, whether living on islands or mainland, it made an exception of "a certain people called Cannibals" who had been asked to mend their ways and to become Christians but who hardened their hearts and continued to eat Indians and kill Christians. For which reason the Queen said: "For the present I give license and power to all and sundry persons who may go by my orders to the Islands and Tierra Firme of the Ocean Sea discovered up

[1] The orders inaugurating the Casa are in Navarrete, II, 285–292. Manuel de la Puente y Olea, *Los trabajos geográficos de la casa de contratación* (Sevilla, 1900), reviewed its activities, with additional documentation.

[2] Antonio Ballesteros y Beretta, *La marina cántabra y Juan de la Cosa* (Santander, 1954), p. 280.

to the present, as well as to those who may go to discover other Islands and Tierra Firme, that if said Cannibals continue to resist and do not wish to admit and receive to their lands the Captains and men who may be on such voyages by my orders nor to hear them in order to be taught our Sacred Catholic Faith and to be in my service and obedience, they may be captured and taken to these my Kingdoms and Domains and to other parts and places and be sold." Specifically mentioned as subject to such punitive action were the harbor of Cartagena, Isla de Barú, Islas de San Bernardo, and Isla Fuerte, as peopled by cannibals who never would admit or listen to her captains.[3]

In so far as known, this Colombian coast had been visited only by the Bastidas-Cosa voyage, which gave the place names still in use. There is no record that this expedition had other than peaceful trade with the natives, or that the Spaniards were unable to enter these islands because of Indian resistance or that Christians had been killed there as the provision claimed. The Queen had been indoctrinated by stories of horrid cannibals. She believed that her rights overseas rested on the mission to establish the Christian faith, and she was told that certain natives would have none of it, not noticing that there was neither clergy nor interpreter. Cosa, the most persistent solicitant, as well as the person selected by the Crown, can hardly be absolved of this trick. The provision was a letter of marque for future expeditions. Any captain could proceed as he wished by affirming that natives were cannibals or resisted the Christians. It approved named areas for taking slaves and opened Europe to Indian slave trade. The results were not slow to follow, with large uncertainty and confusion to the present time as to who the natives of the Colombian coast were. Hostiles, cannibals, and Caribs were interchangeable terms. The taking of slaves had begun with Guerra and Hojeda on the Venezuelan coast. Now all Tierra Firme was available for depredation.

JUAN DE LA COSA TO URABÁ (1504-1506)

Juan de la Cosa, most experienced pilot in the waters of the Spanish Main, consultant to the Casa de Cantratación, lately returned from a mission to Portugal, in short the expert on the lands beyond the sea, was given charge of the new expedition to Tierra Firme. The final papers were signed in February, 1504. Cosa bore the costs and the Crown shared the profits. Although his was a trading voyage rather than one bent on discovery, he was authorized to go to the Gulf of Urabá and any other parts not under prior claim by Portugal or Columbus, the latter still unreported on his last voyage. Cosa was permitted, though not instructed, to make a settlement. He would be high constable of Urabá when such a government was constituted. The previous expedition with Bastidas gave promise that the Gulf of Urabá would be next to colonize.

Oviedo, coming to the same country a decade later, has given the principal account.[4] He censured Cosa as being one of those discoverers who "with better reason might be called alterers and destroyers of the land, since their purpose was not so much to serve God and King as to rob." Cosa entered the Caribbean by way of Margarita and Cumaná, loaded a quantity of superior brazilwood, and went on to Cartagena where he found ships of Cristóbal Guerra. The latter had

---

[3] The document is Appendix No. 17 in Navarrete, II, 414-416.
[4] Oviedo, *Historia*, Bk. XXVII, chs. 1-4.

been killed there in a fight with the Indians; his men were sick and dispirited and wanted to go home. Cosa arranged to transfer his cargo of brazilwood and the slaves he had taken en route. To complement the cargo he attacked the island of Codega in the bay of Cartagena, captured more than six hundred natives, selected those he wished to keep, and turned the rest over to the master of the Guerra ships. Oviedo continued: "it seems to me that this manner to discover and trade might better be called to desolate. . . . This assault and robbery Juan de la Cosa later was to pay for." Cosa then sailed west, took Isla Fuerte by force, tried to raid the coast of Sinú but was repulsed, and continued to the Gulf of Urabá. He captured the town of Urabá and its gold. An Indian prisoner led them in pursuit of the cacique Urabá, which took them through maize fields surrounded by *arcabucos* (thickets) and boscage. They came to a large bohío and in it found a chest containing *atabales* (kettledrums) of fine gold and six masks which together weighed seventy-two large marks of gold, as reported; Oviedo added that when they said four they actually took five or ten. Captives taken at Urabá informed the Spaniards of the town of Darién five or six leagues across the gulf (fig. 21). It also was taken. The treasure chest of its cacique yielded about

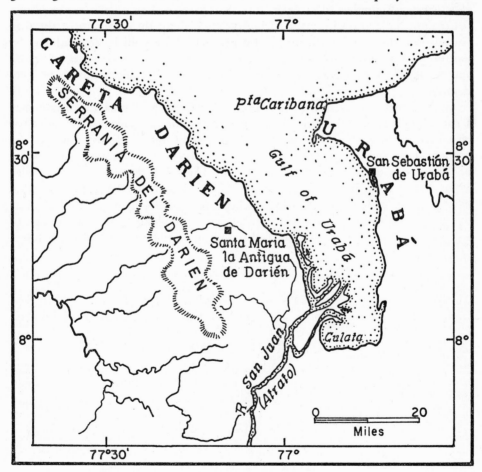

Fig. 21. Darién in 1510.

163

forty marks of worked gold. As they returned to Urabá their ships sank (ship-worms?). Thus stranded at Urabá, they lived for eighteen months by raiding the surrounding country for food and gold. In this time their number was reduced to a hundred by sickness and Indians. Having built new barks, the survivors sailed for Jamaica, where they were restored by good food and rest. Less than fifty reached Española.

Oviedo, who knew participants in the expedition as well as the country, thought it a sorry performance. Cosa followed the coast of Tierra Firme capturing slaves on the way to Cartagena, where Guerra (or the Guerra brothers) had preceded him. Here the notorious Guerras met their end in an otherwise unnoted slaving venture. The Indians about Cartagena, first subjected to a slave raid by Guerra and again by Cosa, thereafter met Christians with hostility and thereby earned the doubtful name of Caribs. Cosa continued raids beyond Cartagena, sacking the Indian towns of Urabá and Darién, the latter first entered at this time. The location of Urabá is indicated as at or near the modern village of Nicoclí by its position and distance from Darién (fig. 22). The damage by shipworms and the difficult return to Jamaica across the trade wind repeated the experience of Columbus in Veragua.

Cosa got back to Spain in the spring of 1506, about three-fourths of the time having been spent at Urabá, mainly by necessity. The gold he secured was by loot of ornaments. Whether he brought slaves from Tierra Firme is not of record and is unlikely. On Jamaica he captured four principal caciques and many commoners.

There is little information concerning the natives. At Urabá the natives had a cacique, his appellation being the same as that of the town, which was not characteristic of Caribs. The gold treasure was of the kind that Bastidas had brought back, and like some of that Columbus obtained in Veragua, the product of artificers from other and unknown parts. The King requested that a golden ax, mask, and kettledrum be sent to him.[5] The land about Urabá was described as having maize fields surrounded by thickets and groves—in other words, clearings under cultivation, groves that implied open land about them, and thickets of second growth, much as Columbus had found the Caribbean coast of the Isthmus.

HOJEDA'S THIRD VOYAGE (1505)

Alonso de Hojeda was licensed to make a third voyage to Tierra Firme in September, 1504. Despite his previous fiascos, he was still the favorite of Fonseca. He was again named governor of Coquibacoa, to which Urabá was added, and once more he was instructed to build a fort.[6] That he made such a voyage is about all that is known. The authorization was given before Columbus returned from Veragua, but probably not before something was known in Spain about such discovery. The whereabouts of Cosa were unknown at the time. It might be good tactics for Fonseca to make a demonstration of authority over the country between the Gulf of Venezuela and that of Darién as a check on Columbus and to discourage interest in the mainland by Ovando. Hojeda was a convenient

[5] Noted in the *Libro de tesorería* of 1506 cited by Puente y Olea, *op. cit.*, p. 26.
[6] CDI, XXXI, 258.

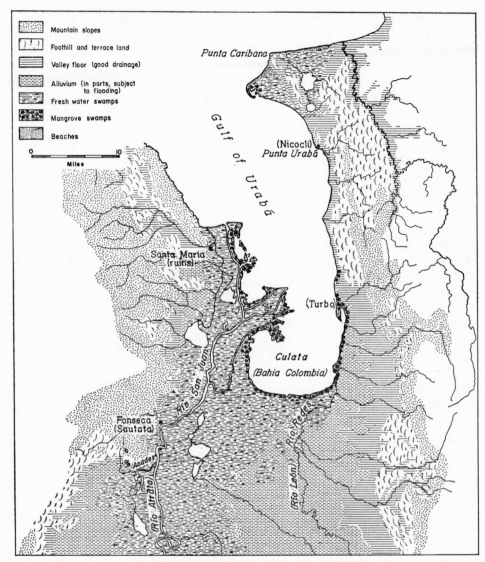

Fig. 22. Topography of environs of the Gulf of Urabá (adapted from map of Instituto Geografico "Agustin Cadazzi," with the location of Santa Maria as given on that map).

tool for the stratagems of Fonseca, who wanted at least a nominal government for this potentially important area. As the bishop had been unconcerned by the prior failure of Hojeda, so would he be about this one.

THE JUNTAS OF TORO AND BURGOS

After the death of the Queen, the King called a conference at Toro to consider, among other matters, affairs of the Indies (1505). The experts were Vespucci and Yáñez Pinzón. Vespucci had been given Spanish citizenship. With Juan de la Cosa in the Indies and Columbus out of favor as well as infirm, those two were the most knowledgeable persons. Both had explored the Atlantic coast of South America, Vespucci far enough to know that it extended well beyond tropical latitudes. Both knew that Tierra Firme was part of the same continental body. Columbus had brought proof that the same mainland continued west and north-west again beyond the Bay Islands of Honduras. However mystified or mystifying the old Admiral may have been about those shores, his mariners knew where they had been. It was the business of Vespucci and Pinzón to keep the Casa de Contratación informed of the geographic knowledge that was brought back from overseas. They must also have heard of the sea that was reported to lie across the mountains from Veragua and Cariay. They were, of course, informed of the progress of English explorations on continental shores in northern latitudes across the sea.

The discussions of the Junta de Toro are not recorded, but they were concerned with finding a way beyond the lately found lands, which certainly were not the Spice Lands or Oriental kingdoms of the tenacious illusion of Columbus. The appointment at Toro of Pinzón to be governor of San Juan makes sense as a base apart from Española from which marine exploration could be undertaken into the unknown sea beyond Honduras and Cuba, the only area where a sea passage might be looked for below the latitudes explored by the English. Puente y Olea, in his study of the Casa de Contratación, located documents showing that Vespucci and Pinzón were sent from Toro to Sevilla with instructions and funds for a fleet to discover the Spice Lands.[7] The ships, it seems, were built in Vizcaya, but did not sail. The death of Isabela resulted in turmoil over the Crown of Castile which forced Ferdinand to flee to the safety of his own Aragón.

In 1508, when Ferdinand was again firmly in the saddle, he called another junta, this time at Burgos. Vespucci, who had continued to work at the Casa de Contratación was again called in as was Yáñez Pinzón. The other pilots summoned were Juan de la Cosa and Juan Díaz de Solís, the latter a native of Lepe who had been in Portuguese service in eastern waters unknown to Spanish ships. This meeting again discussed a route to the Spice Lands and added plans for colonizing Tierra Firme (considered in the following sections). The services of Cosa, Pinzón, and Solís were engaged as participants. Amerigo Vespucci was named on this occasion to be the first Pilot Major of Spain, in effect the head of its office of navigation and coast survey. His duties thereafter were the training of navigators and the making of the *padrón*, or general sailing chart, with which navigators were supplied. Revision of the padrón became a principal duty of his office in the Casa de Contratación. The Casa at that time was expanded from its original services, which were to collect the Crown revenues from overseas, to building a Spanish merchant marine. Vespucci was thus engaged to his death in 1512 and was succeeded by another participant in the junta of Burgos, Díaz de Solís.

FIRST ENTRY INTO THE GULF OF MEXICO?

One of the main results of the Burgos conference was that Yáñez Pinzón and Díaz de Solís were ordered to go in search of the strait. They were told by the

---

[7] Puente y Olea, *op. cit.*, pp. 29–34.

King to sail north and west, Solís to go in the lead because of his knowledge of the Far East. They were not to tarry but to "follow the navigation for the discovery of that canal or open sea which you are sent to discover and which I wish to be sought." [8]

Henry Harrisse, usually well informed, has clouded the enterprise by construing their route as along the south coast of the Caribbean.[9] His bias may be attributed to the documents available in his time. The coast on which Harrisse would have put them, however, was well known to be a continuous land body. Pinzón himself had made major contribution to its discovery east and south. Bastidas, Cosa, and Columbus had established the continuity of Tierra Firme westward, the latter well into the Gulf of Honduras. The only unexplored coast lay beyond this gulf.

The orders were to go north and west, which they did. A joint account was to be prepared and perhaps was not made because of friction between Pinzón and Solís.

Las Casas appears to have been properly informed that they went north and west from the Gulf of Honduras which Columbus had discovered, but credited them only with having discovered the major part of the coast of Yucatán. This is the commonly accepted version of the 1508 voyage of Pinzón and Solís.

Pertinent data are found in the probanzas of the *Pleitos de Colón* taken in 1512 and 1513 at Santo Domingo and in 1513 at Sevilla.[10] Andrés de Morales, always a trustworthy witness, testified that Pinzón and Solís reported on their outbound voyage to Ovando at Santo Domingo. Santo Domingo was a proper port of call for ships going to the west, not for those going to the south coast of the Caribbean that Harrisse construed. Witnesses in number agreed that Pinzón and Solís made discoveries beyond the limits of Veragua that Columbus had discovered. Some added beyond Cape Gracias à Dios; others, beyond Guanaja Island. In this context Veragua was equivalent to the Central American coast found by Columbus.

The deposition by Yáñez Pinzón stated that with Solís he had discovered all the land from Guanaja to a province of Camarón, and named intermediate provinces, a bay, and mountains by names that have not been identified. Harrisse thought he recognized two of these names as those of caciques of Paria and therefore thought the voyage turned east from Guanaja to rerun the well-known coast of Tierra Firme to Paria. His most telling point is that in the transcript Pinzón is recorded as saying that they followed the coast east. This may be an error of the copyist, the exchange of "east" and "west," both usually abbreviated, being one of the commoner errors in transcripts of early documents. Pinzón stated that neither Columbus nor anyone else had reached these provinces, which would have been a patent falsehood. Also, this query concerning the discoveries of Pinzón and Solís, on which many depositions were taken, asked whether these persons "discovered beyond the land of Veragua all that which is discovered to the present and which the Admiral did not touch on nor discover." Had the

[8] CDI, XXII, 5–13.
[9] H. Harrisse, *The Discovery of North America* (Paris, 1892), pp. 453–464.
[10] CDU, VII.

voyage been limited to Yucatán, as Las Casas thought, Pinzón could not have spoken of mountains seen.

The most specific claim of limits attained was by Pedro de Ledesma, whom Harrisse dismissed as "evidently a prejudiced witness, and of doubtful veracity." The reason for such prejudice is not evident. Ledesma had been with Columbus on the Veragua voyage on which he had shown courage and dependability that were praised by Ferdinand Columbus. Ledesma named the landings made on the last voyage of Columbus, and is one of the sources for the course of that voyage. He then accompanied Pinzón and Solís on their voyage. Later he rose to the position of royal pilot as successor of Vespucci and Solís. Of the Pinzón–Solís voyage he testified that they went "on the way of the North" from Guanaja and that "they got by the way of the North to 23½ degrees." He was competent to determine latitude and there is no apparent reason for him to give false testimony. Puente y Olea studied all the documents and concluded that the ships got that far up the Mexican coast.[11] which would have been somewhat to the north of Tampico.

The ships were gone about a year without mishap. On their way home they put in again at Santo Domingo, where Ovando took and kept the Indians they had brought back as interpreters. (The King inquired of Pasamonte why this had been done.) That no word was brought of the great civilization of Mexico has cast doubt on their entry into the Gulf of Mexico. However, the ships were built, equipped, and sent for the purpose of finding a strait that might lead to the Spice Lands, and the leaders were selected for that purpose.

The low eastern coast of Yucatán would have needed close inspection, such reconnaissance being accepted by Las Casas and later students. Beyond the tip of Yucatán the coast turns south of west to the base of the peninsula in the direction they wished to go. There was no point here in scrutinizing the land for a passage here. Their objective being to find a sea route there was no reason to become acquainted with Mayan civilization. From Coatzacoalcos at the northern end of the Isthmus of Tehuantepec the coast was under Aztec domination as far north as the Río Pánuco. Here high mountains formed the western horizon all along the entire coast. There could be no sea passage through them and no reason therefore to land along this coast. A search for a western passage might readily have missed contact also with Mexican civilization.

No further search was made for a western passage within the tropics. When Solís, having succeeded Vespucci as pilot major, turned again to seek the western seaway to the Orient, it was to the far south, where he met his end in the Río de la Plata. When the conquest of New Spain was begun it had no concern with finding a strait. Did the negative results of the Pinzón-Solís exploration suppress further interest in that direction because it had given the last proof that there was no strait in low latitudes?

The Concession of Urabá and Veragua

The last and most important decision of the junta at Burgos dealt with the occupation of the mainland; the authorizations and instructions were given in

---

[11] Puente y Olea, *op. cit.*, pp. 67–83.

June, 1508, before the court moved on to its next seat.[12] The enterprise was to be private, initially for four years, under close supervision as to the share of the Crown, and was to consist of two separate concessions, one to the east of the Gulf of Urabá, the other to the west. The rights given included that of settlement. The venture might lead to Spanish colonization, but this was not of immediate concern nor was there any reference to political and economic organization. The usual prescriptions in regard to rescate and slaves were given, but the first concern was with revenue of "mines," the Crown's share of which was to begin with a tenth and was to rise gradually to the normal fifth. The Crown provided arms and some military support, but most of the costs were borne by the grantees. Each administration was to build two forts, one within a year and a half and the other in the remaining two and a half years of the term of the grant. With bureaucratic thoroughness these forts were ordered to have a first story of stone and a superstructure of tapia. There was no instruction to search for a strait or to engage in exploration. The plan was to resume the activities that had been going on for a decade on these coasts, but now under formal organization. Eight hundred men were to be enrolled from Spain or Española and given free passage. Some trained natives were to be brought from Epañola, and four hundred more could be taken from surrounding islands, as Ovando was doing at the time; their designation as "slaves" was avoided.

In certain matters, not well defined, the new concessions were to be under the authority of the newly-named governor of Española, Diego Columbus, son of the Admiral. Both concessions were to have the right to draw on Jamaica for supplies. Jamaica was still unoccupied, known for its ample production of cassava bread and other foodstuffs, and had been subject to only minor disturbance. The provision indicates that the mainland natives were not expected to feed the Spaniards, having put up resistance to previous expeditions.

The new grant of Tierra Firme was divided between Diego de Nicuesa, who was to have the western part under the name of Veragua, and Hojeda, with Cosa as second in command, who was to have Urabá with rights as far east as Cabo Isleos (Codera). The Gulf of Urabá would serve initially to mark the division. For Hojeda this was a second reconfirmation of the earlier titular governorship he had held of Coquibacoa, including its old eastern limit, doubled in extent to reach west to the Gulf of Urabá. Cosa, as his partner, was reconfirmed in the office of alguacil mayor of Urabá. Hojeda, old favorite of Fonseca and the court, but ever impecunious, was given the first position; Cosa, a commoner whose experience and wealth would be needed and rewarded, was second in command. Enciso, who had acquired wealth in Española as a lawyer and invested it as the third partner in Urabá, was named alcalde mayor by Hojeda. That the new government was named Urabá shows that the principal interest was in its western limits. In fact, no further attention was given to the eastern part of the designated coast (as of Venezuela).

Veragua, gilded by the accounts of Columbus, was considered the greater prize, and Nicuesa, who had become one of the rich men of Española, got it by offer-

---

[12] CDI, XXXII, 25–54; XXII, 23–26.

ing the larger financial backing. Veragua was considered open territory. Columbus had failed in his attempt to occupy it; his expedition had been at the expense of the Crown, and there were no rights to government considered as surviving his death in 1506. The name Veragua was used at the time for all the known land west of Urabá, which carried as far as Honduras.

The two parties got underway from Española in December, 1509, Hojeda and Cosa a few days ahead of Nicuesa. The delay of more than a year had been caused by the difficulty in obtaining the needed capital and men. Hojeda started off with about three hundred men and the experienced Cosa, his main financial backer. According to Peter Martyr, Nicuesa carried 785 men in five ships, indicating that men were more anxious to go to Veragua than to Urabá and that Nicuesa took on more personnel than was prudent for their maintenance or management. Both parties made separate and final preparations at Isla Beata off Española and then took a quartering course to the harbor of Cartagena.[13]

Caribs at Cartagena?

Cartagena had been the most important harbor on Tierra Firme from the first, was known by that name from its discovery by Bastidas and Cosa, and continued to be the leading port of call on Tierra Firme throughout the period of Spanish dominance in the Caribbean. Its name, thus appearing in the Queen's provision against cannibals in 1503, declared its excellence and resemblance to Spain's best harbor on the Mediterranean. It is commodious, well sheltered from storms and river floods, and convenient of entry and exit by sail. The route taken by the ships of Hojeda and Nicuesa was the shortest and best for ships from Santo Domingo, and in winter had the further advantage of northeasterly winds. (When ships came directly to Cartagena from Spain, they usually followed the trade winds all the way, as Herrera noted in his description of standard sailing routes.) Cartagena was also the point of departure to cross over to Central American shores, either directly, with benefit of the trades, or following the shore southward where winds were uncertain. Soon it became known that it was advantageous to steer back to Cartagena from the Gulf of Darién in order to have wind and current abeam for crossing the Caribbean, thus fetching up at the northern islands and going on to Spain. The superior quality and location of the harbor were known to mariners of the southwestern Caribbean from the first; a generation passed before a town was built there.

According to the Queen's license of October, 1503, the Indians of Cartagena and of the coast beyond were to be subjugated, captured, and sold as slaves as having given offense and resistance, having slain Spaniards, and being known cannibals. Spaniards and natives had had repeated bad experiences of one another;

[13] The earliest account is by Peter Martyr, being almost the whole of his Second Decade, written in 1514 after the collapse of both ventures. Oviedo accompanied Pedrarias in 1514 and based his account on his own observations, which are excellent, and on what he heard from survivors, not always reliable (*Historia*, Bks. XXVII and XXVIII). Las Casas, as usual, gave the lengthiest version (chapters 57 to 67 of his *Historia*, Bk. II). Although Las Casas did not know the area, his material was collected with care and includes information not found elsewhere.

the natives were classed as hostile, were thus treated, and so reacted. This was a land where the Spaniards expected to be met with warfare.

The character of the natives living from Cartagena to the Gulf of Urabá has remained obscure, largely because they were declared Caribs and cannibals and were harried by each succeeding party. The Indians about Cartagena were known as Caramairi (alias Calamari, construed as the Spanish word for squid, *calamar*, probably without validity), their inland neighbors as Turbaco, and those farther south along the coast as Tolú. Gregorio Hernández de Alba considers that the coastal population from the Magdalena River to the Gulf of Urabá was Calamari or of similar culture and thinks that probably none of them practiced cannibalism.[14] The point of land at the eastern entry to the Gulf of Urabá was and still is called Punta Caribana, and has been taken to mean "Carib."

The surest information we have about the natives of the coast from the Río Magdalena to the Gulf of Urabá is that they were stout fighters and that they tipped the points of their projectiles in a very potent poison. The arrow poison was a major discouragement to Spanish occupation. The first recorded experience of it was at the landing of the Hojeda-Cosa party in 1510. Whether the poison was used in native warfare as well as hunting is not known. If they waited until 1510 thus to strike back at the Spaniards it may have been desperate retaliation rather than a customary mode of fighting. Padre Pedro Simón in his seventeenth-century *Noticias Historiales,* a major source of information about native conditions of Tierra Firme, thought that the natives from Cartagena west to Acla (in eastern Panama) claimed a common origin, never engaged in sodomy, nor ate human flesh.[15] If he was right this would indicate Chibchan affiliations. Herrera thought they were Caribs, but said also that Indians brought by Hojeda from Española served as interpreters because they understood the language at Cartagena.[16]

Contemporary accounts of their fighting stress the use of bow and arrows, stone-tipped or fire-hardened and pointed shafts, the use of wooden swords, and two kinds of shields; they mention also that women took part in the fighting. The natives were said to be of better than average stature, well built, and of good features. Women wore their hair long, the men short. The women were dressed in cotton from the waist down. Habitation was in villages consisting of multi-family houses, the village was ruled by a chief and surrounded by a stockade of living trees or canes. At a later date, Herrera described in detail the preparation of arrow poison. The bows, he said, were six feet long or more, made of a black and very hard palm wood, and could shoot with great force. The houses, he added, were built in the manner of large *ramadas* with many supports. They did not sleep in beds but used hammocks. Some were great merchants who took inland salt, fish, and herds of peccaries and brought back gold and clothing. Padre Simón concurred, telling of the fish and the cotton hammocks they traded into

---

[14] In Julian Steward (ed.), *Handbook of South American Indians,* IV (Washington, 1948), 329–338.
[15] Pedro Simón, *Noticias historiales de las conquistas de Tierra Firme en las Indias Occidentales* (Bogotá, 1882–1892), Part III, Not. I, chs. 8, 10.
[16] Herrera, Decade I, chs. 14–16.

the interior for gold and other articles. Such are the meager notes that have been preserved on the coastal inhabitants of northern Colombia.

Death of Juan de la Cosa

On landing at Cartagena, Hojeda and Cosa promptly engaged in a *razzia* against the Caramairi killing many, capturing some, and not finding much gold (see fig. 15, chap. v). Before the hosilities began, Hojeda had the prescribed *requerimiento* of submission read and interpreted to the Indians, who had gathered on shore, thus keeping the attack properly legal. Cosa then led a troop inland, taking captives and chasing others into the woods, and thus came to the village of Turbaco, which was found abandoned. Resting there after their easy success, the party was taken by a surprise counterattack in which poisoned arrows were used. Cosa made a stand at the gate of the *palenque* (palisade) that surrounded Turbaco. Hojeda, now no longer brave, made his escape "running so that he seemed to be flying." Cosa and seventy Spaniards were killed—the heaviest loss so far suffered in the Indies. Thus Juan de la Cosa came to his end in February, 1510, the most experienced pilot and cartographer of the Indies, grown rich by trade and loot, and dead because he had been overconfident. Hojeda and the remainder were saved by the timely arrival of Nicuesa's fleet. Nicuesa threw his force into an attack on Turbaco, carrying out "an incredible killing without pardoning anyone." The sack yielded seven thousand castellanos of gold; Peter Martyr noted that their lust for gold was satisfied by what they raked from the ashes of the burned village. The gold, here as elsewhere on that coast, consisted of objects of adornment; Oviedo added that it was good gold, and therefore not guanín.

LANDING OF HOJEDA AT URABÁ AND FOUNDING OF SAN SEBASTIÁN

After ravaging the land about Cartagena, Nicuesa sailed directly for the Panamanian coast. Hojeda and his remnant followed the coast to Urabá, stopping for an assault on Isla Fuerte, a place of Indian salt processing, where they took captives and gold objects. Having entered the Gulf of Urabá, Hojeda kept to the eastern side, which was assigned to his jurisdiction, and debarked his party at the Indian town of Urabá. During the spring of 1510 they built a fort and settlement there, named San Sebastián de Urabá (fig. 21). The site was probably at or near Nicoclí.[17] It had been the town of an important cacique of that name, and probably was the site of Juan de la Cosa's long encampment of six years before, while he built the ships for his return. Nicoclí meets the qualifications: a ridge of high land, called Punta de Urabá, reaching out into the gulf where the fort probably was built, the right distance from Darién on the opposite side of the gulf, and in proper position for incursions into the interior.

---

[17] Eduardo Acevedo Latorre made a reconnaissance of the shores of the gulf ("Breve noticia sobre los lugares donde existieron San Sebastián de Urabá y Santa María la Antigua del Darién," *Boletín de historia y antiguidades*, XXX [Bogotá, 1943], 1096) and arrived at an approximate location.

Hojeda, who had been in a hurry to get away from Española, had come inadequately provided with food and other supplies and without some of the men who were to go with him. His cockiness had resulted in a bad beating at Cartagena and the loss of Cosa. The party arrived at Urabá short of able-bodied men, diminished in confidence, and soon was short of rations. The rain forest then was not the nearly unbroken expanse of modern times, but held numerous Indian villages and cleared lands. The necessity for food, the desire for loot, and boredom led to raids inland. They heard of a town and a chief named Tirisi, or Tirifu, about a dozen miles east into the hills, reputed to have a rich gold mine. (A gold district of similar name was sought in later years in the *quebradas* of these Andean spurs.) Their attack on what was thought to be this place was repulsed with losses. In another food-hunting raid on a village, Hojeda was pricked by a poisoned arrow that disabled him for a good while. Hojeda's original three hundred were reduced to sixty hungry and dispirited men, some of them ill, sitting it out in the sweatbox of San Sebastián. During the summer Hojeda, still suffering from his wound, took a brigantine to Española, ostensibly to search for help, but never to return nor attempt to do so. He had had enough of being conquistador and governor. According to one version he retired to a monastery; at any rate his picaresque career was over. Thus within half a dozen months of its beginning the new government of Urabá lost both of its principals.

The forlorn remnant at the fort was left in charge of Francisco Pizarro, who enters the pages of history inconspicuously at this time. After further weeks of waiting and hunger the decision was made to get out. They retraced their course in two brigantines up the coast to and beyond Cartagena, to be met by the long-awaited ships under the command of Fernández de Enciso, who brought a company of fresh men, a dozen mares, pigs, ample supplies of food and weapons, and new hope. Thus Pizarro's men were induced to return to reoccupy Urabá. It is interesting to note that the fleet was hospitably received by the Indians at Cartagena when Enciso assured them that he came as a friendly and passing visitor.

The new hopes were short-lived. The main cargo ship was wrecked on a bar as it entered the shallow harbor of Urabá and most of its supplies and animals were lost. San Sebastián, meanwhile, had been burned to the ground by Indians. It was reoccupied by about two hundred men, hungry from the start. Peccaries were hunted in palm groves near the coast, and palm fruits and buds were gathered. (This may have been in reference to peach palms—pejibae, *Guilielma* —planted for their starchy fruits in tropical lowlands from Costa Rica to the Amazon.) The Spaniards were forced to range in search of food, the while they were being picked off by bowmen. In a few weeks the position became untenable. Saint Sebastián had not prevailed against the hostile land of Urabá.

Transfer to Darién

The Western side of the gulf was known from former years when Bastidas and Cosa had been there. At least one person remembered it, Vasco Núñez de Balboa, a stowaway on Enciso's ship. His proposal to seek safety on the other shore turned disaster into success. Thus he made his first appearance as a major figure in shaping the fortunes of the New World.[18]

The move was begun early in November by seizing the Indian town of Darién (fig. 22). Unlike Urabá, it was not in an open situation on the coast but on a narrow river channel at some distince inland. The accounts differ somewhat as to the manner of its capture. Peter Martyr, who gave the earliest version, said that the Indians hid their families and household goods on the approach of the Christians. The chief and his men were quickly put to flight. The invaders rested to fill their bellies with the food that was left behind, "bread of roots and seeds like panicum" (maize), whereupon they searched the canebrakes to discover the hidden supplies, including cotton mantas and two hundred pounds of gold and jewels. They then sent back to bring over the rest of their companions from San Sebastián. A new Spanish town was set up on the site of Darién, dedicated to the Sevillan Virgen de la Antigua. This was done before the end of 1510, Enciso being the founder and official head.

Darién was an important and permanent native town, located on a good site. To the south was an intricate system of waterways, distributaries of the Atrato delta, discharging through a swampy lowland that narrows northward to a strip flanked by ridges underlain by bedrock at Darién.[19] The Spaniards found an abundance of root crops, maize, and cotton. The slopes served for growing crops, the swamps and stream channels for fishing and hunting. The permanence of a native town in the tropical rain forest tells of competent selection of site. It does not support the view that in such climates settlements shifted with a shifting agriculture in search of new clearings briefly held against invading vegetation.

The Spanish transfer to Darién was not by planned selection of a suitable site but to find safety from attack by the Urabá Indians and to get food. They also found commodious native houses to shelter them. The hidden gold they discovered gave promise of more, and gold was what they were after. Most significant for a better future, they had come into a land of Indians, soon to be known as Cuna, who did not use poison, wished to live in peace, and would attempt to do the bidding of the Spaniards. Apparently the newcomers did not behave badly and the natives returned to Darién to live with and work for their new masters, to grow food, and to fish and hunt. The temporary refuge promised ease and profit and thus there was no need to look elsewhere to found a town.

Santa María la Antigua de Darién, part Spanish, part Indian, was for years a

---

[18] Balboa has been the subject of much historical and literary study and appreciation. Angel de Altolaguirre y Duvale's *Vasco Núñez de Balboa* (Madrid, 1914) is the basic monograph, with an appendix of eighty documents. Kathleen Romoli's *Balboa of Darien* (New York, 1953) is a spirited and affectionate account, admirable also for its many and original insights into the documents and the geography of the time, both physical and cultural.

[19] A Belgian expedition in 1956 confirmed the location of Darién and made excavations at the site. It was found to be seven and a half kilometers from the coast on an abandoned river channel and located on a low outlier of high land about fifteen meters above the swamp. Beneath the remains of Spanish occupation a native town was discovered, extending to a maximum depth of a meter and a half over an area 650 by 350 meters, showing that a goodly population had lived there for generations. In the absence of native wet-land crops tillage must have been limited to the naturally drained higher land. The Belgian expedition was reviewed by James J. Parsons in *Geographical Review*, L (1960), 274-276.

satisfactory base for Spanish operations of Tierra Firme. As an Indian town its location was superior in resources of coast and soil. For the Spaniards it was a suitable gateway to the unknown south and west for which no other place had equal advantage of distance and passage. The Gulf of Urabá reaches a hundred miles south into the continent; its lower end, the Culata, is sharply constricted by the delta of the Río Atrato building out from its western side. The Atrato, then known as the Río San Juan, gave access by canoe and ship's boat to several hundred miles of the interior. To the northwest of Darién the Caribbean shore leads to Veragua and beyond. Westward an Indian road climbed the serranía of Darién to a pass from which a short descent led to navigable waters flowing into the Pacific Gulf of San Miguel. For the years of reconnaissance the Spaniards were in most favorable position by settling at Darién.

Was the settlement at Darién trespass on the concession of Nicuesa? The colonists were not concerned with the matter of jurisdiction, but Balboa later used it in his denial of the authority of Enciso, who was the official representative of Hojeda. The original grant did not specify limits between Urabá and Veragua. Hojeda and Nicuesa are thought to have come to an agreement that the Gulf of Urabá divided their territories. By royal order of June 15, 1510, the Gulf of Urabá was declared to belong to Hojeda;[20] the colonists at the time not being thus informed, nor caring. The country to the west, however, clearly belonged to the other concession.

THE FAILURE OF NICUESA

Nicuesa, meanwhile, had sailed from Cartagena to take possession of Veragua, landing at Careta, the next native province beyond Darién. Oviedo thought it took three months to make seventy leagues, which might be explained by Peter Martyr's remark that they always followed the coast. At Careta, Nicuesa divided his men and fleet, deciding to push ahead with two brigantines and one fleeter caravel, with himself in the latter. He soon lost sight of the brigantines; the expedition was thus broken into three disjointed parts. Nicuesa missed recognizing the shores of Veragua where Columbus had been, and wound up, thoroughly lost, somewhere on the Mosquito Coast of Nicaragua. Here he lost the caravel and some sixty men, according to Peter Martyr. Meanwhile the two brigantines had reached the actual Veragua and began to establish themselves on the Río Belén, as Columbus had done. A relief party sent ahead to find Nicuesa came back with the remnant of his group. The Belén group also suffered heavy losses. From Belén they retreated to the Portobelo of Columbus, where the Indians repulsed them. So the Spaniards went on to the port of Bastimentos of Columbus, named Nombre de Dios by Nicuesa in supplication. Here a feeble attempt was made to build the fort that was one of the obligations of the concession. Soon all the remainder were evacuated to Darién: The gaily confident armada that had set out from Española for Careta had been reduced to a disorganized handful of refugees within nine months. The accounts differ in their estimates. Colmenares, who took the rescue ships to Veragua, said that of 580 men he found less than

---

[20] Altolaguirre, p. viii.

two hundred alive, the rest having died of hunger.[21] Peter Martyr heard that only forty made it back to Darién.

This second attempt to colonize Central America was a complete and stupid failure, owing almost wholly to Nicuesa. He had with him mariners who had been with Columbus on the last voyage, but he would not listen to them. He was in a tearing hurry to get to the gold of Veragua and passed up the populous and productive districts of eastern Panama. Failing to recognize Veragua, he blundered on along the sandy coast of Mosquitia. Colmenares put it thus: "The cause of his perdition was that this land was discovered by the Lord Admiral [Columbus] who gave information that it was the richest in the world, whereas in fact it has little gold and its coast, most hazardous for more than a hundred leagues, does not permit making a settlement nor to plant the necessary provisions, and therefore its Indians are for the most part fishermen." It was stupid of Nicuesa to scatter his fleet without maintaining contact. He was in trouble with Indians nearly everywhere, perhaps because they had prior sorry experience with the conduct of white men. Some of the expeditionaries were killed by natives, some were drowned, and more succumbed to hardships and hunger. His incompetence to lead was soon apparent and turned into malignance and panic.

OBJECTIVE AND RESULT

The junta at Burgos had made a good plan on paper. The convocation of the major pilots implies that charts of Tierra Firme were studied. (Peter Martyr had manuscript maps in hand, apparently through Fonseca, secured from the Columbus brothers, Cosa, and Morales. By these he computed that it was 140 leagues from Veragua to the place where Nicuesa lost his caravel.) Juan de la Cosa gave his own knowledge of the coast which extended west beyond the Gulf of Urabá. Peter Martyr heard that Cosa had been the first to secure gold from the sands of Urabá, which would indicate that prospects of placer mining were under consideration for both Veragua and Urabá. The junta, and Cosa in particular, could supply a prospectus of the geography and economic potential. When the concessions were given, the first and main concern was with "mines and miners of gold and silver and guanín and other metals." They were permitted "to take and capture slaves from the places which are designated for slaves." There were no plans for establishing colonies, for setting up responsible governments, or for ordered relations with the natives. There was no reference to administrative organization, no provision to explore and report on the status of land and people. In return for a minutely prescribed share of the profits, the Crown gave the concessionaires the right for a term to exploit territory as they wished. The rights were further elaboration of the licenses to trade that Fonseca had begun handing out ten years earlier. The extension of the Christian faith and admonitions that the natives be treated well had disappeared. This sorry business was given into the hands of men who had no better purpose than riches; Hojeda to govern, who never gave a thought to what government should be;

---

[21] *Ibid.*, Appendix doc. 60.

Cosa, who knew how to make maps and navigate but turned to slaving; and Nicuesa, who was a fool. Nothing had been learned about the obligations of power. The one positive result was the founding of Santa María la Antigua by a group that lacked authority but had the will to survive.

IX

EXPANSION FROM ESPAÑOLA

(1509–1519)

•

JAMAICA

With the retirement of Ovando in 1509, the government of the Indies passed into the weak hands of the junior Columbus, whose authority was further reduced by Ferdinand and Fonseca. Miguel de Pasamonte was sent as royal treasurer, to see to it that the new governor did little. The taut rule of Ovando had maintained the production of gold from Española at the cost of natives. By 1509, both gold and natives were getting scarce. Ovando had turned Ponce de León loose on Puerto Rico, and had sent Ocampo on the reconnaissance of Cuba. The transport of Lucayans was well under way. In Spain, Fonseca and the King had taken steps to divide the Indies by giving independent rights to ventures into Urabá and Veragua. Diego Columbus lacked both the personal qualities and the official backing to take over the controls. Colonial policy was dictated from Spain and was carried out increasingly by Pasamonte and his followers.

Only once, and this was at the beginning of his office, was Diego able to assert himself, by ordering the occupation of Jamaica. Jamaica, lacking gold, had not been taken under exploitation. When the new concessions of Urabá and Veragua were granted, the Crown gave them the right to draw on Jamaica for supplies, especially for food. Diego, fearing that this would attach Jamaica to the Tierra Firme administration, rushed Juan de Esquivel to take possession of the island, in 1509. The action was not disallowed by the Crown. The suit of the Columbus heirs against the Crown had begun and Jamaica was hardly the proper place for the Crown to test the Columbus prerogatives. The old Admiral had discovered Jamaica, circumnavigated it, and lived there for a year in the misadventure of his last voyage. There were better places to meet the challenge.

Jamaica was well and favorably known as a pleasant and populous land. As Peter Martyr collected the stories about the western Indies, it appeared to him favored by nature beyond the rest. In his Third Decade he wrote of it as a "fertile island, most fortunate in the benignity of its soil and with only one mountainous part. . . . No one has ever denied its richness." The third book of his Eighth Decade was written in eulogy of the island, which he never saw but of which he had been made titular episcopal abbot. Bernáldez heard Columbus tell of it as most fertile, with many and large native towns, notable for great and finely fashioned canoes. The letter of Cuneo, on the second voyage of Columbus, described the landing at an excellent port (St. Ann's Bay), the country about greatly populated, sixty canoes coming to meet the Spaniards and bringing "bread of their kind in large amount, fishes, roots, and gourds filled with water." He estimated that during the four days of their stay at that harbor sixty thousand persons had come down to visit, all naked and all of one speech. In the return from his final voyage, when Columbus and his men were forced to spend more than a year on the island, they lived comfortably on food the natives supplied, largely without duress. Other parties returning from Tierra Firme, such as that of Bastidas, found Jamaica a haven in which to recuperate at their ease and to supply their needs.

The advantages of Jamaica were obvious, the most important at that moment being its location facing the western parts of Tierra Firme. The island has a benign climate, for the most part without excess of rain or drought. There is only one small mountainous region, the Blue Mountains. Much of the soil is derived from calcareous beds, fertile and well drained. The sea around it is rich in marine life and was phenomenally so in turtles. (The productivity of the island and its seas was well appreciated when the English occupied it in the seventeenth century, as is well described in its natural history written by Sir Hans Sloane.) Jamaica should have had as dense a native population as Española. The inhabitants were of the same stock and culture, practicing the same skills of livelihood, and were organized in cacicazgos. Las Casas thought Jamaica had been a human beehive and held it and Puerto Rico to have been equally attractive and populous.

Juan de Esquivel, sent to take possession of Jamaica, had broken the natives of southeastern Española. Pánfilo de Narváez, another bad actor, was second in authority. There is little record of what took place there. The items mainly are in royal letters of 1511 that mention lost letters from Diego Columbus and are concerned with the conduct of Diego's government.[1] In them it was said that the Indians of Jamaica were very pacific and it was requested that they should be well treated. "It gave great pleasure to see the letter of Juan de Esquivel which you sent me and I give many thanks to our Lord for the mercy there given us in the conversion of so many Christians. Take great diligence and care in giving order to the government there so that those Indians may be Christians in fact as well as in name and may not be as in Española, where they are only Christians by name, except for the boys who are being raised by the friars. It is ordered that the Indians shall not bear burdens or be subjected to other injurious treatment such as was used in the past in Española." Since there was no gold in the island, the natives were to be employed in growing provisions for Tierra Firme and in building roads. The problem of the numerous Spaniards who were unable to meet their debts in Española might be resolved by allowing these to remove to Jamaica, where they could be given Indians. Care should be taken

---

[1] CDI, XXXII, 414–429; CDU, I, 1–14 and 15–26; V, 312–328.

that the Jamaicans "may increase and multiply and not diminish as has been the case in Española." "The main end for which we order the conquest of these parts," it continued, was their conversion to the Faith. These pious hopes were not put into practice, nor is there reason to think that they were honest intentions.

The occupation began in 1509. Esquivel established himself midway of the north coast at the harbor of Santa Gloria where Columbus had made his first landing, near the seat of a major cacique in control of a large population about St. Ann's Bay. A fort was built here and the island for a time was named Santiago. This original "villa of Santiago" was later named Sevilla la Nueva and served for many years as the seat of government.

Las Casas, who had marched under Esquivel in the subjugation of Higüey, blamed Esquivel for the quick ruin of Jamaica. He denied that the natives had the benefit of Christian doctrine (of which there was indeed very little anywhere in the islands), and held that they were put to excessive labor at producing cassava, maize, and cotton for export to Tierra Firme and to Cuba. Jamaican cotton, he thought, was of better quality than in the other islands and therefore the native women were employed in making cloth, shirts, and hammocks.[2]

There is only minor mention of shipping its natives to other parts. The Jamaican natives did diminish rapidly under repartimiento, as was happening in Española and Puerto Rico. Neither Esquivel nor Narváez were humane, nor is it likely that the men who came with them were different. Narváez and his men left Jamaica after two years to take a bloody and ignoble part in overrunning Cuba. Esquivel stayed on until he was replaced in 1515. Garay, who succeeded him, complained of the small number of natives that he found. At the same time Pedro de Mazuelos, royal factor, predicted the total disappearance of the native population in two years' time.[3]

Francisco de Garay, the first governor of Jamaica who held royal appointment, had come to Española with Columbus on the second voyage, had struck it rich in the Minas Nuevas of the San Cristóbal gold fields, and was one of the wealthiest vecinos of Santo Domingo. In 1511 he was given a commission "to discover the secret of Guadelupe," but was repulsed there by the Caribs. On the recall of Diego Columbus in 1515 he obtained the Jamaican post, which yielded neither profit nor glory. In 1519, after Cortés had begun the conquest of the Aztec empire, Garay thought he might block off Cortés at the north and secure for himself the northern shores of the Gulf of Mexico, to which the name of Florida was then applied. How he came to grief there and lost his men to Cortés is part of the story of New Spain. In Jamaica Garay awaited his chance to become one of the makers of Spanish empire and failed.

There was little for Garay to do in Jamaica, with its rapidly fading native population, lack of gold, and limited demand for sale of food or cotton. He founded two more Spanish settlements, villas by courtesy rather than in fact, Melilla and Oristán. Melilla was on the north coast, a dozen or so leagues to the east of Sevilla la Nueva, and lay somewhere in the neighborhood of Port Maria. Oristán was on the southwestern coast about Bluefields. The Crown had the monopoly of minerals and dyewoods, as elsewhere. Neither of the latter

[2] Las Casas, Bk. II, ch. 56.
[3] Francisco Morales Padrón, *Jamaica Española* (Sevilla, 1952), pp. 260, 261.

amounted to anything; the repartimiento of natives was soon completed and the allotments ceased to have value except as they became claims to land.

Livestock was brought over from Española by Esquivel and increased rapidly. The introductions were continued by Garay. When Narváez' men moved on to Cuba, goats and pigs were provided from Jamaica. The shipment of live animals and their dressed products to Tierra Firme and to Cuba soon became the major source of income. Stock ranged all over the island, perhaps with even freer increase than in Española, there being no record of feral dogs. López de Velasco, writing half a century after the time of Garay, was informed that the island abounded in horses, cattle, and pigs, many of the latter being wild.[4] Again a half-century later, Vázquez de Espinosa reported the *campos* of Jamaica filled with ganado mayor from which Tierra Firme and New Spain were stocked, and also with goats, sheep, and pigs. Goats then ran wild, in the montes and especially in the high mountains, where they were killed in large numbers for their hides. Wild pigs were innumerable and free to anyone to hunt, and ships were loaded with their lard. Guinea fowl also had become naturalized.

By 1519 the Indians of Jamaica were nearly extinct. Restless Spanish colonists drifted to Cuba and to Tierra Firme, followed by the larger exodus with Garay to New Spain. The remainder turned to raising and hunting livestock. Small plantings of conucos supplied their other needs. After Garay, Jamaica was a quiet backwater of the Spanish New World.

ENTRY INTO CUBA

Columbus lost interest in Cuba during his first voyage when he found no promise of gold. His exploration of its southern waters in the second voyage was made only at the request of the Crown. Nor was Cuba on the route of early ships, inbound or outbound. In the tedious run from western parts of Tierra Firme across the Caribbean Sea, ships were likely to miss Española and to land on Jamaica or the south coast of Cuba. When able to continue, they turned east to gain an Españolan harbor. Thus parties were stranded occasionally on Cuban shores, as on the Gulf of Guacanayabo, where they well received by the natives. That there was occasional shanghaiing of Cubans is indicated by an inquiry from the King to Ovando (October 8, 1508) concerning a party that had gone secretly to Cuba to capture Indians.[5]

Official attention to Cuba began in 1508, when Ovando sent Ocampo to circumnavigate the island. The Bay of Xagua (Cienfuegos) on the south coast and the harbor of Carenas (Habana) on the north were thereby reported favorably. Perhaps also first notice was taken of gold in Cuba, the King inquiring in May, 1509, concerning "some suspicion of gold in Cuba." [6] Diego at the time wished to send his uncle Bartholomew "to know the secret of Cuba" and thought also

---

[4] When Velasco wrote, there were no Indians surviving, and he attributed to this fact the lack of gold production, of which he thought there was a lot in Jamaica, This myth continued to expand, Vásquez de Espinosa later writing that in the early days of Jamaica great riches of gold were produced by the labor of the many Indians, until these were used up.

[5] CDI, XXXI, 453; XXXVIII, 258.

[6] CDI, XXXI, pp. 388 f.

of sending Diego Velázquez into Cuba.[7] In 1509 the occupation of Cuba was being talked of in Spain and at Santo Domingo, but no action was taken.

In 1511 the King approved an asiento between Diego Columbus and Velázquez to take and govern Cuba. The latter lost no time in overrunning Cuba, which was pretty well accomplished that year, the natives submitting or fleeing. On March 20, 1512, Ferdinand acknowledged the good news contained in letters that Diego Columbus had sent on January 15, according to which the Cubans were much inclined to become Christians. The King wrote Velázquez that he had "done very well in communicating to them that you came only to visit them and convert them to our Faith," mentioning also that search for gold had been carried on.[8] The pious royal tone is like that used when Esquivel went into Jamaica, and the truth was quite the contrary.

The "pacification" of Cuba was given into the hands of one of the more unsavory figures in the annals of the New World. Diego Velázquez de Cuéllar was one of the original vecinos of Español, having come with Columbus on the second voyage. When Ovando marched into Xaragua, Velázquez carried out the massacre of the assembled caciques, went on to subjugate the western part of Española, founded its villas, and gave its Indians into repartimiento. He was the *de facto* lieutenant governor for Ovando of what is now the Republic of Haiti, throughout which the natives were exploited pitilessly. Soon the western villas were failing. The northwesternmost, Lares de Guahaba, was the first to be abandoned; its natives and their cacique Hatuéy fled across the Windward Channel to take refuge in the Maisí district of Cuba. Velázquez, richest and most powerful person in the western region, had had his eye on Cuba for some time. He asked and secured from the new governor the control of Cuba, which was confirmed by the King. Thereby, in the words of Oviedo, he became "mucho mas riquíssimo." [9]

Velázquez assembled three hundred Spaniards at Salvatierra de la Sabana, far out on the southwestern peninsula of Haiti. The destination taken thence to the eastern tip of Cuba perhaps was determined by the desire to capture Hatuéy and his band of refugees. The dramatic execution of the cacique secured for Hatuéy a place as adopted national hero of modern Cuba. From the Maisí region Velázquez went on to establish himself at Baracoa, and founded there his first Cuban villa of Asunción, also briefly his first capital.

Meanwhile, Narváez and his Jamaican party had come by invitation of Velázquez to take part in the Cuban venture. They were joined by others from Española, among them Las Casas, at the time still interested in making his fortune. Narváez and the second group landed at the opposite southern end of Cuba in the Gulf of Guacayanabo, where stranded Spaniards had been sure of help in the past.[10] While Velázquez moved at leisure about the southeast, Narváez led his men the length of the island. Having circled the Gulf of Guacanayabo, they crossed over to the north coast through the large Indian province of Camaguey, where they indulged in an unprovoked massacre at Caonao, word of which

---

[7] CDI, XXXII, 90, 420.
[8] *Ibid.*, pp. 369, 372.
[9] Oviedo, *Historia*, Bk. XVII, ch. 3.
[10] Las Casas, Bk. III, chs. 25–32.

spread quickly. Farther along the north shore (Sagua la Grande) they took to canoes to get as far as Habana. In the latter province the caciques and Indians had fled in fear of Spanish violence, Las Casas going out to reassure them. What Las Casas witnessed on this entrada began his questioning of the morality of subjecting natives. Later he wrote of the expedition of Narváez: "I do not remember with how much spilling of human blood he marked that road." There was no conquest of Cuba other than by terrorizing the natives.

ABORIGINAL CUBA

Aboriginal Cuba is poorly recorded, one reason being that its land and life were much like those of Española, Oviedo saying that the Cubans had the same customs, rites, and ball games as in Española.[11] They were also of the same speech. Las Casas is our principal informant, and his firsthand knowledge extended to most of the island.[12] He noted the extensive savannas studded with clumps of tall palms. (It is uncertain to what extent these are edaphic features or are products of burning. Savannas if of clay soils and matted grass roots were ill suited to native tillage. It may be surmised that Cuban savanna plains were little occupied by Indians.) Las Casas was also impressed by the extent of the woods: "One may go almost three hundred leagues beneath trees; the island being very rich in fine cedars, we were accustomed to say that we had seen a grapevine that extended over the length of the island." This statement is not in conflict with the extent of grassy savannas. The savannas were smooth plains, flanked by woodlands. The multitude of grapevines indicates margins of woods and the abundance of tropical cedars (*Cedrela*) a prevalence of second growth, not virgin forest.

The Spanish villas, here as elsewhere, were placed where there were the most natives. There were no claims of dense population for Cuba such as there are for the other three islands. Las Casas thought its total population about equal to that of Jamaica. One explanation for a smaller population might be that its occupation by agricultural Arawaks came later than in the other islands. Another and perhaps a better reason was that its plains and heavy soils were less well suited to tillage by digging stick.

Las Casas described the tillage as very orderly, with the familiar conuco planting in mounds three to four feet across and three to four palms high; the earth heaped up by fire-pointed poles resembling flails. The staple crops were the same as in the other islands, with yuca most important.

More information is given about animal food, especially for the southern shore, which by reason of its shoal waters, marshes, and low cays may have been more attractive than the north coast. The vast marine pasturage of the green turtles lay on the southern side. One way of taking these was by means of remoras, the suckerfish that attached themselves to the swimming turtles. Captured turtles were kept in corrals built in shallow water, as many as five hundred to a thousand at a time. In the Bay of Xagua (Cienfuegos), near which Las Casas had his estate, he knew of water corrals made of canes fixed in the bottom, in

---

[11] Oviedo, *Historia*, Bk. XVII, ch. 4.
[12] Las Casas, Bk. III, especially chs. 22, 23, and 27.

which *lizas* (mullet) were kept by the thousands. The marshes were frequented by flocks of migrant waterfowl which were taken by swimmers hiding under calabashes (as in Jamaica). In the entrada with Narváez he observed the pueblo of Carahita (in the vicinity of Sagua la Grande), the houses of which were built on forked posts set in the water. Punning, he called the place *casa harta*, "for the abundance of food of many kinds which they had there was to be marvelled at, bread and game, and fish," especially parrots, of which Indian boys knocked ten thousand from their roosts during the fortnight the party stayed there. This is an interesting faunal note. In the early years parrots were frequently mentioned in the islands as well as on Tierra Firme, by the Old World names of *papagayo* and *perico,* and the long-tailed brilliantly colored ones by the Arawak name *guacamayo.* Along with doves and pigeons, they were appreciated as food by Spaniards as well as by natives, and were very abundant. Some were sent alive to Spain for their plumage; others because they had been taught to speak. Parrots have since disappeared from many parts of the West Indies, and elsewhere are rarely seen in the islands.

Living was in villages of multifamily houses. Some of the villages had two to three hundred such dwellings, according to Las Casas. Caonao in Camaguey, where the great massacre took place, had two plazas and on each a great house for purposes of assembly.

As in the other Arawak islands, the society was stratified and organized into cacicazgos. Velázquez in his letter of April 1, 1514 to the King named a score of such provinces in evidence of his success.[13] From this and other sources Cuban students have constructed aboriginal political maps, the information however being insufficient. There seems to have been nothing as extensive or as elaborate as the territories and hierarchies of Española. Camaguey was evidently of greatest extent, with a dependent province of Savaneque to the west along the north coast. To its southwest was the territory of Guamuhaya that ran to the mountains of Trinidad. Habana was a major native province farther west, reaching from coast to coast, as now. In the southeast, Baracoa and Bayamo appear to have been native states. Velázquez did not trouble to treat with any native authority but swept it away at once, possibly an indication that the Cuban caciques were of lesser authority than those in Española.

The western extremity of Cuba was occupied not by Arawaks but by a very different and very primitive people. They were described first by Velázquez: "The life of these people is of the manner of savages, for they have neither houses nor village quarters, nor fields, nor do they eat anything else than the flesh they take in the montes and turtles and fish." Las Casas knew them as "Indians at the Cape of Cuba [Cabo San Antonio] who are like savages, have no relations whatever with others of the island, nor do they have houses, but they live in caves, except when they go out to fish, and are called Guanahacabibes." The long, narrow, infertile peninsula that runs out into Cabo San Antonio still bears that name. That is about all that is known of these primitive people at the coming of the Spaniards.

Kitchen middens and cave remains of rudimentary skills are found in other

---

[13] CDI, XI, 413-428.

parts of the island, where they antedate Arawak remains and indicate rather high antiquity. It has been inferred that these were left by earlier inhabitants of Cuba, who gave way to the Arawak advance out of the East, a remnant remaining lodged in the farthest and least attractive end of the island. A similarly primitive and perhaps related group was noted earlier in the southwestern peninsula of Haiti. Both avoided contact with the Arawaks. Las Casas located Guanahacabibes only in the meager peninsula of that name. In the fertile limestone and terrace lands adjacent to the East, in Pinar del Río and Habana provinces, a number of Arawak place names survive. When Narváez entered the province of Habana he found caciques and conditions like those of the more easterly parts. These remarks are made because modern ethnic maps are likely to assign Cuba about and west of Habana to such primitive aborigines, under the name of Ciboney.

Anthropologists from the United States, discovering middens and cave sites of primitive skills, with no evidence of agriculture or pottery, attached the name Ciboney to such, as they did also to the historical remnants of non-agricultural natives. Thus whatever was non-Arawak or pre-Arawak in Cuba, and also in Haiti, has come to pass in United States usage as Ciboney. The misnaming comes from incorrect reading of Las Casas. In a memorial of 1516 to Cardinal Cisneros, regent of Spain, Las Casas proposed salvaging remnant groups of natives by building one or more monasteries for their care, citing four kinds that might be brought under doctrine and charity: (1) the people of the Jardines or cays off both north and south shores, "many islets lived on by Indians who are accustomed to eat only what they fish"; (2) the Guanahacabibes of the Cape of Cuba; (3) "others who are called Ciboneys, whom the Indians of the island keep as servants, all those of the Jardines being such"; (4) any left on the Lucayas islands should be brought in, being almost of "the same nature and ways" as those of the Jardines.[14] Las Casas set the Guanahacabibes ethnically and geographically wholly apart. The Lucayans were clearly Arawak; the natives of the Jardines were fishermen whom he likened to a servant class known as Ciboneys. What he had in mind was an asylum for groups he knew to be neglected and in distress.

Ciboney was a term for the lowest class in Cuba, perhaps similar to the naborías on Española. In his *Apologética Historia*, Las Casas made this clear: "In the island of Cuba there was a most simple and gentle kind of people, the same as the Lucayos, who were held like slaves." Their name as printed there was *exbuneyes*, which led Loven to think that still another substratum was meant.[15] A copyist or printer set *ex* for *ci*, a type of error common in the poorly printed *Apologética*.[16]

Both in Haiti and in Cuba there was a class unfree by birth and this substratum may have been an earlier stock that had been subjugated. Ciboney should be dropped as an ethnic term along with Taino and Sub-Taino, as only confusing

---

[14] CDU, VI, 6–11; CDI, VII, 5–11.

[15] Las Casas, *Apologética*, ch. 44; Lovén, *Origins of the Tainan Culture*, West Indies (Gothenburg, 1935), pp. 79–84.

[16] There is another such in the statement on Cuba, that there is "no or almost no difference between the *hijos* and those whom these had subjugated." *Apologética*, ch. 44. *Hijos* here can only be a miscopying of *indios*.

the common Arawak ways and people of the Greater Antilles. The Spaniards knew that common speech and habits extended from the Bahamas to Puerto Rico and Jamaica, in contrast to the great diversity on Tierra Firme.

THE SPANISH ORGANIZATION OF CUBA

Velázquez stayed in the south of the island while Narváez carried out the violent possession as far as the province of Habana. Thereupon Velázquez called a general assembly at the Bay of Xagua, writing the King that this bay was "very well known to those who navigate and very necessary and advantageous to those who come from Tierra Firme" (1514). The place was so advantageous that it should have become the center of administration. The Bay of Xagua, or Cienfuegos, midway of the southwest shores, commodious, protected, and well supplied, had been surveyed by Ocampo, who had made clear the existence of a sea passage around the western end of Cuba. There must have been some notion among navigators by that time that this was a good way out from Darién to Spain and that the Bay of Xagua, rather than Santo Domingo, would be the place from which to clear for home.

During the encampment at Xagua, gold was discovered near by. Velázquez "sent to discover mines up the large Río Arimao, which discharges half a league beyond the port, and they found very rich mines of very fine gold, like that in the Cibao but much softer." [17] The Arimao drains the western side of the low mountain mass of Trinidad, geologically similar to the gold-bearing areas of Española and Puerto Rico. Placer gold was located (1512) in numerous stream channels about the high country in the middle of the island. Word of the new gold country spread to Española and Tierra Firme. The Audiencia at Santo Domingo complained in February, 1513, of the rush to Cuba and asked that miners and workmen in Española be denied license to leave.[18] A little gold had also been obtained in mountain streams of the Sierra Maestra to the south, but the new fame of the island came from its central area.

The royal appointment of a master of the mint for Cuba was made in September, 1512. During that year and the next, numerous confirmations of rights were given to Velázquez, including that of allotting the caciques and their subjects in repartimientos, Velázquez being addressed as *capitán* of the island. Most of the correspondence and orders went through the hands of Pasamonte[19] and bypassed Diego Columbus. In his letter to the King of April 1, 1514, Velázquez told of setting out from his villa of Asunción de Baracoa the previous October to call in caciques to be given in repartimiento, of founding the villa of San Sálvador de Bayamo, and of going to Xagua. The choice of Trinidad, already noted as a villa in 1513, had been determined by Indian numbers and gold placers. In the interior to the north, Sancti Spiritus, another center for gold mining, productive streams being within five to ten leagues, became the second mining villa. Puerto Príncipe, a villa on the north coast (Nuevitas Bay) had at its disposal the Indians of Camaguey, seemingly the largest native

---

[17] Las Casas, Bk. III, ch. 32.
[18] CDI, XXXIV, 155.
[19] CDI, XI, 412–429.

"state." In the northwest the villa of San Cristóbal de la Habana was located on the south coast near Batabano. Thus by 1514 Velázquez had founded six villas of Spaniards on the island, to which he added Santiago de Cuba in 1515 to serve as his residence and capital (fig. 23).

Of the seven villas only Sancti Spiritus was an inland town; the original site of Bayamo having been on a navigable channel. It, Trinidad, and Habana faced on the Caribbean. Of the north-shore villas, Baracoa was isolated from the interior by rough terrain; Puerto Príncipe had access to the large Indian province of Camaguey and to the natives on offshore cays. Later it was relocated in the interior to become the town of Camaguey. Santiago has a sheltered and commodious ria harbor across from Haiti and Jamaica. As had been the practice in Española, the villas were placed where there were most natives; Trinidad and Sancti Spiritus had the added advantage of placer gold in abundance. They were spaced so that the entire native population of the island could be given in repartimientos or transported.

Velázquez elected to reside at Santiago and to administer his government from there, committing the tactical error of choosing a rearward location. He had seen only the eastern part of Cuba and was kept informed at long range about the course of events elsewhere. By land or sea Santiago was almost three hundred leagues from the far end of Cuba, with poor communications by land or sea. Velázquez knew of the superior location and advantages of the Bay of Xagua, but passed it up to build his capital where there was no need of one. Thereby he left farther Cuba, at the edge of the unknown, to his subordinates and to the great secession that Cortés soon carried out.

The occupation of Cuba was a repetition of that of Española. The gold Columbus had missed was discovered in arroyos of the central mountains. The placer deposits were numerous and accessible, and for some years yielded good returns. Vecinos of Sancti Spiritus and Trinidad grew rich from working the local gold by native labor. Vecinos of other villas leased their Indians to the mines.

The measures ordered to protect the Indians were not applied. Las Casas had received from Velázquez a good repartimiento on the Río Arimao close by the Bay of Xagua (and near the placers). No one was in a better position than Las Casas to know what was happening. In 1515 he renounced his holdings before Velázquez, to devote his life thereafter to the rights of the Indians. Of his Cuban years he wrote: "The perdition of these people was more vehement and accelerated because the captains went about the island pacifying the people as they said and carrying off many of the Indians whom they were continually seizing in the villages in order to have use of them; all were eating and no one was planting; some of the villagers fled, others were in uproar, caring for nothing else save that they might not be killed as was happening to many. Thus the whole land, or most of it, came to be lacking in food and was abandoned. The men and women in good health were taken to the mines and to other labor, there remaining in the villages only the aged and infirm." One vecino he knew had three hundred Indians who were put to work in the mines in such fashion that after three months only one in ten survived.[20] Church and state in Santiago were unconcerned with what was going on in distant provinces. The decimation of the na-

---

[20] Las Casas, Bk. III, ch. 78.

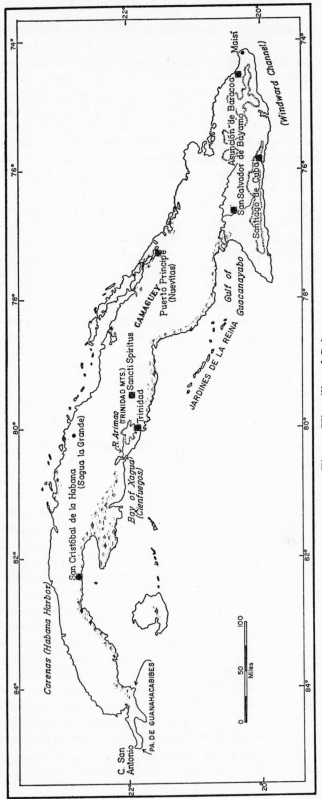

Fig. 23. The villas of Cuba.

tives took hardly a decade; the survivors took refuge in the Sierra Maestra or on cays.

In April, 1514, Velázquez wrote the King that the pigs he had brought had increased to the number of thirty thousand. The figure seems excessive, but is within the range of possibility. Velázquez had collected his men at Salvatierra where pig raising was the chief occupation. Narváez came along from Jamaica, where swine also were plentiful. In the absence of predators and endemic disease, the increase of swine was phenomenal in all the Spanish islands. About the villas then established, pigs, according to this claim soon numbered in the thousands. It may be inferred that as privileged property of the vecinos, they rooted up the conucos on which the Indians depended.

When Cortés began the conquest of New Spain, pigs from Cuba supplied both meat and breeding stock. The long-legged Spanish range hogs were the most adaptable of European livestock, thriving equally well in tropical lowlands and on mountains and dry lands. They provided an ambulant meat supply for Spanish entradas into Mexico, the American southwest, and other parts from the surplus bred in the West Indies.

By the end of its first Spanish decade, Cuba was also well stocked with neat cattle and fairly so with horses. Stock ranches of ganado mayor as well as *menor*, known as hatos, had appropriated a major part of the island.[21]

FLORIDA

Beginning with the Cantino and Canerio maps of 1502, a body of land was represented in about the proper location for Florida and was shown as a peninsula of a northern mainland. By 1509 the evacuation of the Lucayos was well under way, and some knowledge of land beyond the Bahamas was likely. It may have been seen by a strayed Spanish vessel, but is more likely to have been heard from captive islanders.

The Straits of Florida were a major cultural divide of the New World, separating what was ethnically South American from North America. On the one side were the pacific Arawaks, planting conucos, living in multifamily bohíos, and obeying hereditary chiefs. On the other side the natives were of very different physique, language, and habits—warlike, hunters with bow and arrow, depending for plant food on maize as staple, supplemented by squash and beans. These were Indians of our eastern woodlands and of a culture that extended north into Canada. The contrast is illustrated by the change in cultivated plants: yuca, sweet potatoes, peanuts, chile pepper, cotton, and true tobacco were not known in Florida or northward. The Florida channel was crossed, however, by native canoemen, apparently not infrequently. Peter Martyr wrote that natives of the mainland were accustomed to visit the Lucayas islands in order to take pigeons, returning with their canoes laden. Florida archaeology from time to time also is turning up artifacts that are of southern origin. This farther land to the north was first heard of by the Spaniards as Bimini, a name later transferred to a chain of small cays along the western edge of the Great Bahama Bank.

---

[21] Gil González Dávila in 1515 referred to *hatos* of pigs and *hatos* of cattle as belonging to the Crown in Española (CDI, I, 342). *Rancho* is a late Spanish Mexicanism, derived from its original meaning of bivouac.

The ambitions of Juan Ponce de León had been fed by his success in Puerto Rico. He had grown rich there, but also was being charged with having appropriated to himself more than was his right. The King wrote Pasamonte on July 25, 1511, that he was inclined to grant the wish of Ponce de León to undertake a new settlement. New officials had been appointed for San Juan Island and were instructed in November of that year to take the *residencia* of Ponce de León, a regular procedure of inquiry on change of office and one that was always time-consuming. The commission to take the hearings was sent from Spain on February 23, 1512, and on the same date the King wrote Pasamonte to look into them, also that Ponce de León had written his wish to settle the island of Bimini and he enclosed a contract for him to be allowed to do so at the discretion of Pasamonte.[22] Ponce de León was obligated to be present during the hearings in San Juan and could not leave until the process was finished. The process was still going on in October, 1512.

The claim that Ponce de León discovered Florida in 1512 rests on a royal assent, dated September 26, 1512, for him "to settle the Island of Bimini and the Island of Florida which you have discovered by our orders." [23] The events of that year in Puerto Rico however are irreconcilable with such a date. The *Libro de Asientos* gives the date as September 27, 1514, for his right "to settle the island of Bimini and the island of Florida which he had discovered." [24] This accommodates the events of 1512 in Puerto Rico and sets the time of the voyage discovery in the spring of 1513, the acceptable date for the first Spanish landing in the United States. The 1512 date may be considered a slip of the copyist.

The little that is known about the expedition is at second hand. The name Florida, given because of the discovery on Easter Sunday, was applied to the northerly part of the coast, first seen, and the name Bimini to the later discovery of the southern coast. Because contacts were discontinuous, both were thought to be islands. The ships then turned up the west coast of Florida, perhaps for a goodly distance. There was contact with the natives but no entry inland. No gold was found. Ponce, who had financed the venture himself, obtained nothing from it. Being a practical man, he secured his rights to another try by the second agreement (1514), but turned to other activities that promised gain. Peter Martyr first gave currency in 1514 (*Second Decade*) to the story of a Fountain of Youth: "At three hundred and twenty-five leagues from Española those who have explored closely tell of an island, named Boiuca or Agnaneo, having a celebrated spring, by drinking the waters thereof old men are rejuvenated." Oviedo dismissed it as a yarn. Being the kind of story that gives spice to history, it has had perennial life in schoolbooks.

THE PEARL COAST

The Pearl Coast dropped from notice after the time of the Guerras. The native store of pearl ornaments having been soon procured, it required a different

---

[22] The documents comprise a major part of CDI, XXXII; the commission is in CDI, XXXIV, 356 ff.
[23] CDI, XXII, 33–37.
[24] CDU, XVII, 23.

knowledge to find where the pearl beds were and how to exploit them. The local Indians are not known to have been set to work at pearl diving, perhaps a recognition that they had to be dealt with circumspectly. In the final days of Ovando's tenure (May 3, 1509), a letter from the King acknowledged receipt of a shipment of pearls with the comment that they were not very good, but asking for any more that had been fished. The letter continued, "you say the Pearl Island is small for a Christian settlement and that to work it it will suffice to provide encouragement and quit their fears, for if they feel safe two or three Christians can take charge. This seems very proper to me and so it shall be done." [25] The inference is that a party had gone down to the Pearl Coast and located the pearl beds at the Pearl Island, the small island of Cubagua that was to be the great source of pearls in later years. Here pearls had been fished, which implies that Indian divers had been used, probably Lucayans taken from the north. This would also explain the comment about quieting the fears of the divers under Christian protection.

On Ovando's return to Spain he delivered to the Casa de Contratación more than thirty-nine marks of pearls,[26] indicating another expedition. The King accepted the advice of Ovando that no parties going to Tierra Firme (Hojeda and Nicuesa) should be permitted to enter the region of Cumaná (an alternative name for the Pearl Coast). The western parts of Tierra Firme were in process of detachment from the authority at Santo Domingo, but its eastern end remained dependent and so continued into late colonial time, as a part of the Audiencia of Santo Domingo, the original reason having been the control of the pearl fishery.

The successor government under Diego Columbus extended the exploitation of the pearl beds. He was ordered by Ferdinand not to transport natives from Trinidad to Española, in order not to disturb the trade of these islanders with the Indians of the Pearl Coast.[27] The capture of natives for use in Española at this time had spread to farther islands, the King being anxious to keep the Pearl Coast peaceful. That the Spaniards did behave themselves there is shown by the fact that there was no trouble for some years with the Caribs of the Cumaná mainland and also by the continuing friendship of the Guayquerí Indians, of Margarita Island adjacent to the pearl beds. Spaniards from Española and San Juan brought Indian divers, mainly Lucayans accustomed to dive deep for conchs (*Strombus*), Las Casas being of the opinion that this was a principal cause of the extinction of the Lucayans.

In 1512 Diego proposed a fort in "las Perlas," and the King urged that it be built.[28] A settlement seems to have been made on Cubagua during the second decade, perhaps merely a camp occupied during pearl diving. Cubagua was the main source of pearls. Desolate today, it appears to have been less bleak when Oviedo knew it. It lacked potable water, which was brought in barrels from the Río Cumaná, a distance of seven leagues. The island was not inhabited, but Christians from Santo Domingo and San Juan built bohíos in the Indian manner. It was then covered by a scrub of guayacan and columnar cactus, some bearing

---

[25] CDI, XXXI, 428.
[26] CDU, V, 199.
[27] Letter of June 15, 1510, CDI, XXXII, 96.
[28] CDI, XXXII, 422, 337.

good red-fleshed fruit. Oviedo noted flamingos, "hares," iguanas, and many great turtles that came on shore to lay their eggs or were taken at sea by harpoons attached to long cords.

The situation on the mainland appeared timely for converting Caribs. Franciscans established themselves in Cumaná, and Dominicans at Píritu eighteen leagues farther to the west, according to Oviedo in 1516. The promising beginning came to a sudden end when a Spanish ship that had come to Píritu for trade invited the chief and his men on board and made off to sell them as slaves. The Caribs forgot the distinction between good and bad Christians and killed the Dominican friars, the earliest martyrs of the New World. In the year following, the Dominicans built another mission near Cumaná, at Chiribichi on the nearby Gulf of Santa Fé. Depredation by Spanish ships recurred, and in 1519 the mainland Caribs rose to sweep out all the Christians, some eighty of whom lost their lives.[29]

THE "CARIB" ISLANDS

The Lesser Antilles were of little concern. On the second voyage Columbus entered by the Dominica Passage and then turned north in the lee of the Leeward Islands, naming most of them as he passed by. Because this was thereafter the usual approach to Española, the names were remembered and retained, from Dominica to Santa Cruz. A pilot of the second voyage, Pedro Enríquez, testifying in the suit brought by the Columbus heirs, counted the islands off in order, adding that "all lie in one cordillera, extending from northwest to southeast," a very appropriate characterization of their physical geography.[30] The low islands on the Atlantic side of the Leeward Islands, such as Barbuda and Anguilla, were not seen at the time, nor did Harrisse find them on maps earlier than the third decade of the sixteenth century. The current convention that the Leeward Islands (*Sotavento*) run from Guadeloupe to St. Croix records the Spanish practice of sailing to their leeward and may go back to the time of Columbus. All were inhabited by or in the power of Caribs. Santa Cruz (St. Croix) was at times involved in conflict, as when its warriors supported the revolt in Puerto Rico. Because of its position and excellent harbor it was harassed by the Spaniards and soon became depopulated; Ponce de León found it deserted in 1515. Garay undertook an expedition from Española in 1511 against Guadelupe, but was turned back with losses, and Ponce de León also failed four years later.[31]

The discovery and status of the Windward (*Barlovento*) Islands are even more

---

[29] The major accounts are by Oviedo, *Historia*, Bk. XIX, and Las Casas, Bk. II, chs. 18, 33, 34, 45, and Bk. III, ch. 156. Charles Alexander, *Geography of Margarita and Adjacent Islands* (Berkeley and Los Angeles: University of California Publications in Geography, 1958) describes the islands and gives additional historical data.

[30] CDU, VIII, 47; Samuel E. Morison, who retraced the discovery voyage by sail (*The Second Voyage of Christopher Columbus from Cadiz to Hispaniola and the Discovery of the Lesser Antilles* [Oxford, 1939]) came to the conclusion that some of the names became reshuffled. The text accompanying the reproduction of the deteriorated Cosa map (Duke of Alba facsimile atlas, *Mapas españoles de América*) identifies in proper location an *y. de la niebe* (Nevis) and also the island of San Martín. If Morison is correct that the San Martín of Columbus is in fact Nevis, the change in name had taken effect by 1500.

[31] CDI, XXXII, 193, 326; CDI, XXXVI, 379, 393.

obscure. Columbus missed them in his third voyage by sailing from Margarita directly to Española. On his last voyage he touched briefly at Martinique (the Matinino about which he had heard as the Amazon island), stopped on Dominica, and continued to Española. Cosa entered half a dozen islands on his map of 1500 in somewhat uncertain location; their names are forgotten except for the one he called Asensión (Asunción). These may record passages of ships in the 1499 voyages from Spain to Tierra Firme.

As the labor supply on Española declined, attention turned to the southern islands. By authority of the Queen given in 1503, those designated as Caribs might be taken as slaves. In 1511 Ferdinand began to legitimize slaving in these islands, their names thus first becoming of public record. In the earliest order I have seen, he named los Barbudos, Cobaco, and Mayo.[32] The name Mayo continued to appear for a while on maps for an island to the northwest of Trinidad. I do not know what it may have been. Cobaco was Tobago, and los Barbudos, to be discussed below, is Barbados. In a later provision (July 3, 1512) there were designated as subject to capture, because of their resistance to Christians, certain Indians called Caribs in "the island of Los Barbudos, Dominica, Matinino [Martinique], Santa Lucia, San Vicente, La Asunción, and Tavaco [Tobago]."[33] St. Lucia and St. Vincent may be of earliest mention here. Asunción (Asensión of the Cosa map) was Grenada, placed by Enciso under its older name one degree higher in latitude than Tobago. On the Turin map (*ca.* 1523) the name Grenada appeared as the southernmost of the Windward chain. The provisions of 1511 and 1512 threw open to slave hunting all the islands from Dominica to Tobago.

Both Barbados and Barbuda mean bearded, the adjectives more or less interchangeable, *barbudo* signifying long bearded. Barbuda of the Leeward Islands is small, low, and lacks water; even now it has only about a thousand inhabitants. It can hardly have been an island designated as productive of slaves, nor was it in the right position, nor does it appear on the earlier maps. Barbados of the Windward Islands is much larger, and fertile; its present population is a quarter of a million. For both islands, the second syllable was given either as *ba* or *bu*. The important distinction is that the small northern island was always in the singular and feminine, as it is in current English, Barbuda. The large southern island is regularly in the masculine plural, shortened to Barbados in English. The permissions to go slave hunting name the Isla de los Barbudos. The Turin map (1523) distinguishes *de los barbados* from the northern *la barbada*. The *Islario de Santa Cruz* (*ca.* 1541) describes La Barbada as flat and deserted and difficult to see from a distance, and Los Barbados as so called because they found on it Indians with beards. Robert Schomburgk, who wrote his excellent *History of Barbados* (published 1847) too early to have good access to Spanish documents, thought the name came from the hanging air roots of wild fig trees, a fantasy that was accepted into the Oxford Dictionary and remains current. Still unknown to Juan de la Cosa in 1500, by 1511 Barbados was named in first place in the Lesser Antilles as a Carib island open to the taking of slaves, an indication that it was well peopled but not proof that its natives were Caribs. It is remarkable that an island situated a hundred miles out into the Atlantic, to the east of the volcanic

---

[32] December 23, 1511, CDI, XXXII, 306.
[33] CDU, V, 258.

Antillean chain and upwind into the sweep of the trade winds, should have been well peopled.

The second decade of that century was the time of heaviest raiding about the Caribbean Sea. Slaves were required in the large islands of the north, and the importation of Negroes was just beginning. Alonso de Santa Cruz later listed the Leeward Islands from the Virgins to Barbuda as *deshabitadas* or *despobladas*, mentioning only St. Kitts and Nevis as inhabited. To the south, he recorded St. Lucia and Tobago as deshabitada and wrote of the people of Barbados in the past tense.

ISLANDS OFFSHORE FROM TIERRA FIRME

Raids from Santo Domingo, from San Juan, and later from Santiago de Cuba ranged farther and farther about the Caribbean, indifferent to who the natives were. Margarita Island alone remained out of bounds to slavers. By the provision of 1512, Trinidad was designated as Carib, which was not proved. It was not greatly harried, however, for it was too large and too well forested to be raided effectively, and its natives were skilled in the use of bows and arrows. The islands off the coast of Venezuela, known as the Gigantes, and consisting of Curaçao, Bonaire, and Aruba, were harried, although the natives had been amicable and were Arawak. A report of September 6, 1515, from the officials of Santo Domingo rated Caribs as most desirable captives, "few of them dying, good for a lot of use, but hard to guard because likely to escape in canoes." It continued: "of twelve hundred *piezas* [pieces] who had been brought from the Isle of the Gigantes many had died"; the principal cause being the strange notion that they went into the montes to eat *hobos (Spondias)*, and "since they ate nothing else they would come back to the estancias spent and sick." However, they were considered much better than the Lucayo Indians.[34] Half a century later, López de Velasco wrote of Bonaire and Aruba as an encomienda stocked with cattle, sheep, and horses, and of Curaçao that "at the time when Indians were taken as slaves, they say around a hundred thousand Indians were removed from it; today there are about a hundred and fifty married Indians." Another half-century later Vásquez de Espinosa did not mention these islands, the Bahamas, or Barbados in his compendious description.

The political geography of the West Indies is starkly simple: the French, English, and Dutch colonies of the seventeenth century occupied islands that had been emptied of their natives early in the sixteenth century in order to keep Española going. To a great extent the North European successors were able to live off the Spanish livestock that had replaced the Indians.

While Ferdinand lived with Fonseca as his right hand, Isabela's original command that only cannibal Indians should be enslaved was taken as lightly as her declaration that inoffensive natives were Spanish subjects with the rights of such. It was necessary only to declare an island as Carib to legitimize slave raids. The transportation of Indians to forced and unpaid service under the name of naboría did not require even such subterfuge.

---

[34] CDI, XXXVI, 412.

THE CLASSIFICATION BY FIGUEROA

In the reforms of Cisneros the distinction between Carib and non-Carib became a serious concern. In 1518 Rodrigo de Figueroa was appointed judge with plenary powers to determine the matter, enjoining him to ascertain who were in fact Caribs. He reported, "Indians have been taken from los Barbados, the Gigantes, and elsewhere who are not Caribs nor proper to be slaves and whom vecinos of this island [of Española] keep as domestic naborías." Figueroa took his job seriously and rendered an honest decision after two years. For much of Tierra Firme his evidence was inconclusive. He judged that the long stretch of coast from Coquibacoa (Goajira) to the Río Sinú was not proved to be Carib but rather was *guatiao*, with final judgment reserved. Las Casas declared that those of the island of Trinidad were not Caribs, but guatiaos,[35] an Arawak term meaning persons of good will, originally based on a rite by which blood brotherhood was pledged. This was the very country for which the Queen had been persuaded to issue the original order against Caribs. The situation in the islands other than the four large islands occupied by the Spaniards he adjudicated properly: except for Trinidad, the Lucayas, Barbados, Gigantes, and Margarita, the islands were Carib.[36] There is no report whether there were still natives on these exempted islands, Figueroa's inquiry being to find out whether Indians were in illegal servitude. Figueroa came too late, but he does clear up some of the ethnogeography of the Caribbean. His findings, however, have remained largely unrecognized.

[35] CDI, XXIII, 343–344.
[36] CDI, I, 380–383.

X

ISLAND CRISIS AND ITS EFFECTS
(1509–1519)

•

NOMINAL GOVERNMENT OF DIEGO COLUMBUS

Ovando had held the reins firmly and had given the vecinos little cause for resentment, nor had he sought favor at court. The selection of the son of Columbus to replace him meant a deliberate reduction of authority which continued, leaving the young Admiral and his highborn wife little more to do than to play at holding court in Santo Domingo. Pasamonte, with the title of royal treasurer, came in advance of the new governor to be the real representative of King and Fonseca, and to exercise authority which Velázquez, Ponce de León, and others were quick to recognize and to which they allied themselves.

Gil González Dávila, *contino* of the royal household and favorite of Fonseca, was sent over in 1509 to go back and forth between Spain and the Indies on royal commissions. In 1511 three judges were dispatched with plenary powers, constituting the first Audiencia in the New World. One of these, Vázques de Ayllón, later would try to extend Spanish control to the southeastern United States. Both islands and Tierra Firme passed into the hands of Fernandistas, as the clique about the King and Fonseca has come to be known to Spanish historians.[1]

The action overseas expanded as to territory but was otherwise little changed. Occasionally there was a brief interest in a route to the East Indies, sporadic and minor in the continuing search for gold on which Columbus had set the course of the colony. The four major islands were wholly partitioned among private beneficiaries and the Crown. Gold was the staple of the early years under all four governors, and its production depended wholly on forced native labor.

Isabela and Ferdinand as "the Catholic Kings," supported by warrant from the Pope, based their original rights and obligations in the Indies on their Christianizing mission; the Queen taking this duty seriously. After her death in 1504 this sense of responsibility was lost. Ferdinand from time to time expressed concern about the treatment of the natives. He instructed Diego Columbus that the

---

[1] Giménez Fernández has developed this theme in great detail. Men of ambition or of discretion did not align themselves with the Columbus interests. The old Admiral left no legacy of loyalty among Spaniards nor of goodwill among the natives. The young one lacked the ability to attract and to lead men.

caciques were to be assured of good treatment, that these should tell the governor if they were badly treated, and that they should be kept from disposing of their possessions.[2] Repeatedly he urged that the natives should be cared for so that they would not continue to diminish, as they were doing. At the same time he wanted more of them to be put to work in the mines and more to be brought in from islands that lacked gold, and asked that a third at all times to be kept employed at the mines.[3] As he wrote of the discharge of his conscience he also asked for more revenue from mines. Nothing was done, however, to remove rigors and excesses, and almost nothing came of any mission of Christian faith. The state was chronically in need of funds and here revenue might be had in its most desirable form, gold. In the short view of Ferdinand's political urgencies, gold was more important than preserving the natives. The overriding objective remained to secure more gold and this was understood by all officials.

THE DOMINICAN PROTEST

The first Dominican friars arrived in September, 1510. As they found out about conditions in Española they became the first insistent voice to arouse the Christian conscience. The story of how they agreed on the sermon that Fray Antonio de Montesino preached on the last Sunday of Advent in 1511 is well known. Before a congregation of the governor, officials, and citizens of Santo Domingo he declared that they were living in mortal sin because of their treatment of the Indians, who should become their Christian brothers. When protests were sent to Spain asking for the recall of the Dominicans, the friars sent Montesino to the Spanish court to plead the case of the natives. He got scant official hearing but the issue was joined, never to be silenced. A first step was taken in the Laws of Burgos of 1512–1513, to be censured by the Dominicans as ingenuous, unworkable, and evasive, but a first breach in the wall of indifference that was gradually to be widened. The Dominicans found their great ally in Las Casas in 1515 when he abandoned Cuba to go to Spain to begin the defense of Indian rights, accompanied by Montesino. Las Casas continued to work closely with the Dominicans, entering the order in 1522. The old system continued to the death of Ferdinand in January, 1516.

END OF GOLD FROM THE ISLANDS

In the time of Diego the state of Española became more and more depressed, because it became more and more difficult to produce the gold. The yield in Puerto Rico fell off quickly, that of Cuba almost as rapidly. Later writers claimed that it was not exhaustion of gold deposits that caused the abandonment of gold mining but the dying off of the natives. The loss of cheap labor (and forced labor was cheaper than slaves) hastened the collapse but did not cause it.

The island gold was found as placers, waste of weathering and erosion of mountains collected in stream channels, occasionally as a residuum in decayed mantle of bedrock. In the long process of wearing down of the mountains bits of heavy and inert gold were trapped on certain lower mountain flanks by deposit from small streams. The so-called mines were submerged bars (the meaning

---

[2] CDI, XXXI, 388 ff
[3] CDU, V, 312 ff

of the name "placer"), under water or alluvium. The productive districts were few, of small extent, and slight depth. In the islands of Haiti and Puerto Rico they were found immediately by native disclosure. When Cuba was entered, the Spaniards knew how to search the stream beds about the central mountains and also, with less success, those coming out of the Sierra Maestra. There were no further discoveries of importance.

The largest and richest placers, those of the Cibao and San Cristóbal districts, were worked for about twenty-five years; those of Puerto Rico and Cuba lasted about half as long. That they were pretty well worked out in that time is indicated by the fact that gold has never since been of importance in these islands.

The Spaniards used the natives mainly to dig the gold-bearing sand and gravels and do other heavy labor about the camps. The more productive localities were dug over and over year after year by shallow pits, still visible in places. The required input of labor became greater as the yield declined. Diminishing returns and increasing scarcity and cost of labor brought an end to district after district, hastened by the fact that the climate permitted year-round working of the gold diggings. Experienced placer miners were brought from Spain to recover gold by panning, the pans known as *bateas*.[4] They were of greatest benefit in the Cibao where gold was found mainly in fine particles. Whether other improvements in extraction were made has not appeared in the record.

LOSS OF SPANISH POPULATION

Spaniards came to the Canary Islands to live, but to Española at first as employees and then as fortune-hunters who had no intention to stay. The islands were the first example of a highly unstable frontier that attracted the footloose who came to get rich quick, to escape the constraints and boredom of life at home, to get ahead without industry or competence. They were bachelors or, if married, left their families in Spain. Ovando encouraged those who would bring their families, gave inducement to artisans, and tried to establish *labradores*, workers of the soil. Ferdinand thought in 1511 to colonize Basques from his own province of Guipúzcoa, "where there are many people and small means to make a living,"[5] but he did not go to the expense of doing so. The prevailing attitude in the islands was of readiness to take off whenever new opportunities beckoned elsewhere.

Ovando had some success in stabilizing the Spanish population in Española by attaching it to the villas he founded in 1504 and 1505, and by delaying the dispersal to other islands. The villas were temporary, however, because the vecinos were attracted and held only by their allotment of Indians.

Under Ovando, the Spanish population continued to increase to the end of his

---

[4] Las Casas thought this an Arawak word, such interpretation still being commonly accepted. Corominas thought it probably of Arabic origin but could cite no use of the word in Spanish earlier than 1521, from Mexico. It is used in Mexico to the present for wide shallow wooden bowls or trays, usually ornamental and of Indian craftsmanship. Velázquez in his 1514 letter to the King said that Christians had brought a dozen *bateas* to Cuba with good results, giving their daily returns of gold. That he did not explain what a *batea* was suggests that the name was familiar in Spain, and that he gave their number and yield suggests that this was equipment proper to placer mining.

The Haitian natives were skilled in making fine and large trays of polished wood. Perhaps Spanish miners also made use of these as serviceable and available and gave them the name *batea*, and so the name passed over into Mexico for household wooden trays.

[5] CDII, XXXII, 187

regime. In 1509 the governor permitted Ponce de León to colonize adjacent Puerto Rico, and the Crown began the occupation of Tierra Firme by Nicuesa and Hojeda. The second decade of the century was one of continuing and largest emigration from Española, first to Puerto Rico, Jamaica, and Darién. Velázquez was followed into Cuba by so many from the western villas that these were virtually deserted.

The more dissatisfied and adventurous elements abandoned Española, many of them to move on again and again to end up in far parts of the New World, there to acquire the proud title of *conquistador*. Others who had remained after the decade of the large migration left later to acquire fame or infamy elsewhere; Ponce de León and Vázquez de Ayllón in Florida and the Carolinas; Rodrigo de Bastidas in Santa Marta; Juan de Ampués in Venezuela; Gil González de Avila (Davila) on the Pacific coast of Central America; Cristóbal de Tapia and Nuño de Guzmán in Mexico.[6]

In 1514 Pasamonte ordered a new repartimiento, scandalous for its assignment of Indians to his patrons in Spain and making evident that the governor had lost his authority.[7] It affords a look at the old order in Española, after many of the vecinos had dispersed and before reforms were begun. The listing is not really a census of Spaniards in the island for it lists only those who received Indians. The repartimiento was made villa by villa, each donee being named and the number of Indians he was given. Those who were designated as vecinos have been counted. The rest of the donees were specified by occupation, such as miner, mason, smith, or clerk, or were entered only by name. These were lesser folk who had only a few or only a single Indian, often listed as *naboría de casa*. Marital status was recorded with care for the vecinos, irregularly so for the rest which therefore are not here summarized. Both classification of status and totals are here given in my rough compilation, as providing some information about the status of the Spanish towns at the time.

	Vecinos	Wives of vecinos		Other residents who had Indians
		Castilian	Native	
Concepción de la Vega	42	7	7	26
Santiago	35	7	7	8
Puerto Plata	18	3	4	2
Santo Domingo	72	28	5	92
Salvaleón de Higüey	31	16	5	10
Azua	19	4	0	4
Buenaventura	30	9	7	32
Bonao	25	4	4	17
Lares de Guahaba	14	2	1	8
Puerto Real	20	3	2	18
San Juan Maguana	27	1	2	14
Vera Paz de Xaragua	26	6	6	22
Salvatierra de la Sabana	18	0	3	2
Villanueva de Yaquimo	15	2	1	17

---

[6] The trail of desolation that Nuño de Guzmán left from Pánuco through Michoacán and Jalisco into Sonora and Sinaloa was my first introduction to a conquista. In 1514 he was an undistinguished married vecino of Puerto Plata.

[7] CDI, I, 50-236.

The efforts of government and church in support of domesticity had had some success as shown by the number of married vecinos. Wives from Castile were present in all the towns except Salvatierra, from which Velázquez had set out for Cuba. It may be inferred that the friars also had some effect in moderating the conduct of the Spaniards: about one husband in three had a native wife. To my knowledge this is the first record of intermarriage. Families of white and legitimate mestizo offspring were being started and thereby the first roots were put down into the soil of the New World. These were the founding fathers and mothers of a permanent colony.

Only one of the fifteen towns of Ovando's time was abandoned by 1514—Santa Cruz on Samaná Bay, whose vecinos had followed Ponce de León to Puerto Rico, the rest dispersing into villas to the west. Santo Domingo was faring least badly. As capital, it had officials of state and church, lawyers and doctors of medicine, merchants and shipowners, and men of property like Garay, the most successful vecino of Yaquimo, but preferring to live in his town house in Santo Domingo. In 1517 Zuazo found that, except for Santo Domingo, "where there are good houses of stone and good buildings, all the rest consist of houses of thatch and are of twenty to thirty vecinos, like poor villages in Spain." [8]

Concepción was second in importance and size and still had the title of *ciudad*, like Buenaventura having the benefit of what was left of the gold fields. The five villas of the western part of the island were in dissolution. Vera Paz, founded by Ovando to replace Xaragua, Indian capital of the west, was moved in 1515 to the harbor of Yaguana (Léogane), where an occasional ship put in. It was re-named Santa María del Puerto, and the few remaining inhabitants of Villanueva de Yaquimo were brought there. Lares de Guahaba was abandoned at about the same time and its remnant moved to Puerto Real. The depopulation of the island was thus annotated in depositions taken in 1520, which also noted that no vecinos were left at Buenaventura or Bonao and that it was thought those of Santiago would be moved to Puerto Plata.[9] By that time most of the remaining Spaniards had drifted to the coast.

When López de Velasco compiled his geography (1574) the only regular set-tlement in the western part was Yaguana (Léogane); the site of Vera Paz was known, but no sign of it remained; and at San Juan Maguana there was still a church that served the sugar plantations. Of Lares de Guahaba, Salvatierra de la Sabana, and Villanueva de Yaquimo he had uncertain notice of their former existence.

THE LAST OF THE NATIVES

In 1509, when Pasamonte came, there were said to be sixty thousand natives. Diego Columbus a year later knew of forty thousand, both estimates probably referring to those of working age.[10] The Repartimiento of 1514 enumerated 22,726, excluding children and the aged. Slaves were personal property, not subject to repartimiento and therefore were not included. Legally, the Indians

---

[8] CDI, I, 311.
[9] CDI, I, 386–415.
[10] Las Casas, Bk. III, chs. 36, 37.

who had been brought in from the other nothern Arawak islands were not slaves but naborías. The 1514 allotment thus probably included an unknown number who were not natives of Española. The new repartimiento distinguished *indios de servicio* from naborías. The former were identified by their cacique and hence may have been survivors of the local Indian communities under the formula that assigned a particular cacique and his people to a Spanish grantee. The status of naborías is unclear. Many such were assigned singly or in small numbers to individual Spaniards as unfree domestic servants. The 1514 repartimiento breaks down thus by towns, the columns for indios de servicio and for naborías being by my addition, the totals by official summary:

	Indios de servicio	Naborías	Totals
Concepción	2,082	842	2,924
Santiago	1,199	1,024	2,223
Puerto Plata	267	310	587 (*sic*)
Santo Domingo	4,213	1,760	5,973
Higüey	913	285	1,198
Azua	666	137	813
Buenaventura	1,073	450	1,513 (*sic*)
Bonao	719	336	1,055
Puerto Real	540	299	839
Guahaba	266	261	467 (*sic*)
San Juan Maguana	1,107	422	1,529
Vera Paz	502	714	1,266 (*sic*)
La Sabana	692	204	900
Yaquimo	807	232	1,039

The distribution of Indians was greatly changed from early years. A fourth belonged to Santo Domingo. The three towns most convenient to the gold fields —Buenaventura, Concepción, and Bonao—accounted for another fourth. The five western villas, equivalent to what is now the Republic of Haiti, and aboriginally perhaps the most densely peopled part, only for a fifth.

Sex and age distribution are given for the indios de servicio, including those too

REPARTIMIENTOS AT CONCEPCIÓN TO ABSENTEES

	Working age			
	Men	Women	Aged	Children
To the King	47	45	4	7
	62	68	11	26
To Fonseca	52	50	12	17
	28	28	8	5
To Conchillos	37	31	5	5
	41	44	15	7
	24	23	7	12
To Pasamonte	52	34	0	15
	11	11	8	2
	28	24	8	1
	18	5	8	6
	7	6	0	2

young and those too old to be subject to service. Males and females of working age were in fair balance, the percentage of children almost as low as that of the aged. A convenient sample may be taken from Concepción, where the repartimiento began. I have taken the first twelve repartimientos given there, choice plums that were handed to the King, Bishop Fonseca, Secretary Conchillos, and Treasurer Pasamonte, the vecinos being served thereafter.

The number of children of record in these was larger than in all the rest of the grants at Concepción, for some of which the notation is "there were found no children among the people of this cacique." The situation was better at Santo Domingo and Concepción than in the rest of the villas, perhaps best of all in the four royal haciendas at Santo Domingo:

ROYAL ESTATES AT SANTO DOMINGO

Men	Women	Aged	Children
67	88	44	13
77	93	34	63
108	150	21	44
18	20	5	3

In none of these, or anywhere else, was there on the average one child to a family. The island people were clearly marked for early extinction.

Peter Martyr, writing in 1516, said "the number of these unfortunates has diminished immensely; many say that once upon a time a census was made of more than a million two hundred thousand [the allusion being to the enumeration by the Adelantado in 1496], how many there may be today gives me horror to say." [11]

The Licenciado Zuazo reported in January, 1518 that of a million one hundred thirty thousand at the beginning there were then remaining eleven thousand and that in three or four years more there would be none. [12]

Both Zuazo and Gil González Dávila gave independent evaluation of the population catastrophe at the same time and in substantial agreement. [13]

Gil González put major blame on the transfer of Indians from one vecino to another, first because being a delicate people they suffered from such change of place and secondly, because the vecinos, being uncertain how long these Indians would be at their disposal, did not look after them properly. Also the vecinos were likely to be away in town engaged in lawsuits with one another instead of staying at home to look after their natives. Finally, he said, it had always been considered as of first importance to produce and ship as much gold as possible and therefore "There has been no concern about spending money to conserve or develop the island or to give rest to the Indians."

Zuazo criticized the authorities for giving Indians and then taking them away, "from which shifting about (*mudanza*) they have died in infinite numbers." Thus they were taken from place to place, from their homes into strange sur-

---

[11] Peter Martyr, Decade III.
[12] CDI, I, 310.
[13] CDI, I, 290–347; CDI, XXXIV, 237 ff.

roundings, from one end of the island to the other, as from Higüey to Xaragua or Salvatierra, and they died from such *mudanzas*.

Different reasons were given for the dying off of the natives and probably all of them were true. Las Casas stressed the callousness of officials and the brutality of individual masters, citing place and person. There were notorious ruffians who got their start here, even Ferdinand admitting that the men who had come from the Italian wars were a bad element. As in our early American West white men were not brought to account for what they did to red men.

It was not wanton brutality, however, that decimated the natives but a wrong and stupid system, which the Dominicans were first to denounce on moral grounds and which Zuazo and Gil González exposed more tactfully as bad management. It began with the obsession of Columbus with gold and the tribute the caciques were required to collect. It developed as the repartimiento by which the vecinos exacted labor from the natives for the overriding end of producing the gold which Ferdinand demanded. And it was the most capable governor, Ovando, who instituted the most efficient system, that of the demora, by means of which Indian men and women were dragged back and forth across the island to keep up the production of gold.

It was realized and regretted that the natives could not take it. Gil González found them a delicate people, Zuazo said they could endure only "labores de poca resistencia," such as caring for their conucos and looking after their own affairs. A Negro, he thought, could plant ten montones to one that a native did. There was some realization that a deeper trouble lay in the upset of the native way of life.

The concern of the masters was to keep their Indians fully employed in mines, fields, and household service. The success of Spain in the New World depended on the productivity of the natives, not on their removal, as later in the English settlements. The native economy had supported a large population in abundance and ample leisure. This excellent but delicate ecologic balance broke down, quickly and inadvertently, for several reasons, ignorance of diet being one.

Cassava bread was nutritious and could be transported and kept with ease. Also it was produced in ample quantity, there being no indication that the workers were ever on short rations of this staple. They were fed on it with disregard of the needed dietary balance. The supply of protein and fat that had been secured by native fishing and hunting was suppressed. The vecino might send out a trusted Indian thus to supply his own table, but not to provide diversity of food for his subjects. Work gangs were not sent to fish or hunt as it gave them opportunity to run away. The old skills of procuring animal food faded from the knowledge of the younger generation. During the greater part of the period the meat and fat of Spanish livestock was restricted to the masters. Maize and beans were very minor items in native cultivation, and the Spaniards were as yet unaware that these might provide needed variety of food. Indeed, they were innocent of the fact that with a sufficiency of cassava bread and sweet potatoes, their workers suffered malnutrition.

The breakdown of the native social structure took several directions. The caciques were eliminated at the high level; the secondary ones were reduced to the status of overseers or they became naborías of common servitude. The leisure in which they had enjoyed their dances, sings and other communal diversions was lost. Their community life disappeared in the lengthening demoras in the gold fields and transfers from one master to another. A well-structured and adjusted native society had become a formless proletariat in alien servitude, its customary habits and enjoyments lost. The will to live and to reproduce was thus weakened. One way out was to commit suicide by the juice of the bitter yuca. The repartimiento of 1514 disclosed that reproduction was ceasing. The contemporary observers were well aware that the natives died easily, and that they died of other causes than overwork and disease.

The first epidemic of record among the natives was that of smallpox in 1518, which spread to Mexico and Guatemala and cleared the way there for the conquest. The Spaniards being adults, the childhood diseases of Europe perhaps were not disseminated. Since many of the men had soldiered in Italy, outbreaks of malaria might be expected. Nuño de Guzmán had it when he went to Pánuco in 1526 from the islands, but I have not found mention of fever and ague in earlier years. The Europeans must have brought various contagions to the native people, who lacked immunity and resistance. Zuazo thought that moving the Indians from place to place was bad because they suffered from the changes of air and water, which may mean that they suffered from respiratory and intestinal infections such as tuberculosis and typhoid, unrecognized and unnamed as such. One work gang replaced another in mining camps which were innocent of sanitary provision or knowledge. The Indians were herded together in close quarters and then returned to wherever their place of living was. The conditions were highly suited to continuing infection of the native population, living on an improper diet, depressed by overwork, and dispirited by the loss of its own ways of life.

Zuazo foresaw correctly the end of the natives by the end of the second decade of the century, which was apparently true also for Jamaica and Puerto Rico, and mainly as well for Cuba. An occasional remnant survived here and there in a mountain refuge, perhaps to blend obscurely into the later inhabitants. In less than twenty years from the founding of Isabela the impending extinction of the natives was apparent and in another ten it had occurred.

REFORM OF THE GOVERNMENT

On the death of Ferdinand in January, 1516, the rule of Spain passed for scant two years into the able and clean hands of the aged Cardinal Francisco Ximenez de Cisneros, regent for the mad Queen Juana and her young son Charles. The complaints and correctives of Las Casas and the Dominicans at last received attention. Fonseca and his crowd were retired. Cisneros took three Hieronymite monks out of their cloisters to be joint governors of the Indies, a prudent choice of men who had no involvement in the conflict of interests and ideas. He also sent the Licenciado Zuazo as observer with full judicial powers at his discretion, again a discriminating choice. The Hieronymites arrived at Santo Domingo before the end of 1516, Zuazo a little later. The reports that were sent back in 1517 and 1518 are important and have not had their deserved attention. A number are from the Hieronymites, at least two and probably three are from Zuazo, and one is by Gil González Dávila.[14]

The Hieronymites reported on January, 1517, a month after their arrival, that the island was of good quality but was lacking both in Spaniards and Indians. More time and knowledge was needed before they could decide whether the Indians were to be congregated in villages, but the repartimientos to absentees had been canceled, the miners had been put on wages, and the voyages to the Pearl Coast had been stopped, all these acts as they had been instructed to do. In their report of June 22, 1517, they affirmed that the Indians were receiving better treatment than they had had at any time in the past and this they knew because they themselves had gone to virtually all the mines that were being worked. On appealing to the Castilians they found some to be of good heart but others seriously at fault.

By January 18, 1518 they had determined to resettle all Indians in pueblos of four to five hundred persons, old and young, to make their own plantings and to be furnished livestock. Such orders had gone out to all the Spanish villas and had been accepted after some opposition. A year would be required to move and resettle all the natives. A year later, however (January 10, 1519), they had to confess disaster. Thirty villages had indeed been made and the Indians, though few in number, collected into them. These had planted eight hundred thousand montones of yuca, which would have been sufficient to feed at least seven thousand people. In December, when the Indians were about to leave the mines and go to their new pueblos, they had been stricken with smallpox, of which about a third had died in the few weeks that had passed. On May 20, 1519 the officials of Santo Domingo reported that the greater part of the natives were dead of this pestilence. This is almost the last word concerning the Indians of Española and was the end of the attempt to establish free Indian communities.

Zuazo, writing to Xèvres in January, 1518, thought the condition of the natives at the time of his coming a year earlier had been like that of a man on his death-

---

[14] These are in CDI, I, 247–411. One is an unsigned memorial to the Cardinal which the editors of the *Documentos inéditos* were inclined to attribute to Las Casas because of the "terrible accusations" against Conchillos, Pasamonte, and their adherents Velázquez, Ponce de León, and Pedrarias. The memorial has passages strikingly like those in the letter from Zuazo to Xèvres. In the latter Zuazo moreover said that he had written earlier to Cardinal Cisneros about these and other ugly things that had happened. Under date of January 22, 1518, Zuazo addressed one letter to Charles as king-to-be, and another to Monsieur de Xèvres, the name under which William of Croy was known in Spain. The latter was Charles' tutor and accompanied the prince from Ghent to Spain, there to continue to have most influence over the inexperienced young king, an influence that was self-serving as it turned out and contributed to the dislike in which the Flemings came to be held in Spain. (The name Fleming was applied to the retinue Charles brought with him from the North, whether Burgundian, Walloon, or Flemish.) This William of Croy, as Giménez Fernández has documented, shortly formed an association with the Fonseca cabal to undo the reforms of Cisneros. An early illustration of his improper influence is shown by his securing the appointment of his nephew of the same name, a stripling of the age of Charles, as Archbishop of Toledo, the see that Cisneros had held. Both Croys accompanied the young King-Emperor to Diet of Worms and both are reported to have died there, the uncle by poison, the nephew by being thrown from his horse. The Croy family had a long association with the House of Habsburg, some being princes of the Empire, others grandees of Spain. Their coming to Spain had unfortunate results which Zuazo could not anticipate. The aged cardinal had died in November. The young king should be informed, and his mentor seemed the proper person to whom to write in detail about conditions.

bed, "given up by the physicians, with the candle placed in his hand." There was still hope then that they might be saved by settling them in their own communities of three to four hundred, with their own haciendas, and their own fishing and hunting grounds. At this last hour it was realized that if the remnant was to survive it would be by restoring them to their own way of life and freeing them from all servitude. The experiment failed by the chance introduction of smallpox which broke out as the natives were about to leave for their new homes.

The monks, Zuazo, and Gil González were in agreement as to reorienting the Spanish activities. The Hieronymites in particular thought it time that the Spaniards give up their attention to gold, owing in debts whatever they got as returns at the smelter. Instead, they should turn to planting and sowing, from which the Crown might get as great returns from the island as it had from Castile. Agricultural workers should be brought from Andalusia even if these would be few in number.

Gil González urged that such *labradores* should raise wheat, produce wine, and give their attention to the improvement of the pastures. There were range cattle enough to provide oxen to plow the fields of grain. It is of interest that he gave no thought to any crop of the New World, not even to maize. Despite the failure of wheat and other Spanish crop plants he held to the idea that the island should be put under a Mediterranean agriculture. Spanish work and food habits were so well established that it would take more time to find out that tropical climates were ill suited to a simple transfer of tillage and crops from Spain. It is also of interest that neither he nor others thought that white men were unsuited to physical labor in the tropics, a notion that came later out of northern Europe. At the time it was intended to start up agricultural production by Spanish labradores. The disdain of manual labor by Spaniards that soon developed in the New World had nothing to do with climate but was by identification of class with race. Where there were men of dark skin available for the sweaty jobs, the whites found such work beneath them.

A New Population Policy

Under the new dispensation, the old decree of Isabela that good Indians were free was at last in effect. The emancipated natives would take care of themselves and they needed time to recuperate. The basis of the colony would be shifted from gold mining to the products of the soil. A sedentary Spanish population was required on a broad base of artisans and agricultural workers. There would also be need of slaves for which purpose Caribs still were available by proof that they were such in fact and given to proscribed practices. It was evident that scandalous fraud had been going on in the business of hunting slaves.

Negro slaves had long been sold in Europe, especially in southern Europe through Arab, Genoese, and Portuguese traders. At this time the Portuguese were bringing their islands off Africa, from the Cape Verdes to São Tomé, into profitable production by slaves brought from the nearby mainland. Slaves were staple commodities on the Guinea coast, along with gold and ivory (divisions of the coast are still known by those names) and pepper grains.

A few Negro slaves had been introduced into Española in the time of Ovando for use in the mines.[15] Ferdinand thus referred in 1505 to a shipment of seven-teen Negroes, adding that he needed a hundred more so that "all of these be getting gold for me." In June, 1517, the Hieronymites asked that license be given to bring Negro slaves to the islands, in particular to Puerto Rico, and that these be *bozales*, that is, brought directly from Africa. Zuazo seconded and elaborated the proposal, proposing that slaves be brought from Cape Verde under license of the King of Portugal, bozales between the age of fifteen and twenty, male and female, to be placed in villages in which they were to live in marriage. Negroes were suited to heavy labor in contrast to the weak Indians and this was also known to be the best land in the world for them. He had had experience with them and was not afraid that they would revolt: "On my arrival I found that some Negroes were engaged in robberies and others had run away to the monte; some I ordered whipped and others to have their ears clipped and there has been no more trouble."

Negroes had proved hardy in the gold fields. They were next thought of to replace the Indians who had been relieved of forced labor. Las Casas, who had been in Spain during the regency of Cisneros, recalled that vecinos of the island had asked him in 1517 to give his support to the introduction of Negro slaves, to which he agreed as protection for the Indians, the Casa de Contratación approving the importation of four thousand. The exclusive license for four years was bought by Genoese factors.[16] The mass importation of Negroes was already underway in 1518, when the island economy was shifted from gold to agriculture.

If the islands were to be developed and occupied permanently, a sedentary population of white settlers was required. In June, 1517, the monks complained: that "this land is confused and lacking in settled habitation so that it is losing people from day to day and those who are here are like passers by." Zuazo urged the need of married persons who "should feel love of the land; at present two out of three are without wives and have no permanent home." As the King of Portugal had done in Madeira and in the Azores farms (*granjerías*) should be established to take the place of the depopulated mining districts. Artisans and laborers should be brought, along with their wives and households. Zuazo proposed that unlimited immigration be encouraged from all parts of the world, requiring only that the settlers be good Christians (to which the Hieronymites agreed). Ships should be permitted to come from all parts of His Majesty's realm without being obliged to pass "through the needle's eye of Sevilla"—seemingly a suggestion that the islands be opened up to the Low Countries as well as to all ports of Spain and Spanish Italy. The monks again were in agreement with the bold design, which would have changed greatly the course of modern history.

Proposal of a New Economy

Except for lack of people the island prospect was attractive. Zuazo drew a glowing and valid picture for the young King of the productivity and potential

---

[15] Juan Pérez de Tudela Bueso, "Politica de poblamiento y política de contratación de las Indias (1502–1505)," *Revista de Indias*, XV (Madrid, 1955), 387.
[16] Las Casas, Bk. III, chs. 102, 109. The concession is in CDI, I, 371.

of Española. He thought it the best country of the world, always verdant and abounding in streams and springs. Its livestock had increased marvelously. "There are herds of cattle that strayed away numbering thirty or forty, after branding. When they reappear after three to four years they number three to four hundred." Similar increase was true of pigs and other livestock. The sheep were of inferior quality and of coarse wool but could be bred up by introducing merinos. (There are still sheep of archaic breed on the island.) Livestock had multiplied without the usual attentions of the husbandman, was in abundant supply, and available for whatever needs of work animals might arise. The islands would continue to be in a favorable situation as to animal power which would ease its need of manpower.

Zuazo was not thinking of wheat fields, vineyards, and olive groves but of tropical crops which might have a market in Europe and drew up the first outline of a plantation system for the New World. Here and there, vecinos were beginning to grow some things for export, the promotion of which was the concern of the Licenciado. First of these was sugar. He had seen the "fields of sugar cane, greatly to be admired, with their stalks as thick as a man's wrist and twice as tall as a man of middle stature." [17] He had agreed "to build sugar mills (*ingenios*) which will become the source of very great riches." The Hieronymites wrote at the same time that orders had been given to build three sugar mills, for which they had advanced funds.

The cotton of the islands was produced on small trees (the monopodial *peruvianum-barbadense* complex). The *montes* (second-growth woods), Zuazo continued, were full of cotton and he was engaged in making a machine to clean the fiber (ingenio-engine-gin), a forgotten early reference to ginning cotton. A third promising prospect was *cañafistula* (*Cassia fistula*), which lately had "come to be grown, originating from the seed in a purge given to a sick person. There are by now many and fine trees each yielding up to eight arrobas, their branches so heavily laden with fruit that they must be propped, a very handsome thing to see and of the best quality according to physicians." (Cassia pods were an item of importance in the East India trade. Oviedo told the same story of its accidental propagation, placing it at the Franciscan monastery of Concepción. This leguminous tree is of rapid growth and produces pods heavily. It soon became so abundant as to glut the export market. The beautiful tree, well named Golden Shower in English, is a common and conspicuous ornament of the island today, especially in the western parts.) Zuazo was also trying to introduce the cultivation of Oriental pepper. Of several pounds that had been sown, only two seeds had grown, but these were bearing fruit. He was experimenting with the cultivation of a tree that grew in shady places about Puerto Plata, having a bark like cinnamon but of sharper taste (the wild cinnamon of the West Indies,

---

[17] The description is quite unlike the slender Creole cane then grown by Portuguese and Spaniards on the Eastern side of the Atlantic which was soon to be the source of cane sugar in the New World. Zuazo was a good observer, later to be a sugar planter himself. A century later, Père Labat wrote the first full account of cane planting and sugar making in the New World and thought that the Carib islands had a stout sugar cane before the coming of the Europeans. Such a cane was known under the Tupí–Guaraní name of *uba* in parts of Brazil and in Paraguay. Earlier in the twentieth century *uba* cane was of interest to the sugar industry before the development of the hybrid canes.

Canella alba). Sugar, cotton, drugs, and spices would give the islands a new future. Spain indeed might thus have developed its West Indies into a counterpart of the East Indies, having climate and soil that were equally favorable.[18]

Gil González also recommended attention to sugar cane and to cañafistula. He thought a good location for a sugar mill would be at Azua where the Crown had suitable property, and that another might be built at La Sabana (Les Cayes). The proposal of Azua, in a semi-arid region, implied irrigation, which was the practice in Spain. Gil thought the island pines (Caribbean yellow pine) a promising source of income, for lumber as well as naval stores. A water-powered sawmill on the Río Nizao to the west of Santo Domingo could deliver lumber at low cost to ships for export. Pine forests close to Santo Domingo might be tapped for pitch. Such forest resources held greater promise than mining. Considering the ravages of ships' hulls by *broma* (shipworms), notorious for putting a halt to voyages of discovery, the gum of *cupey* (*Clusia*) had been found to give protection and its extraction might give another industry. In such ways Gil González proposed the diversion from gold mining to forms of production that would benefit Spaniard and native and pay for the use of Negroes. The easiest way out of the labor shortage was to turn to stock ranching, for which all that was needed was title to a few animals and a branding iron. Ships returning to Spain were beginning to load cargoes of hides and add tallow and lard, and meat —salted, dried, or smoked. Tierra Firme opened a new market for meat products and live animals. The stock ranged free, the disposal took place at the harbor towns which, partly for that reason, survived better than villas in the interior.

By 1515 private initiative and governmental aid were finding ways out of the dead end of the gold placers.

TROPICAL PLANTATION: SUGAR CANE

Sugar cane had been brought along with many other plants on the second voyage of Columbus. It is unlikely that this was a lasting introduction of any plants from Europe. The starving time that followed resulted in the abandonment of all cultivation. Whatever was edible was eaten. The time of successful plant introductions follows the founding of Santo Domingo in 1496. How such plants were brought and where they were first grown for the most part has gone unrecorded. Vegetables and fruits of Mediterranean origin soon were grown in kitchen gardens, and in these also sugar cane found a place for household syrup. In Spain at the time honey (*miel*) was still a more common sweetening than sugar. (Cane syrup was also known as miel in the island.) Several persons at Concepción and Santo Domingo were growing cane and processing it to syrup.

The credit for beginning the production of sugar goes to a well-to-do physician of Santo Domingo who "at his own cost brought sugar masters to this island

---

[18] At the conclusion of the letter Zuazo wrote that he was sending the King some peregrine falcons, parrots, and "pavos of the kind over here which have a cry very like the yelping of a dog that has been hurt in the head." *Pavo* (peacock) was the name given by the Spaniards to the turkey, its distinctive gobbling cry well characterized by Zuazo. There were no turkeys of course native to the islands. If these were turkeys, as I think they were, they are likely to have been secured from Panama, as will be considered later.

and built a *trapiche* (horsemill), the first in this island, on the banks of the Rio Nigua, and introduced the technicians and art from the Canary Islands." [19] The time was 1515 or somewhat earlier; the place, the valley of the Nigua near San Cristóbal. Oviedo on his first return to Spain delivered the first boxes of sugar manufactured in Española to King Ferdinand on his deathbed.[20] The Canary Islands had begun to share in the sugar boom that brought wealth to Portuguese Madeira. Within a few years sugar came into strong demand in European markets, aided by improvements in processing. Oviedo was correct that this business depended on technical skill. Sugar cane grew readily all about the West Indies without the costly irrigation and terracing of Madeira and the Canaries. To convert its juice into marketable sugar required a capitalist who ventured investment in imported skill. The mill by which the cane juice was extracted was only one and a rather simple step in the operation.[21] Shortly the doctor associated himself with two other local capitalists who had profited from public office and they built a larger water-powered mill (ingenio) at Yaguate in the next valley to the west, that of Nizao. In this broad and fertile valley sugar cane still thrives very well. A modest monument surrounded by handsome cane fields marks the spot where the first ingenio is thought to have stood four and a half centuries ago.

A few residents of means saw an attractive prospect in sugar and brought over men who knew the business. The government of the Hieronymites and Zuazo had the sense to see that this new direction offered a way out for the foundering colony. Jointly, private citizens and the reform group of officials established a new economy of the first factory farms in the New World. It may be noted that in Spanish these establishments were and are known as mills (ingenios and trapiches), not as plantations. Lawyers, doctors, merchants, officials invested in the new venture that required capital for mills and cauldrons, for draft animals and carts, for white technicians, and especially to buy Negro slaves.

It was chiefly the availability of such interest and capital at the city of Santo Domingo that located the new enterprise in its vicinity, first to the west of the city on the Río Nigua, then in the next valley, the Nizao, and soon westward into the region of Azua (fig. 24). Shortly there was a little sugar produced in southwestern Puerto Rico, but none in Jamaica or Cuba.

The islands of the West have marked advantages over those on the eastern side of the Atlantic. Instead of mountain slopes and narrow benches there were fertile valley floors, alluvial cones, and smooth marine terraces, in part former coral reefs, available for planting on a large scale. Some of the land was open fields from Indian days, the rest needed only the removal of its vegetation.

Fuel was required in large amount for the cauldrons, cutting fuel wood being one of the main uses of slaves. These demands were readily met in the early years, but later became a matter of concern as the accessible woods were depleted. Oviedo praised the Azua area "with its favorable disposition of water and

---

[19] Oviedo, *Historia*, Bk. IV, ch. 8; also Las Casas, Bk. III, ch. 129.
[20] Oviedo, *Sumario*, ch. 29
[21] The *trapiche* is still in use under that name in rustic corners of Spanish America. It consists of three, sometimes only of two, vertical cylinders which may be smoothed tree trunks, the cane being crushed as it is passed between the cylinders; these are revolved by the slow circuit of a horse or mule pulling a long shaft geared to the rollers.

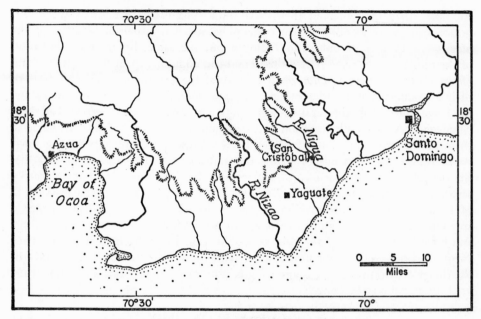

Fig. 24. The early sugar cane districts of Española.

great stands of woods, for the large and continuous fires needed." To the west of Santo Domingo rainfall was adequate to grow cane without irrigation, maturing properly in the dry season following. As cane planting extended into the Azua area, irrigation was necessary but inexpensive in comparison with mainland Spain and the Canaries. Small streams in number come down from the highlands to flow by easy gradients into the Bay of Ocoa across a wide piedmont fan. What Oviedo meant by "favorable disposition of water" was, I think, the ease of diversion of these small water courses onto fields of good natural drainage. To the present time the south side of the island is the superior region for cane sugar. Another asset was the availability of oxen as draft animals, reducing the need of labor and requiring no growing of feed. They have continued to be important in the sugar industry of the island.

Española made the earliest beginning of a plantation economy in the New World. Its promise failed of full realization by no lack of natural advantages, but because shortly the discovery of Mexico, and then that of Peru, again drained away people by lure of gold.

Cane was grown in much the same manner as the Indian natives had cultivated their conucos and as the Negroes cared for their own plantings in Africa. The plow had scarcely a place in the plantation. The earth was dug and piled into ridges or mounds into which the cane cuttings were inserted. Thereafter weeding was done by hand for a few weeks, and thereafter the cane was left to itself until it was ready to be cut. Instead of the native planting stick the Africans were accustomed to the use of hoes of iron, heavy and long bladed.

A cane field was recut year after year, our word ratoon coming from the Spanish *retoño*. Once established, it required labor only at the time of cutting. In the slack season the slaves might be put to other jobs such as cutting wood and, also, they then planted their own food. The early plantations were self-sufficient as to food. The Indian conuco became the provision ground of the blacks, the manner of cultivation being about the same, by digging, and most of the things grown were root crops. The main additions from Africa were yams (*ñame, igname*), that is, *Dioscoreas* of several species, the manner and time of their introduction still undetermined. African guinea fowl were brought in and soon became as happily feral as were pigs and cattle. The Negroes had kept chickens in Africa both for food and ceremonial purposes and did the same in their new surroundings, as they do to the present. There was also a large transfer into Negro hands of plants the Indians had cultivated, implying that the disappearance of Indians and replacement by Negroes were not as sharply separated as is thought. The island of Haiti retains an unusual diversity of forms of Indian plants, and the making of cassava bread in the old Indian manner is still common. This mingling of American and African elements in the village and household gardens of the present would seem to go back to the time when Negro slaves were brought into contact with the last of the natives. A study of the things grown in the provision grounds, how they are processed, and why they are kept, remains to be done.

THE CUBAN FRONTIER

Velázquez was lieutenant governor of Cuba under authority of the government at Santo Domingo, but he did as he pleased, kept in the good graces of Ferdinand, and later ignored the reforms that were ordered. Of all the Spanish Indies, Cuba was perhaps least under control from the outside. Velázquez chose to live in comfort and state at Santiago, where he was in a good position to guard entry from and communication with the Spanish settlements on the other islands. The vecinos of his villas gave him no trouble and were left to their own devices. After the initial occupation he lived a sedentary life and lacked first-hand knowledge of the farther parts of the island. He was not of the stuff of which explorers are made. Where there was prospect of gain beyond his island he would send others.

In his letter of April, 1514, to the King, Velázquez wrote that he "had been informed by the caciques and Indians that on occasion certain Indians had come from other islands beyond Cuba, toward the side of the north, navigating five or six days by canoe and that these gave news of other islands that lie beyond those from which they came," adding that he wished to send someone to discover the secret of the matter. These "islands" could not have been Florida and Bimini, which Ponce de León had discovered the year before, for which he had been given license in 1512, and to the government of which he had been appointed. The secret referred to must have come across the Yucatán Channel, which was little more than a hundred miles wide and could easily be crossed by canoes in five or six days. The island people were capable of such voyages, as they showed in going to and from Jamaica and Barbados, and between the Bahamas and Florida. The claim here was that natives came on occasion to Cuba from the other side of a sea. Very little is known of Mayan seafaring. What Velázquez reported is credible. Las Casas later told of finding a large mass of beeswax in Cuba which must have come from Yucatán. Cuban archaeology has turned up occasional bits of Mayan pottery. The conspicuous seasonal migration of land birds across the Yucatán Channel can hardly have remained unnoticed. It is a reasonable hypothesis that the islanders, freely ranging the seas and knowledgeable of indications of land, also reached Yucatán. That Mayans fared to sea is supported also by the great trading canoes Columbus saw in the Gulf of Honduras. Velázquez may have had thus early a first intimation of Yucátan which he did not follow up.

In 1515 Velázquez was sending out ships on slave raids to replace the Cuban natives who were being used up. The date and data are based on a letter he wrote to Diego Columbus in Santo Domingo.[22] The incident as reported is of interest both as to Velázquez and the Indians involved. A ship and bark were sent from Santiago to hunt slaves in the Guanaja Islands (the Bay Islands Columbus had discovered in 1502); the bark remained to hunt more Indians, and the ship returned to the port of Carenas (the present Habana), with its captured Indians confined below. While most of the Spaniards were taking their ease on the Cuban shore the Indians broke the hatch, seized the ship, ran up the sails, and fled. That they made it back home was known when the wreck of the ship was found on one of the Bay Islands by a party Velázquez sent out to avenge the affront.

This second expedition continued from island to island as far as Utila, which name appears first at that time. It had taken five hundred captives. Again the main body of Spaniards took their ease on shore; the Indians, who were held below deck on the smaller caravel, broke out and seized it, but after a sharp fight were overcome. The two ships returned to Habana with four hundred captives, male and female, and twenty thousand pesos of inferior gold.

A very curious story: the run from Santiago to the Bay Islands, made by sailing with the trade winds, should have been easy and rapid. Indeed, one may wonder whether it had not been made repeatedly since the last voyage of Columbus. Both expeditions returned north through the Yucatán Channel, wind abeam and aided by current, and made for the harbor (north shore) of Carenas, where Habana was soon to be relocated. The repetition of the return course to the same harbor on the Cuban north shore suggests that egress by the Yucatán Channel was known and therefore also the great drift of water through it and past Habana (the Gulf Stream). On the first expedition they raided two islands; on the second they repeated such landings and got west to Utila, from which they returned to Cuba "enriched by not a little." Both operations appear to have been restricted to the Bay Islands. They were in contact with Mayans who were in possession of gold and copper traded in from other parts. The strangest part of the account is the seizure of the ship by the Indian captives at Habana and their success in sailing it home. This, as Las Casas said, was a matter of sailing more than two hundred and fifty leagues and across the wind.[23]

The discovery of Yucatán might have come earlier if Velázquez, instead of

---

[22] Las Casas, Bk. III, ch. 92. Las Casas was quoting from the letter of which he said he had a copy. It was copied by Herrera, Decade II, Bk. 2, ch. 7.

[23] When the second party got to the place where the bark and its crew had been left, they found carved on a tree the words "Vamos a Darien" and thus, Las Casas thought, went to search for their lost men. If they did so they must have turned east and south instead of going west to Utila. The flight to Darién seems improbable. It would have been much more difficult than a return to Cuba.

sitting in Santiago, had been piecing together the intimations of what lay beyond the western horizon.

Bernal Díaz del Castillo begins the epic tale he unfolded with the prologue to the discovery. The old conquistador had a remarkable visual memory as well as uncontrived simplicity. His recall of events and scenes gives the only eyewitness account of the discovery of Yucatán in 1517.

Bernal Díaz tells of his coming to Darién in 1514 with Pedrarias as one of that large band of fortune seekers. Disappointed there, he took passage with a number of companions for Cuba, where they heard that Velázquez would give them Indians, but found that they were too late. "Three years having passed on Tierra Firme and in Cuba and having done little worth mentioning we agreed to join together, a hundred and ten companions who had come from Tierra Firme along with some who had been in Cuba and had no Indians." They pooled their slight resources and made a compact with Hernández de Córdoba, a wealthy vecino of Sancti Spiritus, principal center of gold mining, "to go on our venture to seek and discover new lands in which to engage our persons," Hernández to be their captain. Two ships were bought and fitted out; a third was secured on credit from Velázquez with instructions from him that they should first go to the Bay Islands to take slaves to pay for his bark. Bernal said that the initiative for the undertaking did not come from Velázquez, who, he thought, saw an opportunity to use the adventurers for another slave raid. Bernal commented, from the virtuous station of his old age, that they objected to such disservice to God and King as making slaves of free men. At any rate, they did not take a course to the slaving grounds of the Bay Islands but sailed west.

The motives undoubtedly were mixed. Velázquez was still able to keep the new government at Santo Domingo from interfering, but time might be running out for hunting Indians. Bishop Landa, writing his *Cosas de Yucatán*, thought that Hernández came with his three ships in order to take slaves for the mines of Cuba, which were in need of labor, but added, "others say that he went out to discover." Hernández is thought to have put the most money into the venture. The hundred-odd men were to share according to their means. Bernal said that the ships were stocked with food, chiefly cassava bread and pigs, costing three pesos a head. Trade goods were brought, mainly trinkets. A *veedor* was elected to keep track of the proceeds of the voyage. The participants put their means and persons up for the hope of gaining wealth, in the broad meaning of rescate, peaceful trade or forcible seizure. Also their intention was to go into unknown parts, armed and ready for combat.

By the Bernal version, the three ships set out on February 9, 1517, from the familiar north coast harbor of Carenas (Habana). It took twelve days to get to Cape San Antonio and nine more to cross the Yucatán Channel, including two days in which they were tossed about by a storm, probably a norther, expectable at that season. The landfall was made at the extremity of Yucatán on Cape Catoche, so named on that occasion. The crossing thus was made by the most direct route.

A large town was seen from shipboard, lying about two leagues inland. They called it Gran Cairo from the temple pyramids and houses of stone and mortar. Natives came out in ten canoes, artfully made and holding up to forty persons.

Some were paddled and some came under sail, Bernal recalled. He has been thought in error about the native use of sails in those seas and perhaps his recollection was an unusual lapse. How then however had the captive Bay Islanders stolen the Spanish ship in Habana harbor and succeeded in sailing it back home?

According to Bernal, the Christians were invited into the town, but were ambushed on the way and engaged in a bitter fight. As they continued west and south around Yucatán by way of Campeche and Champotón, they were met by such strong resistance that they lost half of their men, most of the rest being wounded. The angry Indians also kept them from getting fresh water. Returning back up the coast they stopped, in desperate need, to take on brackish water in the Estero de los Lagartos to the west of Cape Catoche. The chief pilot, Antonio de Alaminos, had been to Florida with Ponce de León and urged their escape by that route. Arrived in southwest Florida at a bay that Alaminos recognized, they suffered another sharp Indian attack. The remnant made it back to the harbor of Carenas, Hernández de Córdoba dying shortly of his wounds. Bernal was annoyed that when Velázquez heard of the discovery he took credit for it and said he had spent much money on it.

The rough handling by the natives at Cape Catoche is most unusual and is unexplained. European discoverers, as Friederici liked to point out, were not attacked but were received with ceremony and treated as guests. This was the worst drubbing Spaniards had taken since Juan de la Cosa was killed by the so-called Caribs at Cartagena. Nor is it in character with Mayan ways. The Florida incident was different; Ponce de León had left the memory of his raid there, and those warlike Indians wanted no more of his kind. The Mayans in Yucatán must have had good reason for their hostility. Perhaps they knew of the slave raids against their kinsmen of the Bay Islands or of the treatment of the Cubans. Possibly these were not the first Spaniards other than shipwrecked sailors who had come to their shores. The first edition of Peter Martyr's Decades, not later than 1512, was accompanied by a woodcut map of about that date. This shows a peninsula in the proper position of Yucatán, bearing as its only place name "bahía de lagartos" at the northern tip. The Canerio map (1503?) also had a peninsula to the west of Cuba and on it a "río de lagartos." Was this a strangely coincidental fancy or mapmakers who had heard of caymans and crocodiles about West Indian shores? The Hernández expedition picked up Mayan place names such as Catoche, Campeche, and Champotón, but also one Spanish place name, that of the estuary or river of lagartos, the watering place from which they set sail for Florida, a place name which is in use to the present.[24]

---

[24] Las Casas (Bk. III, chs. 96–98) gave a detailed and in parts divergent account. According to him Hernández de Córdoba, whom he knew as an old friend, and two other named Spaniards got license from Velázquez to hunt slaves in the Lucayas and Guanajas islands, the hundred men who joined being added on wages or shares. The ships left Santiago in late February, 1517, by the north coast and put in at Puerto Príncipe to load supplies. From Cape San Antonio the crossing of the Yucatán Channel took four days to Cozumel. The second question of the Interrogatorio by Cortés in Mexico in 1529 (CDI, XXVII, 301 ff.) asked whether the three ships left Cuba under command of Hernández to hunt slaves in the Lucayas and Guanajas, as was the custom of the vecinos of Cuba, Española, and Puerto Rico. Bishop Landa may have been right that the venture was a slave hunt. The Lucayas having been stripped of natives, the ships would have gone on to the Bay Islands had it not been for the advice of Alaminos, as noted below.

The discovery of Yucatán brought news of a mode of life that seemed reminiscent of the Levant. The people dressed in long cotton garments and lived in compact towns built about pyramids crowned by temples. The houses were of *cal y canto*, dressed stone laid in mortar. The temples were covered with frescos and had a strange form of cross. Priests burned incense in censers. In hurried looting of temples, objects of low-grade gold were found which Bernal thought was half gold and half copper—figures of fish and geese, idols and medallions.

Velázquez lost no time in fitting out a follow-up expedition under his kinsman Juan de Grijalva. This ran out the coast of the Gulf of Mexico to the Río Pánuco, to the end of the land of high culture. Meanwhile Hernán Cortés, serving as secretary to Velázquez, had kept well informed of the course of discovery and got from the latter the appointment to lead the third venture, which resulted in the conquest of Mexico. Cuba was the gateway to New Spain.

Antonio de Alaminos piloted Ponce de León in 1513 to the discovery of Florida and then took Hernández, Grijalva, and Cortés into the Gulf of Mexico. Voyage by voyage he learned the great flow of water that would carry ships northward between Cuba and Florida beyond the reach of the hindering Trades. A native of Palos, which furnished many early mariners to the Spanish Indies, he had gone as a young man with Columbus on the voyage to the Bay Islands and Veragua. No one knew as he did the current that would become known as the Gulf Stream.

According to Las Casas, it was at the outset from Puerto Príncipe that Alaminos informed Hernández that "by way of the west beyond Cuba there would be found a very rich country." This, it may be inferred, was his recall of the cargo he had seen on its way from the west to the Bay Islands, the significance of which Columbus had missed. Las Casas thought it took four days to cross the Yucatán Channel; Bernal remembered it as nine. The crossing demonstrated the northward flow of water from the Caribbean, which moves through that channel at about thirty miles a day and then turns east along the north shore of Cuba. Beyond Cape Catoche they had favoring winds and slight current. As Alaminos continued later to pilot the ships of Grijalva and of Cortés to the western shore of the Gulf of Mexico, he worked out his design of the new course of navigation to Spain. In July, 1519, he left Vera Cruz to sail through the Florida Straits to Sevilla. Thereafter ships returning from Darién and Cartagena also joined the new route, coming north by way of the Yucatán Channel.

The rearrangement of the sailing route from the Indies to Spain caused the relocation in 1519 of the villa of Habana to the north coast at the harbor of Carenas. This superior ria, easily defended at its narrow inlet, sheltered from storms, and able to accommodate any fleet, was soon to earn the name of Key to the New World. Here ships took on their supplies and assembled in convoys for protection against raiders from northern Europe. Habana had become and has remained a pivotal point of the New World.

We should know better how the great sailing route to Europe was established if the time and manner of discovery of the Bermuda Islands were known. The name derives from another notable navigator out of Palos, Juan Bermúdez, who is known to have been in Española as a sailing master in 1498 and continued to be engaged in the traffic of the islands. Oviedo, returning to Spain from Española in the latter part of 1515, said that they tried to land in the Bermudas but were prevented by adverse winds (*Sumario*, ch. 83). By that time, it would appear, there was nothing unusual in a passage rom Española by way of the Bermudas, which sailors had already shortened from the isles of Juan Bermúdez to *las Bermudas*.

XI
ENTRY TO DARIÉN AND
THE SOUTH SEA
(1511–1514)

·

SALVAGE OF THE URABÁ AND VERAGUA CONCESSIONS

The great expectations of western Tierra Firme had broken down in the failures of Hojeda and Nicuesa which came to their disastrous end in 1510. The plan as it had been drawn up in Spain took account of geographic realities. The Gulf of Urabá, being the deep reëntrant of the sea into the southern Tierra Firme, would serve as the most convenient division of the two proposed colonies. East therefrom Hojeda would exploit under the name of Urabá the promise of gold Bastidas had discovered. To the west Nicuesa would follow the golden trail Columbus had believed he had found and called Veragua. Veragua involved the rights of the heirs of Columbus, which were in incipient litigation. The Crown was not committed to either concession, beyond the short term.

The debacle began with the landing of Hojeda at Cartagena to plunder and capture, whereby he lost Juan de la Cosa, his ablest partner, and a large part of his men. Continuing to the Indian town of Urabá on the eastern shore of that gulf to build his short-lived fortified camp of San Sebastián, he raided native villages, lost more men, was wounded, and ran off to Española, abandoning his concession and men. The venture was saved from total failure by the arrival of Enciso with fresh supplies and more men.

Nicuesa fared worse with his larger party and better equipment, wasting both in folly and hysteria. He failed to recognize Columbus' Veragua, scattered his forces along the Central American coast, and took refuge in a makeshift fort at Nombre de Dios, an even more ephemeral shelter than that of San Sebastián de Urabá.

Neither met the terms of their concession. One ran away; the other was stranded at Nombre de Dios. Hojeda had roused the natives to the east, who picked off his men with poisoned weapons. Nicuesa had stirred up the enmity of less formidable people to the west and owed the greater part of his losses to witless blunders.

Enciso persuaded the men who had quit Urabá under the leadership of Francisco Pizarro to return to their abandoned San Sebastián with himself in charge. The foundering of the supply ship, the destruction of the fort by Indians and their continuing harassment made it inadvisable to make a fresh start in the old location. The transfer to the other side of the gulf in order to be among harmless natives was proposed by Balboa, who had come with Bastidas ten years before. This step saved the party, provided it with food, and gave the services of docile natives. The Indian town of Darién was appropriated and remade into the Spanish town of Santa María la Antigua, which proceeded to organize its own government. So much for a retrospect of the Gulf of Darién in 1510.

A rescue ship brought Nicuesa and the remnant of his men to Darién, where Nicuesa promptly asserted that the new settlement was in territory belonging to him and therefore under his authority. By common consent this claim was rejected. In the spring of 1511 Nicuesa and a few of his followers were loaded onto an unseaworthy boat and shipped off to sea, there to disappear. Enciso considered himself in command by the authority he held from Hojeda. Balboa, however, challenged that right and won the support of the self-constituted community, which agreed to oust Enciso and pack him off also, but on a better ship, to Española. In the end this cost Balboa dearly, for Enciso became an enemy against him in Santo Domingo and at court. By April, 1511, Balboa was in complete control of the colony, his authority being the support of the men with him. He was the first *caudillo* in the New World who had no legal status but made himself a leader by ability to win and hold followers.

Santa María began with about three hundred Spaniards, the usual mixed lot of adventurers from Spain and men who had not done well in Española. Poorly supplied, they had to depend mainly on the natives for sustenance. Balboa succeeded in developing their morale and kept them from pillaging and destroying the Indian communities. The Indians at Darién and soon those living to the west came to accept the Spaniards without marked resentment or distress. Balboa would confront the natives with a show of force and, having scared them, would then offer friendship and live up to it. In this part of Tierra Firme the Indians lived under hereditary caciques as did those of the Greater Antilles. Balboa perhaps had learned as vecino in Española the price of upsetting such a system. He did not introduce the repartimiento, nor did he follow Columbus in requiring fixed tribute, nor did he degrade or eliminate the caciques. He established himself as the great white chief who treated the others as vassals and within such limits as his friends. He put an end to the fighting among the native political units—in contrast to the islands, habitually at war. By protecting the natives from violence and abuse by Spaniards, he was able to get food and services pretty well as needed. The relation was a sort of obligate parasitism in which the hosts were not in process of destruction by their predators and apparently were not seriously inconvenienced.

Zuazo, in reviewing the status of Darién as it had been in the time of Balboa (1511–1514), wrote to Xèvres that "Vasco Núñez had labored with very good skill to make peace with many caciques and principal lords of the Indians, by which he kept in peace about thirty caciques with all their Indians, and did so by not taking from them more than they were willing to give, aiding them in their wars they had one with another [he did so as a step in pacification], and thereby Vasco Núñez became so well liked that he could go in security through a hundred leagues of Tierra Firme. In all parts the Indians willingly gave him much gold and also their sisters and daughters to take with him to be married or used as he wished. By these means peace was spreading and the rents of Your Highnesses were increasing greatly." The rare tribute was merited. Equally remarkable was Balboa's success at keeping the Spaniards in line, satisfied, and loyal. The colony prospered during the time of his control and the Indians were not depressed in their living or their numbers. Balboa is reported to have had a romantic liaison with an Indian "princess"; the lack of Spanish women seems to have been willingly supplied by natives.

FIRST ACTIVITIES AND EXPLORATIONS

The first six months at Santa María were occupied in building the Spanish town alongside the Indian town, in setting the natives to plant more fields, and in prospecting for gold. At an undetermined early date, gold was found in streams of the *serranía* a dozen miles to the west, the first effective discovery of placers on the mainland.

By the late spring of 1511 Balboa was ready to begin exploration. The first direction taken was northwest along the coast into the province of Careta, which adjoined that of Darién, the seat of its cacique twenty leagues distant. Like Darién, Careta lay on the Caribbean shore and extended inland into the Serranía del Darién (fig. 21). The mountain crest here was much lower than behind Darién; the foothills extended to the sea, forming a shore of cliffed headlands and rocky islands; and there were no broad inundated lowlands. (The Scottish settlement that took the name of Darién was attempted here in the following century and has left the names Caledonia Bay and Punta Escoces.) Careta was able to provide only small store of food, but gave a welcome tribute of fabricated gold. What was more important, it became and remained a willing Spanish vassal.

At the time, the Caretans were at war with another cacicazgo inland named Ponca after its chief. The montane land of Ponca lay partly astride the serranía, and largely on the interior side, drained by streams joining to form the Río Balsas (Chucunaque). Balboa helped his new friends, taking and sacking the seat of Ponca on the far side of the mountain ridge. In doing so he discovered an easy entry into the longitudinal basin that runs through the middle of the Isthmus from Colombia to the Canal Zone. At the time he could only know that he had gotten across the mountains by a low saddle and that there was a wide and inhabited lowland ahead that stretched along the interior of the mountain range he had been following.

From Ponca the Spanish party, led by its new friends from Careta, turned northwest to visit another cacique, Comogre (fig. 25). This exploration was to point the way to the occupation of the as yet unknown isthmus. Balboa had the sense of orientation in strange terrain that marks the explorer, and this was his first and well-remembered lesson in its topography. The Ponca territory drained into a river that he was to follow later on its southward course, the Río de las

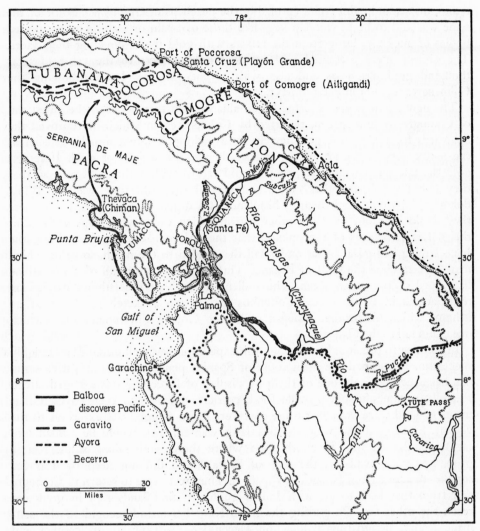

Fig. 25. Early crossings of the Isthmus.

Balsas, now called Chucunaque. The land of Comogre straddled the low divide between the basin of the Chucunaque and that of the Río Bayano. Peter Martyr heard from the participant Colmenares that Comogre held a fertile plain twelve leagues in extent beginning thirty leagues from Darién.[1] The province of Comogre was mainly in the upper part of the Bayano drainage, but also extended north across the low coastal range to the Caribbean, largely an open country except for woods along the rivers and ravines.

The visitors were well received and lavishly feasted at the great house of Comogre, which was a hundred fifty paces long and fifty wide, with ornately carved beams, a finely decorated floor, and a defense of stone walls. Its cellar was stocked with large earthen jars that held wine made from yuca, sweet po-

---

[1] Peter Martyr, Decade II, Bk. 5.

tatoes, maize, and palm fruits (probably the peach palm *Guilielma*). Some of the wine was said to be in wooden kegs like those of Spain or Italy. The desiccated bodies of ancestors hung from the rafters with gold masks covering their faces. The visitors were presented with worked gold objects to the value of four thousand gold drachmas and also with seventy slaves. (I am following the Colmenares account in Peter Martyr.)

The new friendship was sealed by an alliance. On that occasion the eldest son of Comogre made a speech, reported by Colmenares, in which he reproved the Spaniards for taking fine gold jewelry and melting it down into bars, whereas the natives prized the art of the goldsmith, not the weight of gold. If it was gold the Spaniards were after, they should return with a thousand men so that they could subjugate other chiefs and get all the gold they wanted. While doing so, he would lead them to headlands at a distance of six suns. From these they could look out over the other sea on which there were ships as large as theirs. Las Casas was of the opinion that these ships had come from Peru, the Incas having had great balsas under sail that traded to the north, some of which may have reached the Gulf of Panama. Thus, as early as the fall of 1511, Balboa had word of the other ocean. The Indians throughout the Isthmus carried on trade across it. Bartholomew Columbus had drawn a sketch in Rome of an isthmus which his brother thought to be the Golden Chersonese, from which one could sail to the Ganges.

In contrast to previous blunderings, this expedition was well managed and highly successful. It outlined the main route of Spanish penetration. Four native states had been secured, only one of them by display of force and this a staged effect. Friendly caciques would provide food, carriers, guides, and even slaves. Ornaments of gold were in common use and were given as good-will offerings to the visitors. Since gold was what the Spaniards wanted, they would be guided into farther lands and thus to another sea where there were sailing ships. Native provisions were available; the men of Santa María did not need to wait for supplies to arrive from Jamaica or Española. They were free to return to Comogre and from that base to go with Indian guides to find lands rich in gold and reach the other sea. On getting the news King Ferdinand recognized the self-made leader, designating Balboa, on December 23, 1511, as his captain and governor of the province of Darién, without mention of term of tenure.

SOUTH FROM THE GULF OF URABÁ

The promising western prospect could wait while Balboa turned his attention in 1512 to discover what lay to the south. The information is from three contemporary sources. The first is the letter Balboa sent to the King, dated January 20, 1513, telling how he had organized the men who were left stranded by Nicuesa and Hojeda, had made an ordered town of Santa María, had secured the friendship of the provinces to the west and heard there of the other sea, and had started gold mining in the mountain streams to the west of Santa María. He then described his second expedition, which went by canoe and longboat far up great rivers to the south. Another account is by Rodrigo de Colmenares, who had taken part in this second discovery and returned to Spain to tell his version to Peter Martyr in 1513. The third is by Oviedo, who came as an official to Darién in 1514, knew Balboa and many of his men, and had in his possession the records left by Balboa. The accounts mainly agree, their obscurer passages being of the physical geography of the country traversed. The party traveled by canoes and longboats up rivers that flow through swamps and tropical rain forest, a land in which there were few recognizable landmarks. Following sinuous watercourses, they had scant knowledge of how far they got day by day.[2]

The Gulf of Urabá had been known from the time of Bastidas as a major extension of the sea into Tierra Firme. It remained for Balboa to discover how far it reached to the south and what lay beyond. At the southwest the gulf is constricted sharply by the delta of the Atrato River, forming the shallow inner pocket of bay known as the Culata. The Indian town of Darién, remade into Santa María, lay beyond the northwestern margin of the delta. The delta is crossed by numerous and shifting distributary channels. Besides such discharges of water from the Atrato, the Culata also receives the flow of the Río León. Indian Darién had most convenient access by canoe both to the Atrato and León.

The Gulf of Urabá is the seaward end of a structural basin that extends southward for hundreds of miles, three hundred of which are drained by the Río Atrato. The low, wide basin is one of the rainiest regions in the American tropics, and receives the runoff of the western side of the Andean Cordillera Occidental. In volume the Atrato is great, a widely-flooding river with backwater lakes, swamps, and bayous. The expedition to Comogre had been the longest march overland undertaken by a Spanish party. The exploration south from the Gulf of Urabá would be a far more severe test of Balboa's ability to take an expedition on tropical inland waterways. Again he made use of Indian information and guides.

The principal objective of 1512 was to discover the seat of a great cacique or *queví* named Dabeiba, who was thought to live beyond the watery lowlands and was said to be fabulously rich in gold (fig. 26). By way of reconnaissance, Balboa set out from Santa María in a brigantine, skirted the delta, and landed at the mouth of the Río León, called the Río de Redes (nets). They went up this river for about thirty miles to a fishing village amid garden plots. The natives had fled, but left their canoes, nets, and a welcome lot of "encrusted" gold, which according to Peter Martyr, was worth seven thousand castellanos. Whatever these objects of superior goldsmithing were, they are unlikely to have belonged to fishermen. The village was subject to the queví Dabeiba, whom Peter Martyr reported as overlord of the fishermen of the Culata. The notes suggest a political geography of dependence of the Río León basin on a southerly highland state; the river served as a trade route by which worked gold was taken north and dried fish were carried into the southern interior, as was common practice on the Caribbean shores of Tierra Firme. The reconnaissance had been worth while. It had entered the northern lowlands that were reported subject to Dabeiba, had found a substantial amount of gold objects which, it may be inferred, were to be carried to the Gulf of Urabá, and it knew that the seat of Dabeiba must be sought farther south.

---

[2] The Balboa letter is in Navarrete, III, 358–376, and is also reproduced by Altolaguirre. The account from Colmenares is by Peter Martyr, Decade II, Bks. 4 and 6. The main Oviedo version is in *Historia*, Bk. XXIX, with additional items in his *Sumario*, ch. 10.

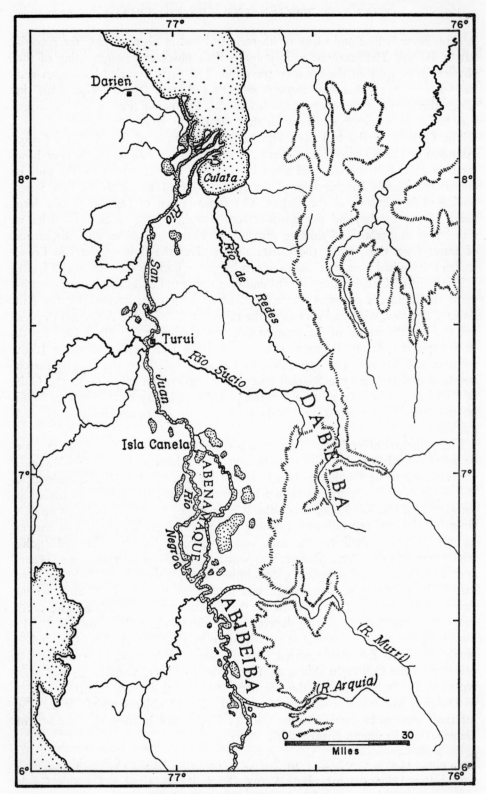

Fig. 26. Balboa's search for Dabeiba.

The next attempt was to go up the Río Atrato, named the Río San Juan by Balboa, perhaps because it was entered on June 24. Oviedo heard from Balboa that this river entered the gulf by ten arms, six of which carried no less water than the Guadalquivir of Andalusia; also that it had great swamps and many lagoons, especially to the east, and that it flooded widely. Balboa wrote the King in January, 1513: "The manner in which this river must be navigated is by canoes of the Indians, for there are many small and narrow arms, some closed by trees, and one cannot enter except in canoes three or four palms wide. After this river has been explored, boats eight palms wide may be made to employ twenty oars, as in fustas, for it is a river of great current and not easy to navigate even in Indian canoes." The blocking of passage by trees came about by their toppling into the stream and intercepting floating driftwood. Balboa mentioned large bends in the river and to the east of the river a lowland that extended to a great sierra which began inland from Urabá, low at first but rising southward "so high as to be covered with clouds. In the two years we have been here the crest has only been seen twice, for the sky is continuously covered. From this highest part it drops away. To that point [i.e., to the north] it is covered with great forests, and beyond [to the south] there are mountain ridges without any tree or brush cover." This is a fair description of the Cordillera Occidental of Colombia, with the interesting observation that it was heavily wooded to the north but not so to the south.

The accounts of the voyage up river make no mention of the arm of the delta by which they entered. Since these arms discharge into the Culeta over a shoreline of many miles, the estimates of distance traveled up the river lack a known starting point. The channels also have shifted through the centuries, as they continue to do. Balboa mentions distances only three times: (1) "Going up this great river of San Juan about thirty leagues there is a province called Abenamaque to the right [west] which has very great promise of gold," the information given by the son of the cacique of that province whom he brought back. (2) "At thirty leagues [apparently the same thirty leagues], there entered a very beautiful and large river on the left [east] side, and two days' travel up this latter the cacique Dabeiba would be found." (3) "I have sure news that fifty leagues up this river of San Juan are very rich mines on both sides."

Colmenares gave Peter Martyr more information, including distances. Having gone with Balboa up the Río de Redes, Colmenares evidently left there to go up the San Juan while Balboa returned to Santa María before beginning his second exploration. Colmenares therefore should have entered the delta by the channel nearest the mouth of the Río de Redes, which provided him also with the shortest passage of the delta (see fig. 25). Colmenares went up the San Juan for twelve leagues to a riverbank settlement named Turui after its chief, there to await the arrival of Balboa. Las Casas had it that Balboa came up by a different river arm. From Turui the joint party continued another such distance (forty miles) to an island of fishermen where there were wild cinnamon trees, and sixty small villages, each of about ten clustered houses. At this place a black-water river came in from the right (west), so open that it could have been navigated by brigantine. At this Río Negro and Isla de Canela they changed to canoes, called *urus*. Fifteen miles farther on they came to a settlement of five hundred dispersed houses of the queví Abenamaque, whom they captured. Las Casas called him lord of the Río Negro. At sixty miles from the Río Negro and Isla de Canela they reached the pueblo of the chief Abibeiba in a region of lakes, where the chief's house was built high in a great tree. In the final thirty miles up river, they reached a country of cannibals, who had abandoned their huts and fled.

There have been various reconstructions of the exploration of the Atrato basin to which I may add another until someone familiar with it provides an informed interpretation (fig. 25). The first topographic point is the site of Turui twelve leagues, or forty miles, from the gulf. If Colmenares took his party from the mouth of the Río de Redes to the Atrato by an eastern arm, the distance would put Turui where he awaited Balboa, about where the Río Sucio joins the Atrato, which would be a sensible spot to wait. The next leg of forty miles was to the Río Negro and Isla de Canela. At this distance the United States Aeronautical Chart shows a large area of islands formed by branchings of the main river, with one major branch at the west and another at the east. They followed a western channel of open and black water, indicating that it was colored dark by humic matter and free of the sediment which the eastern channel derived from the great cordillera to the east. The five hundred dispersed houses of Abenamaque suggest that they were strung along natural levee banks. Sixty miles or so farther, it not being certain from what point, they reached the land of Abibeiba, a land of lakes, where a large and beautiful river entered from the east. Either the Río Murrí or the Río Arquia may be considered as the possible seat of Abibeiba. Both rise in the higher parts of the Cordillera Occidental, and between them a mountain spur nearly three thousand meters high extends to about a dozen miles of the Atrato. When the chief was pressed for gold he offered to go to the mountains nearby to procure it. That his great house was built in a tree does not prove that it was on land subject to inundation. Colmenares told of the store of wine that was kept on the ground, servants entertaining the guests in the tree house by running up and down ladders to bring the wine, the explanation being that the tree house shook too much in the wind for wine to be stored aloft. Having been well fed and wined, the Spanish party went on up river for another thirty miles until they came to the country of the "cannibals." By this tentative reckoning the exploration may have gone as far as the vicinity of Quibdó.

Oviedo considered the discovery of the Río San Juan one of the most important and renowned deeds carried out overseas, and gave Balboa credit for foresight and the care of his men, no captain equalling him in this respect. The natives were roughed up on occasion but the purpose of the expedition was to discover a feasible water route to new gold lands rather than to pillage. No penetration into an unknown interior equaled it until the time of Cortés. The entry was made into an area that has remained to the present one of the least-known parts of the New World.

THE GOLD OF DABEIBA

To the west of Darién, Balboa opened a gateway at Comogre that would give him additional attractive and amenable native states to control, as well as a way to the other sea. He then turned back in the opposite direction to find out what lay south of the Gulf of Urabá where there was said to be the lord of golden treasure called Dabeiba. Having seen and heard enough to feel sure there was such a lord and land, he returned to Santa María. Balboa operated by strategy of limited objectives. Having advanced on his right flank to a favorable position at Comogre, he led a deep penetration on his left to make sure that he could take his men up the San Juan when the time came to move against the land of Dabeiba. He tested out the long water route to his satisfaction and thought that he had gathered enough information about the country beyond it for a future campaign. He had the prudence both to investigate before taking action and not to commit his limited resources beyond their capacity.

In his letter to the King he thought that the "great and beautiful river" out of the East (the Río Murrí?) would lead by a journey of two days to the cacique Dabeiba,

a very great lord of a very large territory and inhabited by many people. He has gold in large quantity in his house, so much that anyone who does not know the condition of this land will hardly believe it. I know this from sure news. From the house of this cacique Dabeiba comes all the gold that goes out through this gulf [of Urabá] and all that the caciques of these surroundings possess. The report is of many pieces of gold in strange forms and of great size. Many Indians who have seen it tell me that this cacique Dabeiba has certain chests of gold each of which requires a man to lift. This cacique collects the gold which is found at a distance from the mountains and the manner by which he gets it is thus: at two days journey farther on there is a beautiful land of very Carib and bad people who eat humans when they can get them. They are a people without a ruler and give obedience to no one. They are a warlike people, each living as he wishes. These are the owners of the mines which according to my information are the richest of the world. These mines are in a country that appears to have the highest mountains in the world, [which leads him to the account of the Cordillera Central previously quoted, forested to the north and treeless farther south, Dabeiba living in the latter country. Continuing with the subject of mines, he located these at two days from the place of Dabeiba toward sunrise, the rising sun shining upon them.] The manner of collecting the gold is effortless and is done in two ways. The one is that they wait until the streams have risen in their narrow valleys (quebradas) and turn dry after the floods pass, at which time the gold is exposed in what is washed out of the ravines (barrancas), carried from the sierra in very sizable nuggets, the Indians indicating the size of oranges or of a fist, and according to their gestures also pieces in the shape of flat plates. There is another way of collecting gold, to await the time of the drying of the herbaceous vegetation (yerba) in the mountains and then set fires in them. After the burning they go to look for it in the heights and likeliest parts and collect the gold in large amounts and in fine nuggets. These Indians who collect this gold bring it as they find it to be smelted and traded to the cacique Dabeiba. As pay in the trade, he gives them Indian boys and girls to be eaten and Indian women to serve their own women, and these are not eaten. He gives them pigs [peccaries] of which there are many in this land. He gives them a lot of fish, and cotton clothes, and salt. He gives them objects of fabricated gold as they desire it. Those Indians trade only with this cacique Dabeiba and not with any other place. This cacique Dabeiba has great smelting of gold in his house and a hundred men continually fabricating gold . . . All this I know by dependable information because I am never told anything different wherever I go. I have learned thus from many caciques and Indians, as well from subjects (vecinos) of this cacique Dabeiba as from other sources, finding it to be true by many ways, putting some to the torture, treating others with love, and giving to others presents of things from Castile.

This is a remarkable document in what it tells of Balboa as well as of Dabeiba. The information was secured from Indians about a country no Spaniard had seen. On the Gulf of Darién, Balboa having heard that their gold jewelry came from Dabeiba, he continued to collect notes about that cacaique and his land. The topographic information was that the seat of Dabeiba was in a somewhat level area within the long cordillera east of the San Juan, a champaign country without monte, meaning trees and brush. There are such basins of subtropical and temperate climate about the upper drainage of the Sucio and Murri Rivers, favored by much less rain than the adjacent lowlands to the west. Later Spanish explorers observed treeless basins and ridges in that region and in other parts of Antioquia. They still exist and are, I think, the result of burning practices. The area controlled by Dabeiba in the cordillera was of unknown extent, and by word of Colmenares extended through the lowlands to the Gulf of Urabá at the Río León.

The information Balboa had was good news, but it also told him that it was time to turn back, although it was only two days to the east to the seat of this lord of gold. They got close enough to the cordillera to see the grasslands. This land of Dabeiba, however, they had been told, was not where the gold was found but where it was brought to be processed into the jewelry and figurines that had been seen in Darién. Dabeiba had the workshops of the artisans of gold and the center of an extensive system of native trade, not the gold mines. Had Balboa been a different sort of captain he would have marched his men off to Dabeiba and looted it, but would have failed in his objective to find the gold fields. These he had been told lay two days' journey to the east of Dabeiba, facing the rising sun, and in the hands of a "very Carib" people. He did not have the men or the means to invade or occupy a land farther overland and inhabited by hostile natives. Balboa had experienced the attacks of such at Urabá; those of the interior were reported to be even worse and to engage in cannibalism.

The hearsay accounts that he collected were true in the main. The eastern slopes of the Cordillera Occidental that drain into the Río Cauca were, in fact, occupied by a very different and uncommonly ferocious lot of natives. A march of two days beyond the cordillera would have taken a party from the temperate western highlands of Frontino-Dabeiba or Urrao to the Río Cauca about Antioquia. Gold placers were worked here aboriginally, became one of the most productive gold regions of colonial times, and still are exploited. The word that these gold fields faced the rising sun, places them west of the Río Cauca. Buriticá, most famous of the early workings, exploited by natives before it was taken over by the Spaniards, is in such location. Balboa had the right information and prudently decided to defer its application to a later and proper time.

In 1536 César, Vadillo, and Cieza de León began their entradas from the Gulf of Urabá across the cordillera to the Río Cauca. Shortly Robledo repeated the passage in the reverse direction. Thus, twenty-five years after Balboa, the Spanish occupation of Antioquia began by placer mining camps along that part of the Cauca from which Dabeiba had been supplied with native gold.[3] The name Dabeiba became a legend, an earlier El Dorado, and in time was even held to have been a native divinity to whom golden offerings were brought (a god or goddess of a golden temple).

PLANNING THE DISCOVERY
OF THE PACIFIC OCEAN

After returning from the Atrato expedition Balboa gave his attention again to the western prospect. His letter of January, 1513, to the King outlined in some detail his plans, which are here abstracted or excerpted in their order in the letter. He asked for five hundred or more men from Española so that with the men he had, less than a hundred of whom were fit for war, he might "enter the country inland and pass to the other sea on the side of the south." Referring to his earlier visit with the caciques Comogre and Pocorosa, the farthest west and inland he had been, he told of mountain country extending into parts as yet unseen. "In those sierras are certain caciques who have gold in quantity in their houses. They say those caciques keep it in cribs (barbacoas) like maize, because they have so much gold that they do not wish to keep it in baskets. They say that all the rivers of those sierras carry gold, and that there are large nuggets in quantity. The manner of taking it is that it is seen in the water and picked up and put into baskets, also they take it from arroyos when these are dry." In support of his statement he sent an Indian who was accustomed thus to get gold. (He had been referring to the serranía along the Caribbean side of the Isthmus.)

From the base of these sierras very smooth plains extend southward, the Indians saying that [across them] the other sea is reached in three days. All the caciques and Indians of that province of Comogre tell me that there are so many pieces of gold in the houses of the caciques on the other sea as to make us lose our minds. They say that gold is found in quantity in all the rivers of the other coast and in large nuggets. They say that Indians come to the house of this Cacique Comogre by canoe from the other sea to trade their gold and that these are people of good conduct. They tell me that the other sea is very good to navigate in canoes, being always pacific and does not turn wild as it does on this coast. . . . I believe that in that sea are many islands and pearls in quantity and large ones and that the caciques have chests full of them. . . . This river which flows from this Cacique Comogre to the other sea, before it gets there, forms three branches, each of which discharges separately into the sea. They say that the pearls are brought by the westernmost of these branches by canoes to the house of the Cacique Comogre. They say that by the branch toward the east the canoes enter into all parts with gold.

If he were given the required men, he offered to procure riches enough "to conquer a large part of the world." At this point he raised his request of men needed to a thousand, listed the arms that would be required, the small ships that should be built, and where forts should be constructed, one to be at Comogre, well palisaded and moated with walls of well-tamped earth (tapia).

The geography Balboa had learned from the Indians was factual and fairly

---

[3] Herman Trimborn, *Vergessene Königreiche* (Braunschweig, 1948) has reconstructed the native conditions in the northern cordillera from the records of these entradas.

specific as to topography (fig. 26). The distance from the land of Comogre to the nearest bay of the Gulf of San Miguel on the Pacific was at most fifty miles overland. This gulf protrudes inland in a series of drowned valleys. The largest river thus discharging is the Chucunaque (Balsas of early days), which has its sources in the land of Comogre and was navigable by canoe to the seat of that chief. Its estuary is joined by that of the Río Tuira, which flows out of the southeast, also navigable by canoe in numerous affluents that yielded gold. The Pearl Islands lie well out to sea west of the San Miguel Gulf. Comogre would serve as his interior base to get south to the Gulf of San Miguel and locate the Pearl Islands. To the west of Comogre the Bayano basin, by way of the native state of Pocorosa, would give access to a farther lowland receiving numerous gold-bearing streams out of the northern serranía, the amount of gold greatly exaggerated in his mind. His eye for the proper strategic location was sure. For west or south, Comogre was the proper starting point for his next operations. The first task would be to take possession of the as yet unseen other sea which was of common native knowledge.

UNEXPECTED REACTION

In composing his letter to the King, Balboa overplayed the prospects of Darién and his own role. It was true, as he claimed, that he had succeeded where Nicuesa and Hojeda had failed. He had, however, usurped authority and had thrown out Enciso, who was lodging complaints against him at court. In the absence of properly constituted authority, the King had named Balboa interim governor in provisional acceptance of an act that was in fact insubordination. Now Balboa asked for a thousand men and formidable military equipment and offered by such means and entry to the other ocean the riches which would conquer a large part of the world. If these things were true, he was asking for a position of power unheard of for a person of his origin and station since Columbus. The time had not yet come for a Cortés or Pizarro to break the bonds of official preferment. Balboa tried too soon and made the mistake of putting his grand design fully and brashly before King and Fonseca.

Instead of getting the acceptance and support he had asked, his letter had the opposite result. On May 31, 1513, Ferdinand ordered the officials at Sevilla not to lose a single day in getting an armada ready for the embarkation of eight hundred to a thousand men under "a principal person whom I shall order to go from here." On June 11 he notified the vecinos of Darién that he would send someone to take charge of the government as they had asked, there being a faction in opposition to Balboa. On June 18 he addressed Pedrarias Dávila as "our Captain and Governor of Tierra Firme." On July 28 he ordered the latter to start proceedings against Balboa in the matter of the complaint made by Enciso. At the same time Pedrarias received the formal and novel title of captain general and governor of Castilla del Oro in Darién.[4] One of his first steps would be to hold a formal inquiry or residencia of Balboa's conduct. The overly ambitious upstart

---

[4] Altolaguirre, Appendix docs. 8–14.

would be replaced by an aged officer of rank and aristocratic origin, also belonging to the circle about Fonseca.

THE JOURNEY TO THE SOUTH SEA

Whatever Balboa might do to protect himself had to be done quickly. There was no time to discover the western gold mines or do the other things about which he had written so confidently. The reality might be much less than he had advertised, but of one thing he could be sure. The other sea awaited discovery and he would gain honor by taking possession of it for Spain. The great rainy season was on, and he could not await its ending. Having gotten his party ready, he set off from Darién on September 1. This would be his page in history; for it he kept record day by day. It passed into the hands of Oviedo to be transposed by him into the *Historia General*.[5]

The expedition lost no time in uncertain wandering. Balboa remembered all that he had been told two years before at Comogre and fitted it into the topography as he went along. The preparations had been properly made. Usually he led or sent a small advance party to lay out the route by which the main party moved up. In the four and a half months of the expedition there was no disaster and hardly a mishap.

The start from Santa María was by nine large canoes trailed by a galleon. According to Oviedo there were eight hundred persons, which meant that Indians were in large majority. They landed at the port of Careta twenty leagues up the coast, where Balboa later founded the Spanish villa of Acla (fig. 26). From this familiar and friendly locality they crossed the serranía in two days to go on to the seat of Ponca, whom they had trounced two years earlier. The place was in the upper Chucunaque basin, probably in the foothills drained by the Río Subcutí or the Río Mortí. They reached it on September 6 and left on the 20th. The province of Ponca supplied provisions, information, and guides freely. Two weeks were thus spent in learning about the unknown country ahead.

The first objective was to cross the lowland of the Balsas by as direct a course as possible, which was southwesterly. The four days thus spent (September 20 to 24) were the most difficult part of the journey, "by bad road and across rivers which the Spaniards crossed on rafts and at great risk," for the rivers were at flood. Peter Martyr noted that natives were taken along to open narrow and difficult passages; there were no beaten tracks because of infrequent communication, but the Indians knew how to follow obscure trails. There was no identification of streams crossed and no mention of settlements. In four days they covered only ten leagues, which would suggest that the difficult going made the distances seem greater than they were, or that they were forced to make detours because of flooded land.

The objective on the far side of the basin was the land of a cacique Quareca, or Torecha, who was an enemy of Ponca, for which reason the Poncans were willing to go along. There is no identification where the seat of Quareca was, other than its distance from that of Ponca. The region is at present an almost

---

[5] Oviedo, *Historia*, Bk. XXIX, chs. 3–5. Other items are in Peter Martyr, Decade III.

unknown wilderness. The *Carta Preliminar* (1957) of the Republic of Panama, based on air photographs, shows a long ridge rising to more than two hundred meters east of Río Sabanas and northeast of the village of Santa Fé on that river, directly across the basin from the Mortí and Subcutí rivers. Location and elevation suggest that this may have been the land of Quareca. The seat of the chief was attacked and taken on the night of the 24th. Peter Martyr took special note of the occasion because he heard that the court of the chief included transvestites, forty of whom were killed by mastiffs, also that there were Negro slaves who had been taken from a province that lay two days distant. These, he surmised, might be the progeny of a ship from Ethiopia that had been wrecked. The province of Quareca he thought poor in gold, sterile, and cold because it was treeless country. (A land of black people was reported again at a later date. A ridge-top savanna within tropical rain forest may have been formed by clearing and burning.)

From Quareca the route turned south. Oviedo obviously made a mistake in his transcription of Balboa's journal. Quareca was seized on the night of the 24th. Gold and pearls were taken, information was secured as to the route ahead, and local natives were assembled to serve as guides. Balboa went on with a party, passed south through the land of a cacique Porque and its bohios, and at ten o'clock on the morning of the 25th, according to Oviedo, climbed the bare ridge from which he had the first sight of the South Sea. The date is obviously impossible, and Mrs. Romoli has properly revised it to September 27.

The march had begun at Ponca on the 20th. The sea was discovered on the morning of the 27th, using this correction. The time available was between six and seven days. Four were required to cross the flooded lowlands between Ponca and Quareca. The events at Quareca took at least another day, leaving less than two days to get to the point of discovery by way of the land of Porque. This tight schedule was made possible only by good leadership and knowledgeable Indian guides. Balboa wanted to get to the Pacific Ocean as fast as he could, and he did so. The geographical knowledge that he had from the Indians and arranged correctly in the map of his mind gave him the proper direction to follow without deviation or delay except for the sack of Quareca.

Late maps of Panama that were not available to earlier studies serve as basis for a relocation of the route of discovery (fig. 26). The most direct and convenient route across the northern serranía from Careta (Acla) led to the western slopes drained by the Río Subcutí or Mortí and thus to the foothill location of the seat of Ponca. From Ponca to Quareca a number of rivers were crossed in making the traverse of the lowland basin. Quareca, situated in a savanna, is tentatively placed on the ridge east of the Río Sabanas; the subsequent crossing of that river is inferred as taking place near the village of Santa Fé, below which a marshy and muddy estuary extends into the Gulf of San Miguel. To the west of that estuary another long narrow ridge runs south to form a peninsula in the inner Bay of San Miguel; United States Aeronautical Chart 769 gives its highest point as 1,200 feet near its tip, across from the town of La Palma and with a view west across the bay. The distance from the inferred ridge of Quareca by way of the Santa Fé crossing to the beginning of the second ridge is about ten miles, with a similar distance along the latter to the high lookout over the gulf. The land of Porque, then, would have been entered west of Río Sabanas as they approached the southern ridge. From a high point on the latter, Balboa had his first look to "the other ocean." This was the nearest and most accessible place for him to see the open sea. Indeed, there was no other such lookout on the north of the Gulf of San Miguel except far away to the west at Cape San Lorenzo.

In Oviedo's version, "Vasco Núñez going ahead of the rest up a bare hill (*monte raso*) beheld from the crest thereof the South Sea." Balboa wished to have the first sight to himself. Thereafter, the rest of the party was called up to join in the first ceremony of possession. They had come by way of a long ridge to a place where they knew they would have sight of the sea, the party being halted so that Balboa might go alone to that lookout. It is hardly a guess that they had been following an Indian trail south, led by Indian guides who had been told to take the white captain to a high open space from which he could see the great water. This grassy eminence suggests another savanna ridge.

They had seen the sea from the high point and, having recorded the discovery by formal ceremony, finished the day by turning westward and seaward (fig. 27). "They continued on their road to some bohíos near the South Sea in the land of the cacique Chape, there to await the coming of the men who had been left behind at Quareca." This was still the day of the discovery. On September 29 Balboa took a party half a league from the bohíos of Chape to the shore of the gulf which he then named San Miguel. Here, on a great wooded bay, they observed the large rise and ebb of the sea. There were wide mud flats at low tide, covered at a rush by the rising sea. The second rites of possession were performed here "by the first Christians who put their feet into the South Sea, all trying the water with their hands and proving that it was salt." The place may be suggested as the bay adjoining the promontory of the discovery at the west. It was close by the latter and was not a mangrove swamp, such as are found almost continuously along the shores farther west. Until the building of modern La Palma this locality of the north shore served as *embarcadero*.

More than two weeks were spent at the seat of Chape, informing themselves of the secrets of the country, sending messengers to different parts, and putting the land at peace. Chape was a major cacique seated in the strategic hub of water communication about the Gulf of San Miguel and the Tiura, Chucunaque, and Sabanas river systems. The current administrative seat of Panama's southern province at La Palma is using the same advantages of location but from the opposite shore. The gulf was named San Miguel at Chape. The small river entering the bay at that place is still called the Río San Miguel.

Two days of long, hard, and dangerous travel in canoes manned by experienced Indians took them across the gulf and north up the open ocean shore to the bohío of the cacique Tumaco. Balboa called its small bay San Lucas, considered the reëntrant of the sea behind Punta Brujas. Here they learned about pearl fishing and saw the manner of taking them demonstrated, though there were few to be had. They spent two weeks here learning about the habits of the pearl oyster. Their hopes to get to the Pearl Islands, twenty miles out to sea, were disappointed by the roughness of the water. The third act of possession took place

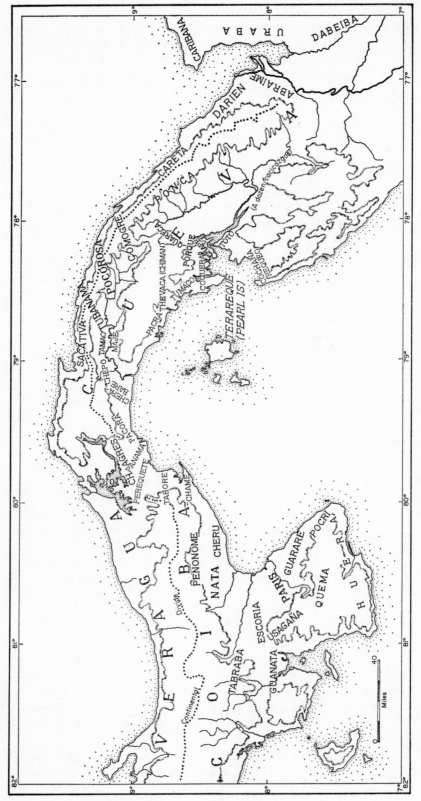

Fig. 27. Native "provinces" of the Isthmus.

on a local headland, perhaps Punta Brujas, on October 29, thereby completing the mission on which the expedition had gone. They were then six weeks out from the start at Ponca, hardly a fourth of which was travel time.

The coast beyond Tumaco was a mangrove swamp through which they followed open channels or cut their way to reach the place of a cacique called Thevaca on the banks of a river in strong flood (the modern town of Chimán). At this point the canoes supplied by the friendly cacique Chape turned back with word that the Spaniards who had remained behind should come overland.

At Thevaca, Balboa left the sea to turn north into a montane country in search of a cacique Pacra, who was reputed to control a gold-bearing land. Balboa gave it the name Todos Santos, which may be taken to mean that it was entered on the first of November. The whole of that month was spent looking for the supposed gold mines. Behind Chimán and paralleling the Pacific coast for about fifty miles is a low and isolated mountain region called Serranía de Maje or Cañazas, both being names of streams rising on its northern slopes. This highland is little known and virtually uninhabited at present. The province of Pacra or Todos Santos lay on the Pacific side of these mountains somewhere to the north of Chimán. I know of no gold produced from that area.

Caciques came to the November camp with presents of gold, offerings of good will which probably were worked pieces. Pacra kept on insisting that he had no gold mines. Peter Martyr wrote that Pacra, who was very deformed and ugly, and three subchiefs finally were thrown to the dogs and their bodies burned, without getting any information from them. Oviedo said that in the papers left by Balboa "the cruelties were not stated, but there were many and he put many Indians to the torture and set dogs on others while on this journey," also that Balboa took their wives and daughters and so set a bad example for others. Oviedo was not motivated by animus. The exploration had turned into outrage.

Balboa left Todos Santos on December 1 to cross the mountains into the interior basin of the Bayano drainage. This was the only time when the party suffered lack of food, because a chief on whom they had counted for supplies had fled and taken his stores with him. On December 8 they reached the familiar bohíos of Pocorosa, where they took their ease for the rest of the month.[6] Chiefs or their messengers came to Pocorosa from near and far bearing gifts to placate the Christians, in whose fear they would live thereafter.

In his earlier letter to the King, Balboa had referred to a cacique Tubanama reported to have gold mines and living beyond Pocorosa. He now made a raid, accompanied by eighty men, into the foothills of the serranía northwest of Pocorosa. Attacking the bohío of Tubanama before daybreak, as was a favored Spanish tactic, Balboa captured the chief and held him for ransom. His Indian subjects complied by bringing in their pieces of gold; one of them, Oviedo wrote, brought fifteen *patenas* (disks) of gold. According to Peter Martyr, the bohío of Tubanama yielded thirty pounds of gold jewels and his subjects brought in sixty more for the ransom; the cacique explained that the treasure was inherited from ancestors. Meanwhile Balboa sent men out to search arroyos and rivers round about for placer gold. It was reported that there was some show of color in all

---

[6] Peter Martyr, referring to the bread of maize here, noted that it was like the panicum of Lombardy.

the *bateas*, this being the first known mention of panning for gold in the Isthmus, a practice however, probably previously used in the placer workings west of Santa María.

Having reassembled his entire party, Balboa reached the seat of Comogre on New Year's Day, 1514. The old chief had died and been succeeded by the son who had earlier told of the South Sea as he reproached the Spaniards for their lust for gold. On January 4 they reached Ponca, where the journey into unknown lands had begun three and a half months before.

The expedition had various objectives and succeeded in all of them. Tactically most important was the discovery of the South Sea and the ceremonies held at three places by which it was claimed for the Crown of Spain. It was shown that the Isthmus could be crossed by a large party in a few days. A richly promising source of pearls was determined. The venture seems to have paid off well also in booty and gifts, so-called. Oviedo said that they returned rich in gold and pearls, in male and female naborías, and in cloth and hammocks of cotton.

Balboa had again proved himself to be a great captain. He brought his men through in good condition and apparently without loss. En route, he might drive them hard, with himself taking the lead, but the greater part of the time was spent at ease in advantageous native localities, at Ponca, Chape, Tumaco, Thevaca, Pacra, and Pocorosa. With its many Indian followers, guides, and captives the party numbered hundreds and was only once in want of food. At no time did it flounder about uncertain where to go or what road to take. This was then a country of a numerous and undepressed people, with settlements, communications, and productive agriculture and fishing. Of these things Balboa took care to inform himself beforehand. Also he appraised shrewdly the structure of the native society. The people were obedient and devoted to their chiefs, as was pathetically evident when they stripped themselves of their gold in order to ransom their cacique Tubanama. Once Balboa had a cacique in hand he could ask and do what he wished.

Corruption by power however also had become evident. Balboa killed some captive chiefs, scared others, and made friends of some; Chape was an illustration of one who gave great and apparently willing aid. Except in the strange and dubious case of Quareca, the Spaniards met with no hostility either as a party or as individuals. Pacra and his subchiefs were put to death because they could not reveal where their nonexistent gold mines lay. Oviedo, best informed and not inclined to tilt the scales of justice in favor of Indians, and not an enemy of Balboa, concluded that gross and wanton cruelties were practiced on the journey.

Balboa, like all the captains of the time, was a seeker after gold. More clearly than most, he realized that the gold objects owned by the natives would soon be at an end and that it was important to locate the source of gold. In the mountains behind Santa María he had established the first placer mining on Tierra Firme. The expedition to locate Dabeiba was made in order to discover the source of supply of gold to the artificers of gold. When he learned that Dabeiba was only manufacturing gold that came from a farther and hostile interior he turned back. On the expedition to the South Sea, bateas were carried to pan placer gold. The cruelty at Todos Santos was exasperation because he believed that Pacra was concealing gold mines, and he held Tubanama for ransom for the same reason. He left Tubanama with some proof that there was native gold and the hope that it would become a gold district—an expectation that was to be revived later with scant success.

At the return to Santa María in the beginning of 1514, Balboa had fairly adequate knowledge of the map, peoples, and resources of the eastern part of the Isthmus. Eastward the Atrato basin had been explored to the Cordillera Occidental.

XII

CUEVAN COUNTRY AND PEOPLE

•

REGIONAL IDENTITY

The Indian "province" of Darién was a strip of about thirty miles of Caribbean coast, from the Atrato delta to Cape Tiburón at the present border of Colombia and Panama. Spanish Darién had no limits other than the extent of Balboa's control, namely the eastern part of the Isthmus and the Atrato basin. The town of Darién lay about midway of an extensive area having a common way of Indian living, found from eastern Costa Rica to the Atrato basin and reaching the Pacific at the Gulf of San Miguel. What Balboa knew of the present country of Panama was then occupied by Cueva Indians, whose lands extended west beyond his ken. Their remnants are the Cuna Indians now living on the San Blas Islands and at a few places in the interior lowlands. (The western Cueva limits, somewhat west of Panama City, will be considered later.) The natives of Veragua and beyond to Puerto Limón, discovered by Columbus and recorded by his son Ferdinand, were also of closely cognate culture. All were of a Chibchan speech which was more or less generally intelligible. This Darién of Balboa and the Veragua of Columbus are the lands here concerned.

The eastern side of the Gulf of Urabá was another matter, how different the Spaniards knew mainly by the menace of poisoned missiles; nor do we know much more today about the Urabaes and that corner of the mainland. On the rivers of León and Atrato, however, the Spaniards were among natives much like those of the Isthmus. The differences were of environment rather than of culture. The indications are that the language was similar. Information was obtained freely and in detail by Spanish parties without mention of any use of interpreters. The names of places and persons sound like those of the Isthmus. Trimborn has identified a native name for the Río Sucio as Tirubi, Tubiri, and Tiribi, to which may be added the Turui of Colmenares for the settlement which I have inferred was at its mouth. Another large river out of the serranía of Darién into the Gulf of San Miguel, called Tuira, has a similar ring. A common toponymy of eastern Panama and northwestern Colombia is suggested at the time of Spanish entry. Trimborn, in fact, has concluded that Chibchan speech and ways extended from the Cueva lands of Panama across the Atrato basin into the Cordillera Occidental of Colombia, the latter the domain of Dabeiba and

238

the "lost kingdoms" with which he has been concerned.[1] This large and important extension of former Chibchan cultures is, I think, borne out by the records.
It also makes sense of Balboa's search for Dabeiba. The thesis here to be considered is of a macro-Cuevan culture dominant from Dabeiba in the south to
Puerto Limón in Costa Rica and extending west to the Gulf of Panama.

The only reference to people of a different sort within these limits is by
Andagoya, who wrote of the Chuchures of strange language, living about Nombre
de Dios, as having come by canoe from the direction of Honduras, but dying off
from the effects of the climate, with few being left when Nombre de Dios was
refounded in 1519. Was this another indication of Mayan seafaring?

SOCIAL ORGANIZATION

To the men who came from Española the structure of the native society was
familiar in major outlines. The provinces, as they called them, were independent
principalities ruled by chiefs, for whom the island title of cacique was appropriate.
The social stratification seems to have been about as strong as in the islands.
No female rulers were mentioned, in contrast to Española. A common title for
a sovereign chief was queví or *quibian*, first heard by Columbus in Veragua.
Balboa was called *tiba*, or great lord. In the *Sumario*, Oviedo called the subordinate chiefs *sacos* and added a hereditary gentry of *cabras*, who had acquired that
rank by distinction in war. The ladies of rank were *espaves*. The Spaniards were
translating the native society into their own terms.[2]

Sovereignty was hereditary and apparently absolute, but was portrayed as
benign. Andagoya, a well-informed source, found that "in these provinces the
lords did not have rent or tribute from their subjects other than personal services.
Whenever the lord required a house or planting or fishing or war, all were
obliged to come thus to serve without receiving anything else than a festival
with food and drink in return." "They lived in much justice by the law of nature,
without any ceremony or adoration. In these provinces the lords in person
determined the judgments." Andagoya noted as an exception to the usual social
structure a district on the Balsas river, "a well-peopled province in which there
was no lord other than that the head of one kindred was the lord of that group,
and all thus lived in amity without the obedience of one lord to another. This
province is part of Cueva and the people are the same." This clan organization
he called by the old Spanish name *behetría*.

There was also a slave class, though perhaps not large. Slaves were traded
and may have been secured as captives in war. Oviedo wrote of the return of
Balboa from the Pacific as bringing many naborías, without explanation.

"The lords of these provinces were small and there were many lords. They had
strong disagreements about their fishing and hunting grounds and so many were
killed." Thus Andagoya, who added that inland beyond Comogre the country was
well inhabited," although the lords were small, one being at from two to two or
one to one league of the other." However, the domains of Comogre and
Pocorosa extended from the interior basin across the serranía to fishing grounds

---

[1] Herman Trimborn, *Vergessene Königreiche* (Braunschweig, 1948), especially pp. 47 and 50.
[2] Friederici has collated references to these titles.

on the Caribbean. A territorial unit and its cacique were usually known by the same name. There is no word that the bellicose people of Urabá and Caribana bothered any of the Cuevan neighbors.

HOUSES

The same scattering of houses first seen in Veragua and Portobelo prevailed in most parts. In general there were said to be no towns or villages. Peter Martyr described the common type of house as of wood, covered and enclosed with thatch and canes of maize and the like, and said, "they live in houses separate and not contiguous because of the wind storms." There may be some sense to this notion. A close grouping of easily inflammable houses was a hazard. His reference to an enclosure about the houses suggests that this may have been an enclosed yard. The dispersed dwelling also suggests that there was no need to congregate for mutual security and thus that the wars between caciques were not formidable.

In the Atrato basin there were clusters or rows of houses, imposed by the amphibious topography of streams, natural levees, back swamps, and lagoons. Oviedo agreed that the isthmian country resembled Viscaya and the Asturias in dispersed habitation. In contrast to these he noted congregated tree dwellings of the Río Grande de San Juan, especially in the province of Abraime. In the latter, he said, were many villages of Indians with their houses built high up in the trees and reached by *escalones*, probably meaning tree trunks into which steps had been cut. Beneath were swamps and lagoons in which the canoes were kept. Elsewhere on the Atrato many people lived together in houses built high up in palm groves, with their canoes moored to the base of the palms. Since these palms were very hard to cut, as he said, one might infer that they were a kind of *Bactris*, about which I am not sufficiently informed to know whether these or some other palm would have been thus available.[3] Oviedo may have been carried away by the novelty of a situation described to him but which he had not seen.

The term bohío was applied by the Spaniards to the great houses of the chiefs. The accounts, speaking of marching from this bohío to that one, refer to the passage from the seat of one chief to that of another, either to treat or to loot. Some of these structures were large and sumptuous. Peter Martyr described the "palace" of Tubanama, mentioned previously. That of Comogre measured a hundred and fifty by eighty *pasos* (steps). (In contrast to the bohíos of the islands, these were rectangular, as most houses of the Isthmus seem to have been.) At Comogre, one room was filled with the dried cadavers of the ancestors, hung by cotton cords from the ceiling, each dressed according to rank and wearing gold and pearls; the manner of drying the bodies on barbecues was also described.[4] The chief's house was the abode of his ancestors, who were objects of reverence. In our Western terms, the seat of the chief was palace, court of law, and temple, the center of authority. When this seat, its head, and part of his family were taken as hostages, the subjects could be dealt with at will. The great house also

---

[3] Oviedo, *Sumario*, ch. 10 deals with houses. In his *Historia*, Bk. XXIX, ch. 2, he wrote of one *bohío* that was supported by a hundred and ten palm trees.
[4] Peter Martyr, Decade II, Bk. 3.

held the main treasure of the native state, a good part of it on the mummies of ancestors, the accumulation of generations, as was explained to the Spaniards. That the new lords should have taken over the insignia and treasured possessions of the old ones was perhaps understandable to the people. Why the new lords should hasten to smelt their treasure into lumps of metal valued only for their gold content was incomprehensible.

The dispersed mode of living in Cueva lands had exceptions, as we know from archaeological studies. The Belgian party in search of Santa María found that the Spanish town had been built on a native site of comparable size and of long occupancy. Linné located a site near the present village of Garachiné on the Gulf of San Miguel that occupied an area of a square kilometer, and to the east another of 80,000 square meters. These are in what was the province of Chochama.[5]

DRESS

The Cuevan dress of Careta was described by Oviedo: "The women went very well clothed from the breasts down, in figured cotton mantas, and they slept on well-ornamented cotton beds. The dresses of the women reached to cover their feet, the breasts and arms being exposed. The men carried their genitals in sea shells (caracoles) of many colors, very well fashioned, by cords that attached the shell about their loins . . . Such shells were objects of trade into the interior, for they were found only on this coast." [6]

FOOD AND DRINK

Oviedo pointed out correctly that there was no bitter yuca grown in western Tierra Firme and therefore there was no staple of cassava bread. Boniata (sweet yuca), batatas (sweet potatoes), and ages (starchy sweet potatoes) were in common cultivation, as they were in the islands. All were easy to prepare by baking in hot ashes at the edge of a bed of live coals. Enciso, describing in his Suma the food production of the southwest coast of Tierra Firme, gave the first account of the regional difference: "The bread and wine is made of the meal of maize, as it is in Cartagena. There are also the roots from which the bread is made in the islands of Cuba, Jamaica, and Española, but here they are of another quality, for those of the islands are dangerous and if one eats of one of them one dies as one would by eating realgar, but those of this land of Sinu and the land beyond to the west can be eaten raw or cooked and are very good food and of fine flavor." In terms of modern geography, Enciso was saying that in Venezuela and to the east bitter manioc was a staple but that it was not known in Colombia and to the west. This is still true. Whatever the place where the bitter yuca was first bred, its acceptance spread along the Atlantic side of the American tropics; only the sweet races were found in western parts of the Caribbean lands, in the intra-Andean lowlands, and along the Pacific. In none of these was cassava bread made from sweet yuca.

---

[5] S. Linné, Darien in the Past (Göteborg, 1929).
[6] Oviedo, Sumario, ch. 10.

The several kinds of roots were very good food and of fine flavor, as Enciso said, but they did not provide the Spaniards with a staple that could be carried easily and stored at will. A proper substitute for the cassava bread of the islands was available locally in maize. Unlike cassava, maize bread does not keep, but the ripe grain stores well, especially on the cob, and is readily transported. Maize also gives a high yield per plant and per unit of surface planted, and in tropical latitudes three or even four crops can be grown in a year. The Spaniards therefore shifted to maize as their staple, both by raiding Indian corncribs and by requiring the natives to plant cornfields for their new masters. As they had depended on Indian women to prepare the cassava bread, so these were needed to grind the grain and bake corn bread. Indian women were taken along on the entradas to prepare the daily bread. The success of an entrada depended on its levies of stored corn.

The best early account of maize and its preparation is by Oviedo, based mainly on his observations in the Cueva country:[7]

> Its ears, more or less a *geme* long [the span between thumb and forefinger] bear grains of the size of *garbanzos* [chick-peas]. The planting ground is prepared by clearing the canebrakes and montes, which are then burned, the ashes leaving the ground in better condition than if it had been manured. The Indians then make a hole in the ground by using a pointed stick, about as long as they are tall, and drop seven to eight grains into the opening, repeating the process as a step ahead is taken, and thus they proceed in a file across the clearing. The grain matures in three to four months and requires watching by boys, for whom shelters are built so that they may scare off the parrots that come to feed on the ears. Continuous vigilance is needed also against *monos gatos* [monkeys, coatis?], wild pigs [peccaries] and deer. . . . The Indian women grind the grain on a somewhat concave stone by means of another round one that they hold in their hands, using the strength of their arms, as painters are accustomed to grind their pigments. They add water little by little which is mixed with the grain as it is ground and results in a sort of paste resembling dough (*masa*). They take some of this and wrap it in a leaf of some plant or in one of the maize. This is put into the hot embers and baked until it is dry and turns into something like white bread, with a crust on the outside, the inside of the roll being crumbly and somewhat softer. This should be eaten while hot, for becoming cold it has neither so good a taste, nor is it easy to chew, being dry and harsh. Such rolls may also be prepared by boiling but are inferior. This bread, baked or boiled, keeps only a few days. In four to five days it moulds and is no longer fit to eat.

Oviedo was writing about a white maize, soft enough to be ground into meal, and therefore not a flinty corn. There was no prior soaking of the grain. The grinding was done by circular or elliptical motion on a concave mealing stone and the *masa* was shaped into rolls, wrapped in leaves, and baked or boiled. The whole procedure was very different from that of Mexico, where the corn was first soaked, then ground on a metate by back and forth motion, and baked into thin cakes (*tortillas*).

The *Sumario* of Oviedo is the first attempt at a systematic account of cultivated and other useful plants about the Caribbean. In this earlier volume his observations were mainly of the Isthmus and especially of "the great province of Cueva," which he knew by residence at Santa María. Some of the descriptions give no

[7] Oviedo, *Sumario*, ch. 4.

indication of the particular area to which they apply. There were more different kinds of fruits, he thought, on the Isthmus than in the islands and they were of better quality, as, for example, were the guayabas (*Psidium*) about Darién (which may indicate a local selection). He also gave the first description of the papaya under the name of *higos del mastuerzo*. These, he said, had been brought from Acla for Spanish cultivation at Darién. From Acla to Cerebaro (Almirante Gulf) they were in native cultivation. (The origin of this important cultigen and of its common name are still unknown.)

Wine making had been observed at the discovery of Veragua. The following quotation is from the Second Book of Las Casas, who said that he was quoting Ferdinand Columbus, presumably from the lost Spanish original. At Veragua they had "white and red wine from maize in the manner in which beer is made in Flanders or in England, throwing into it whatever they hold to be good spices. It is of very good taste, although like a rough wine or one of Gascony. They made another wine from trees that seem to be palms and are of such species. Their trunks or masts are smooth but very full of spines like those of a porcupine. From the tops of these, which are like a *palmito*, by cutting them and extracting the juice they make wine, boiling it with water and mixing in their spices. They hold this to be a very precious wine and the most costly." Wine was also made from pineapples and other fruits "especially from one growing on very tall trees, which is like a grapefruit (*toronja*) or small citron." The account that follows makes certain that the true mamey was being described, which indicates that Las Casas was copying Ferdinand literally without stopping to think that he knew this fruit well from his island experience. In Veragua, therefore, there were two kinds of maize beverage like the beer of northern Europe, another from the terminal bud of a palm armored with spines (probably *Acrocomia*), and still others, all alcoholic, from pineapples, mameys, and other fruits, and any of these might be spiked with spices.

Peter Martyr in his second *Decade* described wine at Comogre. "It was stored in great earthen jars (*tinajas*) or in casks of wood. [This statement is like the one about the wine cellar of the cacique of the tree house on the Atrato. The casks were probably hollow tree trunks]. These receptacles were filled with excellent wines, made of three classes of breadstuffs, yuca, *ages*, and maize, and also from the fruit of palms [perhaps the fruits of the peach palm *Guilielma*]. This wine was the sort of a beverage drunk by the Germans, Belgians, English and Spanish mountaineers, such as Basques and Asturians. Also in the Alps we have seen the Austrians, Suabians, and Swiss make a cider from barley, wheat, or apples. [This interesting aside shows that Peter Martyr, educated in the ways of Mediterranean wine lands, knew little about beer or cider.] They say that in the house of Comogre red and white wines are drunk, and of various tastes, the greater part resembling mead (*aloja*)."

Oviedo reported in the *Summario* that the maize beverage was prepared by soaking the grain until it swelled and sprouted; it was then boiled, taken from the fire after a certain time, and allowed to stand to ferment. It was ready to drink after a day, at its best after four days, and spoiled within a week.

In all three sources, maize was mentioned in first place for alcoholic beverages. Others were made from starchy roots, the sugary sap of a palm, the starchy fruit of another palm, pineapples, and a miscellany of sweet tree fruits. Alcoholic drinks were made in quantity from diverse plants, both starchy and sugary. Mainly these were cultivated. The means of stopping fermentation being inadequate, the supply had to be replenished frequently. The caciques kept ample stores on hand, from which it may be inferred that their subjects were well provided at festivities.

Fish were the most important native food, Oviedo thought, and these were secured from fresh as well as from salt water. Three caciques of the interior, Comogre, Pocorosa, and Dabeiba, were named as controlling fishing coasts on the Caribbean. Nets were made from selected cotton grown "in their settlements and next to their houses." [8] (My recollection is that cotton shrubs are still to be found most commonly growing by the side of a house, from Central America into northern Mexico, a common item in the assemblage of plants that are kept in rural dooryards.) In these humid tropical regions fish and shellfish that were not eaten at once were smoked and dried on *barbacoas*.

A great part of the country then being open land, deer and peccaries ranged freely on secondary growth of grasses, canes, shrubs, and trees. Game was perhaps most numerous near the settlements, by attraction of growing crops and unculti-vated fields. Deer and peccaries were hunted by drives. More information about hunting is available from the cognate region of Coiba to the west (see chap. xiv). The account by Oviedo in the *Summario*, although not localized, is pertinent: "For the deer and pigs they set up traps and snares of vines and other devices of nets into which these fall. At times they organize drives and startle the game by halloing and by means of numerous people cut off their escape and get them to a place where they can be killed by darts [*saetas*, dart throwers, known locally as *estolicas*, being in general use] and by throwing spears." The Cuevans were not bowmen. Oviedo next described the *barbacoa*, a grate or trivet on which the meat was dried over a fire.

Andagoya generalized in similar vein: "In these provinces there are many deer and pigs, the latter differing from those of Spain. They go in large herds, do not have tails nor do they grunt even if they are being killed, and have on their back something like a navel. The chiefs had hunting tracts (*cotos*) to which they went in summer [the dry season] to hunt deer. Fire was set on the windward side and since the plants (*yerba*) grew tall the fire was great. Indians were placed in file at a position where the fire would come to a stop. The deer, massed in their flight and blinded by the smoke, were thus driven by fire to the place where Indians were waiting with their dart throwers and stone points so that few creatures escaped." The dry season was hunting season, when game could be driven by fire to mass slaughter.

GOLD

As in the islands, the wastage of crystalline rocks, especially of quartz veins, left its residuum of native gold in streams. The accumulations of placer gold were slight, as the natives knew and the Spaniards would not believe. When Balboa had the caciques of Todos Santos tortured he believed that they were

---

[8] *Ibid.*, ch. 10.

concealing knowledge of gold mines. When Columbus was told that there was gold in the mountains for great distances, he thought that these held great and widespread riches, whereas he had come upon the one district in Veragua that later was briefly rewarding to placer mining. The Cueva country was only a marginal producer of gold under intensive Spanish search.

The Indians collected gold nuggets at proper places after the rainy seasons. They knew that after freshets stream beds might disclose gold newly washed in or exposed and that certain savanna slopes, being burned over, might expose nuggets. In Veragua it had been noted that ceremonies were observed before setting out to collect gold. The native knowledge of recovering gold was little greater than or much different from that of the islands, but the local interest in finding it was greater since raw gold was important in native trade.

There is no such information as there had been in the islands about the beating of gold into objects of adornment. The Bastidas and Veragua discoveries told more about the kinds of objects that were secured and whether they were of native gold or alloyed than was recorded later in the occupation of Darién. Gold could be beaten into thin sheets and trimmed to desired forms by pounding a nugget as was done in Española, but the casting of gold and its alloying were special skills demanding a metallurgical knowledge of which there is no record in the Caribbean coasts. It is unlikely that had the Spaniards of Darién found such art it would have escaped mention. Indeed, Balboa thought that all the manufactured gold was imported from distant Dabeiba.

In Española the gold districts were known by name. In Puerto Rico and Cuba Spanish villas were established near gold placers. In the territory Balboa explored and in good part controlled, only the gold produced from streams behind Santa María was mentioned as to locality along with the rumored gold district about Tubanama. Oviedo later described how Indian labor was employed to dig and wash in various parts of the Isthmus, but mentioned neither any place nor a notable success. Gold, he said, could be found anywhere within ten leagues.[9] A little native gold was found here and there in the foothills, but the only promising district was the one Columbus had located in Veragua, and it was not exploited until half a century later, nor for long.

Spanish activities in the western parts of Tierra Firme were mostly concerned with getting possession of the gold ornaments owned by the natives. These were melted down and assayed as to their gold content for the payment of the royal fifth. Some of it was pure gold, of 22 carats or more, but the greater part was guanín, or *oro bajo*. In either case they were the products of a metallurgy beyond the competence of ordinary skills. Oviedo came with Pedrarias in 1514 as the King's veedor of gold assays and held that position for a year, during which time the raids were limited mainly to lands previously visited by Balboa. Oviedo wrote that "daily there are [secured] many treasures of worked gold in the possession of the Indians, but the greater part of this worked gold which the Indians have is on a base of copper (*encobrado*) and they make of it many things and jewels which are worn by males and females on their persons and is the thing they most esteem and value." All the loot of the time was promptly smelted to extract its gold. Very little has since been recovered from this area by archaeologic excava-

---

[9] *Ibid.*, ch. 82.

tion. Oviedo knew that copper was the main constituent of the guanín and that some pieces had a film of gold on copper, which he said, was done by the use of certain plants.

The implication is of an Indian trade in metals that was of long standing and extended to distant regions. What was looted or levied from the natives was the accumulation of generations. Balboa knew that the source of such treasure was distant and was produced by craftsmen of metallurgy and concluded that it was all traded in from the workshops of Dabeiba. Where the copper came from was not known or asked. Nor is it known today. Native gold could be collected along streams in various parts of Tierra Firme. Native copper however is found in few parts of the world and rarely in the American tropics. The copper had to be reduced to metallic form from its ores, which required a knowledge of difficult procedures. Central America lacks suitable ores. Colombia had native metallurgists of astonishing proficiency, but did they have access to bodies of copper ores? Vásquez de Espinosa wrote a century later of rich copper mines in the Valle de Upar south of the Sierra de Santa Marta with no intimation of their use by the natives, whom he regarded as Caribs. The smelting of copper required a competent population living near the ore bodies. The two great areas where copper was produced in quantity by natives and from which it was traded were Peru and Mexico. Whether one of these provided the metal for the guanín makers of Tierra Firme remains to be determined. The source of copper, not that of gold, is the more important question.

The copper content of guanín was variable, but was usually estimated as two-thirds or more. The gold-copper alloy was not to economize the gold, but for the sake of hardness, better and easier casting, and especially for the red-gold tones. Spanish Darién and its succeeding government of Castilla del Oro were supported by acquisitions of artifacts of such metal and some of unalloyed gold. For a number of years the chief revenue of Spain from the Indies was from this source that derived from an unknown native commerce in metals out of other parts.

XIII
CASTILLA DEL ORO
(1514–1519)

•

PROVISIONS FOR A NEW GOVERNMENT

The operations on Tierra Firme were undertaken directly from Spain. Little by little the Crown was detaching the western mainland from the administration at Santo Domingo and ignoring the concessions to Columbus. When Balboa attained control of Darién he acknowledged this separation by addressing himself to the King and bypassing Diego Columbus. The King at the end of 1511 named Balboa governor and captain of the province of Darién without intermediate authority.

Except for the entry of Velázquez into Cuba at the time and Balboa's success matters were not going well in the Indies. The new prospect for Tierra Firme brought the decision to send a royal governor, staff, and men directly from Spain.

The title given Pedrarias Dávila on July 27, 1513, as captain general and governor applied to a "land which until now has been called Tierra Firme, and we now order that it shall be called Castilla del Oro, and in it our people have made a settlement on the Gulf of Urabá which is in the province of Darién, which at present is called Andalucia la Nueva and the town is called Santa Maria del Antigua del Darien." [1] The title to Pedrarias is the first designation of Castilla del Oro and included both prior concessions of Nicuesa and Hojeda.

Balboa's temporary government of Darién had been wholly undefined as to limits. The Nicuesa concession had been to Veragua, as beginning west of the Gulf of Urabá and of unlimited extent westward, and was given in disregard of the discovery and title of Columbus. Apparently because the suit of the heirs of Columbus was being pushed strongly in 1513, Veragua was excluded from the new government of Castilla del Oro. The latter was not to have anything to do with "the Province of Veragua the government of which belongs to the Admiral D. Diego Colon, because the Admiral his father had discovered it in person." However, no delimitation was drawn, except for the order to Pedrarias that the villa of Darién lay outside the jurisdiction of Don Diego Colón. [2] Except for

---

[1] Navarrete, III, 337–342, followed by detailed instructions as to conduct of the office.
[2] Altolaguirre, Appendix doc. 11.

Veragua, Pedrarias would take over what Balboa had won, and he was free to move west, south, or east on Tierra Firme.

THE RECORD

The records are unambiguous. The happenings in Castilla del Oro were tragic from the beginning and they are spelled out in large detail. Naked greed and cold cruelty gave rise to protests at court, the sidelights of which give information on what the country was like and what happened to it. The self-serving reports of Pedrarias and his lieutenants are not without geographical value, but there are more and better descriptions by others. What the basis of indignation was is here of less importance than what they told of the country and its people.[3]

The Franciscan Juan de Quevedo, who came with Pedrarias to be Bishop of Darién, lodged vigorous and specific complaints that supported those of Balboa. Oviedo, who had come as veedor, went back to Spain after ten months to tell of the misrule. He returned to Darién in 1520 and remained in the colony for five years, during which time he assembled the materials for his histories. Pascual de Andagoya, who also arrived with Pedrarias, took part in expeditions and became a *regidor* of Panama in 1521. He paid special attention to native ways, the first ethnographer of the mainland.

After the death of Ferdinand the conduct of affairs in Castilla del Oro came to be of serious concern to the Regent Cisneros and the court of Charles. It was thus that Oviedo and Las Casas met, while Peter Martyr was in attendance at court as usual. Las Casas never saw the Isthmus, but he collected the most detailed account of its "pacification" in the third volume of his *Historia*. Although he disagreed with Oviedo in Indian matters, the two made an almost equally grim appraisal of the ruin of Castilla del Oro.

The disastrous management of the colony by Pedrarias was never excused or concealed by Spanish writers or opinion. A century after this time the royal chronicler Herrera y Tordesillas was sued by descendants of Pedrarias for defamation of the character of their ancestor and proved his case.

Commissioned to report and reform the affairs of the Indies, the Licenciate Zuazo sent a lengthy account of Castilla del Oro in the Xèvres letter for the benefit of the young king and his tutor, who were newly arrived in Spain. The relevant parts are here translated, giving a vivid, valid, and quite forgotten view of the Isthmus as it was between 1514 and 1517:

> The armada was prepared and Pedrarias was with it in Sevilla, about to embark. All the party, to the number of [   ][4] lined up to parade through Sevilla. All or most of the men had been in Italy with the Gran Capitán, a very impressive lot,[5] very well dressed, none owning less than a jacket of silk and many one of

---

[3] The competent text of Altolaguirre is accompanied by eighty documents. The third section of Navarrete, vol. III, entitled "Establecimientos de los españoles en el Darién," includes letters from Balboa and the long relación by Pascual de Andagoya.

[4] The number was left blank. Andagoya said there were fifteen hundred; other estimates were higher.

[5] Ferdinand cautioned Pedrarias "concerning the quality of the men who have gone with you, soldiers who have been in Italy, as you know they are accustomed to very great vices, so that you will have some difficulties" (CDI, XXXVII, 281).

brocade. It is said in Sevilla that never was such an assembly of fair and goodly men seen in Spain. The entire armada having embarked, Pedrarias sailed to carry out the plans on which the royal treasury had spent close to forty thousand ducats, as the officials of the Casa de Contratación told me in Sevilla. The King paid all the costs of the armada up to the time of its arrival on Tierra Firme, whereupon each individual was to live at his own cost. When the voyage ended and the ships had safely come into port, provision and maintenance by the Crown came to an end. Therefore the men were obliged to eat what the land afforded, which were roots and a grain called *mahizo*. Darien, where they made port, being in a very wet country, of swamps and overflowed land from which dense and sickly vapors rise, the men began to die and there died two-thirds of them, though dressed in silks and brocade. Those who survived, ill as they were and thinking themselves lost, joined in raids on Indians, robbing and killing, done in this manner: The Council, in order to justify such war, instructed Pedrarias that before major hurt was done to the Indians they should be required to become Christians and subjects of the Catholic King along with other compliances, warning that failing to do so they would be made slaves and subject to killing and plundering.

Thus, as I have said, the armada arrived. An entrada of the survivors was ordered to go into the interior, a certain Ayora being captain. When the Indians saw these and where they were headed they thought them led by Vasco Nuñez, whom they called Tiba, which meant Lord of the Christians. Certain caciques and their men came up, bringing much roast venison on barbacoas (which are their kind of wooden troughs or containers by which they carry cooked and roast meat), many cooked *pavos*,[6] fish in plenty, diverse stews, and other variety of native foods, together with their very white bread which are cakes of maize, and wine also made of maize, enough to feed to repletion six hundred men or more. When the said Captain Ayora got to where a certain cacique was waiting with his provisions, the cacique asked, as they were sitting down to eat, who the Tiba of the Christians was. Captain Ayora being thus pointed out to him, the cacique replied, knowing Vasco Nuñez well, that this was a different man. Having finished the meal Ayora at once seized the cacique, his brothers, and others who seemed to be principals and who had been his hosts. He asked them for gold, otherwise they would be consigned to the flames or thrown to the dogs. The cacique, thus terrified, sent an Indian to bring some gold which Ayora said amounted to little and that he wanted more, otherwise he would carry out his threat to burn them and give them to the dogs. The cacique, thus pressed, sent his Indians out to get all the gold they had, which was brought, but the captain still said that it was a small quantity and that more must be given. At last the cacique said that there was no more, that he would give it if he had more but having given all of his own and of his Indians he begged the captain to be satisfied. Ayora, seeing this, ordered the fire set, burned the cacique, and threw the others to the dogs, an act of greatest cruelty.

This news spread quickly among the caciques round about. Knowing the cruelty done during a friendly reception when food and supplies were brought to Captain Ayora, none of the other caciques or Indians felt safe with any Christian and so they scattered through the country, abandoning their houses and bohios. To the natives thus in flight the requerimiento was displayed from a distance, demanding their obedience to the Catholic King. Ayora had a scribe before whom the requerimiento was read and who certified that the Indians had been thus notified. Thereupon the Captain pronounced them slaves with all their goods forfeit since it was evident that they refused obedience. The requerimiento was read in Spanish of which neither cacique nor Indians understood a word. Moreover it was read at such a distance that had they understood the language they could not have heard what was being said. If they heard the voices they

---

[6] See note 18 in chap. X, above.

would have thought them requests for gold, failing to give which they would be burned as were the other cacique and his brothers. In such manner the Spaniards attacked the bohios at night, robbed them, turned dogs on the natives, consigned them to the flames, and took them away in chains as slaves.

Thus the land has been altered in such a manner that no Christian dares go a league from town except in a company. Continuing the entradas like the one I have described, all the land has become so aroused and alarmed by the grave indignities, killings, brutal robbery, and the burning of settlements that all the Castilians maintain themselves only like birds of prey and all the land is lost and desolate.

The warning Zuazo sent to the new king was proper. The good will Balboa had established was destroyed by the first party that went out from the armada. The rough veterans of Italy, of whom Ferdinand had warned, were on the loose and there was no authority to stay them; the captains set the example for their men.

SICKNESS AND FAMINE

The fleet arrived at Darién at the end of June and within a short time the new personnel began to fall ill. Andagoya, who was one of the newcomers, said that "the men began to sicken to such an extent that they were unable to care for each other and thus in one month seven hundred died of hunger and *modorra*." Oviedo, another newcomer, noted that more than five hundred died, the majority for lack of nourishment but also from modorra and other sicknesses. After seven or eight months, Oviedo thought that more had died or left than remained in the country. Zuazo heard that two-thirds had died and that Darién was an unhealthy site because of the vapors rising from the swamps.

The sickness affected the new arrivals, apparently not the men of Balboa nor the Indians. There had been prior incidents of mass sickening of newcomers. The first was at Isabela in 1493, ascribed by Columbus to change in climate and water, with rapid recovery when fresh food was available, especially fish. The second followed the landing of Ovando and his party at Santo Domingo in 1502 and also seems to have passed shortly. In neither was the mortality high as it was at Darién. In all instances the sickness broke out after the end of the journey. In all cases the ships had been overcrowded for more than a month. In each the voyage had begun from a harbor on the southern coast of Spain. The sickness of the Pedrarias party was called "modorra" by Oviedo and by Andagoya, who did not think it necessary to explain what it meant, thus indicating that it was not new to Spain. (It may be the first mention of the disease in print. Rodrigo de Molina's treatise on pestilence printed at Cádiz in 1554 speaks of a sickness "called modorra by the common people," without describing its symptoms.) The Spanish word means "drowsy." It was a great lethargy in which the afflicted were likely to die. Oviedo said the sickness ran its course with high mortality and then disappeared; "that misfortune having passed, the country was very healthy." The contagion did not take place in the New World, but was brought by the passengers, and the disease did not become endemic; a sleeping sickness of undescribed etiology.

Oviedo continued to maintain stoutly that the Darién country was healthful and good to live in, but Zuazo introduced a note of doubt. When the city of

Panama was settled the Pacific coast was reputed to be healthier than the Caribbean, perhaps only because it had not yet acquired the contagion brought to the north shore. The evil repute of the Caribbean side of the Isthmus was earned much later, chiefly because of fever, cholera, and malignant forms of malaria and enteric fevers. The time was, I think, too early for malaria to have been established; nor is there any note of intermittent fever, or chills and fever. Balboa and his men went through regions that later were notoriously malarial and remained in good health. Pedrarias rushed expeditions out, for which there is repeated mention of illness, perhaps of men who still had not recovered from the great sickness. Also, the men who had campaigned in malarial southern Italy may have established that disease as company after company followed the same routes through country populated by Anopheles mosquitoes.

Famine also followed the coming of fifteen hundred to two thousand men to Darién. This was partly due to a stupid order that the men should not be supplied from ship stores after landing. The old vecinoes at Santa María had been adequately supplied with food by the natives. The new arrivals took to foraging and pillaging, using up the native stores and destroying their plantings. Catastrophe came with the appearance of a plague of grasshoppers. Oviedo observed that to the modorra was added "lack of food for Spaniards and Indians on account of the many locusts that appeared and covered the sky and destroyed the fields of maize,"—the earliest notice of its kind for the New World.

A PREDETERMINED DEBACLE

After twenty years of experience with the New World, the home office had gained little insight. It is true that the instructions to Pedrarias were well drawn, including good treatment of the natives. These might be given in encomiendas, but with carefully prescribed periods of service and of rest, reflecting the rules laid down in the Laws of Burgos. The conditions under which natives might be declared hostile were spelled out to prevent the frauds that had been common. The new villas were to be placed in sites carefully chosen for their healthfulness and convenience to water. They were to be laid out with an orderly street plan about a plaza on which the church was to be built, and the lots were to be assigned according to the rank of the recipient. It was a document to be filed away and ignored.

As had been the case with Columbus in his second voyage and with Ovando, far too many persons were brought without regard given to their capacities or motives. The name for the new government, Castilla del Oro, advertised it as a land of large and quick riches and did so improperly, for there was no knowledge of gold other than in the articles owned by the natives. The appeal was not to sober and industrious colonists but to a *soldadesca* that would raid and move on. The order that the men were on their own after landing was in effect an order to support themselves by levy and loot. Balboa's small group of Spaniards at Santa María and their supporting Indians could not take care of the newly arrived horde of adventurers. Some, "finding the land at peace," like Bernal Díaz, soon left for Cuba. Most went out under sundry captains to destroy the peace wherever they entered.

A sorry lot of men were placed in authority, either to engage in or to permit unlimited violence against the natives. The lieutenant governor, Ayora, was a monster, as Zuazo said, and as the record proved. Gaspar de Espinosa, alcalde mayor and justice, led great raids into undisturbed lands and was the instrument of the judicial murder of Balboa. Not one of the captains of Pedrarias showed moderation in the conduct of an entrada. Pedrarias himself was incapacitated by age and infirmities, unsuited by vanity and vindictiveness, and above all unconcerned about the conduct of his subordinates. Oviedo asked how it could be expected that any would be held to account when Ayora, first and worst of the malefactors, went unreproved and unpunished. The new government started off with unrestrained license and continued in that manner.

KNOWLEDGE OF TERRAIN AVAILABLE TO PEDRARIAS

The instructions to Pedrarias called for the founding of settlements along the Caribbean coast, way stations in the interior, and bases on the Pacific. To the east the coast was well known as far as Cartagena and Santa Marta, as was the peril there of poisoned weapons and bellicose natives. To the south, Balboa had run out the Culata and the delta of the Río San Juan and had gone far inland up that river, henceforth to be known as the Río Grande, Pedrarias suppressing the name, San Juan, that Balboa had given. On the coast to the northwest Balboa had used the harbor of Careta as gateway to the interior. Beyond this port men who had been with Nicuesa knew Nombre de Dios and the mouth of the Río Chagres. Balboa was familiar with more than a hundred miles of the interior basin of the Isthmus and had established relations, in part cordial, with its caciques. He had followed the Pacific coast along the northern side of the Gulf of San Miguel and thence most of the way to Panama, of which he was informed but which he had not seen, as was true also of the Pearl Islands. Pedrarias had available the wide and competent geographic knowledge of Balboa about land and people. Also, he had the services of the veteran settlers of Santa María. He might draw on dependable and adequate topographic information to found the settlements he was instructed to make.

Balboa was interested in a possible settlement on the Gulf of San Miguel and as a last act before he was superseded sent Andrés Garabito with eighty men to find a direct route west from Santa María across the serranía (fig. 26). "Having gone out from Darién they followed the banks of a river they called 'la Trepadera' to the crest of very high mountains, from which Garabito descended by another river that flowed into the South Sea, along which there were many settlements."[7] The start, therefore, would have been up the Río Tanela. The crossing of the Serranía del Darién took them by Indian trail to a western affluent of the Río Tuira, perhaps the Río Pucro, and thence down to tidewater. The name Trepadera indicated the steep climb to the pass, which limited the later utility of this short cut.

FIRST RAIDS INTO CUEVAN LANDS

Oviedo began his account of the entradas of the several captains thus: "It is tiresome for me to write and for others to read, nor would there be paper or

---

[7] Las Casas, Bk. III, ch. 52.

time enough to tell all that the captains did to ruin the Indians and rob them and destroy the land if all were told of the details of the events. However, since I said earlier that in this government of Castilla del Oro there had been two million Indians, or that they were innumerable, it is necessary to say how so numerous a people came to their end in so short a time." He followed this introduction by taking up the captains one by one, their entradas and misdeeds, ending his account as he tired of the minor personalities, where these had been, and what they had done.[8]

The first major raid was directed against the friendly native states of Comogre, Pocorosa, and Tubanama, which had supported the western operations of Balboa. According to Oviedo, who was in attendance, Pedrarias soon after arrival had an amicable session with Balboa to inform himself about the lands and caciques who lived in peace. Within the month he sent his lieutenant Ayora to these, accompanied by four hundred men. They sailed ten leagues beyond the port of Careta to the fishing port that supplied Comogre (which would have landed them about at the mouth of the Río Ailigandi) (fig. 26). Here the main party crossed the mountains with horse and baggage to the seat of Comogre, suggesting an open and well-traveled road. At Comogre the outrage took place as described by Zuazo. Oviedo, in independent agreement, called it a *montería infernal*, "hellish hunting" of Indians. Ayora continued through the territory of Pocorosa and Tubanama, seizing gold and slaves and turning friendly Indians into hostiles. The stage on which to implant the fear of the white men was well chosen. Their most faithful friends were the first victims.

Ayora divided his command among three lieutenants. The first continued by ship from the port of Comogre seven leagues farther north to the fishing harbor of Pocorosa, which would be about Playón Grande, where another convenient pass led across the low mountain range (fig. 26). A second party was left in the "province" of Tamao, bordering Tubanama on the west in the Bayano lowland. The third lieutenant was sent on down that valley to the Pacific coast. Each was to establish a Spanish town according to the instructions given to Pedrarias. The first built a fort of sorts that was called Santa Cruz; the second also established a fortified camp. The third got into previously unvisited country to the east of the Bay of Panama, sat around there for a while, and accomplished nothing.

Ayora was well informed in advance of the logistics of the terrain, of harbors available on the farther Caribbean coast, of two easy routes from coast to interior Comogre and Pocorosa, of the course of the Bayano to the Pacific, and of the strategic position of the three native states in the upper Bayano basin. Having ravaged these, he took the route from Pocorosa to Santa Cruz, returned thence by ship to Darién, and left for Spain with the profits of his raid.

The aftermath was hatred and ruin. The Spaniards at Santa Cruz set off to attack the wealthy cacique Sacativa in the Gulf of San Blas, but were driven off with losses. After Ayora left Santa Cruz, the Indians of Pocorosa and Comogre joined forces to descend on that settlement and wipe it out. The garrison left in the interior at Tubanama held on until a relief party came. The party on the Pacific coast pulled out. The western frontier of Balboa's rule was up in arms, to remain so until beaten down.

---

[8] Oviedo, *Historia*, Bk. XXIX, ch. 10, preceded by the Ayora entrada in ch. 9.

Pedrarias sent another party south from Darién under command of Luis Carrillo, seconded by Francisco Pizarro. In Oviedo's version these went to the province of Abraime above the delta of the Atrato and on to Turui (which I have thought to find at the mouth of the Río Sucio) to plant corn in conucos, but soon came back with many slaves and good gold, practicing cruelties that Pizarro had learned by heart. Las Casas thought that they went only seven leagues south from Darién to found a villa named Fonseca in honor of the bishop in charge of the affairs of the Indies.[9] Nothing more is heard of such a town, which, if it existed at all, was no more than a temporary camp.

The project of such a villa makes sense and suggests that Balboa's knowledge of the Atrato and Garabito's crossing of the serranía were placed in proper context of map. Seven leagues south of Santa María, by a land route that keeps above the swamps, the Atrato is reached at the first high ground above its delta (fig. 22). Here the present village of Sautatá is situated, in what was then Abraime. Above this village the Atrato is joined by the Río Perancho from the west. The latter and its tributary, the Río Cacarica or Cauco, are navigable by canoe to the base of the Tute saddle, which marks the boundary of Colombia and Panama at the divide between Atrato and the Tuira drainage of the Gulf of San Miguel.[10] Across the saddle at a distance of half a dozen miles, a tributary of the Río Tuira is navigable by canoes, thus giving passage by water to the Gulf of San Miguel. A settlement at Sautatá would have given control of the Atrato basin and an easy water route to the Pacific with a single portage (fig. 22).

A third expedition was sent (August, 1514) west to the South Sea in charge of Francisco Becerra, an old soldier of these parts and of the islands, according to Oviedo most practiced in cruelties.[11] The route was by way of the Trepadera from Santa María and therefore followed that of Garabito (fig. 26). Las Casas said that it was known from before and was twenty-six leagues from sea to sea, which is about right. That the descent into the Tuira basin was by the Río Pucro is suggested by Oviedo's listing four rivers named by caciques, joining the main stream (Tuira) as the party went down the river. Crossing to the left side of the Tuira, they got into lands previously unvisited; several more caciques were named and a plains country was noted as having fine savannas and rivers. They turned left up another valley to the seats of four more caciques, the last of whom was in mountain country. Oviedo is vague about the topography; they may have gone south up the valley of the Río Sambú. The next notation is of getting to Cabo Canachiné (Punta Garachiné) "a point or promontory in that gulf, a very remarkable thing, from which a high land is to be seen where the cacique Jumeto said a certain people lived who were Negroes"; the truth of the matter not known because they did not pass beyond that point. This, the second mention of a black people living to the south, refers to the Sierra del Sapo that extends south along the Pacific coast from Garachiné. The cape still retains the name heard at its discovery.

---

[9] Carrillo was related to Conchillos, the right hand of Fonseca.
[10] This pass is on the projected route of the Panamerican Highway.
[11] The accounts are in Oviedo, *Historia*, Bk. XXIX, ch. 10; Las Casas, Bk. III, ch. 62; and Altolaguirre, Appendix doc. 35 (officials of Santa Maria, May 2, 1515).

From this farthest point they turned back to the cacique Toto, where they had been before, and thence crossed to the other (north) coast of the Gulf of San Miguel, and came to the river of the cacique Chape, where Balboa first saw the South Sea. Toto, it may be inferred, was on the south side of the great estuary of the Tuira. They continued west along the north shore of the gulf and then north along the Pacific much as Balboa had done. Becerra saw the coast almost to the site of Panama City but not did get to that place. In the southernmost Isthmus Becerra had entered an unknown land, beyond which a strange and fearsome people were said to live. This is still an almost unknown country. As far as they got they were among Cuevan Indians, passing from one cacique to the next and finding no lack of provisions or canoes. Oviedo mentioned fifteen caciques on the route before they got to the seat of Chape, the presence of fine savannas, and an abundance of deer, wild pigs, and tapirs. The report of the officials at Santa María spoke of the number of caciques on the way to the Gulf of San Miguel, of "well disposed people," and of the point of land that extended into the ocean and seemed to be very near the island of pearls. It added another note about the black people, "how certain canoes came by sea which were manned by black men, large of stature and of great bellies, with long beards and curly hair, who were held in great fear because they killed and ate the natives and fought with lances and clubs." The expedition returned with a satisfactory haul of gold, pearls, and slaves, and information about a country stretching south along the Pacific coast.

MORE EXPEDITIONS INTO THE WEST

Pedrarias had reason to worry that Balboa stood high in royal favor. On August 19, 1514, the King sent a letter to Pedrarias praising the services and discoveries of Balboa. Balboa had written some persuasive letters which have been lost but which moved Ferdinand to an action on September 23 that might leave Pedrarias with an empty title and small profit. On that date six royal orders were sent, to Pedrarias, officials, vecinos-to-be, and to Balboa, naming Balboa Adelantado of the shores of the South Sea and governor of the provinces of Panama and Coiba.[12] These Indian regional names thus entered the historical geography of the New World as the first extension of Spanish designs beyond Atlantic waters. Pedrarias might oppose the advancement of Balboa in three ways: he could deny the existence of such provinces, plead lack of men to put at Balboa's disposal, or establish right of prior possession. He proceeded to do all three, aided by the fact that somehow the order in favor of Balboa took six months to reach Darién.

Ferdinand was informed by Balboa of attractive lands named Panama and Coiba, beyond those seen. This information was sent by Balboa before the arrival of Pedrarias and, it may be inferred, in outline of what would be the next provinces he planned to enter. In appreciation Ferdinand thought to reward Balboa by giving him charge of this western frontier, subordinate to Pedrarias. The latter countered by claiming that Panama was nothing more than some fisheries on the South Sea, the word *panama* meaning "fishermen," and that there

[12] Altolaguirre, Appendix docs. 23–30.

was no land of Coiba, *coiba* meaning merely "far away." [13] To Balboa's request for a hundred men the answer was that none could be spared.

Ayora had taken the first step to block Balboa from the west by sending one party into the lower Bayano valley under orders to make a settlement on the Pacific coast. He was followed promptly by Tello de Guzmán, who relieved the men Ayora had left at Tubanama and continued west through the territories of the caciques Chepo and Pacora to that of Panama, all three preserved in modern place names. The renowned Panama he found to consist of huts of fishermen.[14] Such was the discovery of Indian Panama, a name, as in the case of Darién, applied by the Spaniards to a larger region. It included the lower Bayano drainage and extended along the Bay of Panama. The Guzmán entrada ran from the fall of 1514 into the winter and reached the southern part of the Canal Zone. Oviedo thought Guzmán to have been one of the very worst. Las Casas, followed by Herrera, detailed the outrages and the loot that was taken. (Tello de Guzmán later took part in the pillage of Peru. His milder lieutenant, Diego de Albítez, years afterward became governor of Honduras.) Before Balboa had notice of his assignment of Panama, Pedrarias had established his counterclaim by prior discovery and conquest.

Gonzalo de Badajoz, a survivor of the Nicuesa venture, was sent from Santa María in the spring of 1515 to sail to the ruins of Nombre de Dios. From there he crossed the Isthmus in a southwesterly direction across the Chagres drainage, now submerged under Madden and Gatun lakes (fig. 27). Continuing in the same direction, he climbed the central sierra, then called Sierra de Capira, to descend into and cross the wide and populous lowlands that were the heart of the Coiba country. From cacique to cacique gold treasure was collected until a stouter one made a counterattack that routed the Spaniards and cost them most of their booty. They retreated along the west coast of the Gulf of Panama.

Where Castilla del Oro ended on the Caribbean and Veragua began had been left undecided. Gonzalo gave Pedrarias a claim to Nombre de Dios and Chagres which was not challenged. He was also the discoverer of Coiba, and his defeat there provided Pedrarias with justification for the conquest by Espinosa. The appointment of Balboa to govern Panama and Coiba was countered by a *fait accompli* on the part of Pedrarias.

The other western objective was to secure the Gulf of San Miguel and gain control of the Pearl Islands. To this end Pedrarias sent his cousin, Gaspar de Morales. For the most part the route followed prior explorations. The first part seems to have retraced the path of Garabito and Becerra from Darién across the serranía to tidewater on the Pacific. The narrows of the upper gulf were crossed to the land of Chape, where Balboa had made his first discovery of the South Sea. Thence the north side of the gulf was followed and the open shore of the Pacific as far as Tumaco, and so out to the Pearl Islands. The cacique of Terarequi, its main island, submitted readily, gave Morales a quantity of pearls, and promised to provide a large annual tribute of pearls. One of these was of fabulous size and first quality, and is said to have passed into the possession of the Queen Empress through intermediate owners. On the return across the

---

[13] *Ibid.*, Appendix doc. 52.
[14] Las Casas, Bk. III, ch. 68.

Isthmus, Morales found that the captured natives slowed his travel and had all of them killed. The expedition was a success, bringing the first large treasure of pearls and assuring a continuing tribute from the Pearl Islands.

FAILURE TO THE EAST AND SOUTH

Enciso returned to Darién with Pedrarias. Having knowledge of regions to the east, he was made lieutenant of a well-equipped armada, captained by a nephew of Pedrarias, the objective being the land of Sinú, first named at this time. This Indian land lay midway between Darién and Cartagena. In view of its advanced culture and large population, in both of which it may have been superior to any other part of coastal Tierra Firme, it is curious that it was not mentioned earlier and seems not to have been visited, with the probable exception of Bastidas.

The armada sailed to the Gulf of Morrosquillo, and landed at its western end at a place of sixty bohíos, called Catarapa. Here they were opposed by twenty canoes, which they scattered and then took the town and its cacique. It was learned through an interpreter that Sinú was a very great town nearby "on the banks of a large river that passes near Catarapa and discharges by three arms into the bay, by which the Indians carry salt in canoes and gold which they smelt there and make into large pieces, and that they collect the gold by nets in the river above Sinú and that the mines are in a place called Mocrí." [15] The appended document placed Sinú near the mines of Tarufi (Tirufi).

Tarufi was the name of a cacique rich in gold for whom Hojeda had set out from San Sebastián de Urabá, to be chased back by poisoned arrows. Enciso knew all about that failure and decided to approach from the north. At Catarapa the name Mocrí was added for a gold land, situated up the great Río Sinú. The sources of the Sinú lie to the south in the eastern flanks of the Sierra Occidental across from Urabá at the western base. For years Mocrí and Tarufi continued to be sought as gold lands of the northern cordillera, situated somewhere on its eastern side, perhaps two districts, perhaps two names for the same one. The advice was that the great town Sinú was a center of trade and gold working, but that the source of the gold was farther upstream. (The notes Enciso set down in his *Suma de Geografía* on the Sinú people will be considered later.) The well-equipped party made only a weak attempt to get inland and did not reach the great town, but returned to Darién by November, 1514.

Two expeditions were sent from Darién in the spring of 1515 to go east from the Gulf of Urabá. One, captained by Francisco de Vallejo, entered "toward the part where Hojeda had settled" (Oviedo), and at three leagues from the village of Urabá began attacks on Indian settlements (Las Casas). Thus *rancheando* they secured three thousand pesos of fine gold (Oviedo), entering a distance of twenty leagues into the sierra (Balboa). Harassed by Indians with poisoned arrows, they turned back and got to the Río de Redes (León). Here they made rafts that went to pieces in a flood (Las Casas) and drowned a good part of those who had not been killed by poison.

Franciso Becerra and a larger party took a ship across the gulf to land near Hojeda's former base. The ship returned to Darién in April with word of melt-

---

[15] Altolaguirre, Appendix doc. 30.

ing pots and other apparatus for smelting, the Indians saying that there was no gold there, but that it would be found at Tarufi in the mountains, Becerra having gone on in that direction. Balboa wrote in October that the captain (Becerra) "entered by Caribana to go the way to Sinú; nothing more has been heard of what he accomplished," although a brigantine had gone repeatedly to see whether anything could be learned, concluding: "this entrada has been like sending cattle to the slaughterhouse." Caribana was the northernmost part of the eastern shore of the Gulf of Urabá. It was reported later from Indian sources that the party had gotten across to the Sinú River and had been wiped out. Oviedo, referring to the earlier cruel entrada of Becerra to the Gulf of San Miguel, wrote that thus "he and many others who were lost with him paid their debts."

No further attempt was made in the direction of Sinú until 1534, when Pedro de Heredia moved from the newly founded town of Cartagena to the conquest of Sinú and the rifling of its great mortuary stores of gold. The supposed gold-bearing streams between Urabá and the Sinú drainage were still identified by the names Tirufi (Tarufi) and Mocrí, and in time became vaguely congruent with the gold land of Dabeiba. This northern end of the cordillera, also known as the Sierra de Abaibe, became the mysterious and forgotten kingdoms that Trimborn described in the Spanish entries into Antióquia made twenty years later.

Two more attempts were made from Darién to discover the gold of Dabeiba. Pedrarias continued to deny Balboa access to the west, but commissioned him in the summer of 1515 to go again in search of Dabeiba. The official account says that he was sent with two hundred men to seek the riches of Dabeiba and discover the mines hoped for in that part. As he was going up the Río Grande the Indians stole some of the canoes, and farther on, in another small river, the Spaniards were sharply attacked; one of those killed being Luis Carrillo. The party returned after thirty days, reportedly having gotten as far as the bohios of the cacique Dabeiba.[16] The October letter of Balboa to the King told of the fight on the river and how they got by land to the habitations of Dabeiba only to find that the Indians had fled: "We took there certain people by whom we were told about the mines inland and how Dabeiba got the gold. They say that of a certainty there are large mines as far as ten days' travel thence into the interior, and that all the caciques collect gold. I was unable to get the cacique to come to talk with me, although I stayed there for ten days and sent several times to call him. Most potent Lord, the reason for my return was that in all that land of Dabeiba we failed to find food that would have sufficed for a month because of the many locusts that had destroyed all that country." [17]

The smaller river where they were attacked may have been the Río Sucio—an interpretation that is supported by the remark of Balboa attributing the native hostility to damage done by an unnamed Spanish captain (Vallejo?) who got within two days' travel of Dabeiba. A grasshopper plague had been reported earlier about Darién. Again, no gold mining was mentioned for Dabeiba; the source of gold was now placed farther inland than at the first entry, and as being provided by caciques as far away as ten days' travel, which would include a long stretch of country up and down the auriferous Cauca drainage.

---

[16] *Ibid.*, Appendix doc. 43.
[17] *Ibid.*, Appendix doc. 44.

The last venture up the Atrato to get at the wealth of Dabeiba was carried out by a rich businessman of Santa María, Juan de Tavira, who equipped a large party. Indians blocked their passage on the Río Grande by war canoes. Tavira and others were drowned and again Pizarro took over to lead the return to Darién. This was the end of interest in the south and east. Thereafter Pedrarias turned his attention to the west and mainly to the Pacific.

THE FOUNDING OF ACLA

Beyond Santa María a number of Caribbean harbors had served in entradas— Careta, the port of Comogre, that of Pocorosa, the Gulf of San Blas, and Nombre de Dios. The most familiar and advantageous one was Careta, where the natives had continued to be friendly and in part had become Christians. This and its nearness to waters by which canoes could go into the Gulf of San Miguel were its principal attractions. Also it was close to the land of Comogre, from which canoes had passage down the Río Bayano to the northern end of Panama Bay or from which one could journey by land through open country to Panama and beyond.

Pedrarias, who had not stirred from Santa María previously, decided it was time for him to lead an expedition into the west. He left at the end of November, 1515, with a fleet headed for Careta.[18] carrying two hundred fifty men and twelve horses, the latter of interest as indicating the open country known to lie ahead. A detour was made east across the gulf to "the province of Caribana" to seek news of the party of Becerra, missing for eight months. The word was that all had been killed. Pedrarias played a brief role there as conquistador, naming a river harbor after himself, raising the royal banner in solemn act of possession, and having an Indian settlement attacked and taken. He named the village Aguila because it was on top of what he described as a very high and steep hill that was difficult to climb. Its location is undetermined. The river, swamp, and high cerro may be a dramatized picture of the environs of Punta Urabá and San Sebastián, the present vicinity of Nicoclí.

All who had gone east across the Gulf of Urabá had run into trouble. Many men had been lost, small booty secured, and no gold mines found, only reports of gold fields farther inland. The disaster to the Becerra party put an end to further activities in that direction. The side of the South Sea offered easier and greater gain.

Pedrarias and his four ships sailed on to the port of Careta, which he renamed Acla and ordered a fort and town to be built here. The version given by the governor is confused. The Indians of that province had been stirred up and some had run off. A former pilot of Nicuesa, Lope de Olaño, held the chief cacique in encomienda (a term rarely heard in Castilla del Oro). This chief was persuaded to come to a feast of reconciliation and renewal of allegiance. At that time, Pedrarias wrote, he experienced a "return of the fevers and kidney trouble which did not permit him to continue the journey and thus he stayed in the port of Acla, which is one of the good ports in those parts and very well protected and free of *broma*, where it is possible to build a great city and there are two

---

[18] His report is Appendix doc. 54 in Altolaguirre, dated January 20, 1516.

rivers of good waters." This port, he said, was twenty-two leagues from the South Sea in a direct line with the Isle of Pearls. The treasurer, de la Puente, added that the road from there to the South Sea was known to be passable by foot and horse.[19]

Olaño proceeded to build a villa as instructed, but the once-friendly natives had had enough of abuse, and killed him. When the Espinosa party returned to Acla early in 1517 they expected to find nothing there, having heard of the death of Olaño. Instead they found Balboa peacefully in charge, and Acla "settled in the same manner as that of Darién and food as good as we had in Sevilla." [20] Balboa had again made friends of the Indians and had built the villa, the second on Tierra Firme, which outlasted Santa María by some years.

THE ENTRADA OF ESPINOSA INTO COIBA

The ailing Pedrarias turned the expedition over to Gaspar de Espinosa, as alcalde mayor second in rank after the departure of Ayora. The entrada took more than a year, covered more territory by land than any had done before, destroyed a lot of natives, and made Coiba the center of Spanish exploitation. Espinosa's conduct at the time, and later his sentencing of Balboa, give him a place of infamy along with Pedrarias and Ayora.[21] The route and results of the entrada are considered here; the data on native life, in the next chapter.

Taking along a train of Indians, the party crossed the serranía from Careta to Comogre, Pocorosa, and Tubanama, the several cacicazgos of the upper Bayano basin that had been under the control of Balboa (fig. 27). The familiar tactic was used of attacking the bohíos of the caciques at night. Some were caught and others ran away. Parties were sent out to hunt down the fugitives. (In each case Espinosa referred to a list of the captured Indians to be allotted [repartido]; the list, however, is missing.) The procedure was explained as castigation for the crime of having destroyed the Spanish garrison at Santa Cruz, for which the chiefs and people of Pocorosa were held most responsible. One party raided westward to the north of the Río Grande (in this case the Río Bayano), another along its south side. The natives held most culpable were executed. Little booty of gold was secured, nor was enough maize found to provide the needs. They pressed on to the region of Chepo, Pacora, and Panama and thus to the northern shores of the Bay of Panama. The distances given indicate that the modern places of these names were in about the same location as the Indian settlements. The area had been visited before by Albítez, was thought to have had great friendship for that captain, and known not to have been a party to the rebellion. On this occasion however these natives also ran off and left no food. At Panama a single Indian woman was found and no food. Fear went ahead of them to the end of Cuevan lands.

From Chepo they took about the same route that is now followed by the Panamerican Highway. From Panama it was seven leagues to the cacique Perequete, whose place was captured as usual at night. A river of that name is at

---

[19] Altolaguirre, Appendix doc. 55.
[20] Altolaguirre, Appendix doc. 59; also CDI, XXXVII, 73–74.
[21] The lengthy relación is reproduced in CDI, II and XXXVII and in Altolaguirre, Appendix doc. 59.

that distance west of Panama. Seven leagues farther on the Indian town Chame was reached and again taken at night. Their guides lost the way to the next place, Chirú, so it was well after daylight when they got there to find that the cacique had decamped. From here it was four leagues to Natá, again taken at night, its cacique escaping from his bohío by an unnoticed door. Here many Indians were killed, especially by the horsemen, and about a hundred were captured. Gold was found in some quantity, and there was plenty of food. "The bohíos were so numerous that everyone was astonished and somewhat afraid at seeing so great a population." By this time they were well into the country of Coiba, where the Indians had not been alarmed. Espinosa remained at Natá for four months, to the end of July, well supplied with food by the natives. Many natives were put to work growing maize for Spanish use. From the convenient and productive base of Natá parties went out to loot other settlements.

Meanwhile Espinosa was trying to find out what had become of the golden treasure that Badajoz had abandoned the year before. Badajoz had come into these fertile and populous lowlands by a more northerly route, across the continental divide. He had an easy time until he crossed a large river (now Río Santa María), where he was ambushed and soundly trounced, and had to abandon most of his booty. This experience, new to Spaniards on the Isthmus, made Espinosa cautious in approaching the river.

The crossing was made in force at Escoria, described as six leagues beyond Natá and at the same distance from the sea, which places it near the present town of Santa Maria. The Indians beyond this river were held to be of different ways and bellicose. A cacique Escoria and his household were captured by night attack and taken along for the assault on Paris, who was considered the cacique most to be feared and, together with Escoria, to have caused the rout of Badajoz. The seat of Paris, six leagues farther on, was found to be as empty as though no one had lived there for years, for which reason it was called Asiento Viejo. The name Paris is preserved in the river and town of Parita, the Asiento Viejo being in that vicinity.[22] An engagement took place which was indecisive until the horsemen came up to drive the Indians into retreat.

The country beyond the Río Escoria or Santa Maria had not been seen by Spaniards. It was rich and populous and thought to be somewhat dangerous, being under the control of strong and aggressive chiefs; the cacique Paris thought to be their overlord. Somewhere beyond the river was the loot that had been taken from Badajoz, its value growing with the telling. Espinosa spent about six months going about these new parts and sending parties to explore. His report was accompanied by a map drawn, he said, by compass. The map is lost and not all the Indian provinces referred to have been identified as to location. The key state of Paris extended along the coast beyond the Río Escoria and included the rich lands along the Río del Asiento Viejo (Río Parita) and the Río de Mahizales (Río la Villa). Guarare was the neighboring province in the coastal lowland to the southeast. Somewhere in the interior rim of the lowland basin were Usagaña and Quema, upslope from Paris and Escoria.

Espinosa is credited with the discovery of the Azuero peninsula. One party

---

[22] It is one of the more frequently noted places in Espinosa's second entrada of 1519 (CDI, XX, 5 ff.)

by land, another by canoe, followed the shore from Guarare around to the province of Guera (now Tonosí) "beyond which there was no way by land but only by sea because the land was so rough and the ridges so high." A canoe party, sent on west to explore and map, turned the southwest point of the peninsula and went into the Gulf of Montijo (then unnamed). At the island of Cebaco, lying across the entry to the gulf, there was a brief fight followed by an alliance; its cacique and his fleet of canoes continued with them to another island, which was called Isla de Varones because of its stout defense. This is probably Isla Goberna-dora. The joint flotilla crossed a gulf seven or eight leagues wide and landed on the island of Cabo (now Coiba). There the bohíos of the cacique were attacked and captives and gold taken. The Espinosa account mentions two islands, one as Cabo, the other as Coyba, perhaps mistaking the wide embayment in the middle of the large island for a separation. "This island of Cabo is an attractive island, and the last the Christians discovered is the island of Coyba, which, though tak-ing some Indians who came out from it by canoe, they saw but did not land on. From the island of Cabo they had sight of a long part of the coast of Tierra Firme, all very level land and according to what the Indians said very well peo-pled, cleared and without thickets, a very beautiful country." The party went north from the island "to the coast of Tierra Firme and because it was very popu-lous and its captains great and powerful, although they landed they did not dare to stop there or to make war on its caciques." They were told about a route north across to the northern sea and Veragua that could be traveled in three days. The canoe party having been absent overlong, Espinosa sent a land party west from his camp in the Santa María plain to find out whether all was well with the canoes. It reached Montijo Bay, passing by way of the broad saddle at San-tiago.

Much had been learned about new country during the six months spent beyond the Río Santa María. Espinosa started back from the Asiento Viejo at the begin-ning of January, 1517, via Escoria and Natá to Chirú where the canoe party caught up with the main party. They returned by the same route over which they had come, hurriedly because they found neither food nor service. The na-tives all along the way had fled and taken what stores they could. Espinosa checked the now vacant places off one by one all the way back to Acla, where Balboa had reëstablished production of food. The return was through destroyed or abandoned settlements, a countryside of neglected fields, and a population in hiding. By the testimony of a friar who had been along, forty thousand natives had been killed.

THE FINAL VENTURE BY BALBOA

By the summer of 1517 Pedrarias and his gang had cause to worry. With Cisneros in control of Spain, Fonseca, Conchillos, and their partisans were out. The Hieronymites and Zuazo had cleaned house in the islands and soon would turn their attention to Tierra Firme. The letter Zuazo wrote to Xèvres indicates that he had been collecting incriminating data on Castilla del Oro. Oviedo had re-turned to Spain to ask for reform. Bishop Quevedo kept asking for a new gov-ernment. Las Casas was denouncing their conduct. Cisneros had in hand a report on the Espinosa expedition for which he censured Pedrarias. It was time to be on one's good behavior, and therefore Pedrarias would deal circumspectly with Balboa, even be his friend. The old governor had been successful in keeping Balboa out of Coiba and Panama. Another diversion was indicated that would keep him occupied elsewhere.

Balboa was instructed to build a fleet to operate in the Gulf of San Miguel and serve the Pearl Islands. This would give substance to his title of Adelantado of the South Sea and return him to the scene of his discovery. He was ordered to go from Acla to the river of Ponca (the upper Río Chucunaque) with ship-wrights and equipment to construct the ships. The enterprise was too fantastic to have come from the cool-headed Balboa, but, whatever he thought of it, he undertook the commission.

The task was begun in August, 1517. In all there were about two hundred Spaniards, including Pascual de Andagoya and Hernán de Soto, thirty Negro slaves, and many Indians, especially from Careta. The gear was delivered to Acla and the ship timbers were cut in that vicinity. Why the shipwrights cut and fashioned the timbers on the Caribbean coast is not explained. The heavy materials were carried on the backs of Indians a distance of about thirty miles to navigable water on the Río Balsas (Chucunaque). Andagoya wrote: "on this river we made two ships and thereby used up the Indians of that province, who were numerous, by taking them to Acla to carry the materials for the ships and also by having them provide the food they had in order to feed the carpenters and people who were building the ships." Las Casas was informed by the Bishop of Darién in 1519 that five hundred Indians died while serving as porters; another source stated that the cost was two thousand lives.[23]

The effort was mostly wasted, for the lumber was useless when it was assembled in the brigantines, and a fresh supply had to be cut on the river. Balboa sent out raiding parties to forage for food and to capture more Indians. When the ships were ready it was found that there was no channel open to the sea. Again Andagoya: "We took these ships down to the sea with great labor, for there were many shoals through which we dug channels for them to pass. Having gotten them down to the Gulf of San Miguel they began to founder, for the carpenters did not know the quality of the lumber, which had become rotted and all the planks were honeycombed. Thus with great effort we were obliged to cross in them to the Pearl Island. Here they sank and we built still others, larger and better and of good wood." Balboa then returned "to the Gulf of San Miguel and set up camp in a well-peopled province called Pequeo where he remained for two months taking and seizing Indians whom he sent to Acla to bring more rigging and pitch that was needed for the ships."

The whole enterprise fails to make sense, especially for Balboa, who had never bungled anything he undertook. Only imported gear needed to be transported. Canoes would have floated men, rigging, and stores down to the gulf. Balboa knew the topography of the interior and both coasts. If he was restricted to operating from the Gulf of San Miguel, an easier approach would have been by way of the Atrato and the Tuira. The available crossings of the Isthmus were well known by 1517, and also the harbors on both coasts that might serve as terminals.

[23] Las Casas, Bk. III, chs. 74–77, is the fullest account of the enterprise.

By that time the Gulf of San Miguel was no longer being considered for a Spanish town on the Pacific.

The operation makes no sense as a plan to occupy the Pacific shore, but it does so as a political tactic. The administration of Castilla del Oro was due for an overhaul at any time, the first step of which would be the *residencia* of the governor. As Mrs. Romoli has suggested, Balboa would be the most damaging witness, and so he was given an assignment that would put him beyond reach of the inquiry. Balboa dragged his feet, was absent for about a year and a half, and got little done. The absence was prolonged by his own choice; meanwhile he kept informed of the news from Spain. The Cisneros reforms were underway when his shipbuilding began. The veteran governor of the Canaries, Lope de Sosa, had been named *Juez de residencia* and governor for Castilla del Oro. This promised a strong and competent administration which Balboa would await while keeping at a safe distance from Darién. Andagoya, who was with Balboa, thus interpreted the purpose of their waiting at Pequeo at the southern end of the Gulf of San Miguel: "As we heard the news that provision had been made in Castile for Lope de Sosa to come to govern this land, Vasco Nuñez called together certain friends, persons of honor, and told them in secret that he was sending one Valderrabano to Acla" to find if there was news of the new governor, "because the new governor will not undo what has been done with the fleet, and that we should then go to make a settlement at Chepabar, which is six leagues from Panama toward Acla." This meant that Balboa was merely awaiting favorable news, that he did not intend to settle on the gulf but would use his ships to go to the north end of the Bay of Panama, there to found a town. This would give him access to the territory that had been assigned to him and which Pedrarias had denied him. He had selected a proper site in Chepabar, near the mouth of the Río Bayano, directly south from the Gulf of San Blas, at the shortest crossing of the Isthmus by one of the lowest passes of the continental divide. In these respects it was superior to the later Panama or any other location.

Unfortunately the coming of Sosa was delayed too long. Pedrarias intercepted Balboa's messengers, made a charge of treason, brought Balboa to trial, over which Espinosa presided, and had him executed in January, 1519. The King was informed only after the event. Thus the one person who had insight into what might be made of Castilla del Oro was eliminated.

LIMITS WITH VERAGUA

When Nicuesa was given his limited concession in 1508 to occupy Veragua, it was identified only as "where the Admiral Columbus was at the last." In 1510 Ferdinand declared both shores of the Gulf of Urabá to belong to the concession of Urabá given to Hojeda, without indicating where the western shore of the gulf ended. This in effect legitimized the occupation of Darién by Enciso and Balboa, being successors to Hojeda. The new colony took the name of Darién, and Balboa was appointed to govern without naming of limits. Urabá was dropped as a political term, and so was Veragua for the time being.

Meanwhile the suit of the heirs of Columbus was developing. In naming Pedrarias in 1513 to the government of Castilla del Oro, Ferdinand had excluded

Veragua as belonging to Diego Columbus by right of the discovery by his father, again specifying no limits. In 1514 Ferdinand defined the interior limits between Castilla del Oro and Veragua as the watershed between the two oceans. He did this by naming Balboa to have charge of Panama and Coiba, "which are in the new land draining to the South Sea from the crest of the montanas and sierras, that on the northern side belonging to Veragua." [24] Pedrarias protested both the grant to Balboa and the restriction of Castilla del Oro by the continental divide. "Here we do not consider Veragua to be more than the province which the cacique of Veragua possesses, which is ten to twelve leagues in extent." [25] Ferdinand said nothing about an eastern limit for Veragua. However, limiting Panama and Coiba by the mountain watershed, the Caribbean versant of the Isthmus belonged to Veragua at least as far east as Nombre de Dios.

Pedrarias sent parties along the Caribbean coast to the ports of Comogre and Pocorosa, where the ephemeral place of Santa Cruz had been founded, next to the Gulf of San Blas, and then to Nombre de Dios and the Chagres basin, thus gaining a sort of title by taking possession as far as the Canal Zone. Diego took no steps to occupy Veragua, and the Crown took none to set a Caribbean boundary; Pedrarias was thus left free to extend his dominion to the Chagres basin, but made no intrusion farther west. At the time, the Columbus heirs were asserting rights to all the Indies by virtue of the discovery of their father. Accepting an obscure strip of coast might compromise their claims. Twenty years later they did settle for the dukedom of Veragua in partial satisfaction of their suit.

---

[24] Altolaguirre, Appendix doc. 25.
[25] *Ibid.*, Appendix doc. 52.

XIV

INDIAN LANDS OF FARTHER
CASTILLA DEL ORO

•

EAST OF THE GULF OF DARIEN

Balboa dealt with natives of one culture, having similar speech and government. In the Isthmus these were known as Cueva. There is reason to think that the people of the Atrato basin were much the same. The eastern side of the Gulf of Urabá belonged to Indians whose mode of warfare was so effective that the Spaniards had little opportunity to note anything else than the perils. Unlike their neighbors to the west, the Urabaes fought with bows and arrows and darts and dipped the points of their weapons in potent poison. The name San Sebastián de Urabá given by Hojeda to his ill-fated settlement thus declared the danger of the eastern shore. This the Spaniards were unable to occupy until well after the time of Pedrarias, and did so from other parts of Tierra Firme.

The people east of the gulf came to be considered as Caribs and have been thus accepted in modern ethnology. The case is unproved and unlikely. Hostile natives throughout Tierra Firme were designated Caribs. Poisoned weapons were used by them but as well by others.[1] A specific identification of the eastern shore with actual Caribs was given by Peter Martyr: "The east side of the gulf has the common name Caribana, because all along it live Caribs, who are thus named from the region Caribana." He named five of their pueblos in a stretch of thirty miles of the coast.[2] This was written in 1516, while Colmenares and Oviedo were in Spain, and may have come from either source. Peter Martyr assigned the whole east coast of the gulf to Caribana, which actually was only its northernmost "province." Oviedo later repeated the etymology of the northeastern headland Punta Caribana as giving rise to the name Carib. Both were wrong, of course; Columbus had introduced the name on his first voyage, from which time on it was in use for the Carib islands. In 1503 Carib was made the official designation of hostile Indians subject to capture and sale. Nor is there a Hispanicized adjective "Caribana." This was the name of a territory as heard by Spanish ears, acciden-

---

[1] Friederici has documented variants of the word *curare*, a general term for arrow and dart poison, among Caribs, Tupi, and Arawak of the mainland.
[2] Pete Martyr, Decade III, Bk. 10.

tally sounding like Carib, perhaps originally stressed on the last syllable. Except for the headland, the east side of the gulf soon became known as Urabá.

Urabá was the name of a territory, its cacique, and his seat, or "pueblo." Such was Spanish practice in the Isthmus and the Atrato basin; it was correct for Cuevan-Chibchan societies but not for the democratic Caribs. That this was no merely careless usage as to Urabá is shown by later sources that told of kinship of Urabá caciques and people with those of the non-Carib Sinú to the east.[3] The inference is that Urabá and Caribana were not Carib lands. The cordillera behind Urabá was of uncertain cultural affiliation, perhaps related to Sinú. From Urabá through the Sinú there seems to have been a land of cognate peoples who were not Caribs.

The Sinú country was never regarded as Carib. The definite article El prefixed to the name indicates that it also was considered to be both realm and ruler. When the fleet of Pedrarias stopped at Isla Fuerte on its way west of Darién, Oviedo (who was aboard) observed a salt industry there for the supply of Sinú. They took many salt-filled baskets (cestos) of the size of those carried from the Cantabrian coast into Castile, "but much better-made baskets and the salt very beautiful and white and it is made there from sea water." [4] Peter Martyr had a further account of the trade of Sinú from Oviedo in 1515 or 1516, probably derived from the expedition in which Enciso took part: "This Oviedo tells that in a certain region called Cenu which lies ninety miles east of Darién, a new kind of commerce is used. They found in the houses of the natives hampers, chests, and baskets, attractively made of the leaves of suitable trees, filled with cicadas, crickets, crayfish, marine snails (caracoles), and locusts of the kind that destroy the fields, all dried and salted. Asked for what use they intended these, they answered for the purpose of taking them to people of the interior who desired such things and salt fish." [5] By accident of questions put by Peter Martyr, this unusual commerce in packaged food has been remembered.

The knowledge that the Sinú was rich in objects of gold probably came from the trading voyage of Bastidas. On arriving at Darién this was one of the first parts to which Pedrarias sent an expedition, guided and reported by Enciso. The two documents of 1514 told only of taking the coastal town of Catarapa and of hearing of Sinú as a very large town up the adjacent great river, "by which the Indians take salt in canoes and carry gold to be smelted there and made into large pieces, the gold being taken in nets in the river above Sinú at a place called Mocrí." [6] In the second document the mines are called Tarufi.

In his Suma de Geografía Enciso recalled the process of preserving bodies as seen at Catarapa, in the same manner as in Cueva country. The rest of the account is concerned with gold.

In this land of Zenu there is much gold in possession of the Indians and very good. It is all made of a mixture and base of silver, there being no copper in it and is of a clearer gold color than that which has a base of copper. The Indians

---

[3] B. Le Roy Gordon, Human Geography and Ecology in the Sinú Country of Colombia (Berkeley and Los Angeles, Ibero-Americana No. 39, 1957), pp. 33 and 98.
[4] Oviedo, Historia, Bk. XXIX, ch. 7.
[5] Peter Martyr, Decade III, Bk. 5.
[6] Altolaguirre, Appendix docs. 31 and 31 bis.

say that they bring it from some sierras out of which the Rio Zenu flows from places called Mocri, Cubra, etc., and that the land where these places are is of a reddish color and that the gold is collected in arroyos and valleys. When it rains they spread nets across the arroyos and as the water rises it carries down gold nuggets of the size of eggs which are caught in the nets. Thus they secure the largest nuggets. What has been collected they bring to the place called Zenu, which is on the river ten leagues from the sea. I had captured a cacique who told me that he had gone on three occasions to those places, had seen them getting gold in this manner, and had thus taken some himself.

The unusual claim of a gold-silver alloy free of copper can have been based only on a small sample, the expedition returning with but a modest amount of loot. It was required of the Spaniards to smelt and part the metal so as to determine the royal fifth. Enciso knew whereof he wrote. The notation indicates an importation of silver from other parts, perhaps Peru. The information that the town of Sinú was a major gold-processing center later proved to be correct. Like Dabeiba it imported metal, fabricated it into ornaments and figurines, and traded these to other areas.[7] The men of Castilla del Oro failed to learn that they were on the threshold of an area of higher culture than existed elsewhere in the Caribbean, short of Mayan lands. Sinú gold later became known from their tombs. Their cities remain only partly identified; their cultural ties are still uncertain. I suggest that they were part of the great Colombian complex, El Simú on the coast, El Dabeiba astride the saddle between the Cauca and Atrato rivers, and El Dorado in a remote interior that was still unheard of.

STRANGE PEOPLE TO THE SOUTH

Balboa was told that inland beyond Dabeiba there were "very Carib and bad people who eat as many humans as they can get"—first notice of a major center of cannibalism on the Río Cauca, extending well upstream. The Spaniards of later years who passed up and down that river gave accounts of an almost unbelievable addiction to human flesh. Balboa used the word Carib as an adjective in that sense, not as an ethnic term. The names of such Cauca Valley tribes are of later record, but beyond cannibalistic habits very little is known about them.

On the upper Río Atrato the entrada got as far as a bad and warlike people, according to Balboa. Colmenares added that the natives there lived in huts (chozas), seemingly clustered, which they abandoned at the coming of the Spaniards, and that they were cannibals. This is now territory of the Chocó Indians, but none of the descriptions fits. The Chocó live widely dispersed, preferably on ridges, in houses built on posts or piles and having wooden floors, hardly to be called chozas. They were not cannibals. The information does not indicate that the Chocó were then in the upper Atrato basin. The Spanish party had passed beyond the lands of people connected with Cuevan culture, and that is almost all that is known.

Today the Chocó are the only Indians within the Atrato basin, in the San Juan basin to the south, and in the drainage of the Sinú, thus the only Indians remaining in northwest Colombia. There is no record of their presence in any

[7] Gordon, op. cit., has made the pioneer study of the Sinú country, present and past. He cites Samuel Lothrop for the presence of Sinú products in the archaeology of Coclé in Coiba.

of these areas in the first Spanish decades, nor of any Chocó place or personal names. Gordon has described their northward expansion in historic time and has considered whence they may have come. His conclusion is that they are isolated in language from their neighbors, share some cultural traits with one or another people, but on the whole are markedly dissimilar. He favors the inference "that the Chocó lived scattered through forests of a large territory, then as now occupying the Department of Chocó; that if they were spreading northward, they had reached these districts before the sixteenth century; that their presence was as dependent at that time as it now is on forest cover." [8] In other words, the Spaniards may have overlooked the presence of such dispersed and shy aborigines in their search for gold. If this be so, the Chocó were aborigines in retreat locations within a territory dominated by higher Cuevan culture. An alternative possibility is that their ancestral home lay in a more western hill country between the Atrato and the Pacific, and that they had not settled farther east or north at the time of the first entradas.

The strange story of the black men on the Pacific coast to the south of the Gulf of San Miguel came from independent sources. The first concerned slaves seen at Quareca in Balboa's march to the sea; the second, the report Becerra had at Cape Garachiné. Both placed the "negros" as living to the south, the latter on the open Pacific coast south of the cape. Some years later, when Andagoya set out from Panama on the first leg of the discovery of Peru, he put in at the Gulf of San Miguel, "well inhabited by people of the kind and speech of those of Cueva. Here I learned how there came certain people by sea in canoes to make war at each full moon, and those of this province were so afraid of them that they did not dare to go fishing at sea" because the seacoast south was inhabited by these tall, bellicose people. Andagoya heard or reported nothing of black skins, but only of a tall and dangerous race that prowled the sea on moonlit nights and frightened the Cuevan Indians. Nor did Andagoya land again until well to the south on the Colombian coast. Cape Garachiné was about at the southern limit of Cuevan occupance on the Pacific.

Europe knew of blacks only in Africa; so Peter Martyr wondered about the shipwreck of a crew from that continent. The report by the officials of Santa Maria noted black men of large stature, long beards, and frizzy hair, who fought with clubs and were cannibals, all of which are Melanesian traits. This is the earliest intimation that there may have been landings in the New World from distant parts of the South Seas by men who were accustomed to venture into the open ocean.

COIBA

Coiba was the western part of the Isthmus, on the Pacific side of the watershed. That is the way Ferdinand designated it, as Balboa had requested. Pedrarias objected that there was no such province, which was correct in the sense of province as a political unit. Neither was Cueva a province in that sense. As geographical and cultural terms, however, both are proper.

Coiba was a useful name for the southwestern part of the Isthmus, as was

---

[8] Gordon, *op. cit.*, pp. 50-51.

Veragua for the Caribbean side of the watershed. The central cordillera here rises four to six thousand feet, feeding many streams that discharge south across a broad coastal plain into the gulfs of Parita and Montijo. Between these gulfs the peninsula of Azuero holds a detached highland that fronts steeply on the Pacific. Mainly the land has good natural drainage and is fertile. In contrast to the eastern Isthmus, interior communication is by land rather than by rivers; the main aboriginal east-west route is now marked by the Panamerican Highway. Rainfall is also notably less and the dry season longer. Coiba of Spanish usage was a good natural region. Its undefined western limit included the large island then as now called Isla de Coiba. Andagoya gave these limits: "From the province of Perequete as far as Adechame, which is a distance of about forty leagues continuing to the west, is called the province of Coiba." Perequete was the first native state west of Panama; Adechame lay beyond the Gulf of Montijo.

Culturally Coiba has been regarded as a western extension of Cuevan speech and ways. This was true in large measure, but there were differences and exceptions, the more so the farther west. The interpretation here proposed is that a Cuevan (Chibchan) base of culture was overlaid or overridden by a culture and in part by people intrusive from the north along the Pacific coast. In anthropological terms this would be a mixing of Mesoamerican with Circumcaribbean cultures. This part of the corridor between North and South America has marked attraction over the Atlantic side of the Isthmus. As a land route it has easily passable terrain and much less rain. As a sea route it has light currents and winds and many sheltered bays in contrast to the wild coast of Veragua. The aboriginal migrants always found passage easiest along the Pacific side. It may be inferred, therefore, that not only did the latest intrusions out of the Mesoamerican north enter here, but that there might be survivals of earlier migrations.

Peter Martyr recorded what Colmenares told of the first Spanish entrada, made by Gonzalo de Badajoz.[9] In crossing the eastern end of the cordillera (from the Chagres basin) they entered Coiba *la rica*, finding gold mixed with sand wherever they dug. The slaves found here had been marked in the face by tattooing; a black or red powder rubbed into the pricks made a permanent mark. The party turned south down to the coast to the cacique Chirú, who had excellent saltworks and a country rich in gold. The loot collected as they continued amounted to eighty thousand castellanos of gold and consisted of such things as women's girdles and breast supports, ear pendants, collars, and helmets. Going by way of Escoria they reached the home of the cacique Paris, who defeated them roundly. The account ends with the retreat. The booty, the greatest taken in any raid, was identified as adornments of a kind that suggest that they were stripped from the persons of the wearers. The invaders were trounced so badly that they fled, abandoning most of the loot, and left the country in a hurry. They had been defeated in open battle by Indian valor without the use of poisoned weapons. Gonzalo had made manifest that Coiba differed from the parts previously known.

The following entrada by Espinosa was punitive, by his Relación carried out to castigate and break the arrogance of those who had routed and killed Christians. He came with the largest and best body of troops, foot and horse and

---

[9] Peter Martyr, Decade III, Bk. 10.

artillery, and was accompanied by Indians. He joined the track of Gonzalo at Chirú and followed it to the land of Paris. Here another battle took place, in which the natives fought so well "in battalions" that the fight continued until the horsemen came up "to kill as they wished." Even then the contest ended in retreat, not in rout of the enemy. The captain of the Indians "wore many disks (*patenas*) and armor of gold, also daggers, over a garment (*aljubeta*) of cotton in which he was clothed."

Beyond the Río Escoria (Río Santa María) the natives were more warlike, better disciplined and led, and were thought to be more robust. The chief of Escoria had two giant brothers, one as bearded as any bearded Christian, as Espinosa noted when he executed them. The people of Escoria were very valiant and much given to war; they made all the good arms used in those provinces, somewhat as Milan is noted for its arms. The cacique Paris was held to be very brave and his people very strong. With these remarks of Espinosa, Andagoya was in agreement, acknowledging that the lord of Paris, "a valiant man," gave them a hard day-long battle, had subjected four provinces to the south, and was engaged in fighting with the chief of Escoria. "In this Escoria there was a breed of Indians much larger than the others and better conditioned, among them gentlemen who made great claims of valor . . . some I saw made other Indians seem like dwarfs and were of very fine carriage and build."

The battle dress is reminiscent of that of Mesoamerica, especially the cotton armor. From Cabo (Isla Coiba) Espinosa reported "corselets of cotton which reached from their shoulders to their knees and below, with sleeves to the elbow, as thick as the mattress of a bed, so strong that a crossbow will not pierce them." Such quilted cotton armor was later adopted by the Spaniards in Mexico. Their pikes and lances were as long and heavy as those of Germans, and their lining up with fife and drum was like the Germans.

In the western chiefdoms, palisaded settlements were found to be formidable defenses. Espinosa sent a party inland from Escoria toward the mountains to two caciques who had "forts made with two or three enclosures of timber and large trees and a very great moat around . . . these could well pass for good forts in Italy." Another was on the isle of Varones in the Gulf of Montijo, "with its circles of growing trees and surrounding moat." It was breached by the use of cannon. Andagoya accompanied the second entrada (1519), which got to the peninsula of Buricá, the western limit of the Republic of Panama. The Indian names were transcribed poorly, but somewhere to the east of Buricá and, I think, east of the mouth of Río Chiriquí, there "were three or four lords, bellicose people who had their towns well fortified with moats and palisades (*palenques*) of *cardos* very strong, spiny, and interwoven that make a strong wall." These plants, I take it, were columnar cactuses, still much used to form tight enclosures.

The Pacific side of the Isthmus to the west of Panama City, for which Coiba was and is a useful name, had a population of different breeds and customs from the rest of the Isthmus, the more so the farther west the Spaniards got. What impressed most were their more militant ways, as shown in discipline, arms, and fortified places. Some of the people were larger and stronger than those to the east. In the farthest parts, toward Buricá, Andagoya found them "almost all of one kind in dress and customs, Jewish in appearance." The native states were larger and more populous; that of Paris was the most renowned and feared.

Habitation was in towns rather than in dispersed dwellings, as in the large aggregation of houses at Natá and the moated places farther west. Oviedo described Natá as having large round houses with peaks like spires, topped by an object of pottery resembling a long-necked candelabra. Such bohíos had numerous rooms, walls of thick canes, were lined inside with delicate canes, and had roofs of thatch. Oviedo thought the round houses were an environmental adaptation to the strong winds which they withstood better than did rectangular ones.[10] From the Gulf of Montijo Espinosa reported the first ball game encountered since the bateys of Haiti, implying the presence of ball courts of the Mexican kind, at that time still unknown.

Language and dress were characterized by Andagoya. "The province of Coiba uses the language of Cueva, from which it differs in being more courtly and the people of more formality; it differs only in the men going without the *caracoles* [penis shields] worn in Cueva and without any concealment; the women are well dressed in the manner of those of Acla and Cueva." Farther on, however, he noted distinct languages at Chirú, Natá, and other places farther to the west. Oviedo observed that "in the language called that of Cueva, which is a large province, there are many differences in words, and other than this language those I have known in Tierra Firme are the languages of Coiba, Burica, Paris, Veragua," and others of Central America.[11] Different Chibchan dialects may have been spoken but also other languages. The Espinosa party occasionally had difficulty in finding interpreters.

Both Oviedo[12] and Espinosa noted the privilege of the caciques of Cueva as well as of Coiba to be carried in hammocks slung on poles.

Andagoya gave the summary of food produced: "All these lands are fine and level and a very beautiful country, having large supply of food, maize and ages and melons that differ from ours, *uvas,* yuca, and much fishing in rivers and sea and much hunting of deer; and in these matters the land of Coiba and of Cueva are the same." [13] Espinosa's horde lived at ease for four months on stored maize at Natá. After Panama was founded, his second expedition ranged the Coiba settlements in order to load ships with maize for the new town.

Root crops such as sweet yuca and sweet potatoes were still important. Maize was mentioned oftenest in the accounts, perhaps not only because it was most in demand by the Spaniards but because it probably was the first plant staple. Its cultivation was favored by the marked dry season and by food habits of Mesoamerican origin. Ground corn was toasted, stirred in water, and drunk, which is in fact the *pinole* of Mexico. The preparation of a maize beer was similar to the *tezvin* of Mexico, and was recorded by Espinosa in his first entrada as *chicha.* This word has been considered to be of Quechua origin, but here it was used

---

[10] Oviedo, *Historia,* Bk. XXIX, ch. 27.
[11] *Ibid.,* Bk. VI, ch. 43.
[12] Oviedo, *Sumario,* ch. 10.
[13] There being no grapes, *uvas* must have been an error of the copyist, perhaps for *avas,* the name *haba* being of early use for large seeded beans in the New World. The melons may have been papayas.

years before there was any knowledge of Peru. In interior Coiba, Espinosa knew of "wine" made from a small-grained and flinty corn, perhaps the first identification of a tropical flint corn like the *morocho,* later known from Colombia for alcoholic drink.

Mainly, there is only incidental mention of what was grown. Oviedo was more interested in describing the plant than in telling where it was found. The earliest notice of the papaya may have been from here by Espinosa. Oviedo described it by the name of *higo de mastuerzo* on the Caribbean coast; Andagoya and Espinosa, as Indian melon in Coiban country. It is the only native fruit that might be called a melon, and is still so called in places. Mameys were most abundant in the west, and the greater part of the Isla de Varones was covered with these trees. Also there were many pineapples, especially in the lower central sierra, as Espinosa noted in the second expedition. The utility of pineapples and mameys for making wine may account for their extensive cultivation.

The presence of cocoanut groves on this part of the Pacific coast has become generally known from the *Historia* of Oviedo, as described for the peninsula of Buricá. His earlier *Sumario* adds a locality of cocoanut palms about Chimán to the east of the Gulf of Panama. The earliest account is by Peter Martyr, in 1516, taken from what Colmenares told him of the Coiba expedition of Gonzalo de Badajoz of 1514: "On the South Sea there are various islands to the west of the Gulf of San Miguel and Isla Rica [Pearl Island] in the greater part of which there grow and are cultivated trees that produce the same fruit as the country of Colocut [Calicut], Cochimi [Cochin] and Camemori [Cananore] where the Portuguese have their spice markets." [14] The cultivation of cocoanuts is thereby of record both east and west of the Gulf of Panama. Cocos Island was so named at its discovery in the 1530's. How the cocoanut was distributed thus widely and with so little regard to convenient beaches remains undetermined.

That game was in good supply Peter Martyr learned from the Gonzalo discovery concerning herds of deer and wild pigs. They were taken by digging pits in their trails and covering these with branches. Pigeons were decoyed "by taking a tame one that flies about attached to a cord and so attracts the wild ones into range, or the birds are baited to a clear piece of ground where they are netted, the decoy pigeon in the middle, the feed scattered about." Parrots were taken similarly. The account continued with migratory waterfowl. "In their gardens they grow a tree which produces large calabashes. [By such casual mention it is known that the great fruited cultigen *Crescentia* was grown.] These calabashes are floated in waters where the birds feed, a hunter putting one over his head, having cut eyeholes in the gourd, and thus is able to pull a bird under water, the others thinking it was diving for food"—a sample of the curiosity of the old priest that has preserved many bits of knowledge about the New World.

Deer and peccaries were especially numerous in the Coiba country. Deer were like those of Spain in size and color, usually called *venados,* occasionally *ciervos.* In his second entrada (1519) Espinosa said that they were in herds of thirty to forty. Their herd habit and size identify them as white-tailed deer (*Odocoileus*), not the more solitary and smaller forest brocket deer (*Mazama*), which is still

---

[14] Peter Martyr, Decade III, Bk. 10, ch. 5.

273

present.[15] When Espinoza made his original entry into the town of Natá and looted storerooms, he found "about three hundred deer carcasses, rather more than less, dried and salted (*en cecina*), and the finest meat to eat that has ever been known." Andagoya spoke of good deer hunting and added this curious note: "In this land of Paris there is great quantity of cattle (*vacas*), tapirs (*dantas*), and deer (*venados*); and the warriors there eat no meat other than fish and iguanas, and those of the field and the agricultural laborers eat meat." I do not know what he meant by *vacas* unless he referred to beeves, writing these memoirs after stock ranches had been introduced. Referring to land in the west, he gave a detailed account of hunting peccaries: "It is a country productive of fish and of the native pigs in great quantity, to hunt which they have large nets of something like hemp called henequen, the meshes large and as thick as a finger. They set up this net at the outside of a woody tract (*monte*) where they knew such a herd of pigs to be. These were driven by shouting toward the net, nearing which they were alarmed by the people so that all dashed into the net. As they caught their heads in it and were unable to extricate their bodies, they were enmeshed in the net and were killed by lances so that none escaped." In Coiba as in Cueva deer and peccaries seem to have been secured mainly by drives, both by battue and by fire, each of which requires open spaces.

Besides waterfowl, there were many land game birds, Andagoya mentioning two kinds of *pavos* (*Crax*), pheasants (*Guan*), and doves (*palomas*). The country around Natá abounded in doves, "so numerous that a crossbowman who went out to hunt thought he returned emptyhanded if he brought back less than fifty. There were so many of them taken in nets that we all grew tired of eating them" (Espinosa).

Fish, being abundant everywhere in the coastal areas, were mentioned more casually. When Espinosa was returning from his first raid, finding that the Indians had fled and the Spaniards therefore lacked food, the party had the good fortune to encounter a spawning run at Tabora, to the south of Perequete, "a great abundance of fish and so many that in two hours in truth there were taken two thousand arrobas of fish in such a manner that it seemed to us that there appeared to be more fish than water."

As in Cueva, meat and fish were preserved by smoking on barbacoas and by salting. The land was "well provided with salt, at least the provinces of Chiru and Nata and Paris in which we encountered saltworks (*salinas*) of the finest and best artifice and best organized that have been seen. In these it is possible to make salt for a population like that of Sevilla, as white as snow, as salty and of as good grain as the best there is in Castille" (Espinosa). The manner of evaporating sea water and purifying the salt was not described.

Nothing was recorded of domestic animals until Nicaragua was reached later, for which Andagoya noted the keeping of turkeys (*gallinas de la tierra*) and dogs that were eaten. The Nicaragua of the time included the Pacific coast of Costa Rica. Here, in the peninsula of Nicoya, Philip Wagner tells me that communities which keep to Indian ways still give special attention to raising turkeys. The domestic turkey, derived from the wild turkey of Mexico, was an

---

[15] Oviedo may have had the latter in mind in his brief reference to *gamo* and *corzo*, for which he gave only Santa Marta of eastern Colombia as location.

important element in Mesoamerican culture. It was carried as part of that dispersal south into Nicaragua, which probably meant Costa Rica. May it have been taken farther into Coiba along with other Mesoamerican ways and people? Oviedo said no, that the *pavos* of New Spain had been introduced into the islands and Castilla del Oro by the Christians.[16] He wrote thus in Spain, having ended his second stay in Castilla del Oro in July, 1523. At the time of his writing, *pavos* were kept there, he said, in numbers.

The events do not support Oviedo. The time was too early for Spanish introduction by the Pacific side. By the Atlantic it would have meant the carriage of such birds from Vera Cruz to a West Indian port and thence to Darién. The only island port that a ship from Vera Cruz was likely to enter was Habana, a most improbable port for sailing to Darién. The thesis of Oviedo would require the introduction of turkeys from New Spain to the islands and thence to Castilla del Oro, where they were present in numbers, all within about three years. Another remote possibility is that one of Veláquez' slave raids to the Mayan coast of Honduras brought turkeys from there to Cuba. The one is as unlikely as the other. On the other hand there is the letter of Zuazo of January, 1518, to inform the King of conditions in Castilla del Oro. With it went a present of birds, some of which were turkeys by his description, *pavos* that had a cry like the yelping of a dog beaten over the head. The likelier explanation is that the Mexican domestic turkey had passed, along with other Mesoamerican traits and intruders, into the Coiba country and was taken from there to Darién and so to Santo Domingo, between which places there was frequent communication.

Land routes were open in number to Spanish entries across the Isthmus and along it. The sizable party of Gonzalo de Badajoz crossed from the Chagres basin over the sierra to Chirú by a route that is not now passable. Espinosa led the largest party, with horses, baggage, and cannon across Cueva country that Balboa had pacified, into Panama and thence across Coiba, mostly along the present route of the Panamerican Highway. Side excursions were made at will, partly by horse. The only mention of a bad road was at Huera in the Azuero peninsula, beyond which there was no land road because of rugged country. Almost everywhere they found Indian roads to follow without the need of opening a way. They heard of other routes which they did not take, such as the one across the cordillera from Montijo Bay to Veragua. A network of interior lines of travel covered both eastern and western parts of the Isthmus.

The Espinosa entradas found large seaworthy canoes available and natives to man them. The island of Coiba and the islands of Montijo Gulf were peopled by natives skilled in the use of canoes. The captain who had been sent on the exploration of the coast beyond the Azuero peninsula rejoined the homeward-bound land party at Chirú with sixteen canoes, which Espinosa said were the best that had been seen in Tierra Firme.

Of native gold collected in Coiba there is even less information than for Cueva and Veragua. That there was little placer gold is indicated by the fact that no locality was named as a mining district. Native gangs were put to work getting gold here and there with unrecorded results. The profits of Coiba however were derived from looting golden treasure and these were greater than elsewhere in

---

[16] Oviedo, *Sumario,* ch. 36.

Castilla del Oro. It was the abandoned booty of Gonzalo that directed the course of Espinosa, who recorded from cacique to cacique what he secured. In his entrada of 1519 Espinosa found the burial of the great chief Paris. The body was encased in three shrouds, the finest innermost, and was decked with gold ornaments from the helmeted head to gold bands about the legs. Espinosa reported the value of the gold on the corpse as ten thousand castellanos. Since this declaration was subject to paying the royal fifth, it is not likely to have been exaggerated.

Whether gold was smelted and cast or otherwise fabricated in western parts of the Isthmus is not known. There is nothing in the records of the time to that effect, except for the statement by Pedrarias in which he objected to giving Balboa charge of Panama and Coiba. In it he said "the present cacique of Panama is called Coti. He and all his ancestors are great smelters of gold and masters of working it and very handsome articles are made there. Whatever chiefs, near or far from this province, wish to have worked gold or any delicate things thus fashioned go to that place and therefore they have been accustomed for a long time to say that the gold they have comes from Panama. All the fame is of Panama, although the chiefs collect it in their own lands. In Panama no gold is collected nor is there any. It is because it is founded and fashioned there that they say it comes from Panama. Vasco Nuñez has never seen nor been in those parts or provinces and can only say that he has heard this great fame of Panama and Coiba from Indians." [17] At that time neither district had been seen by Spaniards. When they got to Panama it was found to be a small fishing settlement of little interest for treasure and none for gold-smelting. Pedrarias was right that whatever caciques got native gold in their territories were likely to collect and trade it to a center where there were highly skilled artisans. There is neither evidence nor probability however that Panama was such a place. Balboa knew of Dabeiba and Enciso of Sinú, both to the east. No one other than Pedrarias identified such a center anywhere in the Isthmus.

Archaeological museums have collections of gold work from Panama, especially from Coclé in the Coiba country, and much more from Costa Rica and Colombia, in part identified by their designs as of common origin. The objects were made by master craftsmen who knew smelting, casting, alloying, soldering, plating, gilding, and wiredrawing, and fashioned objects of great diversity, objects of art. The entradas into the west recorded notable features of native life. Thus Escoria was reported as the place where superior arms were made for other districts, without telling what these arms were. Intent as the Spaniards were on getting gold, would they have failed to mention artificers of gold objects if they had found any? They knew that gold was collected in many mountain streams and was carried to a few places to be manufactured and that these centers were not located where the placer gold was found. They knew, as Balboa and Enciso did, that such a manufactory might point to the desired sources of gold. The absence of notice of any such local industry for Coiba as well as for the rest of the Isthmus suggests that none was found.

The loot by which Castilla del Oro supported itself for years to good profit was treasure of heirlooms acquired from parts beyond the Isthmus, a commerce

---

[17] Altolaguirre, Appendix doc. 52.

of unknown antiquity by an unknown exchange of goods. Much of it came from Colombia, where there was a gold metallurgy equalled in few parts of the world. The prevalence of guanín, alloyed with copper and silver, points to even more remote lands, Peru or Mexico, a lost commerce in metals of which the Isthmus was repository rather than source.

XV
ESTABLISHMENT ON THE SOUTH SEA

•

THE DECLINE OF DARIÉN

Santa María de Darién was best situated as first Spanish base on Tierra Firme. No other site would have served so well to find out what lay behind the southwestern shores of the Caribbean Sea. The direct fast sailing route from Spain followed the trade winds through the Dominica Passage to the harbor at Cartagena and continued thence with slight change of direction to Darién under light and variable winds. These were used on the return to get back to Cartagena, and so to Santo Domingo and whatever route was taken north into the Atlantic. By sea the coast of Sinú to the northeast and that of Acla, San Blas, and Nombre de Dios to the northwest were equally convenient to Darién.

At first Darién also was in the best location for getting into the interior. The town lay beyond the western edge of the Atrato delta, safe from floods and having the option of several channels to go up the great river or of entering the Culata to ascend the Río León. There was also the direct land route south to Sautatá above the head of the delta. To the west the Indian trail of Trepadera led directly across the continental divide.

For the support of the Spanish settlement, Darién offered a numerous and tractable Indian population, ample planting and fishing grounds, and gold placers in the Serranía adjacent.

The initial advantage of Darién was soon lost, however. The ventures eastward into Urabá and Sinú ended in disaster. The search to the south for the gold of Dabeiba was disappointing. Profitable returns were found only to the west, first in the gold treasures of the Cuevan principalities of the Isthmus and, after the discovery of the Pacific, in the Pearl Islands. The founding of a second town at Acla was the first expression of westward shift of interest. Acla served two purposes. The first was to descend the Río Balsas (Chucunaque) to the Gulf of San Miguel and get to the Pearl Islands. This line of communication was difficult, hence no town was built on the Gulf of San Miguel, as had been anticipated. The more important use of Acla was as the Caribbean terminus of the easy land route west to the north shore of the Gulf of Panama. This followed through open and well-settled country which was richly rewarding in golden loot and slaves. Darién came to lie farther and farther to the rear of the active front of exploitation.

The natives of the Caribbean coast whom Balboa had preserved were soon destroyed by Pedrarias. They were replaced by gangs of slaves who were brought from the interior, each in turn to be followed by others as the former lot was used up. Food production failed and imports were required by ship. The former Indian provinces of Darién and Careta were ruined. The brutally predatory economy practiced by Pedrarias rested on despoiling Indian areas farther and farther from Santa María and Acla, which thereby were becoming untenable.

Oviedo owned a good home in Santa María, liked the place, was one of the last to leave there, and thought that the abandonment of the town was due to the hatred Pedrarias had for Balboa who had built it, overlooking thereby the westward shift of locational advantage. Oviedo held Pedrarias was motivated by spite in making an end of Santa María, "which city he had dishonored and written that it was unhealthy, which it was not, but he destroyed it for the hatred he held for it . . . since it was built by Vasco Núñez and he wished also to destroy me," Oviedo being the last official there.[1] Oviedo said that after the modorra epidemic of 1514 Santa María again became a healthy place. In this he may have been right. The evil repute of the Caribbean side of the Isthmus came later, and health in fact had nothing to do with the abandonment of Santa María or Acla. As in Española, men were said to return to Spain from Castilla del Oro yellow as gold, perhaps indicating jaundice. At a later time the Caribbean ports of Nombre de Dios and Portobelo became notorious for yellow fever, malaria, and enteric fevers. The records of Castilla del Oro are so explicit that serious morbidity should have had notice as did the sickness of modorra in 1514. Either the Spaniards of the time were remarkably indifferent to ailments or the rainy tropics had not as yet become centers of contagion.

THE CHOICE OF PANAMA

The discovery of the Pacific made it obvious that a Spanish settlement would be needed on the new coast and that it should have the benefit of a convenient crossing of the Isthmus. Hearing of the discovery from Balboa, the King thought that "by the shortest and least difficult terrain" several posts should be built between Santa María and the Gulf of San Miguel, where a settlement was to be made (1514).[2] This crossing, however, was neither short nor easy, and interest shifted farther west along the Isthmus. One proposal of 1515 considered the Gulf of San Blas for the Caribbean port, to connect with an appropriate location on the South Sea, whence the proponent Albítez hoped to sail east to Cape San Agustín in Brazil![3] The Albítez "offer received royal approval in March, 1518, to found two pueblos, one on the north side at the Gulf of San Blas or Nombre de Dios and the other on the side of the South at [the seat of] the Cacique Chepo."[4] From the Gulf of San Blas to tidewater on the Río Chepo the air-line

---

[1] Oviedo, *Historia*, Bk. XXIX, ch. 20.
[2] Altolaguirre, Appendix doc. 23.
[3] *Ibid.*, Appendix doc. 48.
[4] *Ibid.*, Appendix doc. 64.

distance is about twenty-five miles, then mostly open country; the continental divide was passable at less than a thousand feet above sea level. This would have been the best route for the Isthmian crossing and agreed with the one Balboa had in mind while awaiting the recall of Pedrarias on the Gulf of San Miguel. Then, Andagoya said, "we should go to make a settlement at Chepabar, six leagues from Panama toward Acla." Chepabar lay immediately to the west of the lower Río Chepo. The authorization to Albítez and the intent of Balboa were the best solution for paired ports on the two seas. The distance was shortest and the land route easiest. There was no lack of suitable harbors on the Caribbean side. Shoal water, mangrove swamps, and high tidal range on the Pacific side, however, afforded few good anchorages about the Bay of Panama. Here the estuary of the Río Chepo (Bayano), with the island of Chepillo before it, would have been most eligible. Nothing came of these proposals.

In four and a half years as governor, Pedrarias himself had gone no farther than Acla. After the execution of Balboa at the beginning of 1519, he was suddenly in a great hurry to get to the Pacific. Proceeding to the Río Balsas, down to the Gulf of San Miguel over the route of Balboa's discovery, and thence to the Pearl Islands, he took over the ships Balboa had built there. The details of this sudden burst of energy and the ceremonies of possession by which he repeated the acts of Balboa of fourteen years earlier may be passed over. In mid-August, 1519, he founded the town of Panama.

The selection of Panama is unexplained. The Indian fishing village and its vicinity lacked resources, people, and even a fair harbor. The name had gained currency as a vague designation of the farther part of Cuevan territory of which it was a small and undistinguished part. Pedrarias made no search for suitable town sites along the bay, but went directly to this location and declared it to be his future seat. The selection of Panama eliminated the Gulf of San Blas from consideration as Caribbean port. The choice then fell upon Nombre de Dios which Nicuesa had founded and left, a scarcely recognizable ruin. The route between Panama and Nombre de Dios was half again as long as the San Blas-Chepo connection would have been, and crossed more difficult terrain. Nombre de Dios, however, continued to serve for most of the century as the Caribbean gateway to the Pacific.

By 1519 it was evident that the future of Castilla de Oro depended on the exploitation of the Pacific side of the Isthmus, mainly to the west of the Gulf of Panama. Santa María was ordered abandoned. A few Spaniards chose to continue at Acla. A handful sufficed at Nombre de Dios to service an occasional ship and work a few placers in the hills. Most of the Spaniards were transferred to the new seat of government and received repartimientos in its vicinity. Andagoya wrote that having founded Panama Pedrarias "made a division of the land among the 400 vecinos there were at the time in Panama, leaving a certain part of the province of Cueva for the vecinos of Acla. And since in the entradas that so many captains had made through that country as they went to and came from Darien, taking great quantity of Indians, and because the land between one sea and the other was of small extent, there were few Indians at the time it was allotted, he who received most by repartimiento got 90, others 50 or 40."

The removal of Pedrarias to Panama was also in the nature of a tactical retreat to a favorable position from which to await developments in Spain. Pedrarias knew that he was in trouble; his replacement by a new governor meant that his conduct of office would be subject to a searching *residencia*. The accounting of the royal revenues from Castilla del Oro had been highly irregular. Many and specific charges had been lodged against him during and after the regency of Cardinal Cisneros, including those by Quevedo, Franciscan Bishop of Castilla del Oro, and by Oviedo. The veteran governor of the Canaries, Lope de Sosa, had been offered the government of Castilla del Oro, and after long deliberation had accepted; the announcement was made by the King in March, 1519. Pedrarias was not ready to concede the game as lost. He had control of the only ships in Pacific waters, which Balboa had built. He had liquidated Balboa and the men most attached to Balboa. He was attaching the other Spaniards to himself by repartimientos in the west. Official orders were notoriously slow in being put into effect. Sosa was an old man. Fonseca, who had sponsored Pedrarias, had been dismissed by Cisneros, but was again regaining his power. Time might run in his favor.

Luck was with Pedrarias. The departure of Sosa was delayed for a year and the new governor died on arriving at Darién in June, 1520. The subsequent residencia of Pedrarias was a farce and a fraud. The King had his hands full with the Communero revolt in Spain. Under the circumstances Pedrarias was retained in office free to continue as he pleased. Darién was dismantled and Panama took its place, to engage in harrying lands along the Pacific.

THE OCCUPATION OF COIBA

The town that was being founded at Panama would need food, which was not available locally. Espinosa was sent on the ships Balboa had built to requisition food along the west side of the Gulf of Panama. He and a large party had been well provided there earlier, when they roamed about Coiba for a year and never suffered want. They had lived well at Natá for months, long enough to have the Indians plant and harvest a crop of maize for their use. Natá would be his main destination to find provisions for Panama.

Espinosa reported his second entrada in detail and in leisurely manner.[5] It is apparent that he did not expect resistance from the natives and it may be inferred thereby that the violence of his earlier entry had broken their spirit. The expedition took two and a half months, from July 21 to October 3, 1519, and reconnoitered the broad lowland horseshoe about the western side of the Gulf of Panama. The most southerly place reached was Pecora (Pocrí) where a small ship (*fusta*) was loaded with maize and sent back to Panama. From there north to the Río Escoria (Santa María) the country belonged to the native state of Paris. Its two main alluvial valleys, the Río del Asiento Viejo (Río Parita) and Río de Mahizales (Río La Villa) he recorded as very productive of maize, yuca, and excellent melons [papayas], also of cotton that was made into fine cloth. The land abounded in game, deer, peccaries, and game birds. The six leagues of coast were rich in fish, shellfish, and salt. Securing gold was incidental to the purpose of assuring a future food supply for Panama, but the great treasure of gold

---

[5] CDI,XX, 6–44.

found with the body of the former cacique Paris gave awareness of the prospects of grave robbing. On crossing north of the river (Santa María at San Fernando?) at the inner margin of the lowlands, they heard of a mountain state of Esqueva (Santa Fé?) where the pineapples were grown and the small seeded flinty corn. This was an expedition to get supplies, not to explore; and thus they did not enter the mountains but swung eastward through open savanna country to the familiar land of Natá. Here they found fifteen hundred Indians living peaceably in bohíos, people of better understanding and more cleanly than others. The province was small but most fertile of all, with a shoreline of four leagues, in which were excellent saltworks. Again there was abundance of game, also an industry of cotton cloth. On the coast of Natá they loaded twelve hundred fanegas of maize and returned to Panama.

Thereafter the main Coiba country, the fertile and well-watered lowlands west of the Gulf of Panama, became the regular source of supplies for the city of Panama. As long as there were Indians available, these were engaged in planting crops, especially maize, which had replaced cassava as the Spanish staple. The Natá area was most productive and accessible and here shortly a Spanish villa of that name was established.

XVI

NATIVE DECLINE AND ECOLOGIC CHANGE IN CASTILLA DEL ORO

•

DECLINE OF THE NATIVE POPULATION

The evidence of native numbers is not as good as it is for Española, nor is it negligible. There was no count of native tributaries because there was no such system. There is no record of repartimientos and hardly a mention of such until Pedrarias gave allotments to the vecinos of Panama. The island formula that a cacique and his people were to serve a named vecino was not used. After Balboa, there was no semblance of order or restraint in the treatment of the natives. Espinosa's account of his first entrada is mainly of the sacking of settlements and the capture of their people, for which the term *ranchear* was current by that time. Referring to the expeditions inland and to the South Sea, Andagoya said:

> The captains and men who left for those parts, the land being more healthful and more peopled, the Spaniards who went to that part of the land were accustomed to bring back large gangs of people in fetters and all the gold they could get and this state continued around three years. The captains divided the Indians they had taken among the soldiers; the gold they took to Darien. This having been amassed and smelted, each received his share as did the officials and the bishop, as having a vote in the administration, and also the governor. These received also their share of the Indians. Since the captains were appointed by favor of those who governed, and were relatives or friends, no one was punished even if they had done great evil. In such manner the land suffered for more than a hundred leagues from Darien. All the captives brought, and they were in great number, arrived at Darien to be put into the gold mines, of which there were good ones in the land, and as they came over so long a road worn out and broken by the great loads they carried, and the country differed from their own and was not healthy, all died. In all these journeys they never brought peace, nor did they settle, but were interested only in bringing gold and Indians to Darien to be consumed there.

Andagoya's recollection a score of years after the events is supported by others, Oviedo and Zuazo, and in great and angry detail by Las Casas. The time of Balboa had been rather benign, when, as was variously reported a Christian could go throughout the Cuevan lands and be received in friendship. With the coming of Pedrarias the condition and attitude of the natives changed. There-after Balboa as well, building ships under orders of Pedrarias, treated the natives as expendable in excessive labor. In 1607 the Audiencia of Panama, in review of those early years, found the early entrants unconcerned about the future of the colony; it was an invasion by transients whose only concern was to get rich quickly and get out.[1]

Bishop Quevedo in 1515 informed King Ferdinand of seventeen Cuevan caciques who had been at peace with the Spaniards, "each of whom has a province to himself and many principal persons and caciques subject to them." [2] All the Cuevan country, namely the Isthmus to the east of Panama with partial exception of the serranía of Cañazas (between the Bayano basin and the Pacific), was organized into cacicazgos (see fig. 27). The Isthmus was divided about equally between Cueva and Coiba, the division roughly at the Canal Zone. Coiba had the greater native states, the larger population, and the greater production of food.

Oviedo estimated the population of Castilla del Oro to have been two million, "or they were innumerable," and asked "how so many people could have come to an end in so short a time." [3] His guess is not to be taken lightly. He had traveled the length of the Isthmus from the delta of the Atrato to the western peninsula of Buricá. As an official he was conversant with the records, including the papers of Balboa which concerned the Gulf of San Miguel, the major area that he had not visited. No one was in a better position to know what the native population had been.

What happened to the Indians after the founding of Panama received slight attention. Pedrarias continued to govern, or rather to let his followers do as they pleased. A half-century later López de Velasco found no more than five or six Indian villages with a total of three to four hundred Indians, free of tribute because of their poverty. Four villages had lately been reduced to one at Chepo. In the jurisdiction of Natá there were four villages, totaling about a hundred Indians. There were said then to be more than three thousand Negro maroons who had escaped.

The Audiencia of Panama reported in 1607 that the pueblo of Chepo, in other times of many Indians, had been in steady diminution and at the time had thirty-five Indians who spoke only Spanish. To its east, the country was uninhabited. A dozen Indians intermarried with Negroes lived on the Isle of Pearls. The island of Taboga had fourteen householders where once there had been many people.

Vázques de Espinosa (ca. 1628) knew Chepo as an Indian village of thirty houses, the inhabitants speaking only Spanish. It was then, as it has remained since, the eastern outpost of Panamanian settlement. East of Chepo there were only Indios de guerra. In the western part Natá was a small place inhabited by Indians and Spaniards, Parita one of Spanish-speaking Indians, and Coclé and Penonomé were of civilized Indians (de razón).

In the Cuevan country a few Indians survived by hiding out. Their descendants, known as Cuna, live in a few remote spots in the forests of the upper Bayano

[1] Manuel Serrano y Sanz (ed.), "Relaciones historicas y geográficas de América central," Colección de libros y documentos referentes a la historia de América, VIII (Madrid, 1908), especially p. 217.
[2] Altolaguirre, Appendix doc. 53.
[3] Oviedo, Historia, Bk. XXIX, ch. 10.

basin. Others in later times have reoccupied a part of the Gulf of San Blas, where they are now increasing on their own reservation. The remnants of the natives of Coiba were soon absorbed into the mixed population.

SAVANNAS AT THE TIME OF THE INDIANS

The early accounts describe savannas of large extent and in number. The largest open country stretched from the watershed between the Chucunaque and Bayano west through Coiba. Another was the highland country of Dabeiba. Savannas were also noted on the inner side of the Gulf of San Miguel, both north and south.

Andagoya wrote: "The first province to the west of Acla is Comogre, where the open country (*tierra rasa*) and savannas commence; from here on [west] it was well peopled." The province of Comogre straddled the low watershed between the Bayano and Chucunaque drainage. Of Pocorosa, the next province to the west in the Bayano basin, Balboa reported (letter of January, 1513) that to the north at "a day's journey from this cacique Pocorosa are some sierras the most beautiful that have been seen in these parts. They are very open (*claras*) mountains without any woods (*monte*), save for groves (*arboleda*) along some arroyos that come down from the mountains," thus saying that the open country extended up the slopes of the flanking sierra. Espinosa described one great savanna as stretching from Comogre to Guarare to the southwest of the Gulf of Panama: "In the said provinces of Natá and Cheru (Chirú) and from there as far as Comogre is a land as smooth as the palm of the hand, a very healthy country and all savanna without montes other than groves along the banks of the rivers; and from Nata to Guarare it is about the same." Having remarked on the abundance of deer and doves, he continued, "In all this land it is possible to go on horse in summer and winter as well as or more easily than in Castile, to the end of what has been discovered and what can be seen beyond, [perhaps referring to the mainland seen beyond the Gulf of Montijo] very well peopled and very open and without thickets (*arcabucos*)." Looking back on the country west of Chepo, he said, "To here it is the best land as well in being very plain and clear and without thickets, as in being very healthy and agreeable and fresh both in winter and summer and I say this because at all times we were well supplied with all Indian food and much fish of sea and stream and much game." The place at which he made this estimate marked their passing from the new country of abundance at the west back to the devastated lands east of Chepo. He had said previously that the physical aspect was similar throughout the entrada. A more or less continuous savanna reached from the headwaters of the Bayano west all through the lowland north and west of the Gulf of Panama and across the Gulf of Montijo.

Balboa found a treeless land about Dabeiba in the western cordillera of Colombia. Here basins within the mountains, shadowed against rain by enclosing ridges, lie at temperate altitudes. Still another kind of situation of savannas was found when the Pacific was discovered. Balboa had his first view of that sea from the treeless ridge adjacent to the Gulf of San Miguel, a ridge that rises about two hundred meters above the estuarine and alluvial lowland. Such ridges, present in number to the east of that gulf, are structural features, now forest covered. It is suggested that the Río Sabanas, flowing through a depression between them, may have been named at a time in the past when the ridges were capped by savannas. Other savannas were found to the south of the Gulf of San Miguel.

Whether lowland plain, intramontane basin, or ridge top, the savannas were not natural grasslands of climatic origin. In the Cueva country of eastern Panama the rainfall is high; but there is still a dry season. Here the former savannas now support a luxuriant tropical forest composed of many species of trees. To the west, in what was called Coiba, the precipitation is markedly less, but is ample for diverse trees of mesophytic habit and good growth. By the early accounts the sigmoid lowland that runs the length of the Isthmus was more or less continuous savanna from the pluvial upper Bayano drainage west through the moderately rainy Pacific coast to the Gulf of Chiriquí. This open lowland was well drained, for Espinosa commented that it was readily traversed at any time of the year. Whether very rainy or less so, throughout the area there is a season when the rains stop and the ground may become dry. Neither pattern of climate nor structure of soil accounts for the replacement of trees by herbaceous vegetation. This was the result of Indian occupation, and was reversed on their demise.

The flora of Panama is very rich in species of trees that originated in South America; less so in kinds derived from the north. At the lower elevations the Isthmus is by nature a tropical forest except for some marshes, as is also the basin of the Atrato. Such forests provide very little food for man. He might find food where windfalls made openings, along the sunlit banks of streams and in their waters, and especially at the seaside. He might enlarge the advantages at any of these sites by the use of fire to encroach upon the unproductive forest. The aboriginal settlement of South America was by way of Panama in many successive migrations, attested by the diversity of native languages. These migrants, originating in Asia, had crossed the length of North America, employing fire to survive and to aid their collecting and hunting. As they converged in their southward movement on the narrow corridor of Panama they began the alteration of its cover by fire, cumulative through the millennia and effective in particular in the areas that were savannas at the coming of the Europeans. The successive and successful entries took advantage of the attractions of the Coiba region with the food resources of its Pacific coast, many streams, and longer dry season that aided the spread of fires across its plains. Beyond the head of the Gulf of Panama the highly pluvial Bayano basin was gradually converted into savanna, as were lesser tracts farther east and south. The greater part of such extension of savannas may be attributed to the period after agricultural settlement. Their beginnings I should seek far earlier, because this narrow route was the only one by which the people found their way into South America.

The superior advantages of the Coiba over the Veragua side have been noted. East of Panama City there were optional routes, along the Caribbean, through the Bayano-Chucunaque basin, and down the Pacific coast to the Gulf of San Miguel. Farther south, the Pacific coast is most inhospitable in terrain and by excessive and continuous raininess, certainly not a passageway by land. All three routes reconverged on the Río Atrato above its delta, at or above Sautatá. By reasonable premise these early migrations were by landsmen, and the crossing of that great river was as difficult a barrier as they encountered anywhere. If they turned south up the Atrato they were headed for more swamp, water, forest, and continuous heavy rain. The way to survival was to get across the river and head east for the base of the cordillera, and thus come to the attractive high basin of Dabeiba. The primordial route and that of the Panamerican Highway would seem to be about the same. The modern highway still lacks about three hundred miles of crossing the Atrato and the forests of eastern Panama where once there were long stretches of open and inhabited country.

When the cultivation of crops was introduced, fire was the first and main step in preparing the land for planting. Indian planting was easiest by deadening trees and burning the dry debris, which served as fertilizer. Fields were thus advanced farther into the forest. Volunteer vegetation, herbaceous and woody, gradually entered the fields, which might be abandoned to secondary growth if it was easier to make a new forest clearing than to keep the fields free of invading growth.

The early Spanish accounts paid attention to the open country and said little about forests or woody second growth (arcabucos). It would seem that the savannas were not composed of tussocks of bunch grasses or of sod-forming grasses unsuited to the planting of crops, since in general they seem to have been the most populous areas. The Caribbean side may have been less than the painted garden that Columbus described about Portobelo, but it was then largely cleared land. The Gulf of San Miguel and the rivers that drain into it were flanked by agricultural settlements large and numerous enough to provide the large Spanish parties with food and transport.

The modification or elimination of tropical forest cover by man was expressed also in the kinds of game and its abundance. Deer (venados) were hunted in number, and by their size and herd habits are recognized as the white-tailed or Virginia deer of the north, not an inhabitant of forests. Perhaps these deer even followed upon human disturbance into these tropical lands. The collared peccaries, said to range in herds of from forty to three hundred, also bespeak a rather open country. The same applies to the large flocks of ground-feeding doves. Such game may have been most abundant in western parts, but was not restricted to them.

THE RETURN OF THE FOREST

As the Indians died out or hid away, the settlements and fields were abandoned. Chepo soon became, as it still is, the edge of the wilderness. The needs of the city of Panama for cattle, mules, and horses kept the nearer savannas in use. López de Velasco noted the savanna of Pacora (Pacrí) between Panama and Chepo as seven leagues long, two to three leagues wide, and of good pasturage. The report of the Audiencia of Panama in 1607 listed *hatos de ganado* from east to west in these numbers: Chepo 21, Panama 17, Caimito 4, Perequete 2, Capira 4, Chame 6, and the total number of ganado as 53,600, about a hundred per inhabitant, black and white. The land about the head of the Gulf of Panama continued to be open pasture of livestock; the individual properties were still called by the old Spanish name hatos.

East of Chepo the country was of no interest to the Spaniards after the found-ing of Panama, except for a presidio called Bayano, maintained from 1578 to 1611 in the upper part of the river, since known by that name. It was situated in what had been the major Indian province of Pocorosa. The post was established because Englishmen supported by Negro maroons were raiding inland from the Caribbean. The Audiencia report of 1607 noted that all the country from Chepo to Bayano, a distance of about thirty leagues, was depopulated, consisting of swamps and forest of no utility, and that the same was true for many leagues beyond. This was the same country that Balboa, Espinosa, and Andagoya had described as a great savanna, the Cuevan principalities of the interior. When the garrison was withdrawn from Bayano in 1611, Indians promptly attacked and killed all those who had remained as stockmen and lumbermen. The account is from Vázquez de Espinosa, twenty years later, when the country east of Chepo was unpopulated except for a few hostile Indians. Bayano then had *algunos aserraderos y estancias de ganado,* sawpits and stock ranches, utilizing merchanta-ble timber, browse, and grass. The vicinity was reputed to have most fertile land, and there was talk of resettling it, but, like all of eastern Panama, it was left to the readvancing forest.

Lionel Wafer found the Caribbean coast wholly forest-covered in 1681, ex-cept for some cleared and planted ground at Portobelo, which had replaced Nombre de Dios in 1584. The site of Nombre de Dios was overgrown with wild canes, the only indication that there had been a town. The islands to its west that Columbus had named Bastimentos for their abundance of food were found by Wafer to be dense forest. The Bayano basin was forest as far west as Chepo, beyond which there were savannas interspersed with fine groves.

To the west of Panama City the former Coiba country was converted partly to stock ranches, partly to the growing of maize and other supplies for the city. The provisioning was less than sufficient, and Panama City was always depend-ent on imported food. The changes of vegetation in Coiba have not been ex-amined. At the time of Vázquez, its western part beyond Azuero was the prin-cipal source of lumber for shipment to Peru. There were, he wrote, more than four thousand aserraderos, the largest and best found anywhere on the Pacific coast. The wood mentioned by him as most desirable was cedar. This tropical "cedar" (*Cedrela*) ecologically is a very minor item in virgin tropical forest, but is important, even dominant, in an intermediate stage of forest succession. Seeding freely and growing rapidly, it establishes itself readily on open and sunlit ground where moisture and nutrients are sufficient. From the cedar lumbering of the time it may be inferred that stands of merchantable cedar had occupied the open and populous country Espinosa had described a hundred years earlier. The major export of the Isthmus was lumber, mostly from erstwhile Indian farms.

POSTSCRIPT: THE CHOCÓ INDIANS

Early notices of the Chocó Indians refer vaguely to the southern end of the Atrato watershed. If the expedition of Balboa to the upper Atrato got into Chocó country, the few traits it recorded were wrong. I have therefore suggested that the Chocó were not at that time in the Quibdó area. The Atrato basin was occupied mainly by *cacicazgos* of Cuevan character, kinship, and speech, as Trimborn has proposed. These were ruined during the sixteenth century, first by raids from Darién, later by Spanish parties entering from the Caribbean coast of Colombia and from the interior. The depopulated lowland and its marginal hill country were gradually occupied by Chocó Indians.

Vázquez de Espinosa knew of the Chocó as living in the western part of Antioquia, which was then considered to extend to the Pacific coast. The Chocó built their houses on piles on ridge crests, still a characteristic trait. There is no record that they exploited placer gold but they had freshwater pearls. The upper Río Atrato had become known by that time as the Río Chocó. Vázquez heard that these Indians had raided the Spanish villas of Antioquia and Toro on the middle Río Cauca. When attacked in their own territory, he said, they set fire to a palm-thatched pile house by which they gave the alarm to other houses that were then similarly set afire; the Indians fled down the Río Chocó in canoes to hide and live in the swamps until the Spaniards left.

I do not know when the Chocó reached the lower Atrato. Jeffery's *Atlas* of 1775 shows the Atrato River by that name, adding Chocó as one of two Indian names by which it was also known. His other name, Tocomor, may have been that of a multifamily dwelling on piles, Chocó in type.[4] Stream names in *do*, normal in Chocó and not in other languages, are now found as far north as the Culata (Bahía de Colombia), which the Chocó perhaps reached in the eighteenth century.

During the present century a penetration of Chocó Indians has been underway into the eastern part of the Isthmus and so continues at present. They retain their habit of dispersed pile dwellings, preferring ridge tops; they clear a patch sufficient for their subsistence within the forest, and maintain their customs and language. The ancient Cueva country is thus being reoccupied in part by tropical forest Indians of very different breed and culture—one of the very few instances of an Indian people now in process of enlarging their territory.

---

[4] See Gordon, *op. cit.*, pp. 28 and 8 for *do* as terminal or initial syllable in Chocó.

XVII
THE END OF THE ERA

•

THE COLUMBUS HERITAGE

Columbus gave to Spain a New World the existence of which he never admitted. Seamen of western nations had long been voyaging far out into the Ocean Sea and were familiar with its winds and currents. Portuguese had colonized the Azores a third of the upwind way across the western sea. It was well known that in those and higher latitudes westerly winds would speed ships home to European shores. Across the Horse Latitudes of light and variable winds the Madeira and Canary Islands had been occupied. Farther south the Portuguese used the south-westerly set of trade winds into equatorial calms and so crossed into the wind systems of the southern hemisphere. Spanish seamen of the Atlantic ports of Andalusia were accustomed to cross a thousand miles of open sea to the Canaries and return. It was they who would provide the navigating skill for the venture of Columbus. He would direct them to sail west from the Canaries through unknown waters. His objective has never been made clear and perhaps was uncertain. In promoting his venture he proposed to sail west to the kingdoms of the Far East, yet having made the crossing he construed a wholly imaginary geography of Asiatic shores that disregarded everything that was known. Repeatedly he said that he was within a few days' sail of a famous city or country of the Orient, but instead of continuing west turned south. The secret of which he spoke as known to him alone led him south along tropical shores that would become known as the West Indies, peopled by simple natives whom he misnamed Indians.

Columbus had a genius for words, not as to their proper meaning but to cast a spell and to persuade. Soon after getting to Haiti he decided to name it "the Spanish Isle." One of its valleys earliest seen became the Valle del Paraiso. Other parts were likened to the fairest parts of Andalusia in spring. The silvery cloud-capped crest of a northern ridge gave name to Puerto Plata. The outlet of the Gulf of Paria was the Dragon's Mouth. Carib islands took the name of the shrines of Guadelupe and Montserrat. The romantic publicity he gave to the new lands above all was to portray them as lands of infinite gold. All the fabled gold lands of antiquity were relocated in his discoveries or in parts he was about to discover. Columbus was looking for gold mines from the first landing on a coral island to his last days in Veragua. It did not matter that his success was slight. Always and everywhere there was vast promise of gold. The sovereigns and people of Spain became imbued by his obsession, picturesquely and fantastically presented. The course of Spanish empire was first turned to its fateful search for gold by the *idée fixe* that dominated Columbus.

Portugal found its way patiently and cautiously into overseas trade and colonies, guided for forty years by the planning and supervision of Prince Henry. Spain was confronted suddenly with the discovery of land across the ocean without any thought what should be done with it. Spain was unprepared but not so Columbus. He had secured the incredible contract that vested in him and his heirs in perpetuity the almost absolute rule over whatever he might discover and possess, subject to sharing the profits with the Spanish Crown. The inevitable conflict of interest began to develop immediately and troubled the affairs of the Spanish Indies for years.

Columbus, who is not known ever to have managed any enterprise, began in Española with the stupid mistake of building Isabela, which started up the troubles with his Spaniards. He was in trouble with his men most of the time and was engaged in putting down a revolt at the time of his removal. They were his employees, subject to his dictates which considered only his own wishes. The revolt of Roldán broke the control of Columbus who was forced to accept the allotment of native communities (repartimiento) to Spanish grantees (vecinos) and thereby to introduce against his will an institution that was basic to the administration of the Spanish colonies.

His Indian policy was simple, rigid, and unworkable. He found the natives friendly, apt at learning, and timorous. He would put them to work to produce gold, which their caciques would collect on a per capita basis. The impossible demand turned amiability to fear, flight, and retaliation. Many were captured, more died of hunger. Caciques were liquidated, their subjects shipped as slaves. Pacification by terror began thus as an instrument of colonial policy.

The government of Columbus was a continuing series of bad decisions. Always he insisted that he had been right and would have succeeded but for his enemies. Experience taught him nothing. The heritage of his mistakes continued long after him.

CONTROL PASSES TO THE CROWN

Columbus asked for a judicial inquiry at a time when he was especially irritated by complaints against himself at court, confident that his antagonists would be confounded. However, the request charged that there was a conspiracy of forces of evil and its language was wild and disordered. His promises of great revenues had become still more extravagant, unsupported, and improbable. The Crown had borne as long as it would with the expenses, mistakes, illusions, and quarrels of an administration that had proved its incompetence. Columbus was removed from office; Ferdinand and Fonseca took charge in 1498 and held control until 1516.

The perpetual contract of Columbus was not renounced but was ignored by two procedures. Henceforth governors would be named by the Crown, be held responsible to the Crown, and serve at its pleasure. Licenses to discover and trade in other parts of the Indies were issued in number, some with rights to govern, thereby becoming detached from the government in Santo Domingo.

The two years of administration by Bobadilla were the first quiet ones Española had seen. The Spaniards were content and there was no Indian trouble. Also, gold began to be produced in profitable quantity. The next governor, Ovando, made the island an attractive and profitable enterprise. He rebuilt Santo Domingo as a Spanish city, founded the villas that controlled all parts of the island by means of the repartimientos to their vecinos, organized the exploitation of the gold fields, and set up an administration that was efficient and honest. The Spanish population increased in numbers and prosperity to a level that was not again reached for many years. The success was attained by breaking down the native social structure and subjecting the natives to excessive forced labor. The attrition of the native population was so great that other islands began to be raided to provide laborers. Ovando authorized Ponce de León to occupy Puerto Rico and exploit its gold placers, the first Spanish expansion from Española.

Diego Columbus next held the title of governor. The affairs of the Indies, however, were directed by Fonseca and the King through their own men overseas, the royal treasurer Pasamonte, the Audiencia of Santo Domingo, and officials in other islands and on Tierra Firme. The economic basis remained the same, the production of gold by forced native labor which had been reduced to insufficient levels in Española. The Bahama Islands were almost totally depopulated. Slave raids extended as far as Florida, Barbados, Curaçao, and the Bay Islands of Honduras to support the faltering economy of Española and be consumed in the newer gold fields of Cuba and Puerto Rico.

Independent licenses to discover and trade were begun in 1499, equipped and sent directly from Spain. They outlined in short order the existence of a southern continent from Brazil to Central America and showed that there was no sea route to the Spice Lands in tropical latitudes. Tierra Firme was thus parceled out to nominal governments. The treasure of fabricated gold brought back by Bastidas in 1502 indicated the promise of the Gulf of Darién, which thereafter was the focus of attention. Trade and loot of such native treasure was combined with slave hunting along the coasts of Tierra Firme. The successful Spanish establishment at the Indian town of Darién in 1510 resulted in the discovery of the Pacific Ocean in 1513, to be followed in 1514 by the establishment of the government named Castilla del Oro on Tierra Firme.

Criados, which in English is expressed somewhat inadequately as creatures, of Fonseca and the King (the reversed order is preferable) controlled the operations in the Indies. Human predation reached extremes both on the islands and mainland. There was diminishing success in placer mining on the islands but a new and greater source had been found in looting the golden treasure owned by the peoples of western Tierra Firme.[1]

---

[1] The Suma of Enciso is an important source on the southern side of the Caribbean, especially for the years 1510–1515. I do not know that it contains any later items. For the coast of Colombia at that time he is the principal observer. Entitling his work a geography is acceptable because he associated topic and location, as for example his observation that from Cartagena on west the bread was made from maize and a strong maize wine was drunk.

The coastal lands east of Cartagena were of passing Spanish interest after 1510. Enciso

THE TIME OF REFORMS UNDER CISNEROS

The Court and public in Spain were not uninformed of the condition and decline of the native peoples in the Indies. Las Casas and Montesino had been declaiming against the outrages. Oviedo had returned to court, an official of Castilla del Oro, to protest its brutal regime. Bishop Quevedo and Balboa had written from Darién about the abuses that went unpunished and unchecked. Nothing happened until King Ferdinand died in January, 1516.

When Cardinal Cisneros took over the Regency of Spain he moved promptly and vigorously to reorder the affairs of the Indies. He was then eighty years old and the two years that were left to him he used for large and wise reforms. Fonseca and Conchillos, partners in greed and favoritism, were ousted. The government of the Indies was placed in the hands of men who had not been aligned with any party, who had never been overseas or had anything to do with the Indies. The choice of the cardinal fell upon three Hieronymite monks and on the Licenciado Zuazo. The wisdom of this decision, an extraordinary experiment in government, was proved by their intelligent and amicable sharing of authority. They put a stop to the repartimientos, freed the Indians of Española from servitude, and began to reestablish them in communities of their own. Negro slaves were to replace the Indians as labor force. The settlement of Spaniards was encouraged. Instead of depending on producing gold, plantations of sugar cane were developed, other commercial crops were tried, and forest resources were examined. A balanced and permanent economy was in prospect.

The reforms were well prepared and put into operation for Española. Perhaps it was too late to save the Indian population. The steps that were taken were the only ones that had promise. They failed because the epidemic of smallpox swept away much of the remainder. In final reference to the passing of the natives the Dominican Provincial, Pedro de Córdoba, wrote their sorrowful epitaph in 1518, before the final blow by smallpox:

> These islands and lands newly discovered and found so filled with people have been and are being destroyed and depopulated today. People so gentle, obedient, and good have been kept at excessive and unaccustomed labors, so that in Espanola alone more than a million of your vassals have been destroyed. Pharaoh and his Egyptians treated the children of Israel less badly. They no longer conceive nor multiply nor are they able to do so and they do not leave issue. San Juan has been destroyed in the same manner, and in the same way Cuba, Jamaica, and Tierra Firme are being ruined. There are in this island at present ten or twelve

---

supplied information on the districts of Santa Marta and the Goajira Peninsula. Santa Marta he judged to be the best port of the south coast, situated in "a land that is irrigated by hand and by ditches, and all the breadstuffs and things that they sow and plant they grow by irrigation." The country was rather open and abounded in wild pigs and deer. Its natives had much gold and copper, much of the latter gilded by means of a certain herb. They grew a good deal of cotton and made it into cloth of many colors. Also, they made headdresses of the feathers of parrots and other birds.

The large town of Coquibacoa near the tip of the Goajira Peninsula was of good peaceable natives like those about the Gulf of Venezuela [Caquetío Arawaks]. "There have been found balance (*peso*) and touchstone (*toque*) for gold in that place, which is large, and the Indians say that the gold is brought there from as far as twenty-five leagues inland and that when they go there for it they take along balance and touchstone to determine what they are getting."

thousand Indians, male and female. By common consent there will be none left in four to five years.[2]

Zuazo had collected evidence on conditions in Castilla del Oro, his final indictment going to the new King. The cardinal died as young King Charles landed in Spain, without opportunity to induct his successor into the affairs of state. Charles was eighteen, spoke no Spanish, and came surrounded by Burgundian and Flemish courtiers. William of Croy, known to Spain as the Monsieur de Xèvres, was the King's guardian and tutor. The Xèvres influence dominated Charles for several years and restored the Fonseca-Conchillos cabal to power.

The Cisneros reforms were not wholly lost, but they were not carried farther. Velázquez continued in Cuba as he had. Pedrarias was saved by the death of his successor-designate in Castilla del Oro. The affairs of the Indies were again adrift.

FINALE

The Spanish Main was the scene and subject of a tragedy that was played in three acts in classical manner. In the first Columbus was the central figure, moving to the failure for which he had destined himself. The second was of shifting scenes and new persons, manipulated by the hands of Fonseca and King Ferdinand. Beneath an appearance of prosperity the native condition deteriorated to hopelessness. In the third act a gallant attempt directed by Cisneros came too late and for too short a time to stem collapse and desolation.

By 1519 the Spanish Main was a sorry shell. The natives, whom Columbus belatedly knew to be the wealth of the land, were destroyed. The gold placers of the islands were worked out. The gold treasures which the Indians of Castilla del Oro had acquired had been looted. What most Spaniards wanted was to get out and seek their fortunes in parts as yet untried and unknown.

By 1519 a new map of the Indies was taking form rapidly, by which the Islas y Tierra Firme of the older notation came to lie at the eastern edge of activity. It began with the unemployed and restless Spaniards of Cuba, as Bernal Diaz told the story that led to the conquest of Mexico by Cortés in 1519. Alaminos brought the news from Vera Cruz to Spain, following the Gulf Stream and thereby setting the future course of sail homeward-bound from Mexico and Spanish Main. Habana moved across Cuba to take up its location on the new main street of the Indies.

At the same time Pedrarias transferred government and vecinos of Castilla del Oro to the new town of Panama. The former name was soon dropped, the erstwhile village of Indian fishermen giving its name to a colony wholly directed to the exploitation of lands of the Pacific. Pedrarias carried his depredations west along the Pacific side of Central America. Gil González sailed and marched on independent mission well beyond the Gulf of Fonseca without doing violence to the natives. Andagoya sailed south from Panama to bring the first report of Peru.

Magellan sailed from Spain in 1519 to discover the passage into the South Sea by the strait that bears his name and to give Spain title to its Indies of the Far East. And in 1519 Charles V set up the Council of the Indies to take charge of the affairs of Spain overseas.

---

[2] Condensed from CDI, XI, 217–220.

POSTSCRIPT

Fifty years later when López de Velasco compiled the official geography of the Indies he reported a thousand Spaniards in Española, at least half of them in Santo Domingo; two hundred in the island of Puerto Rico, mostly in the town of San Juan; two hundred forty in Cuba; a handful in Jamaica. The government offices and trade in sugar and hides supported Santo Domingo and San Juan. The Spanish population in all the islands did not exceed fifteen hundred, López thought, and most of them were poor. The former Castilla del Oro had about six hundred Spaniards, two-thirds of them in the city of Panama, supported by the trade of Peru. Negroes were the bulk of the population here and in the islands, Española having twelve to thirteen thousand. The old Spanish Main had become a shabby fringe of Peru, New Spain, and New Granada with a few towns maintained in the interest of empire. Most of its land had been repossessed by wild growth of tropical vegetation.

Index

152